CHINA:

ITS STATE AND PROSPECTS

SR *Scholarly Resources Inc.*
Wilmington, Delaware

SCHOLARLY RESOURCES, INC.
1508 Pennsylvania Avenue
Wilmington, Delaware 19806

Reprint edition published in 1973
First published in 1838 by John Snow,
    London

Library of Congress Catalog Card Number: 72-79833
ISBN: 0-8420-1379-2

Manufactured in the United States of America

CHINA:

ITS STATE AND PROSPECTS,

WITH ESPECIAL REFERENCE TO

THE SPREAD OF THE GOSPEL:

CONTAINING

ALLUSIONS TO THE ANTIQUITY, EXTENT, POPULATION, CIVILIZATION, LITERATURE,
AND RELIGION OF THE CHINESE.

BY W. H. MEDHURST,

OF THE LONDON MISSIONARY SOCIETY

SECOND THOUSAND.

Illustrated with Engravings on Wood,
BY G. BAXTER.

LONDON: JOHN SNOW, 26, PATERNOSTER ROW.
1838.

INTRODUCTION.

THE writer of the present volume was sent out by the London Missionary Society, in 1816, to labour for the benefit of China.

The *fundamental principle* of this Institution is, that " its design is not to send Presbyterianism, Independency, Episcopacy, or any other form of church order or government, about which there may be a difference of opinion among serious Christians, but the glorious Gospel of the blessed God, to the heathen ; leaving it to the minds of the persons whom God may call into the fellowship of his Son from among them, to assume for themselves such form of church government, as to them shall appear most agreeable to the word of God."

In conformity with this principle, no question was ever asked, or direction given to the author, as to his personal views of church government ; or what form of ecclesiastical polity he should adopt, in the event of his labours being successful abroad. After residing at Malacca and Penang for several years, he settled in Batavia, where he collected a congregation, and built

a

a chapel, for the worship of Almighty God. In conducting the services of the sanctuary, he invited and obtained the assistance of Gospel ministers from various communions; and when a church was formed, the members who joined it, drew up and signed a constitution; in which, after stating their belief in the Inspired Oracles, as the only sure ground of faith and practice, they acknowledged the standards of the English, Scotch, and Dutch Reformed Churches, as exhibiting those views of Christian doctrine, which they considered the most in accordance with the revealed will of God. Based on this broad principle, the society of Christians thus collected together, though originally of different communions, consented to lay aside their denominational prejudices, and unite on the safe ground of our common Christianity; while Episcopalian, Presbyterian, Baptist, and Independent ministers alternated with each other in the performance of religious services, and the celebration of the holy sacraments. The native church connected with the mission has been established on the same principle.

Should the author, and his esteemed coadjutors, ever succeed in introducing Christianity extensively into China, they purpose spending their utmost energies in spreading the simple Gospel through that important empire, without wasting themselves in dissensions on non-essential points, which have so long and unhappily divided the Christian world. It is on this ground alone, that they can confidently look for the blessing

of the great head of the church, and claim the countenance and co-operation of Christians of every name.
So great is the work, and so feeble the energies that
can be brought to bear on it, that we have no time
" to fall out by the way ;" and it is a pleasing feature of
the protestant mission to China, that hitherto the agents
of various societies, the members of different communions, and the representatives of distant hemispheres,
have consented to merge their national and denominational prejudices, and to join heart and hand in making
known the great doctrine of justification by faith, to the
sceptical and susperstitious Chinese. May brotherly
love continue ; and may one strenuous and persevering
effort be made, till the millions of China be brought
under the influence of Christianity!

But it is necessary that the author should give some
account of the origin and nature of the following work.
Having been called upon in the year 1835, to undertake a journey along the north-east coast of China, in
order to ascertain whether or not that country was open
to the Gospel; and having kept a record of passing
events, he contemplated on his return, the publication of
a journal, with some brief remarks on the situation
of foreigners in Canton, and the state of the native
Christian community there. In the course of his tour
through England, however, to plead the cause of missions, he found it necessary to dilate more at large on
the political, moral, and spiritual condition of the Chinese ; and to relate in order the efforts that have been

a 2

made for their evangelization. These statements having been listened to with some interest, and awakened
a sympathy on behalf of China, the thought suggested
itself, that possibly, the feeling thus created might be
extended and perpetuated by a publication, embracing
the general state of CHINA ; and its STATE and PRO-
SPECTS, with especial reference to the DIFFUSION of the
GOSPEL.

The most important feature in the condition of that
country is its population ; about which so many different
opinions have been held, and for the benefit of which
Christian missionaries so ardently long and labour. The
question of amount, therefore, is discussed, and the suggestion thrown out, that probably the highest census
given of the Chinese people is the right one. Their
civilization and political state next demand attention ;
and some references are made to their singular language, and the state of education among them. As we
contemplate the introduction of a new religion into the
country, it is natural to enquire, what are their present
views of divine and eternal things ; and to shew the
defects of their own systems, as a prelude to the recommendation of another. Before treating on the recent
efforts of protestants to evangelize China, it was thought
necessary to allude to the previous exertions of other
missionaries ; and therefore the devoted, self-denying,
and persevering labours of Syrian, nestorian, and catholic Christians, are briefly enumerated. The missions to
Canton, the Straits, and Batavia, are then severally

described ; and the attempts to carry the Gospel by means of Scriptures and tracts, along the coast of China, are delineated. This review is concluded by appeals for more agents, and increased facilities for the vigorous prosecution of the work ; as it is only when we use the appointed means, that we can consistently look for the Divine blessing on our labours.

The short time that could be spared for preparing this work for publication, must necessarily have occasioned many defects, in point of style and arrangement. Sent forth when very young on this important mission, occupied during his whole stay abroad in studying foreign and difficult languages, and accustomed to write and speak for the benefit of Mahomedans and heathens, it can hardly be expected that the author should be skilled in European composition. Public engagements, for the first year after his return to England, called him incessantly from home ; and it was only during the retirement of the last winter, that he has had the least opportunity for arranging his thoughts on the subject now discussed. Being about to quit his native country during the present summer, to revisit the scene of his former labours, it was necessary that he should begin to print, almost as soon as he began to write, in order to have the book published before his departure. He must cast himself, therefore, on the indulgence of the public, hoping that the circumstances under which the information contained in this volume has been collected and communicated, will be a sufficient apology for the many omissions, and incongruities, which may appear. The critic will perhaps survey with a lenient eye, the productions of the foreign missionary, who by his residence abroad, in regions where the human mind has been long stationary, has not been able to keep pace with the improving spirit of the age. Any observations, however, on his matter or manner, made in kindness and candour, will be thankfully received, and should the work reach a second edition, be carefully improved upon.

Some discrepancy may appear between the diffusiveness of the first few chapters, and the conciseness of other parts of the work; but it is honestly confessed, that finding the matter grow upon his hands, the author was obliged to condense before he had reached the middle of the volume, and to leave out many interesting particulars, regarding his own travels in the Malayan archipelago, in order to introduce what had more especial reference to the evangelization of China. Some difference of style will also appear between the descriptive and narrative parts of the publication; but it was thought better to give the views and impressions of the moment, than to abridge them of their interest, by presenting them in a more laboured style.

As it is, with all its imperfections, the author commits his production to the candour of the benevolent reader, and the blessing of almighty God; hoping that this feeble attempt will be instrumental in awakening an interest on behalf of China, and in promoting the spread of the Gospel in that populous and interesting empire.

In conclusion, the author would gratefully acknowledge the assistance kindly afforded him by the Rev. Drs. Reed and Burder, of Hackney; while he would state the obligations he is under to the following works, which he has consulted in the course of his labours; viz: Sadler's Law of Population, Milne's Retrospect, the Chinese Gleaner and Repository, Morrison's Dictionary, and View of China for Philological Purposes, Du Halde's History of China, and the Reports and Chronicles of the London Missionary Society.

HACKNEY, MAY 1, 1838.

CONTENTS.

CHAPTER I.

CHRONOLOGY AND EXTENT.

Page.

THE Evangelization of China contemplated—General scope of the subject —Antiquity of China—partly fabulous—not credited by Chinese writers —The Traditionary Period—The Ante and Postdiluvian Ages—The Historical Period—The Seven Years' Famine—The Chinese Sampson—The Magnetic Needle—Confucius—Laou Tsze—The burning of the Books —The Building of the Wall—Subsequent Dynasties—The Cycle— Sketch of Chinese Chronology—The Dominions of China—Original Possessions small—Territories enlarged—The Annexation of Tartary . 1

CHAPTER II.

PROBABLE POPULATION.

The Question of Population interesting to the Philosopher, the Politician, the Merchant, and the Christian—The possibility and probability of a large Population, argued from the fertility of the Soil—the extensiveness of the Cultivation—The paucity of the Roads—The manner of disposing of the Dead—The encouragement given to Agriculture—The Industry of the Inhabitants—The Skill of the Husbandman—The Economy in Food, Dress, and Dwellings—contrasted with the scarcity of Provisions—and want of feeling—Emigration, with its difficulties— Bounty on the Importation of Rice—Infanticide—its prevalence— Foundling Hospitals—Conclusion 22

CHAPTER III.

CENSUS OF THE POPULATION.

Testimony of the Catholic Missionaries—and Chinese Authorities—The law of the Census, and the way of taking it—The reason for so doing— its credibility—the different accounts reconciled—increase accounted for—increase sketched—Amiot's estimate—Grosier's—Morrison's—and Sir G. Staunton's—comparison of the whole—which most to be depended on—the discrepancies of some—the most credible Census—The Revenue of China—and its light pressure on the People 48

CHAPTER IV.

REFLECTIONS ON THE POPULATION.

Page.

Their overwhelming numbers—Their sinful condition—the work of Evangelizing them difficult—dependence on Divine aid—The diffusive character of the Gospel—Encouragement drawn from the uniformity of their Government, Language, Morals, and Sentiment—Their extending Population—only checked by Europeans—and the introduction of Opium —The effect of Opium smoking—its rapid increase—Chinese laws against it—Memorial of a Mandarin—Extent of Smuggling—Appeal to the Opium Merchant—and the East India Company—Demoralizing effect of the Drug—Remonstrance to the Government of Great Britain . 71

CHAPTER V.

THE CIVILIZATION OF CHINA.

Comparative Civilization—Soliloquy of a Chinese—Native Politeness—displayed in Conversation—and daily Intercourse—Genius of the Chinese —Discovery of the Compass—The Art of Printing—The invention of Gunpowder—The Sciences—Astronomy—Botany—Medicine—Surgery—the Arts—Painting—Engraving—Manufacture of Silk—Porcelain—Paper—Lackered Ware—Metals—Conclusion. 97

CHAPTER VI.

GOVERNMENT AND LAWS.

The Empire united—The Government based on Parental Authority—The Emperor supreme—The Ministers of State—The Tribunals—of Civil Office —of Revenue—of Rites—of War—of Punishments—of Public Works—The Censorate—The National Institute—The Laws of China—their Character—Civil Laws—Fiscal Regulations—Ritual Enactments —Military Arrangements—Criminal Code—Directions about National Improvements — Imperial Palace — The Forbidden Enclosure — The Gardens and Pavilions—The Northern City—the Southern . . . 122

CHAPTER VII.

LANGUAGE AND LITERATURE.

Origin of Language—Hieroglyphics—Phonetic Characters—Chinese mode of recording Events—Six classes of Characters—Number of Symbols—reducible to few Elements—Modes of Writing—Question about Egyptian origin—Porcelain Bottle—Inscription explained—Date ascertained—Chinese Classics—Authorized Commentaries—Esteemed Works—Heterodox productions—Oral Language—Monosyllabic mode of Spelling—initials and finals—variety of tones—collocation of phrases—Chinese Grammar—Figures of Speech—Poetry—Literary Examinations—Hono-

Page
rary Degrees — Village Inspection — First — second — third — and fourth
Examinations—Effort necessary—Advantages and disadvantages of the
system 148

CHAPTER VIII.

THE RELIGIONS OF CHINA.

Three Systems of Religion—Confucius—his life—moral and political opi-
nions—Notions about Heaven—and the Supreme—His Theory of the
Universe—The two Powers of Nature—The Diagrams—Scheme of Meta-
physics—Material Trinity—Ideas of Spiritual Beings—of the Future
World—and of Human Nature—The Religion of Taou—Eternal Reason
— Incarnations of it—Philosopher's Stone — Ghosts and Charms—
Treading on Fire—Demoniacal Possessions—Magic Arts—Religion of
Buddha—History of its Founder—Entrance into China—Buddhist
Temples—Meditation on Buddha—Repetition of His Name—Absorption
of a Blacksmith—Form of Prayer—Compassion to Animals—Feeding
Hungry Ghosts—Paper Money—and Houses—Scrambling for Holy
Food—Doctrine of Annihilation—despised by the Confucians—Resem-
blance to the Catholics—Review of the three Systems 181

CHAPTER IX.

CATHOLIC MISSIONS IN CHINA.

The Gospel designed for the World—Early Diffusion in India and China—
Ancient Intercourse—The Marble Tablet—its contents—its authenticity
—Efforts of the Nestorians—and of the Catholics—Mission of Xavier—
Arrival of Ricci—his journey to the Capital—his success—Christian
Mandarin—his daughter Candida—Death of Ricci—Arrival of Schaal
—Illustrious Converts—Arrival of Verbiest—Persecutions—Revival—
Cannon Cast by the Missionaries—Patronage of the French king—Death
of Verbiest—New Persecutions—again allayed—Disputes among the
Missionaries—Papal Bulls— Romish Legates—Failure of Negotiations
Expulsion of the Missionaries—New efforts—present state—number of
Converts—Mode of operations—Character of the Catholic Missionaries—
and their adherents—Conclusion 220

CHAPTER X.

PROTESTANT MISSION TO CANTON.

Mission projected—Want of information—Morrison appointed—Sails for
Canton—Mode of living there—Pious breathings—Extreme caution—
Marriage and appointment— religious services—Printing commenced—
Adverse Edict—Arrival of Milne—Voyage to Java—New Testament
completed—Baptism of a Convert—Genesis printed—Removal of Milne
— Embassy to Peking—Old Testament completed—character of the

Page.

translation—Dictionary finished—Morrison visits England—Presented to the King—Reception by the Society—Returns to China—Labours of Afah—his letter—Baptism of Teen Ching—Agang—and Choo Tsing—Death of Morrison—Persecutions of Afah—Proclamation of the Magistrate—Afah's account—Conclusion 251

CHAPTER XI.

MISSION TO CANTON, CONTINUED.

Situation of foreigners in Canton—Surveillance of the Hong-merchants—and Compradores—Confinement—and Insult—Restrictions on Missionaries—Study of the native language prohibited—Difficulties of printing native books—Mode of obviating them—State of Macao—How far open to Missionary operations—Enquiry after native Converts—The literary graduate—The printers—The family of Afah—Agang and his son—Edict of the Emperor—Commission of enquiry—its fate—Missionaries not involved—Need of caution—Little interest in behalf of Canton—Recommendations 283

CHAPTER XII.

THE MISSION TO MALACCA.

Resolutions regarding Malacca—Occupation of the Station by Mr. Milne—Baptism of Afah—his experience—Arrival of the Author and other brethren—Schools—Tracts—and Translations—Anglo-Chinese college—Various labours—Rescue of a Malay family—Death of Milne—Morrison visits Malacca—Arrival of Kidd—Visit of the Deputation—Death of Collie—Baptism of a Malay slave—and a Chinese youth—Tomlin's superintendence—Arrival of Evans—Fresh Baptisms—Dyer joins the Mission—More encouragement—Twenty individuals Baptized—Ten more added—Their experience—Mission to Penang—Station at James Town—Labours of Dyer—Mission to Singapore—Joined by the American Missionaries 306

CHAPTER XIII.

MISSION TO BATAVIA.

First three Missionaries—Supper's labours—Slater's misfortunes—The Author's arrival—Schools—Printing—and other exertions—Christian village—Conversations with Heathen—Malay Judge—Napoleon's picture—Visit of the Deputation—Desultory labours—Tract against the Missionary—Journey to Soerabaya—The Tanggar Mountains—Japanese Books—Chinese preaching—Ironical arguments—Communication of the Gospel—Work on Chronology—Javanese types—Journey to Pahang—Tringano—Klintan—Patani—and Songora—Voyage to Pontianak—State of Borneo—Chinese under convictions—another incensed—Visit

Page.
to Bali—Erection of the Chapel—Preaching to convicts—Accessions to
the Church—Baptism of soldiers—Covenant with the Dyaks—Baptism of
a Chinese. 329

CHAPTER XIV.

VOYAGES UP THE COAST OF CHINA.

Summary of Missionary attempts in the Colonies—Desire to benefit the
Mother Country—Gutzlaff's voyages—Different views—Anxiety for more
information—Author's arrival in Canton—Disscussion regarding opium
vessels—Reasons for not embarking in them—as disreputable, inconvenient, and involving the Missionary in difficulty—The propriety of
hiring a vessel, or purchasing a Missionary Ship—Offer of the Huron—
Preparations for departure .   .   , ... 361

CHAPTER XV.

NARRATIVE OF THE VOYAGE.

Embarkation—Apprehension of a storm—Water-spouts—Chinese ideas of
them—Voyage up the Yellow Sea—Arrival at Shan-tung and Wei-hae—
First landing—Visit of the Mandarins on board—Second landing—Difficulties in the way—Discussions on the beach—Adjournment to the
temple—Excursion to the interior—Amicable conference—Eagerness for
books—Ramble over the Island of Lew-kung-taou—Visit to a peaceable
village—Second day's operations—A burial ground—Description of the
villages—and state of the country—Curiosity of the people—Quiet distribution of books—Anxiety for more—Attention to preaching—second
visit of the Mandarins on board—Summary 381

CHAPTER XVI.

PROCEEDINGS AT KE-SAN-SO.

Providential deliverance—Events on landing—Suspicions of the people—
Arrival at the town—Eagerness for books—Dispute with an officer—A
temple and a stage—Permission to purchase provisions—Tour through the
villages—Objections of a Confucian—Hospitality of a peasant—Rapid
distribution of books—A Chinese fort—Excursion to an adjoining bay
—Exhibition of an armed force—Invitation of the Mandarins—Second
visit to the town—anxiety to see the strangers—Discussion about ceremonies—Introduction to the principal Mandarins—Etiquette observed—
Questions proposed—Objections to our enterprise—Advice of the General
—Discussion about presents—Conversation on politics—Magisterial dignity and meanness—Presents received and return made—Disturbances
on board 406

CHAPTER XVII.

PROCEEDINGS ON THE SOUTH OF SHAN-TUNG.

Page.
Voyage round the promontory—Landing at Tsing-hae—State of the town
and defences—Interviews with the people—and Mandarins—Excursion
through the villages—Simplicity of the natives—Calmness of the women
—Voyage prosecuted—A second landing—Annoying interference—Suspicions of the inhabitants — Solitary journey—Interesting group of
villagers—Various adventures—A new harbour discovered—Visit to
Nan-hung—Enquiries and alarms—A Chinese fort described—Geological
formations—Disposition of the natives—and reception of the Missionaries
—Dress and habits of the men—Appearance of the women—their
dwellings—Temples and cemeteries—Productions of the soil—Domestic
animals—State of the people—Reflections 435

CHAPTER XVIII.

PROCEEDINGS IN KEANG-SOO PROVINCE.

Voyage to the southward—Arrival at Woo-Sung — Appearance of the
country—Reception on shore—Journey to Shang-hae—Interview with
the officers—Books distributed—Arrival of the chief magistrate—Refusal
to stand before him—Discussion about ceremonies—Reasons for decision
—Attempt to enter the city—Unpleasantness at parting—Operations
among the Junks — Remarks on Woo-sung — and its inhabitants —
Arrival of a General—Description of the military—and fortifications—
Visit of one Mandarin—Cunningness of another—Unsuccessful voyage
—Pleasant tour—The people eager for books—and the soldiers for gain
—Difficulties and disappointments 456

CHAPTER XIX.

OCCURRENCES IN CHE-KEANG AND FUH-KEEN.

Departure from Keang-soo—and arrival at Kin-tang—Visit of war-boats
— Operations on shore—Perishing boy—Proceedings at Choo-sans—
Eagerness for books—Coffins scattered about—Voyage to Poo-too—
Picturesque appearance of the island—its consecration to idolatry—
Description of the temples—Character of the priests—Conversation with
naval officers—Liberal views of a Mandarin—Providential escape—
Arrival at Nan-yih—Appearance of the women—The town of Tung-
san—Free distribution—Disorderly conduct of a Mandarin—and sub-
sequent alarm—Surprise of the people—Return 491

CHAPTER XX.

SUBSEQUENT OCCURRENCES.

Restrictive policy of the Chinese—Exclusion of foreigners—Anger at their
intrusion—Edict against the Huron—Appeal to the British authorities

Page.

—Complaints against the English—Disapprobation of our books—Threat
of stopping the trade—Late voyage of Gutzlaff—Tung-San bay—Description of the country and its inhabitants—Barren region—Extensive
valley—Mountain ridge—Deserted village—Intestine broils—Chinese
temple—Fertile spot—Populous city—Ravenous labourers—Character of
the Mandarins—Tsin-kang district—Eagerness for books—Visit to
Amoey—Anxiety for more labourers 508

CHAPTER XXI.

CLASS OF LABOURERS REQUIRED FOR CHINA.

Comparative claims of China—Need of more labourers—for the colonies—
and the coast—Offers invited—Objections met—Regarding the climate—
and the language—The oral and written mediums—compared with the
English—Exhortations to engage—Educational agents needed—Schools
for schoolmasters required—Pious physicians—Efforts already made—
Opthalmic hospital—More practitioners wanted—The probability of their
success—Speech of Sir H. Halford—Moral influence of physicians—
Deference paid them—Interesting anecdote—Importance of medicine to
Missionaries—Inferiority of Chinese practice—Union of the clerical and
medical professions—Persons who should offer 532

CHAPTER XXII.

DESIDERATA FOR THE CHINESE MISSION.

Translation of the Scriptures—Difficulties in the way—Efforts already
made—Need of a revision—Opinions of Chinese converts—and European
students—Resolution of the Bible and Missionary Societies—Steps to be
taken—Importance of the subject—Chinese printing—Moveable types
Mode of preparation—Necessity of punch-cutting—and casting—Dyer's
fount—Parisian type-founding—Various cost of block, stone and metal
type printing—with the advantages and disadvantages of Xylography—
Lithography—and Typography—Superiority and importance of the latter
—Missionary Ship—Concluding Appeal 555

ILLUSTRATIONS.

PAGE.

Frontispiece.

Title.

Summary Execution 122

Judicial Process . . . . ib.

Buddhist Priest on a Stage 181

Adoration of a celebrated Devotee. . . . . ib.

Service in a Chinese Temple . . . . ib.

View of the Mission Chapel, at Batavia 329

Map of the Maritime Provinces of China 381

Chinese Fort 406

Guard-room with Soldiers . . . . ib.

Cluster of Temples . . . . ib.

Landing at Woo-sung 456

CHINA:

ITS STATE AND PROSPECTS.

CHAPTER I.

CHRONOLOGY AND EXTENT.

THE EVANGELIZATION OF CHINA CONTEMPLATED—GENERAL SCOPE OF
THE SUBJECT—ANTIQUITY OF CHINA—PARTLY FABULOUS—NOT CRE-
DITED BY CHINESE WRITERS—THE TRADITIONARY PERIOD—THE ANTE
AND POSTDILUVIAN AGES—THE HISTORICAL PERIOD—THE SEVEN
YEARS' FAMINE—THE CHINESE SAMPSON—THE MAGNETIC NEEDLE—
CONFUCIUS—LAOU TSZE—THE BURNING OF THE BOOKS—THE BUILD-
ING OF THE WALL—SUBSEQUENT DYNASTIES—THE CYCLE—THE DO-
MINIONS OF CHINA—ORIGINAL POSSESSIONS SMALL—TERRITORIES
ENLARGED—THE ANNEXATION OF TARTARY.

BEFORE entering on the prospects of China with regard
to the ultimate diffusion of the Gospel, it may be well
to offer a few remarks on its former and present state,
as introductory to the consideration of its future destinies, and with the view of encouraging those exertions
which, by the Divine blessing, may result in its universal evangelization. The conversion of the Chinese
to the Christian faith must be viewed as an object
every way desirable, and some observations on so important a theme from the pen of one who has long
devoted his energies to this work, may not perhaps be
considered altogether unacceptable.

In contemplating the evangelization of China, the

B

field spreads itself out before the mind, as one of vast extent and interest; the importance of cultivating this field appears to be of incalculable magnitude; the difficulties which threaten to impede the progress of Divine truth in those regions ought not to be overlooked, while the existing facilities for conducting a series of operations for the benefit of that interesting people should be allowed to animate and encourage us. An allusion to what has been done, to what is doing, and to what remains to be done, may not be unsuitable; and a prospective view of the contemplated results, when these designs shall have been fully carried out, may properly conclude the whole.

China demands the attention of Christian philanthropists, with regard to the antiquity of its origin, the extent of its territory, the amount of its population, and the advance of its civilization. In nearly all these respects, we shall find that it rises superior to every other unevangelized country, and stands forward with a prominence, which bespeaks it the greatest of pagan nations.

Commencing with the early history of China, we may be allowed to correct an error into which many have fallen, relative to the assumption of an extravagant chronology by the Chinese. It has been generally supposed that the Chinese maintain an antiquity of myriads of years, and that their historical records, stretching far back into the vista of more than a thousand ages, are at such variance with the comparatively recent account of Moses, as to oblige us either to question the one or the other. This was, at one time, gladly caught at by the sceptics of Europe, and they thought that they had discovered, in the high antiquity of the Chinese, combined with the Hindoo and Egyptian races, an argument which threw discredit on the chronology of the Bible, and weakened the evidence of its Divine authority. The fact, however, is, that the Chinese, like most other heathen nations, have a mythological as well as a chronological period; the one considered by themselves as fabulous, and the other as authentic; the one connected with the history of their gods, and the other with that of their men. In the former they speak of their celestial emperor, who reigned 45,000 years; their terrestrial emperor, who reigned 18,000 years; followed by their human emperor, who reigned as long: without condescending to enlighten us as to the names, characters, events, or circumstances of these wonderful individuals, or their still more extraordinary reigns: nay, without so much as telling us whether their dominions were established in heaven or on earth, or whether they referred exclusively to China, or included other nations. In short, the vague account they furnish us of these fancied emperors shews that they were merely the figment of the imagination, introduced to supply a deficiency, and to amuse the credulous. Indeed, so little credit is attached to this fabulous period by the Chinese themselves, that one of their most respectable historians, Choo-foo-tsze, does not venture to allude to it, but passing by these extravagant assumptions, commences his relation at a much later period, when events and circumstances of a connected character stamp the records of the age with greater marks of credibility. Another Chinese historian, named Fung-chow, remarks, "How is it credible that more than 10,000 years elapsed before the yang, or ' superior principle' was produced, and the heavens spread;

and that 10,000 more elapsed before the yin, or 'secondary principle' was produced, and the earth formed; that 10,000 more passed away, before 'the yin and yang' united to produce the various material existences; and, further, that 40 or 50,000 years more passed away, before the process of the two principles was finished, and the sages appeared! Such a tale is contrary to all sense and reason. From the time of the sages Yaou and Shun, to the present age is not more than 3000 and odd years. How can it be believed that 40 or 50,000 years elapsed after the formation of the heavens and the earth, before man appeared, or the earth and water were adjusted, and food supplied to human beings? or that, if the world had existed so long, these things should not have been arranged before Fŭh-he and his successors? It is evident that Pwan-koo, the first man, according to the fabulous records of the Chinese, who acted at the separation of heaven and earth, could not have been long before Fŭh-he, perhaps a thousand years, certainly not ten thousand; and the time of Fŭh-he must have been very near Yaou and Shun, perhaps a hundred years certainly not a thousand. No scholar should decline a thorough enquiry." Sze-ma-tsëen, another very celebrated historian of China, does not record anything relative to the three emperors above mentioned; how much less then might he be expected to refer to Pwan-koo, who is placed before them.

Thus Chinese authors of the greatest reputation agree in considering the first part of Chinese history as entirely fabulous. Whilst, however, we fully coincide with them in this opinion, we cannot help, on a review of their brief allusion to this period, suggesting the idea, that the whole is probably based on some indistinct recollections of the theory of the creation. Of the first man, they say, that soon after the period of emptiness and confusion, when heaven and earth were first separated, Pwan-koo was produced; his origin is not ascertained, but he knew intuitively the relative proportions of heaven and earth, with the principles of creation and transmutation. During the supposed reign of the celestial, terrestrial, and human emperors, they allege that the year was settled, the months and days arranged, and the hills and rivers divided; all which may be but distant allusions to the formation of the heavenly bodies, and the settlement of the earth and waters.

The next period of Chinese history is that which is said to have elapsed between Fŭh-he and the sages Yaou and Shun, which the Chinese denominate the age of the " Five Rulers," and at which Choo-foo-tsze begins his history. There is much difference among historians as to the arrangement of this era, and Choo-foo-tsze himself says, that " several things affirmed of this epoch were all pushed up by people who lived in subsequent ages." While, therefore, we might be unwilling to give full credit to what Chinese writers say of the events of this period, it is not improbable that much of it is drawn by tradition from the correct account of the antediluvian age handed down by Noah to his posterity. The coincidence of ten generations having passed away, the institution of marriage, the invention of music, the rebellion of a portion of the race, and the confused mixture of the divine and human families, closed by the occurrence of the flood, in the time of Yaou, might lead us to conclude, that in their allusions to this period the Chinese are merely giving their version of the events that occurred from Adam to Noah. When Yu ascended the throne, the lands were drained, and China became habitable. About this period wine was discovered; Yu tasted it, and found it sweet, but rejected it, saying, "at some future period wine will occasion the ruin of the country." If now we should consider this to be a description of the antediluvian period, down to the age of Noah, traced according to Chinese recollections, and illustrated by Chinese fancy; and if we should account Yu to be the first founder of the Chinese empire, we should then be assigning them a very high antiquity, without giving any countenance to the extravagant pretensions which their fabulous writers have assumed. These thoughts are merely thrown out as suggestions, in which some sober and judicious men have concurred, who have considered the highly wrought relations of the times of Yaou and Shun, as mainly imaginary, not according with the state of improvement in other parts of the world at that period, nor even with the condition of China itself, at subsequent epochs of her history.

If then we consider Yu to be the first real character in Chinese history, and place the beginning of his reign at B. C. 2204, or one hundred and four years after the flood, about the age of Peleg, when the earth was divided, we shall find that it just gives time for such an increase of the human family as would admit of emigration, and yet allow for China being in such a state of marsh, as to require draining for the sake of culture, which service was ascribed to the labours of Yu. Thus the empire of China, even when deprived of its fabulous and traditionary periods, is still very ancient ; the Chinese must have branched off from the great human family immediately after the dispersion, and travelling to the farther east, settled down on the borders of the Yellow River, coeval with the establishment of the Babylonian and Egyptian monarchies. The mention made in their early history of the draining of the land, as one of the first acts of the primitive rulers of China, and the allusion to the discovery of wine about the same period, shew that their first kings must have synchronized with the immediate descendants of Noah ; and the recorded fact that a seven years' famine took place in China nearly coeval with that of Egypt proves that their chronicles are entitled to some degree of credit. Thus, ere Rome was founded, or Troy was taken — before Thebes or Nineveh were erected into kingdoms — China was a settled state, under a regular form of government; with customs and institutions, similar in many respects to those which it possesses now.

From that time to this, revolutions and wars have frequently occurred ; the country has been exposed to foreign invasion, and torn by intestine commotion ; dynasties have changed, and the people are even now subject to a Tartar yoke,—yet China is China still. Her language and her customs remain unaltered ; and the genius and spirit of the people are the same they were in the patriarchal age. No nation has undergone less change, or been less affected from without ; and they seem to have grown up as distinct from the rest of mankind, as if they had been the inhabitants of another planet ; retaining all their peculiarities just as much as if their exclusive wall had surrounded their whole empire, and debarred all others from intercourse with them. Those who are accustomed to attach veneration to antiquity, will probably regard the Chinese with some degree of interest on account of their patriarchal character; and those who love to survey human society in every possible stage, will be gratified with the contemplation of it, as it existed not only centuries, but milleniums ago. The modern kingdoms of Europe are but of yesterday, compared with the Chinese; and though western nations have grown rapidly since their origin, yet they cannot look back to any very distant period when their ancestors laid the foundation of their present greatness, and established systems which still exist and characterize their populations. The Chinese, on the contrary, have derived their veneration for parents, and their subjection to rulers, with the arrangements of domestic life, from the first founders of their monarchy; and embody in their present conduct principles which were laid down four thousand years ago.

A few allusions to Chinese history may not be amiss here. Of the great Yu, the founder of their first dynasty, B. C. 2204, they write, that " seeing his father had been put to death, for not completing the work of draining the waters, he applied himself more assiduously to that undertaking, which kept him from home thirteen years; and though during that period, he thrice passed his own door, he would not enter. When he was appointed ruler, he rose ten times from a single meal to listen to complaints, and thrice tied up his hair while in the bath, to attend to some urgent affair, with the view of encouraging his people to an instant and energetic devotion to business."

Of Ching-tang, the founder of the second dynasty, B. C. 1765, the Chinese write, that " he ruled the people gently, and abolished oppressions, complying with the predilections of the multitude, so that all parties reverted to him. In his days, the seven years' drought occurred; the principal scribe observed, that prayer should be offered up. Ching-tang said, ' I only wish for rain on account of the people. If prayer will avail, I will present it myself! ' He then fasted, and cut off his hair and nails, riding in a mourning chariot; and binding white reeds around him, that he might represent a sacrificial animal, he went forth to the wilderness of mulberry-bushes, and invoked, saying, ' Let not the lives of the people be forfeited, on account of the neglect of one individual!' He then acknowledged his six faults, saying, ' Is it that my government is extravagant? or that the people are not properly attended to? or that my palaces are too lofty? or that my ministers are too numerous ? or that presents are too frequently sent? or that sycophants abound?' He had scarcely ceased, when the rain fell, to the distance of several thousand furlongs."

At the close of this dynasty, B. C. 1153, the tyrant Chow presided over the empire; he was said to be endowed with supernatural strength, so as to be able to conquer the fiercest beasts, and yet he was deluded and ruined through the fascinations and extravagances of a wretched woman. It is very remarkable, that the age of this individual should agree so exactly with that assigned, in sacred history, to Sampson.

The founders of the third dynasty are described as

virtuous, patriotic, and brave, exterminating the tyrant of the preceding dynasty, and scattering the wealth and provisions which he had accumulated among a starving people. About this time, B. C. 1121, foreign ambassadors came, from the modern Cochin-China, to court, presenting a white pheasant to the emperor: on returning they missed their way, when the prime minister furnished them with a "south-pointing chariot," by means of which they reached their own country, after a year's journey. Thus we see that the polarity of the needle was known and applied to useful purposes in China, at that early period.

In the twenty-first year of the emperor Ling, of the third dynasty, B. C. 549, Confucius was born, in the state of Loo, now the province of Shan-tung. He had a remarkably high forehead, on which account his name was called Kew, or "hill." One of the nobles of his native state, when on his death-bed, addressed his posterity, saying, "Confucius is a descendant of the sages, and must certainly understand human nature; when I am dead, let my children repair to him for instruction." When Confucius was in the Chow country, he went to Laou-tsze, to enquire about propriety. Laou-tsze said, "a clever merchant conceals his stock, and appears empty; so an advanced scholar puts on the appearance of stupidity." Confucius, addressing his disciples, said, "There is something remarkable about Laou-tsze." When he was nearly fifty years of age, the ruler of his native state, Loo, employed him to govern a certain district: he had not been thus engaged above a year, when the surrounding nobles began to imitate him. His sovereign said, "Had I not better follow your example in the government of the Loo country?" Confucius replied, "With such principles you might pacify the world, how much more the Loo country." In a few years, Confucius became the prime minister of his sovereign; but seeing his prince carried away with the love of women and music, he resigned his office, and quitted Loo. At the age of seventy-five, he died. The writings compiled by Confucius and his followers are the most ancient Chinese records that have been handed down to the present time. Some of these are, professedly, collections of earlier documents, and refer to the traditionary period of Yaou and Shun, as well as to the times of Wan Wang, B. C. 1120; but it is more than probable, that some of the odes and speeches, collected by Confucius, were merely traditionary notices, found in the mouths of bards and statesmen, and not documents actually committed to writing before his time. Confucius' history of his own times, commences with the reign of the emperor Ping, B. C. 720, and is as much to be depended on as the recitals of the Greek and Roman historians;—it not only bears on itself the stamp of credibility, but laid the foundation of all the subsequent historical works which China has produced. The well known "Four Books" are written by the followers of Confucius, and contain an account of the sayings and doings of the sage and his immediate disciples, something similar to our Gospels and Acts, or as has been observed, corresponding to Boswell's Life of Johnson.

It is very singular, that China should have given birth, at the same time, to two remarkable men, differing essentially in their doctrines and views, each the founder of a system of religion and morals, which has overspread and divided China, from their days to the present time. These individuals have been already referred to, viz., Confucius and Laou-tsze, and their interview with each other recorded. Though they seem to have had a respect for each other, yet they do not appear to have combined or coalesced in the plans they laid down for the instruction of posterity. Of Confucius it is said, that he never spoke of the strange and marvellous, and sought to fix men's attention on the duties of the human relations; while the other inculcated a contempt for worldly greatness and domestic happiness—placing the chief good in mental abstraction, and professing to deal much with the spiritual world. The one erred in being too sceptical, and the other in being too superstitious; yet they have both retained their hold of the mind of China, even to the present day, and it is difficult now to say, which system is most prevalent throughout the empire.

About the same period, Buddhism arose in India; and though it did not immediately spread into the ultra Gangetic nations, it diffused itself rapidly on its subsequent introduction, and now exerts as great an influence over the minds of the vulgar, as the other two sects do over the learned and the superstitious.

A little more than two hundred years before the Christian era, China became subject to a fourth dynasty, called Tsin, from which Chin, or China, the name by which that country is known in the western world, is probably derived. The ruler of Tsin conceived the insane idea of establishing a dynasty, which should extend from the beginning to the end of time. With this view, he collected and burnt all the records of previous ages, and buried alive four hundred and

sixty learned men, wishing to make posterity believe
that the dominion of the world commenced with himself, the first universal emperor of China. The object
of obliterating all remembrance of antiquity was, however, defeated by the subsequent discovery of the books
of Confucius, in the wainscoat of an old house ; and
the intention of perpetuating his rule to succeeding
generations was also frustrated by the demise of his
son, only two years after his own death, by which
means the empire passed into other hands, and his
dynasty became extinct. Though the writings of Confucius were recovered, yet they were much injured,
and, in many parts, defective; which has greatly detracted from the integrity, intelligibility, and, in the
opinion of some, from the credibility of the whole.

During the life-time of this monarch, the famous
Chinese wall was erected, in order to keep out the Tartars, who then infested the northern frontier. Almost
every third man was drafted, throughout the empire,
for the accomplishment of this undertaking ; and being
but poorly supplied with provisions, many of them
died in the work. Hence the Chinese call it, " The
ruin of one generation, and the salvation of thousands."
However true the first part of this sentence may be,
the latter is not so exactly correct, as the Tartars
have several times invaded China, notwithstanding
their wall, and are now in possession of the empire.
Still it is a stupendous work, stretching over fifteen
hundred miles of country, crossing hills and rivers,
and provided with gates and towers, at certain inter-
vals, so that if well manned and guarded, in a country
where artillery is seldom employed, it might still be
serviceable in keeping out an enemy, were not the

dreaded Tartar hordes now on both sides of the wall, and in possession of the palaces and capital of the empire. The name of the first ruler of the Tsin dynasty is, however, held in detestation by the Chinese.

Since the days of Tsin, a succession of dynasties have swayed the destinies of China: among the most celebrated of which are Han, Tang, Sung, and Ming, with the two Tartar dynasties Yuen and Tsing. The dynasty Han, lasting from B. C. 205 to A. D. 226, is distinguished for the military prowess and courage at that time displayed; hence the Chinese are still fond of calling themselves sons of Han. After the downfal of this race of kings, six smaller dynasties followed, of whom little remarkable is recorded. During the Tang dynasty, from A. D. 620 to 906, learning was extensively cultivated, and the literary examinations were then first established. Between the age of Tang and Sung, five smaller dynasties intervened, during which period printing was invented by one Fung-taou; A. D. 924; while the practice of binding the feet of women appears to have commenced about the same time. At the close of the Sung dynasty, A. D. 1275, Marco Paulo the venetian traveller, visited China. While the Mongolian Tartars had possession of China, the grand canal was dug, which proved of such incalculable service to the empire; and the Yellow River was brought back to its former bed, by which means much land was brought under cultivation, and former inundations prevented. Under the reign of the Ming dynasty, from A. D. 1638 to A. D. 1643, the Portuguese visited China, and settled themselves at Macao. The present Tartar race have possessed the throne one hundred and ninety-four years.

To the above brief allusions to the principal events of Chinese history, a regular list of Chinese emperors will be added in the appendix, with some of the remarkable occurrences of each successive dynasty. This list is made up from the Kang-këen-e-che, a Chinese historical work, and is calculated according to the cycle of sixty years, compared with the eras of the western world, that both the Chinese scholar and the European reader may be alike assisted in referring to it. Some explanation of the cycle will be required, for those who wish to consult the list. This mode of reckoning has been adopted by the Chinese from the commencement of their monarchy. They ascribe its invention to Hwang-te, who lived in the traditionary period, before the flood of Yaou The latter is said to have commenced his reign in the forty-first year of the fifth cycle, while the cycle itself is said to have begun with the sixty-first year of the reign of Hwang-te. During the period anterior to Yaou, however, the events of history, in Chinese books, are not marked by the years of the cycle, while subsequent to Yaou's accession, every important occurrence is carefully noted down by the appropriate horary character, so that a student can easily ascertain the date of any given event, by a reference to this mode of calculation. The inference therefore, is, that the cycle was not known before Yaou, if so early ; and that the assumption of the forty-first year of the fifth cycle, for the accession of that monarch is merely arbitrary, for the sake of fixing the date of subsequent, rather than of preceding events. The sixty years of the cycle are made out by joining ten horary characters, called the " ten celestial stems," with twelve others, called the " twelve terrestrial branches." These united together,

of course, exhibit an excess of two branches, after
every ten stems, which, being carried over to the next
row, vary the associations, until the ten stems are
repeated six times, thus forming sixty: when the process has to begin again. The origin of the ten stems
may be ascribed to the ten digits, and of the twelve
branches, to the twelve signs of the zodiac, which are
to be met with in all the primitive nations of antiquity,
and are supposed, by some, to be antediluvian. Indeed, the twelve stems, are, in calendars and astronomical books, used for the signs of the zodiac, beginning with Aquarius. As the characters, denoting these
twelve branches, have little or no signification in themselves, the common people, in order to remember them
the more easily, have attached to each branch-character
another word, with the meaning of which they are
familiar; as mouse, ox, tiger, rabbit, dragon, snake,
horse, sheep, monkey, pig, fowl, and dog, which were,
probably, the ancient terms for the Chinese signs of
the zodiac: so that the supposition that they were,
originally, derived from that source, is not altogether
without foundation. The Chinese make frequent use
of these horary characters in the notation of time, not
only as designating years, but months, days, and hours.
Thus there are in each year twelve months, and three
hundred and sixty days; while in each day there are
twelve hours, all exhibiting numbers easily denoted
by peculiar modifications of twelve. These characters
are frequently used in designating the age of individuals, and most requisite in calculating destinies;
while in chronological matters, they form the only safe
method of denoting time.

The history of China exhibits many traits of human

character, and a variety of incidents that would well repay the perusal. It was thought sufficient, however, in the present work, merely to allude to the system of chronology adopted by that people, partly to remove an erroneous notion entertained by some, that the Chinese boast of a chronology extending through an almost indefinite period, and partly to establish the fact, that, exclusive of their fabulous and traditionary periods, they do possess a series of historical records, extending back to the very first ages of the world, agreeing, in many important points, with the astronomical and chronological calculations of the west, and entitled, in some degree, to confidence and credit.

It will not be unsuitable now to call the attention of the reader to the dominions which have been possessed by these successive dynasties. A glance at the map of China Proper, exhibits it as bounded on the south and east, by the ocean; on the west, by Thibet and the desert; and on the north, by the great wall. Two mighty rivers are seen rising, nearly together, in the mountains of the west, one flowing north and the other south; and, after a lengthened and tortuous course, approaching each other nearly about the centre of China, from whence they flow side by side till they empty themselves into the eastern sea not far from each other; the one is called Hoang-ho, or the Yellow River, and the other, Yang-tsze-keang, or the Child of the Ocean.

At the first settlement of the Chinese in their patriarchal regions, they doubtless occupied but a small portion of that space which they now call their own.

The first part of the country possessed by their primeval ancestors, soon after the dispersion, was that portion of territory now included in the provinces of Shan-se and Shen-se, on the banks of the Yellow River, just after it crosses the great wall; or the northwestern part of China Proper. Here the land was laid out in portions which were divided into nine equal squares, the outer allotments of which were cultivated by eight separate husbandmen, while the middle plot was wrought by the united strength of the whole, and the proceeds given up for the service of the state. As the population increased, they spread themselves farther eastward, occupying the lands that lie between the Yellow River and the modern wall, as far as the sea; until, in the time of Confucius, the whole of the territory north and south of the Yellow River, as far as the Yang-tsze-keang, was inhabited by tribes speaking the same language, and adopting the same customs, separated into different states, and acknowledging one federal head. In process of time, these were all brought under the dominion of Tsin, and the foundation of that empire was laid, which has been long known to the western world, under the appellation of Sin, Chin, and China. It was long, however, before the emperors of China extended their sway over the tribes lying to the south of the Yang-tsze-keang, and, for many ages, the provinces of Fŭh-këen, Canton, Kwang-se, Yun-nan, and Kwei-chow, were in a state of barbarism, scarcely submitting to the Chinese yoke, and deriving little benefit from the civilizing influence of their northern neighbours. Education, however, and superior tactics, gradually won over the southern states, and the emperors of China became lords of all within the wall and the ocean, and extended their influence from the desert to the eastern sea.

Having thus far progressed, China was soon enabled to enlarge her territories by that which generally circumscribes dominion. She spread, not by conquering, but by being conquered. For many ages, the effeminate Chinese had been exposed to the incursions.of the Tartar hordes, which infested their northern border. To keep out these, the great wall was built, but built in vain. First, under the Moguls, and, subsequently, under the Manchows, the Tartar race invaded the territory, and ascended the throne of China. In this however, the superiority of knowledge over ignorance—of civilization over barbarism—has been apparent. Mencius, a Chinese philosopher, who flourished before the Christian era, has a passage in his works to the following effect: " I have heard of barbarians being improved by the Chinese, but I never heard of the Chinese being improved by barbarians." Thus the Tartars, after subjugating China, instead of altering its institutions, and changing its maxims of government, conformed themselves to the customs and laws already existing in the country, and were, in fact, subdued by the Chinese: while China remained what China was, having only changed its rulers, and gained a great accession of territory.

The modern empire of China assumes a peculiar interest and importance, on account of the extent of its territory. In addition to China Proper, which, with its eighteen rich and fertile provinces, each of them equal in extent and population to some European kingdoms, covers an area of 1,298,000 square miles, the empire is now swelled by the annexation of Chinese Tartary, a thinly peopled, but outstretched region, extending from the sea of Ochotsk, on the east, to Bukaria, on the west; and from the Altay and Nershink mountains on the north, to the great wall, on the south.

The power of China is strengthened, by having Thibet on the one hand, and Corea and Loo-Choo on the other, almost entirely subject to its influence; while its importance, in the eyes of eastern nations, is augmented by claiming to include Cochin-China, Camboja, Burmah, and Siam, among its tributary kingdoms. What an enormous and overgrown dominion is thus presented before us, extending over thirty-five degrees of latitude and seventy of longitude, and covering an area of upwards of 3,000,000 square miles.

The Chinese empire occupies no inconsiderable space in our map of the earth's surface, and fills up nearly the whole of their own; no wonder, then, that the Chinese should consider their country as the middle kingdom, including all within the four seas; and that, with them, the world and their empire should be synonymous terms.   It is true, that a great part of these territories are uninhabitable deserts, and Chinese Tartary may have only four inhabitants to a square mile; yet the government of that country extends an influence over nearly as much of the earth's surface, and more of its population, than either England or Russia, and makes its orders heard and obeyed from Peking to E-le, and from the capital to Canton, amongst several hundred millions of people.   By its new accessions of territory,

China has come into the neighbourhood of the British possessions; and, though originally so distant from us, seems to shake hands across the Himalaya mountains,—and invite western nations to publish amongst them, the glad tidings of great joy, which shall be to all people.

CHAPTER II.

PROBABLE POPULATION.

THE QUESTION OF POPULATION INTERESTING TO THE PHILOSOPHER, THE
POLITICIAN, THE MERCHANT, AND THE CHRISTIAN—THE POSSIBILITY
AND PROBABILITY OF A LARGE POPULATION ARGUED FROM THE FER-
TILITY OF THE SOIL—THE EXTENSIVENESS OF THE CULTIVATION—
THE PAUCITY OF THE ROADS—THE MANNER OF DISPOSING OF THE
DEAD—THE ENCOURAGEMENT GIVEN TO AGRICULTURE—THE INDUS-
TRY OF THE INHABITANTS—THE SKILL OF THE HUSBANDMAN—THE
ECONOMY IN FOOD, DRESS, AND DWELLINGS—CONTRASTED WITH THE
SCARCITY OF PROVISIONS—AND WANT OF FEELING—EMIGRATION,
WITH ITS DIFFICULTIES—BOUNTY ON THE IMPORTATION OF RICE—IN-
FANTICIDE—ITS PREVALENCE—FOUNDLING HOSPITALS—CONCLUSION.

SCARCELY any thing has been the subject of so much controversy, and at the same time of so much interest, relative to China, as the number of its population. The philosopher, the politician, the merchant, and the Christian are alike concerned to know, how many individuals are congregated together in that immense empire, and what is the rate of increase of its inhabitants. The population of China has formed the basis of numerous hypotheses among those who treat of the wealth or poverty of nations, and its exceeding populousness has been assumed or denied, according as different writers have sought to establish various propositions relative to the rapid or slow growth of the human family ; and in proportion to the amount of their fears lest the increase of population should entrench upon the means of subsistence and produce an extensive and insupportable famine. The Malthusites have caught at the fact, that China, already over peopled, is yet increasing in population and is doubling the number of its inhabitants every twenty-five years; which, connected with the circumstance of the scarcity and misery which already prevail, have led them to form the most gloomy apprehensions for the future, and to discourage marriage and encourage wars, lest the world should, like China, become overstocked, and universal want and misery envelope and engulph the whole family of man. The anti-Malthusites, on the other hand, shocked at this dreadful picture, and still more alarming prospect, have greedily embraced the suggestion thrown out by some writers, that the population of China has been exaggerated; and finding different returns given by various authors, have argued that the subject is questionable and undecided; then taking the lowest census they can find they have come boldly forward and declared that China is one of the most thinly peopled countries of the globe, that her soil is not one tenth part cultivated, and that her peasantry and mechanics are enjoying an ease and luxury, devoid of all appearance of want or penury, unknown and unequalled in any other part of the world. These extreme differences of opinion, established as they both appear to be by irrefragable arguments, tend to perplex the enquirer; but we must remember that the advocates of opposing systems generally go to extremes in defence of their favourite propositions; and that the truth usually lies between the two, to be elicited only by a dispassionate research, and an unprejudiced mind; determined to judge according to the evidence adduced, independent of previously existing opinions.

The politician is not less interested in the question of China's population ; for, if it be true that that empire contains its hundreds of millions, it will become an important enquiry how she is to be dealt with ; and what precautions are necessary to prevent her enterprising, though not warlike people, from pressing with their teeming myriads upon the neighbouring populous and fertile states.   If they be so numerous, and if they threaten to become doubly so, not only will the restrictive policy of the Chinese, which would prevent its inhabitants from emigrating, be broken down, but the welfare, if not the peace of surrounding nations be disturbed by the influx of a mass of shrewd and hungry intruders ; who, if they cannot obtain a livelihood by honest competition, will first by petty thefts, and then by more daring robberies, become dangerous to the colonies where they reside ; and in time present such annoyances as can only be checked by their exclusion from the scene of their chosen residence.

There are already two colonies in the eastern archipelago, one under the Dutch and the other under English authority, where the annual influx of Chinese colonists has, whether right or wrong, been the occasion of much alarm ; and in one district in particular the revolt, or supposed revolt, of the Chinese has ended in the utter extermination of the suspected tribe ; while in Borneo the Chinese have settled themselves down in the interior —have made head against the European authorities— and carried on the war for a considerable time ; concluding with an honourable peace, by which they have retained full possession of a rich province,— abounding in the precious metals,—and secured the mouth of a river, affording a favourable outlet for

foreign trade.   Hence European colonies in the east
have begun to forbid the introduction of Chinese emigrants, some levying a heavy fine on all new comers,
which amounts to an actual prohibition, and others
sending whole cargoes away, bidding them to seek
another home.

To the merchant and manufacturer, this subject is
not devoid of interest; particularly at a period when by
the invention of machinery, goods are manufactured
more than doubly sufficient for all the civilized tribes
of Europe and America; when even our East Indian
possessions are overstocked with the productions of
art; and when a new market for our manufactures
becomes a matter of serious concern to those who
have already exceeded the necessities of neighbouring nations, and who are compelled to look out for
purchasers in new and untried fields of commerce.
But if China really contain so large a population as
is assigned to it, in a climate where warm clothing is annually required, how large a field is thus
opened to the speculations of capitalists and the energies of operatives, which for years and ages they would
not be able fully to exhaust.   Say not, the Chinese are
poor and cannot pay for our goods; they already pay
four millions of pounds sterling for our opium, which
only injures and destroys them; and how is it that they
cannot afford to purchase useful and necessary commodities, the wearing of which will as much promote
their interests, as the sale will ours.   It is true, their
system is exclusive, and commerce with them is carried
on under numerous restrictions; yet if such a vast mass
of people exist and must be clothed; and if our merchants and manufacturers can furnish them with the

necessary articles cheaper and better than they can supply themselves, the trade must extend, and our manufactures gain admission.

But the Christian philanthropist is still more interested in this important question. When each individual possesses a never dying spirit, and each sinner is exposed to endless wrath, the greater the number of persons involved in the calamity, the more serious the evil; and the more must the contemplation of it oppress the mind of the thoughtful Christian. As this view of the subject, however, will be more fully enlarged upon in the sequel, it will be sufficient now, to discuss the question of China's population; and endeavour to ascertain the real state of the case, leaving the deduction of inferences to the close.

To clear the way to this important subject, it will be necessary, first, to shew the possibility and probability of China's containing the assumed population; and then, the reality of its existence.

That it is a possible case that China contains as many inhabitants as even the largest census would give, few who have paid any attention to the subject will be disposed to deny. Though there have not been wanting those who strenuously affirm, that the soil is incapable of sustaining so vast a population; yet, by a comparison of that land with others, calculating the number of occupants and the area of their territory, we find that such *a priori* reasonings are not founded in fact, nor entitled to our regard. China Proper is said to contain 1,297,999 square miles, or 830,719,360 English acres of ground. If then we allow only one-half of the land to be capable of cultivation, (though some would allow two-thirds,) and each acre of cultivated ground to be capable of sustaining one individual, (though some say each acre will support five,) then we have cultivable ground in China sufficient for the support of 415,000,000, of persons. Thus by a very moderate calculation, we see that it is by no means impossible for China to contain the full population which the highest census assigns to it.

Again, if we compare China with other countries of the globe, and calculate the population of each square mile, we shall find that that empire is not more thickly peopled than some other countries ; and if it be possible for other regions to sustain their population, then is it also possible for China to do the same.   In Holland, for instance, we have 210 inhabitants to the square mile ; in England, including the army and navy, 244 ; in Ireland, 256 ; and in Belgium, 333.   While in China, if we take the population at the highest census, given in 1812, namely 361,279,897, we shall find that its population is about 278 individuals to the square mile, being somewhat more than the population of Ireland, but by no means equal to that of Belgium.   Now as the people of Ireland can live, and those of Belgium can afford to maintain a separate and expensive government, and keep a large army on foot,—there is nothing extravagant in the supposition that China contains and is able to sustain the population assigned to it.

We next come to consider the probability of such a supposition ; and in so doing we shall find that it is not unlikely that China contains a large amount of population from the fertility of its soil, combined with the great quantity of land under cultivation ; the encouragement that is given to agriculture ; and the industry and skill of the inhabitants, contrasted with the economy observed; notwithstanding which the people in many provinces are reduced to the most abject state of want and misery, many dying of actual starvation, and thousands emigrating every year, in order to procure a precarious subsistence abroad.

It is true that China is in some parts hilly, and in others marshy; that wild men and wild beasts occupy the higher regions, and reeds and rushes the lower; in such situations we do not of course expect to find fertility; yet the vallies and the level plains, which are by no means circumscribed, are proverbially productive, and in some favoured spots, the fertility is amazing. Barrow says, "that an acre of land, in China, with proper culture, will afford a supply of rice for ten persons for a whole year, in the southern provinces; and sufficient for the consumption of five in the northern; allowing each person two pounds a day."* This estimate may be considered high; but on minute enquiry of the natives, who are acquainted with the cultivation of the interior, it appears, that an acre of land in China, well cultivated, will produce 3600 pounds of rice, in two crops, per year; which is equal, at two pounds a day, to the sustenance of five individuals. But the Chinese peasantry generally cannot calculate on two pounds of rice a day, or scarcely one, and are obliged to make up the deficiency by sweet potatoes, pulse, or any thing else that will satisfy hunger. The observation of travellers, who have visited the country, tends to shew, that the borders of the grand canal, and the two gigantic streams—the Yellow River, and the Yang-tsze-keang—are extraordinarily productive, yielding two crops in the year, without needing to lie fallow

* Barrow's Travels in China, pp. 577, 578.

a single season. The provinces of Keang-soo and Gan-hwuy, Shan-tung and Shan-se, Chĕ-keang and Ho-nan, are those which yield the greatest revenue to the emperor, and consequently those which are most productive to the people; while the thick set stalks of waving corn in the vicinity of those places fully substantiate the character given of them by foreign travellers and native documents, as being the granary of the land.

To the fertility of the soil, we may add the consideration that it is very extensively cultivated. China contains, as has been before observed, 830,719,360 English acres; and if we allow one third of this area for hills, rivers, marshes, and waste lands, we shall have 553,812,906 acres for cultivable ground. In ascertaining this, however, we are not left to conjecture; as there exists a report made to the emperor Këen-lung, in the year 1745, of the amount of land then under cultivation, according to which it appears, that, reckoning the land belonging to individuals, with that in the possession of the Tartar standards, the military, the priests, and the literary, there were, at that time, 595,598,221 English acres under cultivation; since which period, a new estimate has given 640,579,381 English acres, as the total extent of occupied land in China. Thus it appears that more than three-fourths of the surface are owned and tilled by man, allowing, according to the highest census, nearly one acre and three quarters to each individual. The greatest part of this area is laid out exclusively in arable land, and devoted to the production of food for man alone. In China, the natives make no use of butter or cheese, and very seldom of milk; the principal animal food is pork, which is generally home-fed; they have few horses for travelling, pomp, or war; and the only cattle they keep are such as are needed in husbandry: hence, there are no grazing farms, no meadows, and very little pasture; while every acre of ground, capable of cultivation, is turned up by the spade or the plough, in order to afford sustenance for the teeming inhabitants. The few beasts of burden, or of draught, which they keep, are either tethered to a string, by the side of the road, or turned out to graze on the hills; while they are supplied, by night, with a little straw or bean stalks, which is also their principal food during the winter   A common is quite unusual throughout the eastern half of China; while parks and pleasure grounds are proportionably scarce, as the anxiety to satisfy the appetite prevails over the desire of amusement.

Wheel carriages being rare, particularly in the south, the roads are comparatively few and narrow; generally consisting of raised pathways through the rice fields, or of winding lanes over the mountains. The statement of Barrow, that "the imperial roads are triple," with the declaration of Le Compte, that "they are fourscore feet broad, or near it," does not interfere with the general assertion, that the roads of China are narrow; for the two writers just quoted, are speaking of the public roads in the vicinity of the capital, and of the royal way from Peking to the imperial residence in Chinese Tartary. Broad ways may comport with a high state of civilization, but where the people are little accustomed to luxury and self-indulgence, they will be content with narrow paths; particularly when every particle of improveable soil is needed to sustain the population. What an immense quantity of land is occupied in England, in order to indulge the locomotive propensities of the inhabitants, and to enable them to move, with ease and expedition, from one place to another. This expenditure of the energies of the soil, in feeding millions of horses, and this laying out of good ground, in constructing several thousand miles of road, is almost entirely spared in China, where the public are content to walk, or carry each other about, if they may but get enough to eat and to wear.

It has been objected to the statement regarding the occupancy of a great proportion of the land in tillage, that the cemeteries of the Chinese are both numerous and extensive ; and much of the soil being consecrated to the service of the dead, there must of necessity be a smaller quantity left for the support of the living. The force of this objection seems to be heightened by the consideration, that the Chinese never allow old graves to be disturbed ; and, generally speaking, dig a new pit for each individual. But, an acquaintance with the fact, obviates the supposed difficulty ; for, the Chinese seldom select, for burial places, situations capable of agricultural use and improvement ; and inter their deceased friends on the hill side, or under the craggy precipice, where little else could be made of the soil. During the various excursions, which the writer has made into the interior, along the shores of three or four maritime provinces, he was particularly struck with the extreme paucity of graves. In one part of the province of Shan-tung, a cemetery was discovered in a sequestered glen ; and, here and there, a white monument presented itself by the road side ; but by no means equal to the hosts of living inhabitants, everywhere

met with.   Near the populous city of Shang-hae, coffins
were seen in the corners of the fields, kept above ground
till the body should decay ; when the bones might be
collected into jars, placed by the cottage door, and the
coffin and the room might serve for other occupants.
At the great island of Choo-san, scores of coffins were
observed under a precipice, scattered about in confusion,
some fresh, and others in a state of decay, all denied
the right of sepulture, from the crying necessity of a
want of room.   In the neighbourhood of Peking, the
cemetery may be large because the population is great,
and the ground round the capital comparatively barren;
but generally throughout the country, and particularly
in the more level and fertile provinces, the living
cannot afford much room for the dead, and the cemeteries are therefore contracted and few.

The encouragement given to agriculture would also
argue a dense population.   It is an ancient maxim with
the Chinese, that when people are hungry there is no
attending to the dictates of justice and propriety, and
only when a population is well fed, can they be well
governed.   Hence from the earliest antiquity, the emperor has set an example of industry to his people, by
personally and publicly holding the plough once a
year, while the empress does the same with regard to
the loom.   In arranging the various classes of the people, the Chinese place the literati in the foremost rank,
as learning is with them the stepping stone to honour ;
but immediately after the learned, the husbandman
takes the precedence of all others, because being engaged in raising the necessaries of life, he is abundantly
more important than the mechanic, who merely changes
the forms of matter ; and the merchant, who originates

nothing, and only barters and exchanges commodities for the sake of gain. This honour put upon agricultural employments is evidently the result of design; and shews that the country, being over stocked with inhabitants, needs cultivating to its utmost extent, in order to provide the people with sustenance.

The industry and skill of the Chinese, striving to produce as many of the necessaries of life as possible, would also argue a dense population, ever struggling against threatening want, and compelled to exert themselves for their daily bread. In tropical climates, where the ground is fertile, and the population scanty, the natives find that, by a few months labour, they can produce sufficient food for a whole years consumption and are therefore indisposed to exert themselves further. But in China, the inhabitants are incessantly employed, and every individual is obliged to be busy in contributing his quota to the common weal. Every one, in the least acquainted with the manners of the Chinese, knows that they are untiring in their exertions to maintain themselves and families. In the business of agriculture, they are more particularly active, raising two crops from the ground every year, extending their cultivation in every possible direction, and bringing the most unpromising spots into use, in order that nothing may be lost. Their skill in effecting these objects, is not, considering their few advantages, contemptible. They thoroughly understand the importance of varying the crops; they know perfectly well the seasons and soils adapted for certain productions ; and they are fully sensible of the importance of manuring the ground, in order to maintain its fertility. A stranger is struck with this, on first setting his foot on the shores of China.

Almost every individual met with, in the paths and
fields, is provided with a basket and a rake; and every
evening, the cottager brings home a certain quantity to
add to the mest heap, which is a most important appendage to every dwelling.   Having but few sheep and
cattle, they are obliged to make the most of the sterco-
raceous stock of men and swine.   This is carefully
collected, and actually sold at so much per pound, while
whole strings of city scavengers may be seen cheerily
posting into the country, every successive morning, with
their envied acquisitions; little heeding the olfactory
nerves of the less interested passengers.   Every other
substance likely to answer the end, is anxiously collected, and carefully disposed, so as to provide for
future exigencies; such as decayed animal and vegetable matter, the sweeping of streets, the mud of canals,
burnt bones, lime; and, what is not a little singular,
the short stumpy human hair, shaven from millions of
heads, every ten days, is industriously gathered up,
and sold for manure throughout the empire.   In the
high importance placed on stercoration, in China, we
see an illustration of that passage in II. Kings, vi. 25,
that when there was a great famine in Samaria, " the
fourth part of a cab of dove's dung was sold for five
pieces of silver."

The skill of the Chinese husbandman is also manifested in the arrangement and irrigation of his rice lands.
In the centre and south of China rice is the staple com-
modity; and it is well known that rice will not thrive
unless supplied with water.   From the preparing of the
ground for the seed, almost to the reaping of the harvest, the rice fields must be overspread with water.   In
order to this, each field is made perfectly level, with an

elevated ridge or border, and a stream of water constantly flowing into it, to provide against the loss by evaporation, and to yield an overplus for the fields around and beneath it. For this purpose water must either be raised by artificial means, such as pumps, levers, wheels, &c., from a lower to a higher region; or conducted with great skill and care from some elevated position, along the sides of hills, and across vallies, to the desired spot; where, introduced into the highest field of the series, it gradually flows down to the lower terraces, until it is lost in the river or the sea. The very ingenious methods which the Chinese employ for raising water have often been illustrated; and shew at once their adroitness, and the necessity which has thus driven them to their wits ends, to increase the produce of their soil. The water brought over the land, brings fertility along with it, and the debris accompanying the fluid thus conveyed from the surrounding heights, tends alike to moisten and fructify the soil. The Chinese may be considered adepts in terrace cultivation, notwithstanding the observations of Barrow, that he saw but few instances of it in his route. From all the information that can be gathered from the natives, the contrary is the fact; and though in places where a supply of water cannot be commanded at an elevated spot, the natives necessarily leave the hills uncut into terraces; yet in every instance in which the locality is favourable, they do not fail to adopt a mode of cultivation so essential to the production of rice in southern latitudes. All travellers agree in the opinion that in minute spade husbandry, the Chinese more than equal Europeans; and Lord Macartney denominates them the best husbandmen in the world. The activity and acuteness of the Chinese husbandman, therefore, tend to shew, that so much energy and mind have been necessarily called into display by an overflowing population.

Not less remarkable, nor less available to our argument, is the economy observed by the Chinese in the use of the necessaries of life, in order that they may make them go as far as possible. This is apparent in their food, their dress, and their dwellings; in all of which they avoid extravagance, and restrict themselves to such kinds as need the smallest quantity of ground to produce and rear them. It is not meant by this, that the Chinese are not fond of good food, and plenty of it, when they can get it; they are, in fact, both epicures and gormands, when good things fall in their way; but they manage to do with little and coarse food, when necessity compels them, which is, alas! but too often. The diet of a Chinese is generally a little rice and salt fish, or salted vegetable; a species of *brassica* being commonly used for this purpose, which being thoroughly impregnated with salt, helps to flavour the insipid rice, and enables them to relish their food. This mess is sometimes varied by certain preparations of pulse or millet, and more rarely a few ounces of pork are stewed down with the vegetable preparations, in the proportion of one to five. The common food of the poor, however, is sweet potatoes or yams, with occasionally a little rice boiled in a large quantity of water; and once a month, it may be, a pork meal, or on grand festive occasions, a little poultry. Against the eating of beef they have a strong prejudice, not so much on account of religious scruples, as because oxen are used in husbandry, and they think it a shame, after a poor animal has been

labouring all his life in their service, to cut him to pieces
at last, and then to feed upon his flesh, and make shoes
of his hide. Hence in the hortatory tracts, which they
sometimes publish, they draw the figure of an ox, composed entirely of words or characters, which set forth
the complaint of the cow kind, relative to their hard
usage during life, and their still harder fate at death,
concluding by assigning the lowest place in Pandemonium to the villainous beef-butchers, who mercilessly
cut them up for gain.

Having no inclosed pastures, they cannot breed
many sheep or goats, which, wandering over the corn
fields and gardens, would destroy more than they are
worth. It is only in hilly and barren regions where
these animals are allowed to roam, and even there not
beyond the shepherd's eye; hence in the more fertile
and more populous parts of the country, mutton is scarce
and seldom eaten. Instead of beef and mutton, however, the Chinese have recourse to dogs and cats, the
flesh of which animals is equal in price to that of swine.
In default of these, they have no objection to make a
dish of rats and snakes; and cockroaches and other
reptiles come in to be used either as food or medicine,
by a people who are driven frequently to great straits
for want of sustenance; animals that die of disease,
and those already far gone in a state of decay, are when
discovered eagerly devoured by a hungry peasantry in
search of food. In short the Chinese have the most
unscrupulous stomachs imaginable; every thing animal
from the hide to the entrails,—and almost every thing
vegetable, from the leaves to the roots, is made available to the support of life; and even some parts of the

mineral kingdom are laid under requisition for this important purpose.*

In their dress, the Chinese are alike anxious to economize the soil. Barrow says, " that an acre of cotton will clothe two or three hundred persons:" and as cotton can be planted between the rice crops, and thus vary the productions, and relieve the soil, the Chinese prefer such clothing as they can raise, at the least expense of ground and labour. Were the hundreds of millions of China to be clothed in woollens, an immense tract of grazing land would be required, which would deduct materially from the area devoted to food, and greatly exceed what the Chinese could afford. In their dwellings, likewise, they are particularly frugal of room: living together in a very small compass, and crowding into closely built cities, as though ground with them were an object of great moment. A room twenty feet square would afford sufficient space for a dozen people to eat, drink, work, trade, and sleep; while the streets of their towns and cities are so narrow, that it is quite possible to touch each side of the way with the hand as you pass along. Now if we compare this frugality with the extravagance of European nations in regard to room, living on beef and mutton, and wearing woollen clothes; we may easily see that the ground which would sustain one Englishman, would be sufficient for the support of three or four Chinese. Amongst such a selfish and sensual people, so much economy would not be observed, did not stern necessity compel; and what greater necessity can exist

* The Chinese use great quantities of gypsum, which they mix with pulse, in order to form a jelly of which they are very fond.

than the difficulty of sustaining a crowded population from a contracted soil.

Notwithstanding all this diligence and care, however, the people in most of the provinces find a difficulty in procuring the necessaries of life; many die of actual want, and many more are obliged to emigrate: while every encouragement is given to the importation of grain, in order to relieve a needy population. The general poverty of the people has already been alluded to, in shewing them to be content with a diminished quality and sometimes quantity of food; yet many of them can hardly find food enough, and numbers die annually of sheer starvation. When a drought, or inundation occurs, when locusts invade the coasts, and the crops fail from blight or mildew, imperial bounty is obliged to be extended to the sufferers; otherwise a people, considerably straightened on common occasions, would in a season of scarcity actually perish for want. For this purpose, a great quantity of grain is annually left in the various provinces, besides that which is forwarded to Peking, in order that the supply may be ready when necessity demands it. According to one statement, there are reserved in different parts of the country about 26,000,000 bushels of grain, and 12,000,000 bushels of rice, to be sold out at a low price to the poor in seasons of scarcity; a quantity sufficiently indicative of the wants of the people, and of the straits to which they are sometimes driven, to need such a supply. And yet this royal munificence sometimes proves inadequate to the relief of the wretched; or being pillaged by underlings in its way to the necessitous, leaves the hungry to starve ere the provision reaches them. The extreme poverty of the people in the south of China is well

known to all who are acquaintedwith those regions, and
the piteous scenes presented in winter by whole hosts
of peasants almost destitute of food or fuel, are enough
to affect most deeply the minds of the compassionate.
The common wages of the day labourer is but four
pence a day, and the remuneration to a schoolmaster
from each of his scholars is only ten shillings a year;
while provisions are sometimes nearly as high as they
are in Europe.

The want of feeling generally apparent among the
Chinese, argues their deep poverty; for where provisions are scarce and dear, the human heart, unsanctified
by Divine grace, soon becomes closed against the cry
of distress, and the sick poor are allowed to perish by
the road side, without a helping hand to relieve them.
There is some charity manifested towards kindred, but
none to strangers, who are left alike destitute of public
provision and private benevolence.   Canton is infested
with beggars, who gain a scanty relief by their untiring
importunity; and, in other parts of the country, the
needy present their dismal tale of miseries to the too
heedless spectators.

Persons in danger of being drowned, or burnt, are
seldom rescued; and numbers are turned out to die in
the open air, to save the trouble of tending them while
sick, and the expense of cleansing the house of their
ghosts, when dead.   This disregard of the wants and
miseries of others, must be partly occasioned by the
pressure of personal want, and the great number of
individuals needing relief.

The subject of emigration, is one which considerably
affects the question of the population of China.   The
government of that country being restrictive and exclu-

sive, have gone on the principle of forbidding alike the emigration of natives and the immigration of strangers. Standing in need, however, of foreign supplies; and being unable to provide for their own subjects, they have, in the first place, been induced to allow a sort of restricted commerce at Canton; and, finally, to wink at the departure of natives to foreign lands. Still they consider those who go abroad, as forfeiting all claim to the protection of their own government, constituting themselves outlaws, as well as aliens, by the same act of expatriation. When a misunderstanding occurred between the Chinese colonists and the Dutch authorities, at Batavia, some years ago, and a massacre of the Chinese followed; the colonial government afraid, lest the emperor of China should take umbrage at the transaction, sent an embassy to that country, explaining the matter, and attributing the blame to the emigrant Chinese themselves. The emperor, however, coolly replied, that, as they had chosen to place themselves without the pale of his benign and fostering sway, they were no longer entitled to his protecting influence; thus, whatever happened to them, he should not interfere. Those who return to their native land, after having amassed considerable property, if not screened and sheltered by their friends and relatives, are liable to be accused of having had intercourse with barbarians; when their crime increases in malignity, according to the amount of their possessions, until, by repeated extortions, they are deprived of all. Notwithstanding, however, the original restrictions on emigration, the forfeiture of the rights of citizenship which they thereby incur, and the prospect of a good squeezing when they return; yet, such is the difficulty many of them find in procuring a subsistence, that they willingly quit friends and home, and brave the dangers of the deep, with the inhospitalities of a foreign clime, in a state of poverty, rather than stay at home, and drag on a miserable existence in want of all things. Hence they have not only removed from the more populous provinces of China, to those more thinly peopled; but have crossed the wall, the desert, and the ocean—pouring forth their hordes to the east, west, north, and south—occupying the waste lands of Tartary—colonizing Thibet, Burmah, Camboja, and Siam, and basking under the fostering care of European governments, in the islands of the Malayan archipelago. What stronger proof of the dense population of China could be afforded than the fact, that emigration is going on, in spite of restrictions and disabilities; from a country, where learning and civilization reign, and where all their dearest interests and prejudices are found—to one where comparative ignorance and barbarity prevail, and where the heat or cold of a tropical or frozen region, is to be exchanged for a mild and temperate climate; added to the consideration, that not a single female is permitted, or ventures to leave the country, when consequently all the tender attachments, that bind heart to heart, must be burst asunder, and perhaps for ever. Where is the country—where, under such circumstances, emigration would prevail, unless stern necessity compelled, and unless the ever-increasing progeny pressed on the heels of the adult population, and obliged them to seek a precarious subsistence in a less thickly peopled part of the earth?

The breaking through of another restriction, in the otherwise unalterable system of Chinese policy, proves

the existence of a dense population in that country. It
has been before observed, that the Chinese discourage
intercourse with foreign nations, and only permit a
limited and heavily burthened commerce at Canton.
All foreign vessels, trading to Canton, have to pay a
measurement charge, amounting, on vessels of eight
hundred tons, to two thousand dollars, and an entre-
port fee of nearly equal value ; but, by command of the
present emperor, in the year 1825, the former, and by
previous orders, the latter charge, were both dispensed
with, in case of all vessels loaded with rice, in order to
encourage the importation of so necessary an article
from abroad.   This permission is taken advantage of
by foreign merchants at Canton, and great quantities
of rice are thus imported, to supply the wants of a
needy population.   Nothing but necessity will induce
the Chinese government to swerve from its usual regulations, and to grant any immunities to foreigners :—
when they do so, as in the case alluded to, it shews
that rice is greatly needed in the country ; and, if rice
be needed in so fertile a region as China, it is evident
that China is overstocked with inhabitants.

In addition to the above mentioned considerations,
the prevalence of infanticide, in China, has been adduced, by some, as a proof of that empire's extreme
populousness. While, however, we would by no means
argue, that this abominable practice is kept up, in
order to keep down the population, or that it has any
considerable influence in diminishing the numbers of
the people, we may still contend that infanticide in
China, is more the result of poverty than prejudice, and
has to do with economical, rather than religious considerations.   In the first place, it is to be observed, that

infanticide in China, is wholly confined to the female
sex; boys, it is imagined, can provide sufficiently well
for themselves; are likely to repay, by their labour,
the care and expence bestowed on them; and contribute to the building up of the family name and fortunes; in all of which matters, girls are of little value.
Hence the birth of a son is hailed in every Chinese
family, with delight; while the house is only filled
with lamentation, on the appearance of a wretched
daughter. A son is, therefore, valued and cherished,
while a daughter is despised and neglected. This feeling carried to excess, leads many, in extreme poverty,
to perpetrate infanticide, in the one case; and to practice forbearance, in the other. Again, the abominable
custom alluded to, is not taught or enjoined by any
religious system prevalent in China — either Confucianism, Taou-ism, or Buddhism; it is not done to
propitiate the gods, as was the case, formerly, amongst
the cruel worshippers of Moloch; nor do the natives
expect to reap any spiritual advantage, by giving " the
fruit of their body for the sin of their soul;" but the
Chinese perpetuate this infernal custom merely from
parsimonious motives, and just to save themselves the
care and expense of bringing up a useless and troublesome being, who is likely to cost more than ever she
will fetch, on being sold out in marriage. It prevails,
therefore, in proportion to the general indigence of the
people, and affords by its prevalence, a criterion by
which to judge of the density of the population, and the
poverty of the inhabitants. Hence, we find that it
obtains more in the southern provinces, where the
numbers of human beings exceed the powers of the
soil to produce sufficient sustenance; or, in a crowded

capital, where the myriads of citizens find hardly room to live or to breathe. In the southern parts of the empire, the natives themselves, who might be supposed anxious to conceal the fact, bear ample testimony to its existence, and that in a proportion which it is fearful to contemplate; while the lightness, with which they treat the murder of female infants, shews that it must have prevailed, in no ordinary degree, in order so far to blunt their sensibilities on the subject, as to lead them to contemplate the drowning of a daughter, as far more excusable than the treading of printed paper under foot. The extent of infanticide in the capital has been calculated, by the number of infants thrown out every night, and gathered by the police in the morning, to be buried in one common hole, without the city. One writer informs us, that ten or a dozen infants are picked up every morning, in Peking alone; hence, the murders in that city must amount to several thousands annually.

Some writers and travellers have questioned the prevalence of infanticide in China, because they have never, in their intercourse with the Chinese, seen any instances of it. Thus, Ellis remarks, "that in passing along the populous rivers of China, through upwards of 1600 miles of country, they met with no proofs of its existence." De Guignes has been brought in, also, as saying, "that in his route, through the whole extent of China, in travelling by water, he never saw an infant drowned; and, in travelling by land, although he had been early in the morning, in cities and in villages, and at all hours, on the highways, he never saw an infant exposed or dead." But, this negative kind of evidence is contradicted by the direct testimony of Messrs. Bridg-

man and Gutzlaff, who have both met with instances
of what neither Ellis nor De Guignes could trace or
discover.

The fact, that foundling hospitals are more easily
filled in China than elsewhere, is corroborative of the
little regard in which female infants are held. The
more tender hearted parents, rather than lay violent
hands on their offspring, prefer giving them away; or if
they can find no one to receive the charge, depositing
them in some temple, or monastery, where there is, at
least, a chance of their being noticed and preserved.
The Buddhists, in China, avail themselves of this circumstance, to fill their nunneries; while the Catholics, in that country, increase the number of their
adherents, by rescuing the outcast daughters of the
inhabitants, and bringing them up for wives to the
native converts. Others, actuated by base motives,
pick up the abandoned children, and rear them for the
purpose of sordid gain, which they accomplish by selling them for domestic slaves, or training them up for
wanton gratifications, or condemning them to beg
through the streets, after having cruelly put out their
eyes, to make them objects of charity.

It is not meant to be argued, that the Chinese murder, expose, or sell their female infants to prevent the
country becoming overpeopled; or that the practice is
so general as to have any material effect on the population. Whatever the motive be, it is altogether personal, and not patriotic; it is merely to save themselves
pains and money, and not to benefit the country by
decreasing the number of consumers. To whatever
extent, also, the practice may prevail, it is not likely
materially to affect the aggregate of the population.

For if we allow that one per mille only of the female infants born in China are smothered, which is much below the mark in the populous provinces and crowded cities, while it would exhibit a fearful estimate as the aggregate of murders, it would still be very inconsiderable as affecting a population, which amounts to several hundred millions, and which increases at the rate of three per cent. per annum. The object of the argument is to shew, that the children being sacrificed to Mammon rather than to Moloch, the prevalence of the custom indicates the great poverty and overwhelming numbers of the people,—that there is a disproportion between the supply of food and the number of consumers,—that human life is cheaper than human provender,—and hence the conclusion, considering the fertility of the soil, that China is immensely populous.

CHAPTER III.

CENSUS OF THE POPULATION.

TESTIMONY OF THE CATHOLIC MISSIONARIES — AND CHINESE AUTHORI-
TIES — THE LAW OF THE CENSUS AND THE WAY OF TAKING IT — THE
REASON FOR SO DOING—ITS CREDIBILITY—THE DIFFERENT ACCOUNTS
RECONCILED — INCREASE ACCOUNTED FOR — INCREASE SKETCHED —
AMIOT'S ESTIMATE — GROSIER'S — MORRISON'S — AND SIR G. STAUN-
TON'S — COMPARISON OF THE WHOLE — WHICH MOST TO BE CREDITED
— THE DISCREPANCIES OF SOME — THE MOST CREDIBLE CENSUS — THE
REVENUE OF CHINA — AND ITS LIGHT PRESSURE ON THE PEOPLE.

BUT we have somewhat more than probability to guide
us, in endeavouring to ascertain the population of China.
We have the evidence of men who have long resided in
the country, and a variety of estimates taken by the
natives themselves, and published by imperial authority.
While the learned of Europe are sitting at home, and
calculating what may or may not be, which they decide
according to their several hypotheses, and partialities;
we have the testimony of eye witnesses and actual
residents, as to what really exists.   Between these bare
supposers and personal enquirers there can be no difficulty in determining on whom most reliance is to be
placed.   The speculators on China's population, however, aware that facts are against them, have sought to
throw discredit on the witnesses produced on the other
side, by bestowing on them the most opprobrious
epithets, and calling their veracity into question on
every occasion.   The authorities most likely to furnish

information on the subject of China are the catholic missionaries, and the Chinese themselves. The former who penned the " Edifying and curious letters," are sometimes spoken of jocularly as " reverend gentlemen" telling their " pleasant stories ;" at other times more cavalierly, as " stupid and lying missionaries, who contrived to impose upon Europeans with their absurd and ridiculous notions." Malte Brun, however, describes them as " weak and credulous, rather than wilfully mendacious." It must be confessed, that these are rather hard terms to bestow upon men who have left their native land, and ventured all, to spread what they conceive to be the truth ; men, at the same time, of much learning, and, one would hope, of some sincerity —who have deserved better than to be denounced as downright liars, in matters where they had neither interest or inclination to deceive. Their opportunities for ascertaining the fact, were many and great, as they were engaged, by imperial authority, in travelling through the various provinces, and drawing up a statistical view of the empire ; so that they were not likely to be easily imposed upon by accounts inconsistent with truth.

The Chinese authorities have been treated in a still more unscrupulous manner, and the estimate given by a principal mandarin, to Sir G. Staunton, is described as complete an example of Chinese mendaciousness, as any ever afforded ; and, as a document, bearing on its very face, the marks of fabrication. It is comparatively easy to get rid of adverse testimony, by throwing discredit on the judgment or veracity of the witnesses ; but though the Chinese may be, generally, given to

E

fabrication and exaggeration, yet, in a matter where the only trial of veracity is to transmit returns from the people to the government, and to record them in public documents, we do not see why they may not be believed. The documents, thus drawn up and published by the Chinese executive, are not intended for the eyes of foreigners, or meant to exalt native resources in the estimation of surrounding nations; on the contrary, the emperor, in the edicts referring to the population, does not speak of its amount in a boasting, but a complaining tone; for, like another Malthus, he is afraid lest the increase of population should entrench on the means of subsistence, and a famine be produced; he, therefore, exhorts the people to diligence in husbandry, that they may raise as many of the necessaries of life as possible, and to economy in their expenditure, that they may make them go as far as they can.

Now, however mendacious the Chinese may generally be, we can only expect them to gratify their lying propensities when interest allures, or when they have no means for ascertaining the truth. That they can have no interest in deceiving the world, is evident from their unconsciousness of these statements being published to the world; and that they have every possible means of ascertaining the amount of the population, will appear from the manner in which those returns are made, and the census obtained. The law on this subject, is as follows:—

" All persons whatever shall be registered, according to their respective professions or vocations. When a family has omitted to make any entry in the public register, the master thereof, if possessing lands chargeable with contributions to the revenue, shall be punished with one hundred blows; but if he possess no such property, with eighty blows. When any master of a family has among his household strangers, who constitute, in fact, a distinct family, but omits to make a corresponding entry in the public register, or registers them as members of his own family, he shall be punished with one hundred blows, if such strangers possess taxable property; and with eighty blows, if they do not possess such property; and if the person harboured is not a stranger, but a relative, possessing a separate establishment, the punishment of the master so offending, shall be less than as aforesaid by two degrees, and the person harboured shall be liable to the same punishment. In all these cases, the register is to be immediately corrected. In all the districts of the empire, one hundred families shall form a division, in order to provide a head and ten assessors, whose duty it is to assist and oversee in the performance of all public matters. These 'elders' must see that all the families in their respective divisions, have been registered, and failure in doing this, exposes them to the bamboo. The returns of population are to be made annually."

On this subject, Dr. Morrison observes:—

" In the Chinese government, there appears great regularity and system. Every district has its appropriate officer; every street its constable; and every ten houses, a tything-man. Thus they have all the requisite means of ascertaining the population with considerable accuracy. Every family is required to have a board, always hanging up in the house, and ready for the inspection of authorised officers, on which the names of all persons, men, women, and children, in the house, are inscribed. This board is called a mun pae, ' door tablet,' because where there are women and children within, the officers are expected to take the account from the board at the door. Were all the inmates of a family faithfully inserted, the amount of the population would, of course, be ascertained with great accuracy. But it is said, that names are sometimes omitted, through neglect or design; others think that the account of persons given in, is generally correct."

The census thus annually called for, by the Chinese

government, and published in their official accounts of
the empire, is demanded with the view of enabling the
ruling powers to ascertain the state of the country, in
order that they may apportion the due amount of
government officers, and police force, to each district,
and make suitable provision for the necessities of the
people, in case of famine. According to the system
adopted by the reigning dynasty, a considerable proportion of money and grain is retained in the provinces
for the service of the state, and the exigencies of the
people ; and it would be difficult to know what amount
should be reserved, unless the average number of the
inhabitants were ascertained. It is, then, to assist the
government, in making proper arrangements for the
home administration, and not to impose either on themselves or foreigners, that this census is taken. It is
published in a work, given out by imperial authority,
called the Ta-tsing-hwuy-tëen, or "Collection of statutes
for the present dynasty," where the various arrangements, for the direction of the six tribunals, are
fully particularized. Under the item of revenue, the
account of the population occurs ; and as this work has
been published at different periods, it affords a criterion
to judge of the state of the population through successive years.

Now the question occurs. Are these official documents to be believed, or are they not? When any
European government orders a census to be made, and
publishes a state paper, declaring that such and such is
the result of their researches and calculations, it is
generally believed. No one objects to the statement,
on the ground of that government professing the reli-

gion of the Romish or Greek church, or professing no
religion at all; but since it is a matter of mere
civil polity, with which they must have a much better
acquaintance than others can possibly have, they are
allowed to make their own statement, and are believed
accordingly. In negociating with foreign powers, or
in managing matters which immediately concern their
individual interests, the Chinese do sometimes practice deception; but, in matters of sober fact and actual
calculation, we do not see why the Chinese should not
be credited as well as others. We receive, without
scruple, their account of the number of their provinces,
counties, and districts; the aggregate of their officers,
and the amount of their revenue; and why not take
their estimate of the population? at least, until we can
find one made by those who have better opportunities
of ascertaining the fact. It will not do for us, who
have only supposition to guide us, to contend with
those who are in the habit of counting the people every
year, and have such efficient means for arriving at the
truth. We may make some deductions for the extravagance of eastern nations, and receive with caution
the statements of different years, which we can compare together, and endeavour to ascertain the rate of
increase; but we are not at liberty to call them liars,
till we can prove them to have erred wilfully in this
matter.

It is now time to introduce to the notice of the
reader, the various estimates which have been given by
the Chinese themselves, with the authorities on which
they rest, in order that a complete view may be formed
of the gradual growth, and present state, of the Chinese population.

Dynasty.	Emperor.	Year of reign.	A. D.	Population.	Authority.
Ming	Tae-tsoo	27	1393	60,545,811	Kang-këen-e-che.
Tsing	Shun-che	18	1662	21,068,600	⎫ Ta-tsing-hwuy-tëen,
,,	Kang-he	6	1668	25,386,209	⎬ old edition, extracted
,,	,,	49	1710	23,312,200	⎭ by the author.
,,	,,	50	1711	28,605,716	⎫ Ta-tsing-hwuy-tëen,
,,	Këen-lung	18	1753	102,328,258	⎬ new edition, extracted
,,	,,	57	1792	307,467,200	⎬ by Dr. Morrison and
,,	Këa-king	16	1812	361,221,900	⎭ his son.

The above items are taken from regular Chinese works, and depend on the authority of official documents. By these, it will be seen, that before the Tartar conquest, when the Chinese dwelt under their native emperors, the population amounted to 60,000,000 ; and that after the invasion of the empire, by the rulers of the present dynasty, the population suddenly fell off to twenty or thirty millions ; at which state it continued for fifty years, when it gradually rose, till it reached a hundred, and, subsequently, three hundred and odd millions. In order to account for this, it may be necessary to observe, that the wars which took place on the transfer of the empire into new hands, greatly diminished the number of the people : that, for scores of years, a great part of the empire remained unsubdued, on which account, the Tartars could not reckon on the inhabitants of the southern and western provinces as their subjects ; and that, at the commencement of the present dynasty, the revenue was levied in the shape of a capitation tax, which, of course, led a great number to evade enrolment, lest they should be held responsible for the impost demanded by the government officers. Hence, it is not difficult to account for the great falling off in the population, during the first years of the present dynasty, and for the amazing difference between the forty-ninth and fiftieth year of Kang-he, when the capitation tax was removed, and converted into a land tax.   Indeed considering the change of measures, adopted by the government, it was rather to be expected that the returns for the following year, would exhibit an increase of twenty instead of five millions, as all those who had been previously deterred from giving in their names, had now every motive to concealment removed, and would willingly allow the registration of their signatures.

From the year 1711 to the year 1753, a period of forty-two years, the population appears to have advanced, from twenty-eight millions and a half to a hundred and three millions.   This may be accounted for, partly in the way above mentioned, and partly by the gradual increase of the population.   This increase will not appear very great, if it be considered, that an excess of three per cent. per annum, of the births over the deaths, will make the population treble itself in the time specified.   The next increase, according to the official returns, is of a like character: viz. from 102,328,258 in 1753, to 307,467,200, in 1792; or a triple sum in about forty years.   And, when we consider, that during these two periods of forty years each, the dominions of the Tartar-Chinese monarch were extending, and more and more persons were inscribed on the population list;   besides the perfect tranquillity which the empire enjoyed during the whole series of years, it is not to be wondered at, that the population should advance at such a rapid rate.

The customs and institutions of the Chinese, doubtless, contributed much to this increase; for, according

to the precepts of Confucius, " of the three degrees of
unfilial conduct, to be without posterity, is the greatest;" hence the Chinese of every class and degree marry
when quite young, and rejoice in nothing so much as in
the increase of their families. Added to the strong desire
of issue, we may allude to the bounties offered by the
Tartar rulers, when fully established in the dominion
of the empire, proposing grants of the land which had
been previously deserted by the terrified population, to
any who would settle down and cultivate it; which has
induced many to spread over the country, and to prosecute the quiet and healthy arts of husbandry; by
which their industry has been exercised, and their
increase promoted; until now the whole land is full of
inhabitants, and they are bursting their bounds on
every side.

From 1792 to 1812, a period of twenty years, the
increase has been inconsiderable compared with former
years, being only one-sixth of the whole, and scarcely
an addition of one per cent. per annum. This diminution in the rate of increase, during the last twenty
years, previous to 1812, may be accounted for, partially
by the growth of emigration, and, more fully, by the
introduction of opium, which since the latter part of
the last century, has been smuggled into the country,
at an enormous rate. Those who have not seen the
effects of opium smoking, in the eastern world, can
hardly form any conception of its injurious results on
the health, energies, and lives of those who indulge in it.
The debilitating of the constitution, and the shortening
of life, are sure to follow, in a few years, after the
practice has been commenced; as soon and as certainly,
if not much more so, than is seen to be the case with

those unhappy persons, who are addicted to the use of
ardent spirits.   The dealers in opium are little aware
how much harm they are the instruments of doing, by
carrying on this demoralizing and destructive traffic;
but, the difference between the increase of the Chinese
people, before and after the introduction of opium,
ought to open their eyes, and lead them to ask themselves whether they are not accountable for the diseases and deaths of all those, who have suffered by its
introduction.   And if it be true that the Chinese increased at the rate of three per cent. per annum, before
the commencement of the traffic, and at the rate of one
per cent. per annum, since, it would be well for them
to consider, whether the deficiency is not to be attributed, in some degree, to opium, and the guilt to be
laid at the door of those who are instrumental in
introducing it.   They may flatter themselves, that if
the growth of population were not thus checked by the
introduction of opium, its increase would be curtailed
by wars or pestilences ; or the superabundant populace
would perish by famine, and starvation effect what
opium would not accomplish.   Still, whatever cause
might contribute to the balancing of the population
with the means of subsistence, human life could not be
sacrificed, without blame being attached somewhere ;
and blame, in proportion to the greatness of the evil
which might result from the measure.

   In addition to the official returns of the population
above given, there are others furnished by different
European writers, which as they appear to be derived
from native sources, deserve some notice here.   They
are the following.

Amiot's estimate, for the year 1743, amounting to 157,301,755
Grosier's ditto 1762,   ditto   198,214,553
Morrison's ditto 1790,   ditto   143,125,234
Staunton's ditto 1792,   ditto   333,000,000

With respect to the first it will be seen that it
exhibits a greater population in 1743, than is found
by the official returns to have existed in 1753.   Amiot
professes to have drawn his estimate of the population
from the Ta-tsing-yih-tung-che, "an account of what is
essential to be known respecting China," published in
the eighth year of Këen-lung, A. D. 1743.   Grosier,
who seems anxious "to justify the assertion of the
learned missionary, and to free him from all suspicion
of exaggeration," enters more into detail respecting
Amiot's estimate, and remarks that the Yih-tung-che
shews only the number of the jin ting, or those who
are taxable in each province, which amounted to
28,516,488; and as these are the heads of families,
Grosier suggests that Amiot multiplied these by five,
in order to shew the number of individuals in the whole
empire, thus making 142,582,440 ; then including the
inhabitants of Füh-këen, about seven millions, which
he had before omitted, and the civil and military
officers, literati, &c., he makes the sum total amount
to 157,301,755. This, however, is a very unsatisfactory
method of ascertaining the population of a great country;
and will not warrant us, on the ground of such calculations to call in question the authority of official
returns.   But it is more than likely that Amiot, or his
friend Grosier for him, has entirely mistaken the case.
Jin-ting is not the expression employed to designate
families in Chinese statistical works, but *men :* the

word for *families* being hoo, " doors," in distinction
from kow, " mouths," which is the proper word for
individuals. Again, the work to which he refers, though
published in 1743, may refer to a census of the population at a previous date, and thus nearly synchronize
with the census given in the year 1711, which we have
seen by authentic records to have been 28,605,716.

Grosier's own enumeration was taken from an estimate of the population in " the tribunal of lands " at
Peking, which was made in the twenty-seventh year of
Këen-lung, A. D. 1762, and was received in France in
1779. It was written both in Chinese and French,
and was translated into the latter at Peking. By this
estimate it appears that the population amounted to
198,214,553. Upon this we may remark, that Grosier
himself does not appear to have consulted the work
referred to, but only an extract from it, or a translation
of it. It is possible, therefore, that there may be some
mistake, either in the number, or the date. Still as the
census is placed between the years 1753, when the
population was 102,328,256, and 1792, when it was
307,467,200, the intermediate number of 198,214,553
is not an unlikely estimate.

The account published by Dr. Morrison, in his view
of China for philological purposes, exhibits the population as amounting to 143,125,225 in 1790. This
estimate was taken from a new edition of the Ta-tsing-
yih-tung-che, or " a complete statistical account of the
empire under the present dynasty," published about the
close of the reign of Këen-lung, probably A. D. 1790;
which is the identical work referred to by Amiot, only
a later edition. The edition which Dr. Morrison consulted exhibits the original amount of the population,

at the beginning of the present dynasty, and then the
increase since that time. The first, says Dr. Morrison,
was probably about A. D. 1644, and the last about
1790. In a note at the bottom of the page, Dr. Morrison observes, "that the work itself does not state
what the time of the original census was; that it was
at the beginning of the present dynasty rests on the
verbal authority of the natives." Neither does it appear
that the work states the precise time when the second
census was made; we only know that it was taken prior
to the publication of the book in 1790, but how long
previous to that date we are not aware. The dates,
therefore, of 1644, for the first, and 1790 for the second,
are merely hypothetical; and, as much depends on the
period when a given census was taken, we cannot, in
estimating a population which is constantly and rapidly
increasing, take a census without date, and oppose it to
the authority of those the dates of which are clearly ascertained. The first census quoted by Dr. Morrison is
27,241,129; while the second amounts to 143,125,225.
Now if we refer to the official returns, the dates of
which are determined in a foregoing page, we shall find
that about the year 1711, the population amounted
to 28,605,716, which is not far from the first statement
furnished by Dr. Morrison; neither does it differ very
materially from the number of jin-ting, or men, quoted
by Amiot, and which he has mistaken for families, and
multiplied to 157,301,755. The probability therefore
is, that as both Amiot and Morrison consulted the
Yih-tung-che, only in two separate editions, the number
quoted by the French missionary, and the first estimate
produced by Dr. Morrison, refer to one and the same
period; and that that period instead of being 1644, as

supposed by Dr. Morrison, or 1723, as Amiot imagined, was most likely the intermediate date of 1710, which would make it agree with the estimate given of the population for the following year in the Ta-tsing-hwuy-tëen, quoted above. Dr. Morrison's second estimate of 143,125,225 need not be placed exactly in 1790, because the work in which it was found appeared about that time: it might as well be assigned to the middle as the close of Këen-lung's reign, and fall more about the year 1765, which would allow for the gradual increase of the people from 102,328,258 in 1753, to 143,125,225, twelve years afterwards. Besides the indefiniteness of the dates in the account furnished by Dr. Morrison, there are some inconsistencies hard to be reconciled with other returns, or with the state of the country, which will be noticed in a subsequent page; it is due to Dr. Morrison, however, to observe, that the statements above given were published in 1817; and that in a paper drawn up by him, and inserted in the Anglo-Chinese College Report, for 1829, he has given an estimate of the population as amounting to 307,467,200, in 1792.

The account furnished to Sir G. Staunton, by the Chinese mandarin, Chow-ta-jin, has been frequently referred to, and not a little reprobated and called in question. Malte Brun thinks, that because the numbers, in each province, are given in round millions, and because, in two provinces, the number of millions is precisely the same, that, therefore, the whole document is a fabrication. But, how can these be considered as the marks of fabrication? The mandarin professed to derive his information from a particular friend at Peking, and merely gave it as a general estimate, without entering into particulars on the subject; and this is, by no means, an uncommon case with ourselves. The population of England, France, Germany, or Spain, is frequently given in round millions, without the specification of the units, except when a census is particularly demanded or published by government; and when a population is thus roundly stated, it does not throw discredit on the whole, to say, that two different regions, Austria and France, for instance, contain the same number of millions. With regard to Sir G. Staunton's informant, we may look upon his statement, as entitled to credit, as far as general estimates go; and while it does not profess to give a particular account of the population, we may take it as corroborating or explaining some cotemporaneous statement derived from more authentic sources. Now this account of the population was delivered to Sir G. Staunton, in 1792, and does not materially differ from an official return, published in the same year, which makes the population amount to 307,467,200 ; and, considering that the one was a rough guess, in round numbers, and the other, the result of a minute investigation, we need not be surprised at the discrepancy that appears in the aggregate. The two together are sufficient, however, to prove that the population of China, at that period, exceeded three hundred millions.

We shall now present the reader with a comparative statement of the number of inhabitants in each province, according to the various accounts, accompanied by other statistical returns, calculated to throw light on the subject.

VARIOUS ESTIMATES COMPARED.

Names of the Provinces	No. I. Census taken about the beginning of the present dynasty, extracted from the Yih-tung-che, by Dr. Morrison. probable date, 1710.	No. II. Census taken in the 50th year of Kang-he, according to the Ta-tsing-hwuy-tëen, extracted by J. R. Morrison, Esq. 1711	No. III. Census taken in the 18th year of Kёen-lung, from the Ta-tsing-hwuy-tëen, new edition, by Rev. E. C. Bridgman. 1753	No. IV. Census taken from the Yih-tung-che, by Dr. Morrison published about the latter end of Kёen-lung's reign, probable date, 1760. 1760	No. V. Census taken from the Yih-tung-che, by Grosier, published about the 27th year of Kёen-lung, and referring to the year 1765. 1765	No. VI. Census furnished by the Chinese mandarin to Sir G. Staunton. 1792	No. VII. Census taken in 1812, according to the Ta-tsing-hwuy-tëen, extracted by J. R. Morrison, Esq. 1812	No. VIII. Land Tax paid in money, calculated at 6s. 8d. per tael, and forwarded to Peking. Taels.	No. IX. Land Tax paid in grain, calculating the Chinese shih at 160 lbs. weight. Shih.	No. X. Customs taken at passes, remitted in money, calculated at 6s. 8d. per tael. Taels.	No. XI. Grain retained in the provinces, calculating the Chinese shih, at 160 lbs. weight. Shih.	No. XII. Number of square miles in each province. Miles.
Shing-kйng	4,194			486,634	668,852		942,003	38,708	111,672	78,660	296,314	
Chih-le	3,260,075	3,274,870	9,374,217	3,504,038	15,222,940	38,000,000	27,990,871	3,000,210			1,960,269	58,949
Keang-soo	3,917,707	2,656,465	12,618,987	28,967,233	23,161,409	32,000,000	37,843,501	3,257,676	1,431,273	779,584	2,514,602	92,961
Gan-hwuy		1,357,829	12,435,361	1,438,023	22,761,030	19,000,000	34,168,059	1,770,693	795,063	220,351	1,019,163	
Keang-se	1,350,131	2,172,587	5,055,251	5,922,160	11,006,640	21,000,000	23,046,999	1,888,302	678,320	181,190	1,927,143	72,176
Chè-keang	5,528,499	2,710,312	8,662,808	18,975,099	15,429,690	15,000,000	26,256,784	3,426,640		73,549	2,119,268	39,150
Fйh-kёen	2,710,649	706,311	4,710,339	1,684,528	8,063,671	14,000,000	14,777,410	1,184,809		9,644	2,011,434	53,480
Hoo-pïh	1,468,145	433,943	4,508,860	24,604,369	8,080,603	13,000,000	27,370,098	1,283,671	96,934		562,475	
Hoo-nan	469,927	335,034	4,336,332	9,098,010	8,829,320	25,000,000	18,652,507	947,505	96,214		1,508,420	144,770
Ho-nan	375,782	3,094,150	7,114,346	2,662,969	16,332,507	24,000,000	23,037,171	3,177,408	221,342		2,443,341	65,104
Shan-tung	2,005,088	2,278,595	12,769,872	25,447,633	25,180,734	27,000,000	28,958,764	3,396,885	353,963	29,680	1,445,190	65,104
Shan-se	1,792,329	1,727,144	5,162,351	1,860,816	9,768,189	18,000,000	14,004,210	3,528,803		10,919	1,306,987	55,268
Shen-se	240,809	2,150,696	3,851,043	257,704	7,287,443	27,000,000	10,207,256	1,699,323	218,550		3,334,143	
Kan-suh	311,972	368,525	2,133,292	340,086	7,412,014	21,000,000	15,193,125	320,102			3,482,246	154,008
Sze-chuen	144,154	3,802,089	1,368,496	7,789,782	2,782,976	10,000,000	21,435,678	651,614			1,055,019	166,800
Canton	1,148,918	1,142,747	3,969,248	1,491,271	6,797,597	8,000,000	19,174,030	1,317,804		97,420	2,585,000	79,456
Kwang-se	205,995	210,674	1,975,619	2,569,518	3,947,414	9,000,000	7,313,885	489,429			1,117,646	78,250
Yun-nan	2,255,666	145,414	1,003,058	3,083,459	2,078,802		5,561,320	243,837			750,401	107,969
Kwei-chow	51,089	37,731	1,218,848	2,941,891	3,402,722		5,288,219	122,548	227,626		157,808*	64,554
	27,241,129	28,605,716	102,328,258	143,125,225	198,214,553	333,000,000	361,221,900	31,745,966	4,230,957	1,480,997	31,596,769	1,297,999

* Besides this quantity of grain, 28,705,125 Taels are retained in the Provinces.

With regard to the foregoing lists of the population, published at various periods, and adduced by different writers, we may observe, that the second, third, and seventh columns, being extracted from official documents with the dates annexed, may be considered as most worthy of regard; and, by a comparison of these three, it will be seen that, in almost all the items, as well as in the sums total, they advance in a progressive ratio, from 1711 to 1753, and 1812. It is a matter of regret that we are not able to furnish the particulars of the census taken in 1792, and extracted by Dr. Morrison from the Ta-tsing-hwuy-tëen, but the aggregate 307,467,200 corresponds with that system of progressive increase which has evidently been going on in China, for the last century. It will be seen also that the revenue derived from the various provinces, in the eighth, ninth, and tenth columns, is in such proportions as we might anticipate from the population of the respective regions as exhibited in the second, third, and seventh columns; considering that some of the provinces are more fertile than others, and therefore produce more, both in money and kind. From these considerations, therefore, we may venture to conclude, that the three columns above referred to, exhibit the most authentic and credible account of the population, at the periods specified.

Next to them in importance and credibility is the account given by Grosier, and the rough sketch brought home by Sir G. Staunton, in the fifth and sixth columns. Grosier's account exhibits a progressive increase in the various provinces, such as we might expect to find, and thus greatly corroborates the statements which precede and follow, in the third and seventh columns. The estimate brought home by Sir G. Staunton tends in some measure to the same end, though as a round statement, it cannot be expected to exceed in accuracy; and is merely introduced to shew the general opinion entertained by Chinese officers, respecting the population.

We are sorry, however, to observe, that we cannot derive so much advantage from the censuses in the first and fourth columns; inasmuch as, in several points, they differ from every other account of the population, and from what is known of the state of the country. In the first column, it will be observed that no inhabitants are assigned to Shan-tung, though that is so near the seat of government, and has always been considered a fertile and populous region; while, however, the first column exhibits Shan-tung as entirely destitute of inhabitants, the fourth column, derived from the same authority, presents the same province as swarming with more than 25,000,000 of inhabitants. During all this time, however, the province of Canton, which for the last century has been the seat of foreign commerce, has been nearly stationary; both columns exhibiting that province as containing little more than a million of inhabitants; when it is well known that Canton is one of the most populous regions of the empire, and possesses between the provincial city and Macao, more inhabitants than are assigned to the whole province. Again, Yun-nan, which is known to be deficient in population, and which was at the beginning of the present dynasty but imperfectly subjected to the Tartar yoke, is said in the first and fourth columns to contain more than double the population of Canton; while the neighbouring province of Kwei-chow, which

F

is similarly circumstanced, contained according to the first census but 51,089, and according to the next estimate of the same writer nearly 3,000,000. There is also much inconsistency with regard to the returns for Fŭh-këen; the population of that region contained according to the fourth column but 1,684,528; while we may venture to say, that there are a million emigrants from Fŭh-këen in various parts of the Chinese coast, and the Malayan archipelago, and more than ten times that number in the province itself. Lastly, the province of Hoo-pih, in the centre of China, fertile, populous, and one of the first that submitted to the Tartar yoke, is rated at 469,927 in the first column, and at 24,640,369 in the fourth column. These incongruities compel us to hesitate respecting the estimates in question, and incline us to depend more implicitly on those accounts the dates of which are certain, and the items consistent with each other.

It will easily be seen from what has been before stated, that the author inclines to receive the highest estimate that has been given of the Chinese population, and to rate it at 361,221,900: and thus after the fullest consideration of all that has been said on either side of the subject,—after the most patient investigation of native documents,—and after extensive enquiries and observations among the people for more than twenty years, he cannot resist the conviction which forces itself upon him, that the population of China Proper is as above stated; besides upwards of a million more for the inhabitants of Formosa, and the various tribes of Chinese Tartary, under the sway of the emperor of China.

We cannot dismiss the preceding table, without

adding a word or two respecting the revenue of China as therein exhibited; shewing us, at the same time, the resources of the country, and the share of the burthen of government sustained by each individual. Before making up this statement, however, it will be necessary to explain what is meant by the denominations of money, and the measures of grain employed in the table. The *tael* is a nominal coin among the Chinese, representing something more than an ounce of silver, and may be rated at six shillings and eight pence, or the third part of a pound sterling. The *shih* is a measure of grain, containing 3160 Chinese cubic inches, or 3460 English cubic inches. The Chinese frequently weigh their grain, and then the *shih*, in Canton, is supposed to weigh 130 catties, or $162\frac{1}{2}$ pounds; while in the interior a *shih* weighs 180 catties, or 225 pounds. The value of such a measure of grain is generally about one pound sterling. The revenue is derived principally from the land-tax which is paid partly in kind, and partly in money; it is generally a very light impost, amounting not, as some suppose, to one tenth, but more usually to one fiftieth or one hundredth of the produce. There are also taxes on pledged articles, and more particularly a heavy impost on salt; while custom-houses are established on the sea coast, and at the most important passes in hills, and junctions of rivers, so as to secure the mercantile as well as the agricultural population. Some of the revenue thus derived is kept in the provinces, to pay the army, navy, and police, and to provide against famines, while a considerable proportion is forwarded to Peking for the immediate service of the emperor and his officers. We cannot, therefore, form a correct estimate of the resources of China, unless we consider all that is sent to the capital and expended in the provinces, as being alike drawn from the labour of the people, and devoted to the service of the state. Thus the revenue of the Chinese empire will appear to be as follows:—

Land-tax, paid in money, and sent to Peking . . .	31,745,966 taels, or	£10,581,755
Ditto, paid in grain, ditto . .	4,230,957 shih, worth	4,230,957
Customs, paid in money, and sent to Peking . . .	1,480,997 taels, or	493,666
Grain kept in the provinces .	31,596,569 shih, worth	31,596,569
Money ditto ditto .	28,705,125 taels, or	9,568,375
		£56,471,322

This revenue, when divided amongst 361,221,900 persons, amounts to three shillings and three half-pence per head: and if that only which is sent to Peking be reckoned, namely £15,206,378, it will not amount to much more than ten pence per head. Some persons may doubt, how a government over so great a country can be maintained for so small a sum, and how a people under an arbitrary rule can be let off with such insignificant imposts; particularly when in a free country like our own, and in a time of profound peace, each individual contributes upwards of two pounds, annually, as his share of the public burthen. But it must be remembered, that China has few or no re-sources beyond itself, that her foreign commerce is limited, and compared with the population insignificant, that comparatively few subsist by manufactures, and that almost all the inhabitants are dependent on agriculture. In a country, therefore, where the con-sumers fully equal the capabilities of the soil, and where every production is hastily devoured by a needy population, there is little left for a government to glean, or, to use a Chinese simile, to squeeze, out of the already exhausted pockets of the people. It is not unlikely, also, that the present peaceful state of the country, and the willingness with which the Chinese submit to the Tartar yoke, is to be ascribed mainly to the light and insignificant burthens pressing on the people, who would soon complain, and perhaps revolt, if more heavily taxed. But how can the government manage to maintain an immense establishment of civil and military officers, besides an army and navy of nearly a million of men, upon fifteen or even fifty-six millions of pounds sterling? To this it may be replied, that the pay of a Chinese soldier is only four pence a day; that the salary of the highest officer under government does not exceed £8,000 per annum, of which there are not many; that there is not more than one officer to ten thousand people; and that most of these have not more than £50. per annum: thus it is quite possible for the government to manage a country so thinly officered and so poorly paid, upon a comparatively small sum of money. Besides which, there is no national debt in China, so that all that is gathered goes to the actual maintenance of the government, and is not expended in paying the interest on obligations formerly contracted, to be defrayed by future generations.

In the report of the anglo-Chinese college, for 1829, there is an estimate of the amount of land-tax paid in different provinces, extracted from the Ta-tsing-hwuy-tëen, or " Collections of statutes of the Tartar dynasty," by which it appears that the average rate of land-tax per mow, (or Chinese acre, somewhat smaller than an

English acre,) is from fifteen cash to one hundred, or from one penny to sixpence: this when calculated at its highest value, and multiplied by the number of acres in China under cultivation, will amount to about £12,000,000 sterling.   This statement agrees with the common report of the natives, who affirm that from one to two per cent. of the produce is the utmost of what is exacted by the government in the shape of land tax.

CHAPTER IV.

REFLECTIONS ON THE POPULATION.

THEIR OVERWHELMING NUMBERS — THEIR SINFUL CONDITION — THE WORK OF EVANGELIZING THEM DIFFICULT — DEPENDENCE ON DIVINE AID — THE DIFFUSIVE CHARACTER OF THE GOSPEL — ENCOURAGEMENT DRAWN FROM THE UNIFORMITY OF THEIR GOVERNMENT, LANGUAGE, MORALS, AND SENTIMENT — THEIR EXTENDING POPULATION — ONLY CHECKED BY EUROPEANS — AND THE INTRODUCTION OF OPIUM — THE EFFECT OF OPIUM SMOKING — ITS RAPID INCREASE — CHINESE LAWS AGAINST IT — MEMORIAL OF A MANDARIN — EXTENT OF SMUGGLING — APPEAL TO THE OPIUM MERCHANT — AND THE EAST INDIA COMPANY — DEMORALIZING EFFECT OF THE DRUG— REMONSTRANCE TO THE GOVERNMENT OF GREAT BRITAIN.

IF the population of China really amount to such overwhelming numbers, then what a distressing spectacle presents itself to the eye of the Christian philanthropist. Three hundred and sixty millions of human beings huddled together in one country, under the sway of one despotic monarch, influenced by the same delusive philosophy, and bowing down to the same absurd superstition. One third of the human race, and one half of the heathen world, held by one tie, and bound by one spell; one million of whom are every month dropping into eternity, untaught, unsanctified, and, as far as we know—unsaved. How unaccountable it appears that one individual should be allowed to fetter the minds of so vast a portion of immortal men, and to forbid the introduction of evangelical liberty. How

distressing to think, that this nation has been for ages
in its present demoralized and degraded condition, with
no light beaming on the people, but that derived from
atheism and polytheism, with now and then an obscure
ray from a questionable form of Christianity.   If we
were sure that this state of things would always continue, or that the Gospel was not destined at an early
period to subjugate and renovate China, we might
almost be led to grow weary of such an unimproving
and unimprovable world.   To see the demon of darkness reigning in one soul is painful, but to see him
rampant over a whole nation, and that nation constituting one third of the human race, is beyond measure distressing, and might well induce one to exclaim,
" Oh that my head were waters, and mine eyes a foun-
tain of tears, that I might weep day and night for the
slain of the daughter of this people."

There are, doubtless, amongst such a vast concourse
of human beings, numbers, who, according to the light
they have, lead tolerably decent lives, as it regards
moral and social duties ; but they must all be destitute
of right views of divine and eternal things ; and where
these fundamental truths are misapprehended, there
can be little hope of the claims of human relations
being properly sustained ; in fact, experience forces
upon those who have had the most frequent and intimate intercourse with them, the unwelcome truth, that
amongst them, in a remarkable degree, " there is none
righteous, no, not one : there is none that under-
standeth, there is none that seeketh after God ; they
are all gone out of the way, they are together become
unprofitable ; there is none that doeth good, no, not
one.   Their throat is an open sepulchre, with their

tongues they have used deceit; the poison of asps is under their lips, whose mouth is full of cursing and bitterness; their feet are swift to shed blood; destruction and misery are in their ways, and the way of peace have they not known;" and why? but because " there is no fear of God before their eyes." Now, if it be true, that they have " all sinned and come short of the glory of God;" that " without shedding of blood there is no remission," and that " without faith, it is impossible to please God;" if they cannot " call on him in whom they have not believed, nor believe in him of whom they have not heard, nor hear without a preacher;" then, how wretched must be the condition, and how dismal the prospect of a nation of sinners, and so great a nation, involved in one common ruin with ourselves, and yet ignorant of the only way of salvation. We are not warranted by divine revelation to conclude, that wilful and determined sinners will be forgiven without an interest in the great atonement; and we have no reason to imagine, that such interest can be obtained, by adult transgressors, without a knowledge of, and faith in, the Divine Mediator. How truly affecting and heart-rending is it, therefore, that so large a portion of the human race should be shut up together, under one tyrannical government, whose exclusive policy forbids all intercourse with foreigners, and whose proud self-sufficiency imagines their native institutions fully adequate to all the requirements of the present and the future world. Really, if the apostle Paul, speaking under the influence of inspiration, could express himself so feelingly and so strongly, relative to God's ancient people, as to " wish himself separated from Christ, for his brethren and kinsmen according to the flesh;" and if his "heart's desire and prayer to God for Israel was, that they might be saved;" then, surely, Christians in the present day, may be excused for feeling strongly on the subject of China's danger, and for panting eagerly after China's salvation.

But the population of China, in its present condition, not only distresses—it appals the mind. The man, who shall set himself to reform his household, or to enlighten his neighbourhood, has assigned himself a task of some difficulty; but of proportionate ease, compared with the great object of arousing a whole nation, turning the current of popular opinion, and bringing the mass of a people to think aright on the subject of religion. The difficulty is increased, however, when the reform of such a nation is attempted, and that in opposition to early and long cherished prejudices, backed by all the array of political power and philosophical cunning. Where shall we begin, or where can we hope to end the Herculean task? And what proportion do our present means and efforts bear to the end in view? Some score of individuals, is all that the churches of England and America now devote to the conversion of China—one thousand persons are thereby brought under instruction, and not more than ten converted every year. This is a very small proportion, and protracted will be the period, ere we can expect at such a rate to succeed. Could we bring one thousand individuals under instruction every day, and give them only a day's teaching each, it would take one thousand years to bring all the population of China thus under the sound of the Gospel; and if even ten of these separate thousands were every day converted to God, it would require one hundred thousand years to make all these mighty hosts savingly acquainted with divine truth.   This is a startling view of the matter, but a more affecting consideration still, is, that the ranks of heathenism are increasing at a thousandfold greater ratio, than we can expect, by such a system of proselyting, to thin them.   For, even allowing an increase of only one per cent. per annum, on the whole population, we shall find that they are thus adding three and a half millions, yearly, to their number; so that according to our most sanguine calculations, the heathen would multiply faster than they could be brought over to Christianity.   Besides which, while we are thus aiming to rescue a few, the many are still perishing for lack of knowledge.

Thus, the very magnitude of the object disheartens and depresses the mind.   The multitude of individuals to be benefited, astonishes—and the distance to which the supposed accomplishment of the design is removed, sickens—so that men of common mould, and the usual energies, would hardly venture on such an undertaking; and Christians, in general, despairing of success, are tempted to restrain prayer before God.   And what shall we say to these things?   Shall we give up the attempt as hopeless, and leave the Chinese to perish, unpitied and unaided?   God forbid.   It must be remembered, that we depend not on human resources; for if we did, we never should have attempted the work: and had we thus rashly ventured on the undertaking, we should speedily have sounded a retreat. Our hope is in the Father of Lights, from whom cometh down every good and every perfect gift, and with whom there is no variableness, neither shadow of turning. He hath said, " I have sworn by myself, the word is gone out of my mouth in righteousness, and shall not return, that unto me every knee shall bow, and every tongue shall swear." And hath he said, and shall he not do it? hath he spoken, and shall he not bring it to pass? He can cause a nation to be born in a day, and even the conversion of so great and populous a nation as China, is not beyond the compass of Almighty Power; for, is anything too hard for the Lord?

But God does not need to be at the expense of a miracle, or to step out of the way of his ordinary providence to accomplish such an event. The plain preaching of the Gospel, by humble unassuming individuals, accompanied and blessed by the powerful energy of his Holy Spirit, will accomplish, in due time, the desired end; but, in such a way, that the power will, after all, appear to be of God, and not of men. The character of the Gospel is *diffusion;* it is compared to a little leaven that gradually spreads itself, till it leavens the whole lump. The very instinct of Christianity is *propagation;* and no sooner does one obtain a knowledge of divine things himself, but he is anxious to make it known to others. Thus an individual converted under the preaching of the word, on the shores of China, like Andrew, on the coast of Galilee, first finds out his own brother Simon, and tells him of Jesus of Nazareth. In this way, one may be the means of awakening ten, and ten of communicating the same blessing to a hundred; and so they may go on, without any miracle, except that of grace, spreading and increasing in a tenfold ratio, till a district—a county—a province—and the whole empire is evangelized. In this view of the case, numbers no longer appal, nor difficulties dishearten; and though China contained double the amount of inhabitants, fenced around by much severer restrictions, we need not fear attempting, nor despair of succeeding, in the work of evangelizing that people.

On the contrary, there is something in the very abundance of the population which constitutes a ground of encouragement; for, the inhabitants of that empire, though numerous, and spread over eighteen provinces, must be considered as a great whole; and what bears on the political, intellectual, moral, and religious condition of the people bears upon them as a whole. Thus China, though vast, is under one despotic form of government, and if measures could be adopted that would influence the ruler of so vast an empire, the whole mass of his subjects would, in a great measure, be affected thereby. It is not a fanatical suggestion, that the prayers of pious Christians, on behalf of the " Son of Heaven," would be heard in the court of heaven, particularly if all the available means be employed to inform, enlighten, and affect his mind. It is not impossible that a remonstrance drawn up by Christian missionaries, may reach the " dragon throne;" or, that a devoted and zealous preacher of the Gospel should get introduced to court, and plead the cause of Christianity in the imperial ear: and though the expression of his " holy will " might, at first, prove unfavourable, yet the repetition of such attempts, might, in time, prove successful ; and induce the government to grant free toleration to the profession of real godliness, through the length and breadth of the land. The man, who should make this the business of his life, and expend his talents and energies in seeking such an introduction, and procuring such an edict, would effect, under God, more than Archimedes contemplated, when he speculated upon moving the world.

But the Chinese are not only living under one form of despotic rule, they possess, likewise, one universal language and literature. It is a remarkable fact, that notwithstanding the spoken dialects of each province and county vary so materially, that the Chinese of different districts are absolutely unintelligible to each other; yet, the written medium of the whole empire is easily understood by all, and writing instead of speaking, constitutes the universal method of exchanging ideas. The Chinese written language, being symbolical, and the same symbols being used to designate certain significations, whatever sounds be attached to the character, each instructed person readily understands a book, though he may use a different dialect from the writer. It is remarkable, further, that not only are the same signs employed for certain ideas, in all parts of the country, but the same style is used. The disposal of the characters, as well as the characters themselves, is according to one uniform method; so that a person able to write well, in Chinese, no matter what may be his native dialect, is intelligible to the remotest borders of the empire. Yea, even beyond the limits of Chinese rule, the Chinese character and style are understood, and throughout Cochin-China, Corea, and Japan, the same mode of writing is current and legible. Thus a book, once composed in the customary Chinese style, if intelligible to one learned man, would be intelligible to all; and might travel among the hundreds of millions inhabiting south-eastern Asia, communicating intelligence throughout the whole region. What a stimulus does this afford to an active and energetic mind, while engaged in studying the Chinese language, or inditing a book for their instruction, that he is doing what may be available to the benefit of so many millions, and that to the latest generation? Such a book needs only to be multiplied and circulated, without undergoing the slightest alteration, in order to enlighten and edify one-third of the human race.

The morals, also, of this numerous people have one striking characteristic, and their religious views and practices are precisely similar throughout the empire. When a man has studied the main features of the Chinese character in one place and one person, he has studied them in all; and when he has discovered a train of argument that will silence the philosophical and superstitious objections of one individual, he has provided himself with materials that will be serviceable on all occasions. This uniformity and unvariableness of the Chinese mind is to be traced to their possessing one set of opinions on philosophy and religion; which being laid down in their ancient books, and stereotyped from age to age, constitutes the public and universal sentiment on the above topics, and runs through the whole mass of society. Hence the missionary finds the Chinese always using the same arguments and starting the same objections, which having been often answered before, may be easily replied to again. In this view of the matter, the multiplicity of their population dwindles into insignificance, and affords an advantage to the missionary not to be met with elsewhere.

Whilst considering the population of China in all its

bearings, it may be well to observe, that it is possible
to draw encouragement from its very increase.   It has
been before observed, that China, partly by additions
to the number enrolled, and partly by the preponder-
ance of births over deaths, has doubled its population
several times during the last century.   Such has been
the rapidity and extent of the increase, that all the
waste lands, within the empire, capable of cultivation,
have been occupied ; and the surplus population, unable
to gain a subsistence at home, have been compelled to
emigrate by thousands every year, to the islands and
countries around.   Now, the number of inhabitants is
still increasing, and the Chinese in spite of their exclusive and restrictive system are bursting forth on every
side, and, without our asking it, are coming in contact
with Christians, and seeking shelter under European
governments, where missionaries may labour unimpeded
and unprohibited among them.   If the same causes
continue to operate, without any counteracting influence, there seems nothing to prevent the Chinese from
crowding into the British possessions in Hindostan, and,
under the mild and just sway of our Indian rulers, multiplying still more fast and plentifully than they have
done in their own country.   They have already their
hundreds of thousands in Siam, and will soon occupy
Birmah, Pegu, and Assam.   They have long colonized
the islands of the Malayan archipelago, and what
should hinder them from pushing on to New Holland,
where millions of acres await their assiduous and energetic cultivation ; while the extensive and fertile regions
of New Guinea and New Ireland lie still more con-
tiguous to their mother country.   A nation increasing
as does the Chinese, cannot be long confined within

narrow bounds, and restriction with them is impossible. Imperial edicts are already weak and inefficient, but will soon be flung to the winds. Hunger cannot be controlled, and necessity knows no law. Let but another age roll by, and China double her population once more, and her very increase will break down her political barriers, and bring her myriads in contact with the Christian world. Let vigorous measures be taken for the thorough instruction of the Chinese emigrants, and, while coming adventurers get an acquaintance with the truth, returning individuals will carry with them what they have learned; and thus, within and without the limits of the empire, all will gradually be evangelized. The multiplication of their numbers, therefore, viewed in this light, presents an encouraging aspect, and would lead us to anticipate the period as not far distant, when China shall stretch out her hands unto God.

It has been suggested, that this would be the case, if no counteracting influence intervened. We lament to say, that such an obstacle to the increase of the population does exist; and that it is to be found, not in external wars, or intestine commotions,—not in the oppressive measures of the Chinese government,—not in the unwholesomeness of their climate, or the confined nature of their buildings,—not in the general neglect of the poor, or in the awful prevalence of female infanticide,—but in the extensive and still advancing introduction of an *intoxicating medium.*

It has been observed, that wherever Europeans come in contact with their less skilful neighbours, and bring superior intelligence, enterprize, and, we may add, cupidity, to bear on the tawny nations of the globe; the result has been the gradual decline and disappearance of the one before the other, till the hardy and energetic white has taken the place of his coloured brother. In some places this has amounted to complete extermination, and in others the process is rapidly going forward, with the same gloomy prospect. Not one of the race formerly inhabiting Newfoundland is now in existence. The same may be said of the Caribs; while the Indians of North America, and the aborigines of New Holland, will soon be in the condition of those unhappy races. But was it intelligence alone which enabled the tutored tribes to prevail over the untaught? Were not other means employed, and did they not prove most lamentably successful? Was not the rum cask called in to the aid of the scheming colonist, and did not the red man fall but too easy a prey to the insidious allurement? Did not ardent spirits prove the ruin of the Indians, undermining their energies, shortening their lives, and decreasing their numbers? All this is well known fact, and will soon become matter of history. In China, territory is not sought, nor lands coveted; there Europeans do not aim at conquest or colonization; they have no need, therefore, to use an intoxicating medium, in order to subserve their designs of political influence, and territorial enlargement. The only inducement, that English merchants can have to lead them to carry on the opium trade in China, is the desire of gain; and yet that gain is so considerable as to draw them on with increasing eagerness in its pursuit. It is with them not a means to an end, but the end itself; they do not contemplate the wasting away of the population in consequence of the traffic, and yet the terrible effects of the traffic may be the same as though they did contemplate it. Facts induce us to believe that it is so. Those who grow and sell the drug, while they profit by the speculation, would do well to follow the consumer into the haunts of vice, and mark the wretchedness, poverty, disease, and death which follow the indulgence; for did they but know the thousandth part of the evils resulting from it, they would not, they could not, continue to engage in the transaction. Previous to the year 1796, opium was admitted into China on the payment of a duty, when a few hundred chests annually were imported. Since that time, the drug has been openly interdicted, and yet clandestinely introduced, at the rate of 20,000 chests annually, which cost the Chinese four millions of pounds sterling every year. This quantity at twenty grains per day for each individual,* would be sufficient to demoralize nearly three millions of persons. When the habit is once formed, it grows till it becomes inveterate; discontinuance is more and more difficult, until at length, the sudden deprivation of the accustomed indulgence produces certain death. In proportion as the wretched victim comes under the power of the infatuating drug, so is his ability to resist temptation less strong; and debilitated in body as well as mind, he is unable to earn his usual pittance, and not unfrequently sinks under the cravings of an appetite, which he is unable to gratify. Thus they may be seen, hanging their heads by the doors of the opium shops, which the hard hearted keepers having fleeced them of their all, will not permit them to enter; and shut out

* Some take a great deal more than this, but this is the average for the poor, and therefore for the many. Besides which the properties of the drug are not destroyed by once smoking, but will bear to be used as an anodyne twice over.

from their own dwellings, either by angry relatives or ruthless creditors, they die in the streets unpitied and despised. It would be well, if the rich opium merchant, were sometimes present to witness such scenes as these, that he might be aware how his wretched customers terminate their course, and see where his speculations, in thousands of instances, end. When the issue of this pernicious habit is not fatal, its tendencies are to weaken the strength, and to undermine the constitution; while the time and property spent in this voluptuous indulgence, constitute so much detracted from the wealth and industry of the country, and tend to plunge into deeper distress those weak and dependent members of society, who are already scarcely able to subsist at all. In fact every opium smoker may calculate upon shortening his life ten years from the time when he commences the practice; one half of his physical energies are soon gone; one third of his scanty earnings are absorbed; and feeling strength and income both diminishing, while the demands upon his resources are increased, he seeks to obtain by duplicity what he cannot earn by labour, and thus his moral sense becomes blunted and his heart hardened, while he plunges into the vortex of ruin, dragging with him his dependent relatives, and all within the sphere of his influence. Calculating, therefore, the shortened lives, the frequent diseases, and the actual starvation, which are the result of opium smoking in China, we may venture to assert, that this pernicious drug annually destroys myriads of individuals. No man of feeling can contemplate this fearful amount of misery and mortality, as resulting from the opium trade, without an instinctive shudder. But the most appalling fact of all is, that the trade is constantly increasing. The following statement exhibits the consumption of opium during the last twenty years:—

1816	.	Chests,	3,210	.	Value,	3,657,000	dollars.
1820	.	,,	4,770	.	,,	8,400,800	,,
1825	.	,,	9,621	.	,,	7,608,205	,,
1830	.	,,	18,760	.	,,	12,900,031	,,
1832	.	,,	23,670	.	,,	15,338,160	,,
1836	.	,,	27,111	.	,,	17,904,248*	,,

By this it will be seen, that while the consumption has been increasing, the price has been falling, from 1139 to 660 dollars per chest or nearly one half its original value. Still the enterprising speculator has been pushing his article into the market, determined to furnish the Chinese with it at any price, rather than lose so large a customer. Thus the appetite has been created, and is largely fed, until nearly three millions of victims have been drawn into the snare; and there is every prospect of its increasing still more, until the consumers dying off in proportion as the consumption extends, the country will be thinned of its inhabitants, and Mammon at length be disappointed of his prey.

But is there no remedy? The emperors of China have wisely and patriotically determined, from the very moment they spied the onward march of the threatened evil, to denounce and resist it: and instead of admitting it, on the payment of a duty, have as rulers, resolutely refused to derive any profit from the vices of the people. In the first year of the late emperor, Këa-king, 1796, the introduction of opium was interdicted

---

* The quantity introduced up to the year ending in the spring of 1837, was 34,000, and the deliveries during the month of July, of the same year, amounted to 4,000 chests.

by law; those who were found guilty of smoking it, were pilloried and bambooed; and the venders and smugglers made liable to the severer penalties of banishment and death; so late as the year 1833, the amended law upon the subject, was as follows:—

" Let the buyers and smokers of opium be punished with one hundred blows, and condemned to wear the wooden collar for two months. Then, let them declare the seller's name, that he may be seized and punished; and, in default of his discovering the vender, let the smoker be again punished with one hundred blows, and three year's banishment, as being an accomplice. Let mandarins and their dependants who buy and smoke opium, be punished one degree more severely than others; and let governors of provinces be required to give security that there are no opium smokers under their jurisdiction; and let a joint memorial be sent in, representing the conduct of those officers, who have connived at the practice."

Thus, as far as law goes, the government of China has, ostensibly, done every thing in its power to check the growing evil; and one would imagine that these regulations were sufficiently severe to ensure the entire exclusion of the article from the empire. Yet, in the year 1836, a Chinese officer, high in rank, presented a memorial to the emperor, in which he tells him,

" That, recently, the number of chests imported has exceeded 20,000, and that the sum paid, annually, exceeds eleven millions of dollars. Within the last few years, he adds, foreign ships have visited all the ports along the coast, from Canton, as far as Chinese Tartary, for the purpose of disposing of their opium, and though the local authorities immediately expelled them, yet the quantity clandestinely sold, is by no means small. The foreigners have, besides, a depôt, for opium, at Lintin, in the entrance of the Canton river, where they have seven or eight large vessels, called receiving ships, anchored all the year round. In Canton, the native brokers pay the price of the opium to the foreign merchants, when they obtain orders for the drug from the receiving ships. They have also convoys,

plying up and down the river, which are called fast-crabs, and scrambling dragons. These are well armed, with guns and pikes, and
manned with desperate fellows, who go as if they had wings. All
the custom-houses and military stations which they pass, are literally
stopped with bribes; and if they chance to meet any of the armed
cruisers, the smugglers do not scruple to come to an engagement,
and bloodshed and slaughter ensue. The governor of Canton lately
sent a naval officer, with a sufficient force, and captured a boat laden
with opium, seized one hundred and forty chests, and killed and took
prisoners, scores of smugglers; yet, the traffic was not at all checked.
Multitudes of the people, have but little dread of the laws, while they
use every device to escape punishment, and are eager after gain:
indeed, the laws are, sometimes, utterly without effect."

When a Chinese mandarin undertakes to make, and
the emperor consents to receive, such a statement as
the above, we may conclude that this, and much more,
is true. In fact, opium is not only regularly introduced, but openly sold, in all parts of China. Notwithstanding the prohibition, opium shops are as
plentiful in some towns of China, as gin shops are in
England. The sign of these receptacles, is a bamboo
screen, hanging before the door, which is as certain an
intimation there, as the chequers are here, that the
slave of intemperance may be gratified. Into these
shops, all classes of persons continually flock, from the
pampered official to the abject menial. No one makes
a secret of the business or the practice, and though the
officers of government are loud in denouncing the
indulgence in public, they privately wink at what is
patronised by their own example, or subservient to
their own interests. It is a well-known circumstance,
that the government officers come regularly on board
the receiving ships at Lintin, and demand so many
dollars per chest, for conniving at smuggling; while
it is currently reported that even the viceroy of Canton

receives a very respectable consideration, for winking at these illicit transactions. The military and naval officers sometimes get up a sham fight, in order that they may have to report their vigilance and strictness to Peking; and when the smugglers are remiss in paying the accustomed bribes, they now and then seize a boat or two, to keep them regular and submissive. Thus, it is evident, that the imperial government is absolutely powerless, in aiming to prevent the introduction of opium; and that the traffic does and will increase, notwithstanding the most violent and sanguinary edicts to the contrary. Surrounded by corrupt and venial officers, the emperor's best efforts, if indeed, he use any, are entirely nugatory; and bribery laughs at imperial proclamations, which universally forbidding and never punishing, become, in fact, so much waste paper. Every one acquainted with China knows, that as long as the appetite for opium exists there, the traffic cannot be put down by the present inefficient police; and should the naval and military force of China be resolved to use their utmost efforts to prevent the intoduction from abroad, they cannot overcome the force of well manned and armed European vessels, nor elude the vigilance of the *fast-crab* and *scrambling-dragon* native smugglers.*

To the foreign community of Canton we would appeal, did we not fear that most of them are now

---

* Late accounts from Canton inform us, that the Chinese government were taking very vigorous and decisive measures to break up the opium trade at Lintin. The receiving ships had been compelled to quit their usual anchorage, and to remove to a place forty miles to the eastward. More edicts had been issued: and it was expected that the superintendent of British trade would be appealed to, with the assurance that the whole of the foreign trade should be stopped, unless the orders of the native government were complied with, and the smuggling of opium discontinued.

actively engaged in the traffic; and should the present residents, influenced by principle, abandon the trade, there are not wanting others, who will gladly embrace the opportunity of enriching themselves at the expense of the miseries of thousands. Many, doubtless, are deluding themselves with the idea, that if they do not deal in it, others will: and as the Chinese will have opium, whether or not, they may as well furnish them with it, as let others reap the profit of what their over scrupulousness would deprive them. They are fully aware that opium is injurious to the constitution, and that, imported in such quantities, and consumed by so many, it must tend to the destruction of life, and the dimunition of happiness. But, then, they plead that they were involved in the trade, before they were aware of the extent of the evil; and, now that they are embarked in it, they cannot well retract; besides they intend soon to return to their native country, when they will leave the Chinese, and future opium dealers, to do as they please. The principle, sanctioned by all this special pleading, it will easily be seen, is untenable: it is simply this, that immediately we can ascertain that a thing will proceed, whether we take part in it or not; or that others will carry on a measure, if we abstain from abetting it; it then ceases to be an evil in us to participate in the transaction, however ruinous or destructive it may be. True morality will lead us to enquire, whether the thing be right or wrong; and, if the latter can be established, it is ours to renounce it, however lucrative to ourselves, or grasped at by others. The golden rule, of doing to others as we would be done by, will teach us to avoid being accessory to the spread of allurements, and incentives to vice, when we pray every day for ourselves, " Lead us not into temptation, but deliver us from evil." When Mammon has less hold on the hearts of civilized men, and when educated merchants begin to be more scrupulous about the craft, by which they get their wealth, then we may expect that opium dealers will be diminished, even in Canton ; and the time is not, we hope, far distant, when it shall be considered as disreputable to administer to the vicious indulgences of the Chinese, as it is now to those of the British — and as creditable to abstain from opium dealing abroad, as from distillation at home.

As the Chinese government cannot put down, and the foreign community of Canton, it is to be feared, will not abandon, the illicit traffic in opium, we must look for a more immediate remedy to another quarter. It is well known, that the greatest part of the opium is grown within the territory, and transported through the dominions of the Honourable East India Company. It is, in the Bengal presidency, a monopoly in the hands of our Indian government, who dispose of it to our merchants, at the annual sales. The profit derived from the transaction is, doubtless, great ; and as a comparatively small quantity of the article is consumed by the immediate subjects of the company, and the evils consequent thereon, are confined to foreign lands, it is possible, that the Board of Directors, at home, and our Indian government, abroad, may have overlooked the enormity. Now, however, neither the company, abroad, nor the directors, at home, can plead unconsciousness in the matter: it has been told, and it shall be rung in the ears of the British public, again and again, that opium is demoralizing China, and becomes the greatest barrier to the introduction of Christianity which can be conceived of. Not only are the wretched victims of the indulgence, themselves, impervious to remonstrance, and callous to all feeling—not only must we despair of the conversion of an opium smoker, almost as much as if his doom were already sealed—but the difficulty of convincing others of the truth of Christianity, and of the sincere intentions of Christians, is greater, in proportion, to the extent of the opium trade to China. Almost the first word uttered by a native, when urged to believe in Christ is, " Why do Christians bring us opium, and bring it, directly, in defiance of our own laws ? That vile drug has poisoned my son—has ruined my brother—and, well nigh led me to beggar my wife and children. Surely, those who import such a deleterious substance, and injure me for the sake of gain, cannot wish we well, or be in possession of a religion that is better than my own. Go, first, and persuade your own countrymen to relinquish this nefarious traffic ; and give me a prescription to correct this vile habit, and then I will listen to your exhortations on the subject of Christianity." Alas ! they little know, that the one is almost as impossible as the other ; and that the work of persuading the growers and venders of opium, to relinquish the source of their ill-gotten wealth, is as difficult as the task of curing a confirmed opium smoker of his evil habits ; and that both are to be effected, alone, by that Power which can cause the Ethiopian to change his skin, and the leopard, his spots ; and make those who have been accustomed to do evil, learn to do well. But, surely, when the evil is known, and its effects seen, the rulers of an empire which professes to be governed by the principles of mildness and equity, will never lend themselves to the promotion of a measure which demoralizes a population, in such a wholesale manner; and, still less, condescend to derive a profit from that which ruins myriads. The East India Company might, if they would, greatly diminish the trade in opium. If they were to discontinue the growth of it, in their own territories, and to bind down the native princes in alliance with them, to do the same; while they forbad the transport of it through their dominions, India would, then, no longer be what it now is,—the great source from whence the evil originates. Were the supplies from India cut off, the inconsiderable stock, and inferior quality, yielded by Turkey, would be far from supplying and satisfying the market, and the practice sink into desuetude, from the fewer facilities afforded for its gratification. The lands now employed in the cultivation of the poppy, being necessarily rich and fertile, would, if laid out in the raising of other productions, be equally valuable to the possessors; and, while the revenue was not diminished, the happiness, health, and industry of the people, would be increased; in addition to which, the divine blessing would, doubtless, be doubly bestowed on those, who renounced an apparent benefit to themselves, in order to extend a real good to others.

If unsuccessful with the East India Company, we would carry up our remonstrances to the government of Great Britain. Since the discontinuance of the company's trade with China, and the consequent withdrawal of its establishment, the English government have placed a superintendent of British trade at the port of Canton. The attempt of Lord Napier to fix his

residence in the provincial city, and to open a negocia-
tion with the native authorities, together with the
failure of the same, is well known. Since that period,
the viceroy sanctioned the residence of his successor
in Canton, for the purpose of watching over the
conduct of Europeans, though he is still unwilling
to treat with our agent on political matters. It is
possible, however, that in the course of time these
jealousies may diminish, and the British superintendent
come into correspondence with the native authorities on
state business. The English have much to ask of the
Chinese, and are anxious to place the trade on a secure,
respectable, and advantageous footing; to have the
rights of British subjects recognized, and the security
of British property acknowledged. When, however,
the representative of our government makes a demand
from the Chinese of increased privileges and advantages, the first requisition made by them will be that
we aid them in putting down the illicit traffic in opium
carried on by our own countrymen, who, in defiance of
Chinese laws, introduce an intoxicating medium into
the country, and seduce their subjects into disobedience
and voluptuousness. They will not believe, that with
all the power of Britain, and while the drug is grown
in our own territories, we are unable to suppress the
trade; and nothing will dispossess them of the idea,
that the British government is accessory to the production and introduction of the article. We must then tell
them that we will or will not, strive to put down the
traffic in question, before we can venture to make any
demands from them in our own favour. If we refuse
to curb the evil, we give a public and official sanction
to what is in their eyes vexatious and abominable; and

cannot with any grace, ask them to assist us. If we consent, however, to do what we can to assist the Chinese in excluding opium, we are bound in all honour and honesty, first, to discontinue the growth of opium in our own colonies ; next, to prohibit the transport of it through the company's territories; and then to restrict British vessels from trading with it along the coast of China. The mere issuing of a decree of the governor in council at Calcutta would effect the former, and a very small force stationed on the coast of China, would accomplish the latter. In putting down the slave trade, it was not considered too much to maintain a naval force on the coast of Africa ; and to abolish slavery in the British dominions, the sum of twenty millions was willingly sacrificed ; yet slavery was not productive of more misery and death than the opium traffic, nor were Britons more implicated in the former than in the latter. In the case before us, however, no compensation money could be demanded; and only a few light armed vessels would be required ; while the real compensation would be, the turning of four millions annually into another channel, to the benefit of our manufactures and the mother country. By paying four millions for opium, the Chinese shew that they have money to spend, and if we can but induce them to take our cottons and woollens instead of our opium, we shall be blessing them and enriching ourselves. The money paid for opium is equal to what we give for our teas; thus the Chinese are parting with their produce for what is worse than useless, while it impoverishes their country and diminishes their population.

The ruin it threatens to China has already arrested

the attention of her greatest statesmen, and they have devised various schemes for remedying the evil. One recommends, that opium be admitted on the payment of regular duties, in order that the clandestine trade may be stopped, and the practice be brought under the control of government. This would increase the public revenue, and by raising the price to the consumer, would place the drug out of the reach of the poor. The emperor has hitherto resolved to reject this plan, and thinks that increased rigour in prohibiting the article will avail. But the Chinese laws are already sufficiently severe, and yet the traffic increases at the rate of four thousand chests per annum. The remedy, then, is not with them, and if neither the East India Company nor the British government interfere, the British public must be appealed to; the cry of " no opium" raised, and be made as loud as the cry of " no slavery," until the voice of humanity prevail, and end in the abolition of the whole system.

But to return to the population, we shall find, that though checked in its growth, it is still immensely great, and claims the attention of the Christian evangelist, as much, or even more than other parts of the heathen world. In attempting to do good, we should do it on the largest scale, and to the greatest number of persons. The physician is most needed where the malady is most distressing, and the diseased most numerous; and so the missionary is principally required where the heathen most abound. Upon this principle, China requires our first attention, and will exhaust our most strenuous efforts. There, all the disposable labourers in the Christian church may employ their energies, without fear of over working the field, or standing in each other's way. Piety, the most exalted,—talents the most splendid,—may there find ample room for display ; the greatest trophies of Divine grace will there be obtained, and the Gospel is destined to achieve more in China than has ever been witnessed elsewhere, mainly on account of the number of individuals to be brought under its influence. This then is *the* field for missionary exertions ; the sphere where the most influential societies should direct their chief efforts, for until some impression is made upon China, it will matter little what is achieved in other more confined and thinly peopled regions. The conversion of a few islands to Christ, and the introduction of the Gospel to the extremities of a continent, resemble an investing of the outworks of heathenism ; but the strong hold remains still untouched, and until China is evangelized, the greatest half of our work remains to be begun.

CHAPTER V.

THE CIVILIZATION OF CHINA.

COMPARATIVE CIVILIZATION—SOLILOQUY OF A CHINESE—NATIVE POLITE-
NESS — DISPLAYED IN CONVERSATION — AND DAILY INTERCOURSE —
GENIUS OF THE CHINESE — DISCOVERY OF THE COMPASS — THE ART
OF PRINTING — THE INVENTION OF GUNPOWDER — THE SCIENCES —
ASTRONOMY—BOTANY — MEDICINE — SURGERY — THE ARTS—PAINTING
— ENGRAVING — MANUFACTURE OF SILK — PORCELAIN — TEA—PAPER—
LACKERED WARE — METALS — CONCLUSION.

In seeking to evangelize the heathen world, two des-
criptions of people claim our attention; namely, the
barbarous and the civilized. China belongs to the
latter class. Instead of a savage and untutored people
—without a settled government, or written laws,—
roaming the desert, and living in caves,—dressed in
skins, and sitting on the ground,—knowing nothing of
fashion, nor tasting luxuries; we behold in the Chinese
a quiet, orderly, well-behaved nation, exhibiting many
traces of civilization, and displaying them at a period
when the rest of mankind were for the most part sunk
in barbarism. Of course we must not look for that
high degree of improvement, and those well-defined
civil rights, which are in a great measure the effects
of Christianity; neither are we warranted to expect in
China any of those advances in science, or improvements in the arts, which now distinguish Europe, and
which are the result of that march of mind so charac-

teristic of the age we live in.   Railways, tunnels,
machinery, and all the ramifications and operations
of gas and steam, are not to be looked for in China.
With these exceptions, however, China possesses as
much civilization as Turkey now, or England a few
centuries ago.   Indeed, were the question proposed
to a Chinese, as to which he considered the most
civilized nation, while he might acknowledge the superiority of Europeans in cunning and force, he would
not scruple to claim for his own countrymen the praise
of a superior polish.   They denominate China, " the
flowery nation,"—" the region of eternal summer,"—
" the land of the sages,"—" the celestial empire,"—
while they unscrupulously term all foreigners " barbarians," and sometimes load them with epithets still
more degrading and contemptuous ; such as swine,
monkeys, and devils.

The soliloquy of one of them is rather amusing ;
" I felicitate myself," says Tëen Ke-shih, " that I was
born in China; and constantly think how very different
it would have been with me, if born beyond the seas, in
some remote part of the earth, where the people, deprived of the converting maxims of the ancient kings,
and ignorant of the domestic relations, are clothed with
the leaves of plants, eat wood, dwell in the wilderness,
and live in the holes of the earth ; though living in this
world in such a condition, I should not have been different from the beasts of the field.   But now, happily,
I have been born in the middle kingdom.   I have a
house to live in ; have food, drink, and elegant furniture ; clothing, caps, and infinite blessings ; truly the
highest felicity is mine ! "

The Chinese have a proverb, that he who judges of

the circumstances of others, without a thorough acquaintance with them, is like a man at the bottom of a well, attempting to form an opinion of the heavens. It is to be feared, that the Chinese have been at the bottom of the well, with regard to foreigners, and that we are not unfrequently at the bottom of the well, with regard to them. The writer would fain bring each party to the brink, and exhibit them to each other. Without acceding, therefore, to the extravagant pretensions of the Chinese, or submitting to their unjust reflections upon foreigners, we must allow them a degree of civilization, which would awaken an interest in their behalf, and favour not a little the attempt to promote their evangelization.

The civilization of the Chinese will be seen in their complaisance towards each other. In no unchristian country do we find such attention paid to ceremony, such polish in daily intercourse, and so many compliments passing to and fro, as among the Chinese. In associating with friends, and in entertaining strangers, their politeness is remarkable. The poorest and commonest individual will scarcely allow a passenger to cross the door without asking him in; should the stranger comply, the pipe is instantly filled and presented to his lips, or the tea poured out for his refreshment; a seat is then offered, and the master of the house does not presume to sit down, until the stranger is first seated. The epithets employed, when conversation commences, are in keeping with the character of the people. The familiar use of the personal pronoun is not indulged in; on the contrary, " venerable uncle," —" honourable brother,"—" virtuous companion,"—or " excellent sir,"—in addressing a stranger, are used

instead of the pronoun " you ; " and " the worthless
fellow,"—" the stupid one,"—" the late born,"—or the
" unworthy disciple," instead of the pronoun " I," are
terms of common occurrence. " What is your noble
patronymic ? " is the first question ; to which the usual
reply is, " my poverty-struck family name is so and so ;"
again, the question is asked respecting the " honourable
appellation, the exalted age, and the famous province,"
of the stranger; which queries are replied to by applying
to one's self the epithets of " ignoble, short-lived, and
vulgar ;" and thus the conversation proceeds in a strain
of compliment, the very commonness of which proves
the civilization of the people.   The titles bestowed
upon the relations of others, together with the humiliating light in which persons speak of their own connections are also remarkable. " Honourable young gentleman," for a friend's son ; and " the thousand pieces of
gold," for his daughter, are usual appellations ; while
the individual replies, by bestowing the epithet of
" dog's son," and " female slave," on his own offspring.

The ceremonies observed on the invitation and
entertainment of guests are still more striking ; complimentary cards are presented, and polite answers
returned, all vieing with each other in the display of
humility and condescension, On the arrival of the
guest, considerable difficulty is found in arranging
who shall make the lowest bow, or first enter the door,
or take the highest seat, or assume the precedence at
table ; though the host generally contrives to place his
guest in the most elevated position. When conversation
commences, the mutual assent to every proposition, the
scrupulous avoiding of all contradiction, and the entire
absence of every offensive expression, or melancholy

allusion, shew what a sense these people entertain of politeness; while the congratulations or condolence lavished on every prosperous or adverse occasion, and the readiness displayed to "rejoice with them that do rejoice, and to weep with them that weep," manifest the degree of interest they appear to take in each other. Any one, who would examine the style of their epistolary correspondence, the form of their invitation cards, and the phraseology of their polite discourses, must see, that, professedly at least, " they esteem every other better than themselves," which is the foundation of politeness. Their civility may indeed verge towards adulation, and their compliments assume the air of flattery; but, when we see a whole nation thus externally soft, affable, and yielding, we must acknowledge that they have made some advances in the art of good breeding.

But the civilization of the Chinese appears in a more substantial form, in the discoveries they have made, and the arts and sciences which they have cultivated. Their inventive genius has been manifested in various particulars, and at early periods. Three most important discoveries, which have given an extraordinary impulse to the progress of civilization in Europe, were known to the Chinese previous to their being found out by us. First of all ranks the invention of the mariner's compass, with which the Chinese seem to have been long acquainted. The earliest allusion to the magnetic needle is met with in the traditionary period of their history, about 2600 years before Christ; when the Yellow Emperor, having missed his way, invented a carriage, upon the top of which was a gallery, surmounted by a little figure, pointing to the south, which-ever way the carriage turned.

At a later period, we have a more credible account of this discovery, in the reign of Ching-wang, of the Chow dynasty, B. C. 1114; when it is said, that some ambassadors came from the modern Cochin China, affirming, that having experienced neither storm nor tempest in that country for three years, they imagined it was in consequence of the sages then existing in China; and therefore had come to pay court to them. On the return of these ambassadors, they knew not what course to take; and the prime minister of China gave them five close carriages, all provided with instruments that pointed to the south: with these they were enabled to find their way, and in a year arrived at their own country. "Hence," adds the historian, "these south-pointing carriages have ever since been used as guides to travellers." There are several other references to this important invention at later periods, so as to make it evident that they possessed the discovery before the people of Europe, and it is not improbable were the means of communicating it to us; for it is well known that Marco Paulo, the Venetian traveller, visited China A. D. 1275, and that the mariner's compass was not invented by Gioia, of Naples, until A. D. 1302, so that it is not unlikely that the Italian communicated it to his countryman. Though the Chinese have not much improved the art of navigation, and have allowed us to exceed them in nautical science, yet we should remember from whence the grand invention was derived, and accord the due meed of praise to those who so early possessed it.

Next in the order of utility stands the art of printing, which it appears was known to the Chinese upwards of nine hundred years ago. Some say, that it was invented by one Fung-taou, the time-serving minister of the first ruler of the Tsin dynasty, A. D. 937 ; though by a reference to Chinese history, it appears, that eleven years previous, the ruler of Tang ordered the nine classics to be engraved, printed, and sold to the people. The historians of those times do not seem to have any doubt about the art having been then in use, and merely discuss the propriety of selling the books, rather than giving them away, on the principle that it would be difficult to supply so many millions gratuitously.

In the time of Confucius, B. C. 500, books were formed of slips of bamboo, upon which they wrote with the point of a style. About one hundred and fifty years after Christ, paper was invented, when the Chinese wrote on rolls, and formed volumes. A. D. 745, books were first bound up into leaves ; and two hundred years afterwards they were multiplied by printing; so that the Chinese appear to have made early advances in civilization, whilst we only discovered the art of making paper in the eleventh, and that of printing in the fifteenth century. The mode of printing adopted by the Chinese is of the simplest character. Without expensive machinery, or a complicated process, they manage to throw off clear impressions of their books, in an expeditious manner. Stereotype, or block printing, seems to have taken the precedence of moveable types in all countries, and in China they have scarcely yet got beyond the original method. Their language consisting of a great number of characters, they have not thought it worth while to cut or cast an assortment of these ; which they might distribute and recompose, as the subject required ; but have preferred cutting the characters for each separate work, page by page.   This stereotyping of their books, has caused the stereotyping of their ideas ; and kept them in the same eternal round of uniform notions, without variety or improvement.   While the discovery of printing therefore, has enabled them to multiply copies of their ancient books, it has discouraged the compilation of new works, and tied them down to an imitation of antiquity, without assisting them to burst the fetters which custom has laid upon them.

Still the use of wooden blocks has not been without its advantages : among which we may enumerate speed and cheapness.   The first part of the process is, to get the page written out in the square or printed form of the character.   This having been examined and corrected, is transferred to the wood in the following manner.   The block, after having been smoothly planed, is spread over with a glutinous paste ; when the paper is applied and frequently rubbed, till it becomes dry.   The paper is then removed, as much of it as can be got away, and the writing is found adhering to the board, in an inverted form.   The whole is now covered with oil, to make the letters appear more vivid and striking ; and the engraver proceeds to his business. The first operation is, to cut straight down by the sides of the letters, from top to bottom, remove the vacant spaces between the lines, with the exception of the stops.   The workman then engraves all the strokes which run horizontally ; then, the oblique ; and, afterwards, the perpendicular ones, throughout the whole line : which saves the trouble of turning the block round, for every letter. Having cut round the letters, he proceeds to the central parts ; and, after a while, the page is completed. A workman generally gets through one hundred characters a day, for which he will get sixpence. A page generally contains five hundred characters. When the engraver has completed his work, it is passed into the hands of the printer, who places it in the middle of a table : on one side, is a pot of liquid ink, with a brush ; and, on the other, a pile of paper : while, in front, there is a piece of wood, bound round with the fibrous parts of a species of palm, which is to serve for a rubber. The workman then inks his block with the brush ; and taking a sheet of dry paper, with his left hand, he places it neatly on the block ; and, seizing the rubber with his right hand, he passes it once or twice quickly over the back of the paper, when the impression is produced, the printed sheet hastily removed, and the workman proceeds with the next impression, till the whole number be worked off ; and, thus, without screw, lever, wheel, or wedge, a Chinese printer will manage to throw off 3,000 impressions in a day. After the copies are struck off, the next business, is to fold the pages exactly in the middle ; to collate, adjust, stitch, cut, and sew them ; for all of which work, including the printing. the labourer does not receive more than ninepence a thousand. The whole apparatus of a printer, in that country, consists of his gravers, blocks, and brushes ; these he may shoulder and travel with, from place to place, purchasing paper and lamp-black, as he needs them ; and borrowing a table anywhere, he may throw off his editions by the hundred or the score, as he is able to dispose of them. Their paper is thin, but cheap; ten sheets of demy-size, costing only one half-penny. This connected with the low price of labour, enables the Chinese to furnish books to each other, for next to nothing. The works of Confucius, with the commentary of Choo-foo-tsze, comprising six volumes, and amounting to four hundred leaves, octavo, can be purchased for ninepence; and the historical novel of the three kingdoms, amounting to 1,500 leaves, in twenty volumes, may be had for half-a-crown. Of course, all these prices are what the natives charge to each other; for all which Europeans must expect to pay double.

Thus, books are multiplied, at a cheap rate, to an almost indefinite extent; and every peasant and pedlar has the common depositories of knowledge within his reach. It would not be hazarding too much to say, that, in China, there are more books, and more people to read them, than in any other country of the world.

Another discovery, which is supposed to have originated with the Chinese, is that of gunpowder. Soon after the commencement of the Christian era, this people were in the habit of using what they called " fire medicine," which they employed for the purpose of making signals, and affording amusement, in the shape of rockets and fire-works, but do not appear to have used it to project bullets to a distance, in order to attack an enemy.

The historian of the Yuen dynasty, A. D. 1280, says, that " fire engines" commenced about that period. Wei-ching, constructed machines for throwing stones, in which he used powder, made of saltpetre, sulphur, and charcoal. Some time after this, guns and powder were invented in Europe; and, it is not unlikely, were introduced into this part of the world, in consequence of the statements of Marco Paulo.

With regard to the sciences, the Chinese cannot be said to rank high, though they have made some advances in a few; fully equal to what has been accomplished in other eastern nations. To astronomy they have always paid some attention; and even during the reigns of their earliest kings, the five planets, the twenty-eight constellations, and the twelve signs of the zodiac were well known. They were in the habit of regarding various celestial phenomena, and eclipses and comets were regularly observed, and faithfully recorded, as will be seen by a reference to the scheme of chronology in the Appendix. A. D. 900, a comet appeared, which was considered as ominous of some change in the government, when the sovereign put thirty men of influence to death, and threw some of the literati into the Yellow River; closing the bloody transaction, by murdering the former empress, in order to secure to himself the possession of an usurped throne. A. D. 996, an eclipse of the sun, which had been predicted by the astronomers, did not take place; on which occasion, the courtiers congratulated his majesty, suggesting, that the very heavens had altered their courses, out of compliment to his virtues.

In all the periods of their history, the Chinese have thought that the heavenly bodies moved in their orbits, for no other purpose, than to point out the rise and fall of dynasties, and to indicate some change of rule in their empire. Famines and pestilences, wars and commotions, droughts and inundations, are with them prognosticated by falling stars and shooting meteors; and so close is the connection between the celestial empire and the powers of nature, that nothing can happen to the one without affecting the other. The science of astronomy, therefore, is studied mainly on account of the influence of the stars on human affairs ; and hence the astronomical board is intimately connected with the government, and interference with that department is considered as treason against the state, and punished accordingly. The arrangement of the calendar is a matter of much moment with the Chinese, and lucky and unlucky days are regularly noted in that important document, by which all the business of the empire is regulated. We must not, however, rate the Chinese exceedingly low, on account of their partiality to astrology ; when we remember that even in England, in the nineteenth century, there are numbers of persons who continue to place implicit confidence in Francis Moore, and his precious prognostications, which are sure to happen " the day before or the day after."

Of botany they have sufficient knowledge to enable them to collect and arrange a vast number of plants, whose appearance and properties they minutely enumerate, though they do not describe or classify them in a philosophical manner.

In the commencement of Chinese history, we find some allusion to the " Divine Husbandman," who cultivated the five kinds of grain, examined the various plants, and compounded medicines. Before that period the people lived on the fruits of trees, and the flesh of animals, knowing nothing about husbandry ; until Shin nung pointed out the varieties of the seasons, and the properties of the soil, making ploughs of hard wood, and teaching the people to plant grain : thus

commenced the business of agriculture.   When sickness invaded, and remedies were needed, the sovereign
tasted the various plants to ascertain their cooling and
tranquillizing properties, and in one day discovered
seventy kinds of poisonous shrubs, with their antidotes,
which he described in a book; and the science of
medicine began to flourish.   Since then, the Chinese
have published a very compendious work on botany,
called the Pun-tsaou, which is certainly the result of
much labour, and, considering their disadvantages,
does them great credit.   In this work they distinguish plants into class, genus, and variety.   Their
classes are five; viz., shrubs, grains, herbs, fruits, and
trees.   Under the first class they include the following
genera: wild, odoriferous, marshy, poisonous, rocky,
scandent, watery, cryptogamous, and miscellaneous
plants; under the second class they enumerate wheat,
barley, millett, maize, and other grains; under the
third class are found alliaceous, mucilaginous, creeping,
watery, and fungous vegetables; under the fourth class
we meet with cultivated, wild, and foreign, as also
aromatic and watery fruits; and under the fifth class
are included odoriferous, gigantic, luxuriant, parasitic,
flexible, and miscellaneous trees.   All these genera are
subsequently divided into 1094 species.   This arrangement will be seen to be far from scientific; but that
they should have examined the vegetable kingdom at
all, and made any sort of classification, shews that they
are by no means an unthinking or an uncivilized
people.

  To the science of medicine the Chinese have paid
some attention, but, as usual, were more celebrated for
it in former than in latter times.   The systems of their

earliest physicians have mostly died with their inventors, and posterity have scarcely been able to equal, much less to exceed, the ancients. Some allusion has been made above to the " Divine Husbandman," who discovered the noxious and healing qualities of various plants, and laid the foundation of the Chinese pharmacopœia. About the same time lived a statesman, to whom the invention of the puncture is attributed; this man left on record two fragments, which are looked upon as the most ancient notices on the cause and cure of diseases in China. In these fragments the circulation of the blood is recognised, and compared to the unceasing revolutions of the heavens and the earth, which begin, end, and begin again from the same point at which they originally set out; thus, they say, the blood goes round and round the human body, till its dissolution. It must not be imagined from this, however, that the Chinese understand the circulation of the blood, as the phrase is used in Europe; or know anything distinctly about the veins and arteries through which it flows. Not having practised anatomy, they are unacquainted with the internal structure of the human frame, and remain satisfied with the fact of the blood's circulation, without attempting to explain it.

To the pulse, however, they have paid close attention, and are enabled to discover its variations with a nicety and precision, scarcely equalled by European physicians. They affect to distinguish twenty-four different kinds of pulsations, and will frequently proceed to prescribe, without asking a single question, or examining any other prognostic. The system which they have imagined to themselves, is more the result of fancy than experience; and the connection they pretend to trace between the five points at which the pulse may be felt, the five viscera, the five planets, and the five elements, is the fruitful source of innumerable mistakes in their practice; but we must remember, that it is not long since Bacon opened the gate of experimental science in Europe, and that our forefathers once united astrology with medicine, by which they blundered quite as much as the Chinese!

In the earliest classics of the Chinese, several physicians of eminence are referred to, and during the period of the "contending states," a medical man was called "the nation's arm," because he rescued so many from impending death. When China was divided into three kingdoms, about the third century of the Christian era, the father of Chinese surgery, Hwa-to, flourished. He is said to have laid bare the arm of a wounded chieftain, and to have scraped the poison off the scapula, while the unmoved warrior continued to play at chess, and to drink wine, with the other arm. A jealous tyrant of that age cruelly murdered this useful man, and his wife burnt all his manuscripts, by which means his valuable art perished with him. In the fourth century, the well-known work on the pulse, quoted by Du Halde, was published. In the sixth century lived Chin-kwei, who is said to have cut into the abdomen, removed diseased viscera, and stitched up the part again, curing the patient in a month's time. The most eminent writers on medicine in China are the "four great masters," who flourished—the first in the third, the second in the thirteenth, the third in the fourteenth, and the fourth in the fifteenth centuries. The first is considered the father of physic, and has left numerous writings behind him. From the various treatises on medicine, one imperial work has been compiled, in forty volumes, called "a golden mirror of medical practice," which was completed nearly a century ago, after four years labour. Other works on medicine have successively appeared; and a gentleman in Canton, wishing to obtain all that was procurable in that city, made a collection of eight hundred and ninety-two volumes of medical books: so that if the Chinese know little of the science in question, it is not for want of books or theories.

We are not, however, to estimate the value of medical knowledge in China by the aggregate of treatises on the subject; or the efficiency of their practice, by the number of doctors' shops throughout the country: for though the celestial empire literally swarms with medical works and apothecaries' shops, yet the number of successful practitioners we believe to be small. For the most part, their medical practice is mere quackery: and their surgery, in modern days, does not extend beyond puncturing, cauterizing, drawing of teeth, and plastering, without attempting any operation in which skill or care is required.

The advance which the Chinese have made in the fine arts has been more considerable than in the sciences. To begin with painting, we may observe that the graphical representations of the Chinese are not altogether despicable. It is true they lamentably fail in the knowledge of perspective, and the differences of light and shade have not been much noticed by them. But their colours are vivid and striking, and in delineating flowers, animals, or the human countenance, they are sometimes very successful. The Chinese drawings brought to this country on what is called rice paper, have been much admired for the striking characteristics, and brilliant tints which they display. If instructed in the art of shading, and taught the nature of perspective, the Chinese might become good artists ; and one of them, who had the advantage of a few lessons from an eminent English painter, has produced some pieces which have been thought worthy of a place in the Royal Exhibition at Somerset House.

In the art of engraving the Chinese excel. The rapidity with which they carve their intricate and complicated characters is really surprising, and not to be imitated by European artists, in the same style of execution, and at the same low prices. A London engraver was surprised when he learned, that what would cost sixty or eighty shillings in England, might be accomplished by a Chinese workman for half-a-crown. In seal engraving they are not behind our own countrymen, and in ivory and ebony, tortoiseshell, and mother-of-pearl, their carving surpasses that of most other artists. The celebrated Chinese balls, one in the other, to the amount of seven or nine, all exquisitely carved, have puzzled many of our English friends ; who have been at a loss to know, whether they were cut out of a solid piece, or cunningly introduced, by some imperceptible opening, one within the other. There can be no doubt, however, of their having been originally but one piece, and cut underneath from the various apertures, which the balls contain, until one after another is dislodged and turned, and then carved like the first. The ivory work-boxes and fans, commonly sold in Canton, exhibiting the various figures standing out in very bold relief, may be considered as fair specimens of Chinese skill.

ɪ

In the useful arts, the Chinese are by no means deficient; and in what contributes to the necessaries, comforts, and even elegancies of life, shew themselves to be as great adepts as their neighbours. The manufacture of silk has been long established among them; and thousands of years ago, when the inhabitants of England were going about with naked bodies, the very plebians of China were clothed in silks; while the nobility there vied with each other in the exhibition of gold and embroidery, not much inferior to what they now display. In the fabled days of the Yellow Emperor, at the commencement of the Chinese monarchy, " the empress taught her subjects to rear the silk-worm, and unwind the coocoons, in order to make dresses; so that the people were exempted from cold and chilblains." When Confucius arose, the Chinese had long been in the habit of cultivating the silk-worm, and the general rule then was, for " every family that possessed five acres of ground, to plant the circumference with mulberry trees, in order that all above a certain age might be clothed in silk." Down to the present age, the Chinese are still celebrated for the abundance, variety, and beauty of their silk fabrics, equalling in the richness of their colours, and the beauty of their embroidery, anything that can be manufactured in France or England, while the crapes of China still surpass the products of this western world. But they are not only skilled in making, they are also attached to the wearing, of gay apparel; the Chinese are confessedly a well-clothed nation, and except where poverty prevents, the people are seen attired in silks and crapes, as commonly as we appear in cloth and leather. Their fashions differ indeed from ours, but the dress of a Chinese gentleman or lady is as elegant in its way, as the external appearance of a modern belle or beau in Europe.

The manufacture of porcelain commenced with the Tang dynasty, A. D. 630: and the first furnace on record is that at Chang-nan, in the province of Keang-se, from whence a tribute of porcelain was sent to the court of Han Kaou-tsoo, and called "imitation gem ware." The district now most famous for the production of this article, is Kaou-ling, a hill to the eastward of the town of King-tih, in the district of Yaou-chow, which came into repute in the time of the third ruler of the Sung dynasty, A. D. 1000. The material from which porcelain is made is called tun, " clay," or pih-tun, " white clay," from whence is derived the *petuntse* of European books; its nature is " stiff and white, without much sweat," and the porcelain made of it does not crack. The best sort is known by breaking and examining the ware, to see if the fracture be smooth and even, without veins or granular coarseness, and just as if cut with a knife. What commonly goes under the name of Petuntse is divided into red, white, and yellow. The red and white are used for the finer wares; the yellow only for the coarser sorts. The people who procure it always avail themselves of the mountain streams, where they erect mills, and pound the material; after which they wash it clean, and mould it into the form of bricks, called Petuntse. The yellow clods are large and hard, while the white are rather loose and fine.

The government of China has, for the last thousand years, paid great attention to the manufacture of porcelain; and the emperor Këen-lung, about fifty years ago, sent a person from court to make drawings of the

process.   The first business is to procure the stones,
and make the paste, which is commonly done in the
district of Hwuy-chow, in the province of Keang-nan.
The paste is then scoured and worked, and the glaze
ashes prepared.   These are formed of a sort of fern,
with the powder of a blueish-white stone, to which a
portion of fine Petuntse is added; forming together a
thick paste.   The next process is to form the earthern
boxes in which the ware is baked, and the moulds for
the round ware.   The biscuit is then turned on a lathe,
and formed into vases and other articles.   After this
the unburnt shade-dried biscuit is fitted to the mould,
and the excrescences cut and pared off.   These broken
bits are pounded to a milky consistency for the use of
the painters.   Numbers of lame and blind, old and
young, earn a scanty livelihood by pounding these
pieces, — their wages being only half-a-crown per
month; though some by working two pestles, and
continuing half the night, get double wages.   The
ware is then painted, which work is divided amongst
two sets of artists, the one drawing the outline, and the
other laying on the colours, " in order to render the
workman's hand uniform, and keep his mind undiverted."   They glaze by the brush, the dip, or the blow
tube.   The latter is a recent invention, consisting of a
bamboo about eight inches long, having its end covered
with a thin gauze, through which the workman blows a
certain number of times, according to the size of the
ware, or the consistence of the varnish.   Till this period,
two or three inches of earth are left at the bottom of
the vessel as a handle; but now the handle is taken
away, and the foot formed   After this, it is put into the
furnace and burned for some time, when the process is

finished.   To this succeeds the packing, and the whole
is closed by sacrificing to the gods, on which ceremony
much stress is laid.   On one of these occasions, a lad is
said to have devoted himself to the flames, by which
they imagine that great blessings were procured.   The
concourse of people at King-tĭh is very great.   There
are from two to three hundred furnaces, and several
hundred thousand workmen, who wait as anxiously on
the fire, as the husbandman does for the early and latter
rain.—See Morrison's Dictionary, part iii.

For some time, porcelain was a regular article of
export, from China to Europe, and much prized in this
country.   Since, however, the improvement in our
own manufacture, and the discouraging duty levied
on imported porcelain, the introduction has greatly
diminished; though the value of real China ware still
keeps up.   Whatever advances we may have made in
the whiteness of our porcelain, and the brilliancy of
our colours, we must remember, that the Chinese were
the first to practise the art, and still exceed us in the
compactness of the material, and the fineness of the
ware.

The Chinese have not only furnished us with cups,
but with tea.   It is not exactly certain, when this
beverage was first used by the Chinese; it is presumed
however, that, in early antiquity, the use of the plant
was unknown; as the ancient classics, and the history
of the middle ages, make no mention of it.   Ever since
the intercourse commenced with western nations, this
leaf has formed more or less an article of export; and,
in England, especially, the use of it has grown with a
rapidity, only equalled by the advance in the opium
trade, to China.   We find mention made of tea, in

England, in the year 1661; a century ago, the export of this article did not much exceed half a million pounds weight, but of late years, it has risen to nearly fifty millions. The sorts commonly known, are seven kinds of black, and six of green. First,—Woo-e, or Bohea, so called from a famous range of hills in the province of Fŭh-këen, where this tea is grown. Second, —Këen-pei, or Campoi; literally, choice fire-dried teas. Third,—Kang-foo, or Congo; literally, work-people's tea. Fourth,—Pĭh-haou, or Pekoe; literally, white down tea. Fifth,—Paou-chung, or Pouchong, wrapped tea; so called from its being wrapped in paper parcels. Sixth,—Seaou-chung, or Souchong, small seeded tea. Seventh,—Shwang-che, Souchi, or Caper; literally, double compounded tea. The green teas are,—First, Sung-lo, fir-twig tea; probably from its resemblance to fir-twigs. Second,—He-chun, or Hyson; literally, happy spring tea. Third,—Pe cha, or Hyson skin; literally, skin tea. Fourth,—Tun-ke, or Twankay, literally, stream-station tea; probably from the place where it is collected. Fifth,—Choo cha, pearl tea, or gunpowder tea. Sixth,—Yu-tsëen Ouchain, or Young Hyson, literally, tea collected before the rains. The black teas are, generally, grown in the province of Fŭh-këen; and the green, in Chĕ-këang, or Găn-hwuy. The whole are brought overland to Canton, where they are shipped for the European market. The process of making tea has been delineated, in a succession of pictures, corresponding to those on the manufacture of porcelain; and a variety of books have been written, describing the growth and manufacture; but the exact manipulation of the leaf, is a secret still possessed by the Chinese, which foreigners have not been able fully to develope. Some workmen have lately been brought from the tea districts, and conveyed to the island of Java, and the province of Assam, under the Dutch and English governments respectively; but, it remains to be seen, whether they can completely succeed in equalling the inhabitants of the celestial empire, in the preparation of tea. It is a matter yet in dispute, whether the green and black teas are made from the same tree; or, whether an entirely different plant is used. Most persons incline to adopt the former opinion; though, from the circumstance of the two sorts coming from different provinces, it might be inferred that the green and black are gathered from different shrubs.

In the manufacture of paper, the Chinese have been early active. In the first century, mention is made of paper, which the Chinese employ, not only in making books, and wrapping up articles, but in sacrificing to the gods and departed spirits; in which service millions of bundles are annually consumed by this superstitious people. This forms a principal article of internal commerce, and of export trade to the Chinese colonies, whither the native junks proceed, almost entirely laden with sacrificial paper.

In lackered ware, the Chinese do not equal the Japanese; though, until lately, they far exceeded the Europeans. They are enabled to excel in this art, in consequence of their natural advantages, possessing a varnish tree; which yields them a material better adapted for their purpose, than any which can be manufactured by art.

In the working of metals, the Chinese are not unskilled, and produce implements for use, suited to all

the business of life.* Metallic mirrors have been made
by them, for the use of the fair sex, by which means the
ladies of China were enabled to survey their features
and adjust their dress, before the invention of glass,
or its introduction into that country. The Chinese
still imagine that they possess, so exclusively, the
material, and the art of working in iron and steel, that
a standing order, in Canton, to this day, is, that the
barbarians shall not export iron from the country.

From what has been before advanced, and much
more which might be adduced, we are led to accord to
the Chinese, a certain rank among civilized nations.
But, let us now see how their civilization is likely to
affect their evangelization. When missionaries proceed to a nation altogether barbarous, they have many
difficulties to contend with. Their lives and property
are, in the first instance, in great jeopardy. Instances
have occurred, of savage tribes falling upon the messengers of mercy ; and, immediately on their arrival,
proceeding to plunder, murder, and, even eat them.
But, this is not likely to occur among a people, in a
great measure, civilized. Where order prevails—where
law is respected—and where the forms of justice are
observed, a person is not likely to be summarily deprived of life or liberty, without the assignment of a
reason, or the shadow of a trial. Again, amongst uncivilized tribes, there are a great many difficulties in
the way of communicating religious knowledge. The

---

* In the traditionary period, the Chinese relate, that the Yellow Emperor
made twelve bells ; and, afterwards, having discovered a copper mine, he cast
three tripods, which have been much venerated by the Chinese, and, for ages,
considered the regalia of the empire.

barbarian has first to be taught to think, before he can ponder religious truth; but, civilized men are, perhaps, too subtle and metaphysical in their speculations, and we find more difficulty in restraining, than in exciting their imaginative faculties. In the savage state, the relations of life are scarcely recognized, friendly and family feelings are almost unknown, and subordination and fidelity are exceedingly rare. But, in such a country as China, where marriage has been instituted for upwards of three thousand years, and filial respect cherished from the first settlement of their monarchy; where the reciprocal duties of sovereigns and subjects, friends and neighbours have been known, and, in some measure, acted upon, for milleniums—a sort of foundation is laid for benevolent and moralizing exertions, —and affords manifest advantages to the propagator of Christianity. In going amongst such a people, he finds a set of commonly acknowledged axioms, which, though in some instances, erroneous and overstrained, are yet of sufficient stability to serve him for a stepping stone, in order to pass on to greater and more important topics. It is possible, in such cases, by reasoning on principles which the heathen readily acknowledge, to convince them, by divine assistance, of their deficiencies; and thus to point out the necessity of a mediator to those who have evidently offended against the dictates of natural religion. This is a vantage ground which civilized nations present, and of which the missionary ought gladly to avail himself.

CHAPTER VI.

GOVERNMENT AND LAWS.

THE EMPIRE UNITED — THE GOVERNMENT BASED ON PARENTAL AU-
THORITY—THE EMPEROR SUPREME — THE MINISTERS OF STATE — THE
TRIBUNALS — OF CIVIL OFFICE — OF REVENUE — OF RITES — OF WAR —
OF PUNISHMENTS — OF PUBLIC WORKS — THE CENSORATE — THE NA-
TIONAL INSTITUTE — THE LAWS OF CHINA — THEIR CHARACTER —
CIVIL LAWS — FISCAL REGULATIONS — RITUAL ENACTMENTS — MILI-
TARY ARRANGEMENTS — CRIMINAL CODE — DIRECTIONS ABOUT NA-
TIONAL IMPROVEMENTS — IMPERIAL PALACE — THE FORBIDDEN EN-
CLOSURE — THE GARDENS AND PAVILIONS — THE NORTHERN CITY —
THE SOUTHERN.

THE civilization of China will further appear from the
consideration of the stability, regularity, economy, and
efficiency of their government. The country, no longer
torn by the contentions of rival princes and independent
states, is united under one regular and established authority. The emperor, residing in his capital, extends
his influence to the remotest corner of the land. Every
officer that presides in the most distant district is especially appointed by the court, and every measure of
importance is the result of arrangements issuing from
the centre of power. To exert an influence over such
an extent of territory, and for such a length of time,
argues a minuteness of arrangement and a comprehen-
siveness of system, which could not have place in an
uncivilized country.

The question has frequently been asked, how do the

Summary Execution.

Judicial Process.

Chinese, ignorant as they must be of the science of political economy, and destitute as they are of the knowledge of Christian ethics,—manage to keep such a mass of people in order, and preserve their empire free from encroachment and diminution? In attempting to solve this difficulty, we cannot but assign to the Chinese an intimate acquaintance with human nature, and an unusual skill in the application of well-defined principles to the business of life. The secret of their success in political matters is the establishment of the patriarchal system of government, grounded on the basis of filial obligation. The first principle in their moral code, is the duty of children to submit to their parents, and the right of parents to dispose of their children. Having been the instruments of bringing them into the world, and providing for their support and education, parents are considered as entitled to the unreserved respect and submission of their children; while disobedience to parental authority is punished with the severest rigour. From the dependency and inferiority of the infantile state, when this authority is naturally recognised and easily enforced, to the more advanced stages of life, the idea of an almost divine superiority is cherished, and no circumstances can arise in which the child is absolved from unqualified and undisputing obedience to the parent.

This principle forms the basis of their political code also. For though the emperor stands in no natural relation to his people, and is rather cherished by them than contributes to their support, yet he has induced the belief that he is their parent and protector, and as such possessed of unquestionable authority over them. In order to strengthen this assumption, the idea of divine right is superadded to that of earthly supremacy. Heaven and earth are considered the parents of all mankind, and the emperor, as the Son of Heaven, is of course next in authority, and reverenced accordingly. Whosoever, therefore, obtains the decree of Heaven, to ascend " the dragon throne," has a sort of mysterious dignity thrown around him ; and it is in their opinion as wicked to dispute the authority of the supreme on earth as the supreme in heaven.   Both parents and rulers are by the Chinese infinitely exalted above children and subjects, and receive not only homage but adoration.   Moral feeling, therefore, carried to an excess, and strengthened by superstitious awe, lead the Chinese without questioning to yield to authority; and this submissive, unresisting spirit is the source of that peace and good order which prevail throughout the empire. Thus to establish, and thus to sanction the most absolute despotism, and to render it subservient to the pacification of a great country, certainly argues a degree of penetration and discernment which does not comport with a barbarous state of society.

We are not here defending the justness of the principle, or maintaining the doctrine, that, because a ruler chooses to call himself the parent of a nation, therefore all his subjects are children, and to be treated as if they were in their nonage ; but if it be an object to secure the submission of the populace to a few rulers, we say, that a more convenient and effectual plan could not have been adopted.   Grounding the authority on the most readily acknowledged title, that of the parental prerogative ; and demanding obedience on the most powerfully constraining principle, that of filial affection ; it is not strange, that subjection is attained, and confidence won. This has been the foundation of Chinese politics from the earliest ages of antiquity; it has prevailed through every successive dynasty; and even now succeeds in binding together their vast and increasing population. We could tell them of a better system, which, inculcating universal love, is equally effectual in restraining oppression on the part of the ruler, as well as insubordination on the part of the subject; which, while it requires servants to be " obedient to their own masters," insists on " masters doing the same things to them, forbearing threatening, knowing that they also have a master in heaven." But for a heathen country, where the light of the Gospel has never shone, we cannot but admire the wisdom of a legislative principle, which so effectually unites and tranquillizes so vast a nation.

The policy of the Chinese government will appear in the mutual responsibility, and universal espionage which prevail throughout all the offices of state, and to the remotest corner of the empire. Though the " Great Emperor,"—the " Imperial Ruler,"—and the " Holy Lord," as he is called, claims and exercises universal and unlimited control over all " within the four seas;" though he dwells in the " pearly palace," and sits on the " dragon throne;" with the designation of " Ten thousand years," for his title, and the meed of divine honours for his gratification; yet he finds that he cannot rule the empire without assistance, or regulate its multifarious affairs without the aid of his ministers. These he calls his " hands and feet," his " ears and eyes," and to these he condescends to delegate a portion of his authority; holding them responsible for its exercise, with their fortunes, their liberties, and their lives. The highest minister of state, being the creature of imperial power, can be degraded, bambooed, banished, and beheaded; subject to the whim of the only one, who claims and exercises irresponsible authority in China. Hence the Chinese have a proverb, that 'tis safer sleeping in a tyger's den, than basking in the sunshine of imperial favour.

The prime ministers of state, are called the "inner chamber," or cabinet; the first is a Mantchou Tartar, to which race the present royal family belongs; the second is a Chinese, who is likewise president of the imperial college; the third is a Mongul Tartar, also superintendent of the colonial office; and the fourth is a Chinese. This mixture of Chinese and Tartars in the great offices of state, with the latter always taking the precedence, is a specimen of the general system pursued by the Chinese, of setting the two races to watch over, and be responsible for, each other. They admit native Chinese to high and important stations, in order to satisfy the people, but they take care to have them associated with, or superintended by, Tartars; so that the former cannot devise schemes of rebellion, without being instantly discovered, and betrayed by the latter.

Under the cabinet they have the six tribunals, which take cognizance of their several departments, and report to the emperor for his decision and approval. The first is the tribunal of civil office, the presidents of which enquire into and report on the conduct of all magistrates, recommend persons to vacant stations, and suggest the propriety of promoting or degrading deserving or undeserving individuals. A vast amount of patronage and power necessarily falls into the hands of a chamber which has the general superintendence of several thousand civil officers, from the viceroy of a province, down to the magistrate of the smallest district.

The second tribunal is that of revenue, appointed to take cognizance of the amount of the population, which the government is very careful to ascertain, in order to know what income may be expected from the various provinces, and what supplies should be transmitted to different parts of the empire, in case of famine. This tribunal also sees to the due collection and transmission of the land tax, which is paid partly in money and partly in grain; the coin of the realm is under their inspection, to see that it be not adulterated, and to "take care that the silver does not leak out of the country." Salt, on which a heavy duty is levied, and over which special officers are placed, is under the care of this board. The expenditure, as well as the income of the country, comes under their controul; and the payment of the various officers, with the maintenance of the state sacrifices, is arranged and provided for by them.

The third tribunal is that of rites, taking cognizance of all religious ceremonies, court etiquette, and astrological predictions. For though there be no established religion, or paid hierarchy in China, the rulers think it necessary to perform certain ceremonies, in order to propitiate the gods and overawe the people, of which this board has the superintendence. According to Chinese notions, the supreme in heaven can only be worshipped by the supreme on earth; and in doing this, the emperor is his own priest, presiding at the sacrifice and announcing his prayers, while the people look on in silent awe. At the accession of a monarch, at each of the four seasons, and in times of felicitation, or calamity, the ruler of China appears as the high-priest of the people, and constitutes himself the chief medium of intercourse between earth and heaven.   At the same periods, throughout the provinces, the various officers and magistrates pay their adorations to the presiding divinities of their several districts, the gods of the land and grain, the god of war, of literature, &c. all of which rites are determined by the board in question. The ceremonies to be observed on court occasions; the introduction and arrangement of nobles at the levees; the number of prostrations each is to make, and when; the clothes, caps, and boots they are to wear; the paths by which they are to come and go, to and from the imperial presence; and all other such like important minutiæ, are gravely and accurately specified by this board.   The imperial astronomers are also placed under its superintendence; for as these gentlemen have to calculate celestial phenomena, as well as to prognosticate terrestial affairs; as they have to fix the lucky and unlucky days for the performance of civil and religious ceremonies; their labours come necessarily under the cognizance of the board of rites.

The fourth tribunal is that of war; taking the superintendence of the army, navy, and ordnance; appointing the number of troops assigned to each province; and inspecting the state of the forts, and other defences of the country.   The army of China is rated at 700,000; who may rather be termed militia, being employed part of the year in cultivating the ground, and contributing to their own support.   These generally clothe and arm themselves, according to their own fancy; and are distinguished by the character " robust," being stitched on to their jackets in front, and the word "brave," behind!

The regularly organized troops of the present dynasty, are the Tartar legions, which amount to 80,000 effective men, arranged under eight banners, and always at the disposal of government. Their standards are yellow, white, red, and blue; each of which are doubled by being provided with a border. These are so distributed throughout the empire as to keep four thousand times their own number in order. The naval force is numerous, but inefficient; the ships of war are generally about the size of trading junks, but better built and manned; though it would require an indefinite number of them to cope with one of the smallest frigates of the British navy. As to their forts, those only at the Bogue, on the Canton river, deserve the name; but the incapability of these to resist the entrance of the British ships, a few years ago, was most clearly manifested. The management of all these defences is confided to the military tribunal.

Next comes the tribunal of punishments, which appoints and removes judges, takes cognizance of all judicial proceedings, and sees to the carrying out and execution of the laws. It is rather singular, that the supreme court of justice, in China, should be termed the tribunal of punishments, but it shews that the government of that country is more active in chastising the people for breaches of the law, than anxious to dispense justice to the injured and innocent. Every province is provided with a criminal judge, at a salary of £2,000 a year; this officer goes the circuit of his district periodically, and holds his court in the provincial city. There is a shew of some solemnity, and certainly of terror, in a Chinese court of justice; but one looks in vain for the jury box. A man is not tried by his peers, in China; while examination by torture is generally employed; and the criminal is punished on his own confession.

The last tribunal is that of works, to which is committed the care of public buildings, the excavation of canals, the embankment of rivers, and the construction of bridges and locks. Any one who considers the immense trouble and expense necessary to maintain some of the above, with the ruin and devastation sometimes consequent on neglect in this department, will see, that a branch of public service of such importance ought to be placed under a separate board of management.

In addition to the above tribunals, there are other public offices, to which important affairs are confided. Such as the colonial or foreign office, for the superintendence of the extensive districts, which, by the annexation of Tartary to the empire, have been brought under the imperial sway. There is also the public censorate, the officers of which are appointed to oversee the affairs of the whole empire, and are allowed to reprove the sovereign, or any of his officers, without being liable to punishment. Full liberty is given them to descant on the general affairs of government, though not to interfere with the private concerns of the monarch; and they are frequently sent into various parts of the empire, to inspect and report on the conduct of some of the highest officers of state. Such an institution as this, where the expression of public opinion is generally suppressed, is certainly of great value, and indicates the wisdom of those statesmen who established, and the magnanimity of those rulers who endure it.

In addition to this, we have the grand national college at Peking, the members of which are all the chief of the literati of China. After having passed through the three public examinations with honour, a select few are again tried, in order to their admission into this college. All matters which respect literature, and many which regard politics, are referred to this board, while the principal officers of state are chosen from among its members. Every individual in the empire is eligible to this distinction, and every scholar looks forward to it, as the consummation of all his wishes.

The laws of China are numerous, minute, and circumstantial, and give the best idea of the character of the people, and their advance in civilization, which could possibly be furnished. The present dynasty have published three works on law. The first contains the general laws of the empire, an elegant translation of which has been furnished by Sir G. Staunton. The next contains the bye laws, or particular regulations for each department of government; and the third is the work already alluded to, viz. " a collection of statutes for the present dynasty." As the general laws of China are best known, it may be well just to allude to them, as illustrative of the genius of the people from whom they emanate. The following testimony in their favour is by a writer in the " Edinburgh Review."

" When," says he, " we turn from the ravings of the Zend Avesta, or the Puranas, to the tone of sense and business of the Chinese collection, we seem to be passing from darkness to light; from the drivellings of dotage, to the exercise of an improved understanding; and redundant and minute as these laws are, in many particulars, we scarcely know any eastern code, that is at once so copious and so consistent, or that is nearly so free from intricacy, bigotry, and fiction. In every thing relating to political freedom, or individual independence, it is indeed wholly defective; but for the repression of disorder, and the gentle coercion of a vast population, it appears to us to be in general mild and efficacious." " There is nothing here of the monstrous verbiage of most other Asiatic productions; but a clear, concise, and distinct series of enactments, savouring throughout of practical judgment and European good sense; and, if not always conformable to our improved notions of expediency in this country, in general approaching to them more nearly than the codes of most other nations."

These encomiums are certainly high, and the general laws of China are, undoubtedly, much indebted to their elegant translator, and still more lavish admirer. In our humble opinion, many of the penal laws are just and good, and indicative of a knowledge of human nature, not to be met with in the savage state. Among the Chinese, the code is highly prized; and their only wish is, to see its enactments justly and impartially administered. The whole is divided into six sections, according to the six tribunals above named; and regard civil office, revenue, rites, military proceedings, punishments, and public works.

The *civil laws* refer to the system of government, and the conduct of magistrates. According to these statutes, hereditary rank is allowed, but only such as commenced with the present dynasty, and has been purchased by extraordinary services to the state. The appointment and removal of officers depend entirely on the will of the emperor. No officer of government can quit his station without leave, and no superior can interfere with his subordinates, except in the regular discharge of his duty. All officers engaging in cabals, and state intrigues, are to be beheaded; while those who neglect the orders of government, or fail in their duty, are liable to the appropriate penalties of the law. No magistrate can hold office in his own province;

each officer is removed every five years; and, however high and dignified, they must always state, in every public document, how many times they have been degraded, in order to keep their delinquencies in remembrance.

Some of the *fiscal laws*, regarding the enrolment of the people, have been quoted in a former chapter. Under this head, the regulations relative to the land-tax are included. This impost is supposed not to exceed one fiftieth of the produce. The enactments regarding the lending of money, limit the interest to three per cent. per month; and licences are granted to money-lenders and pawn-brokers, by which no inconsiderable revenue is realized. The maker of false weights and measures, is threatened with sixty blows; and the individual, who passes inferior articles for good merchandize, with fifty blows.

The *ritual laws* assign to the emperor the exclusive privilege of worshipping the Supreme, and prohibit subjects from offering the great sacrifices. Magistrates are required to superintend the sacred rites, in their various districts; and, on such occasions, are to prepare themselves, by fasting, self-denial, and abstinence from every indulgence, under penalty of forfeiting one month's salary. The neglecting to prepare the proper animals and grain, for the sacrifice, is punished with one hundred blows; and a wilful destroying of the public altars, is visited with as many strokes, and perpetual banishment. The deities to be worshipped by the magistrate, are the local gods, the genii of the hills and rivers, and of winds and rain, the ancient kings, and holy emperors, faithful ministers, and illustrious sages,—who are all to be honoured with the accustomed rites, by the respective officers of each district. While, however, the government requires its ministers to worship the gods, according to the state ritual, it strictly forbids the performance of unauthorized worship; and will not permit private persons to usurp the ceremonial exclusively claimed by the ruler. If it should be objected, that all this does not much display the wisdom of our Chinese legislators; we can only reply, that they are not the first who have failed, in attempting to legislate about religion.

The *military laws* commence with drawing a cordon around the imperial residence, and threatening any person with the bamboo who shall enter its precincts without authority; while those who intrude into the apartments actually occupied by the emperor shall be strangled. No person is allowed to travel on the roads expressly provided for his majesty; and during the imperial journey, all persons must make way for the state equipage. This regulation is intended to keep up the impression of awe, with which the Chinese invest their rulers, as though they were too divine and majestic to be beheld by mortal eyes; and is no doubt designed to preserve the person of the ruler safe from harm, which under a despotic government is not at all unnecessary. The code next proceeds to legislate on the government of the army, which it places entirely at the disposal of the emperor; and takes up the subject of nocturnal police, which prohibits all persons from stirring abroad, from nine in the evening till five in the morning. In order to protect the frontier, it is enacted, that whoever without a license passes the barriers, and holds communication with foreign nations, shall be strangled: and whoever introduces strangers into the interior, or plots the removal of subjects out of the empire, shall, without any distinction between principals and secondaries, be beheaded. No law is more frequently or more lightly broken than this; the natives emigrate by thousands annually: while dozens of catholic priests are every year clandestinely introduced into the country, and protestant missionaries land frequently on all parts of the coast, and walk over hill and dale, unhurt and almost unhindered by the natives.

Respecting the policy of this regulation, however, much may be said. Though the Chinese flatter themselves with the idea, that they are the greatest of nations, and almost the only people worthy of being called a nation; they cannot but see, how easily they have been overcome by a barbarous tribe from the north; and how much they are disturbed by every petty insurrection on their mountains, and every paltry piracy on their coasts. Contrasted with their own weakness, they must be aware of the power of foreigners. They see the rapid strides which Europeans are making towards conquest and power, in the eastern world; and how the English in particular, from the establishment of a factory, have proceeded to the erection of a battery; and then sending out their armies, have subdued whole kingdoms to their sway; till they number a hundred millions among their subjects, whom they keep in awe by a few thousand European troops. The Chinese, seeing this, could not but be alarmed for their safety, and the integrity of their empire. They, therefore, decided on checking the threatened evil in its infancy, and resolved to keep at arm's length a power, with which they knew that they could not successfully grapple. They judged, that if they could but keep out the barbarians, they might preserve at once their dignity and territory; but if they once let them in, their fair dominions would fall a rapid and an easy prey to the encroaching strangers, and their majesty remain the mere shadow of a shade.   And can we blame them? and can we say, that they had no reason for their conduct?   Their policy is for them the wisest that could have been pursued; and if China is closed against us, we may thank ourselves for it.   They might by admitting our commerce and our manufactures, still confer a mutual benefit on both countries; but if, by permitting the introduction of these, they lay themselves open to the infection of our intoxicating drugs, and afford an opportunity for the establishment of our colonizing system; they may have to regret, when they see their population diminishing, and their lands passing into other hands, that they did not adhere to the exclusive system, with which they commenced.

The *criminal laws* are particularly severe in the matter of high treason, which is either against the established government, or against the person of the sovereign.   All persons convicted of having been principals or accessaries, in this heinous offence, are to be put to death by a disgraceful and lingering execution. Besides which, all the male relations of the offender, above the age of sixteen, shall be indiscriminately beheaded;   while the female relatives and the children shall be sold into slavery, and the property of the family, of every description, confiscated.   In order to lead to the speedy discovery of the offence, any person who shall be the means of convicting another of high treason shall be immediately employed under government, besides being entitled to the whole of the criminal's

property.   This severe and sanguinary law is indicative
of the fears entertained, by the rulers, of assassination
and rebellion.   Under an absolute despotism, however,
it is the best dictate of policy ; and where the people are
deprived of the privilege of thinking and speaking for
themselves, nothing less than the terror of such a law
will ensure the safety of the sovereign.   All those who
enter into the service of a foreign state, who aim by the
practice of magic to bewitch the people, who sacrile-
giously abstract the implements used in the public
sacrifices, or who steal the imperial signet, shall be
indiscriminately beheaded.   All the above offences are
included under the head of theft, in the Chinese code,
because they reckon all those to be thieves, who oppose
the established government, or who attempt to invade
either the honour, authority, or personal security of the
reigning monarch.

Stealing in general is punished by blows ; but above
a certain amount, (£40.) by strangulation.   Kidnap-
ping persons, and selling them for slaves, is punished
with blows and banishment.   The disturbing of graves
is visited with the same infliction ; and whoever muti-
lates or throws away the unburied corpse of an *elder*
relative shall be beheaded.   With regard to murder and
homicide, the Chinese are very strict and particular.
Preconcerted homicide, is punishable by death.   Killing in a fray or sport, is denounced as murder ; while
homicide that is purely accidental, is redeemable by the
payment of a fine.   All those who cause the death of
others by poison, magic, or terror, shall suffer death
themselves ; and all medical practitioners, who kill
their patients, through ignorance of the established
rules of practice, shall be fined, and prevented from

exercising the profession; while those who do this designedly, and aggravate the complaint, in order to extort more money for the cure, shall be beheaded.

The offences of the inferior relations against the superior, are visited with a tenfold heavier punishment, while those of the latter against the former, are scarcely noticed. A parricide is to suffer the most lingering and shameful death that can be devised; and should the criminal even die in prison, the body is to be subjected to the same process, as if still alive; but if a parent put to death his own offspring, the offence is comparatively trivial. Whoever is guilty of killing a son, grandson, or slave, and charging another person with the crime, shall be punished by blows and banishment; but nothing is said about the crime of smothering female infants, which is so prevalent, because entirely unchecked, in China. Quarrelling and fighting is strictly prohibited in a country, where the rulers being few, and the subjects many, it is necessary to keep the people as quiet as possible. The bamboo is the remedy for the pugnacious propensities of the plebeians, and the number of blows is proportioned to the injury done, or the situation of the offending individual. A difference is observed, between striking with the fist or with a club; and the loss of an eye, tooth, finger, or toe, is visited with punishment, according to a graduated scale. A slave, beating or abusing his master, shall be put to death; while nothing is said about the master's beating his slave. A husband is not amenable for chastizing his wife, except he inflict a wound; while a wife, striking her husband, is to receive one hundred blows. A child, striking or using abusive language to a father or mother, shall be put to death;

while a parent, chastening a disobedient child, so as to cause death, shall be punished with one hundred blows. This distinction between the claims of the superior and inferior relatives, is in unison with the system which they have adopted, of raising rulers and parents to the rank of gods, and of depressing subjects and children to the level of slaves or brute animals. The policy, however, of these enactments, considering their design, will be easily seen.

Magistrates are forbidden to receive presents of any kind, except eatables, from the people, under the penalty of forty blows. Police officers, neglecting to apprehend offenders, are to be subjected to the bamboo. In judicial examinations, torture is not to be employed with respect to the eight privileged classes; and persons under the age of fifteen or above seventy, as well as those suffering under any bodily infirmity, are exempted; but in all other cases it is allowed and practised. This enactment goes upon the principle of not allowing offenders to be punished, until they acknowledge the fact of which they are accused, the justice of the sentence pronounced against them, and the parental kindness of the ruler in thus inflicting the necessary chastisement. Considering also the utter dereliction of truth, and the consequent want of confidence among the Chinese, the policy of this regulation, whatever may be the justice of it, will be acknowledged.

The laws relative to public works provide, that granaries should be built in every province, supplied with a sufficient store of rice, for the sustenance of the people in time of scarcity; which, being sold at a reduced rate, keeps down the price of grain, and brings the necessaries of life within the reach of the indigent.

This benevolent arrangement not only carries out the idea of parental care, which the Chinese rulers profess to have for their numerous family, but entitles them as much to the appellation of " discreet and wise," as was Joseph in the house of Pharaoh, when he recommended a measure of a similar character to the sovereign of Egypt. The laws relating to this department also require, that the canals, roads, embankments, and bridges, should be kept in due and thorough repair. The Chinese are necessitated, by the circumstances of their country, to pay much attention to the draining and irrigation of their lands. Water, like fire, is with them a good servant but a bad master. Without it they cannot raise their produce or transport their goods; and yet, when their mighty rivers accidentally burst their bounds, or the sea makes any encroachment on their thickly peopled territory, devastation and ruin, with a fearful loss of life, are the immediate consequences. Especial care, therefore, has from the earliest antiquity been taken to prevent inundations; and the individual who first drained the waters of the Yellow River, was raised to the rank of emperor, and almost deified. The labour and expense still bestowed on this department of public service, is scarcely equalled in any other unevangelized country. Some of the embankments are strong and well constructed; and though built centuries ago, still stand the test of time, and prove of incalculable benefit to the surrounding peasantry. Their bridges, over rapid streams and broad arms of the sea, composed of solid blocks of granite, fifteen or twenty feet long, and standing erect amidst the raging tide, bear testimony to the skill and perseverance of those who contrived and completed the design: while the enactments, requiring these to be kept in constant repair, shew that the rulers of China are not altogether indifferent to the welfare of the people. Considering the nature of the present work, it would be impossible to enter more into detail respecting the laws of this singular people, but the slight sketch we have given is sufficient to shew, that the Chinese are not devoid of sagacity, and that they deserve to be classed among civilized nations. A people possessed of written laws, of whatever character, must be considered as a grade above barbarians; but those who descend to the minutiæ of legislation, and provide for every possible exigency in the administration of an extensive empire, must have advanced to a stage of improvement, not far inferior to what is witnessed in this western world.

As another proof of their civilization, we may mention the state maintained by the emperor, who dwells in the interior of his splendid palace, secluded from the gaze of the populace, and surrounded by extensive parks and gardens; with the solemn parade of ministers, and the pompous pageantry of processions; which bespeak indeed a sort of barbaric grandeur, but a grandeur delighted in by some of the most powerful European monarchs of the nineteenth century. In order to form some idea of the degree of civilization attained by the Chinese, it may not be unsuitable here to allude to the extent and magnificence of the imperial city, where the lord of one third of the human race holds his court. The capital is divided into two parts, the northern section of which covers an area of twelve, and the southern of fifteen square miles. Within the northern enclosure is the palace, which is

the most splendid, as well as the most important part
of Peking.   According to the Chinese, this is a very
superb residence, with "golden walls, and pearly
palaces," fit for the abode of so great a monarch : to
the unprejudiced eyes of strangers, however, it presents
a glittering appearance, with its varnished tiles of brilliant yellow, which, under the rays of the meridian sun,
seem to constitute a roof of burnished gold : the gay
colours and profuse gilding applied to the interior, give
the halls a dazzling glory, while the suite of court
yards and apartments, vieing with each other in beauty
and magnificence, all contribute to exalt our apprehensions of the gorgeous fabric.   We must not expect to
find much there that will gratify the taste, or suit the
convenience of those accustomed to admire European
architecture, and English comfort; but in the estimation of the Chinese, their scolloped roofs, and projecting eaves, and dragon encircling pillars ; with their
leaf shaped windows, and circular doors, and fantastic
emblems, present more charms than the Gothic and
Corinthian buildings, or the curtained and carpeted
apartments of modern Europe.   "There reigns," says
father Hyacinth, "among the buildings of the forbidden city, a perfect symmetry, both in the form
and height of the several edifices, and in their relative
positions, indicating that they were built upon a regular
and harmonious plan."

The grand entrance to the " forbidden city," is by
the southern gate, through the central avenue of which
the emperor alone is allowed to pass : within this gate
is a large court, adorned with bridges, balustrades,
pillars and steps ; with figures of lions, and other
sculptures, all of fine marble.   Beyond this is the

" gate of extensive peace," which is a superb building
of white marble, one hundred and ten feet high,
ascended by five flights of steps, the centre of which
is reserved for the emperor.   It is here that he receives
the congratulations of his officers, who prostrate themselves to the ground before the imperial presence, on
the new year's day, and the anniversary of the emperor's birth.   Two more halls and three flights of
steps, lead to the palace of the sovereign, which is
called the " tranquil region of heaven," while that of
his consort is entitled " the palace of earth's repose ;"
to keep up the idea of the inseparable connection sub-
sisting, in the Chinese mind, between the powers of
nature, and the monarch of China ; the latter of whom
is, in the estimation of that idolatrous and superstitious
people, the representative and counterpart of the
former.   Into this private retreat of the emperor, no
one is allowed to approach, without special leave ; and
here the graet autocrat deliberates upon the affairs of
state, or gives audience to those who solicit his favour.

The Russian traveller, Timkowski, represents this
as the " loftiest, richest, and most magnificent of all
the palaces.   In the court before it, is a tower of gilt
copper, adorned with a great number of figures, which
are beautifully executed.   On each side of the tower,
is a large vessel, likewise of gilt copper, in which
incense is burned, day and night ;" doubtless, to flatter
the vanity of the imperial inhabitant, who fancies himself a god though he must die like men.   Beyond the
residence of the emperor and empress, is the imperial
flower-garden, laid out in beautiful walks, and adorned
with pavilions, temples, and grottos ; interspersed
with sheets of water, and rising rocks, which vary and

beautify the scene. Behind this garden, is a library of immense extent, vieing with that of Alexandria, in ancient, or of Paris, in modern times; and, further on, stands the gate of the flower-garden, which constitutes the northern outlet to the forbidden city.

The above comprises the buildings in a direct line between the northern and southern gates. To the east are the council chamber, and a number of princely palaces; with a temple, designed to enshrine the parental tablets of the present imperial family. To the west of the principal line of buildings, stand the hall of pictures, his majesty's printing-office, the principal magazines of the crown, and the female apartments; which fill up this division of the inclosure, and render the whole one, compact and extensive establishment. This magnificent residence, though described in a page or two, is about two miles in circumference, surrounded by walls, thirty feet high and, twelve wide; built of polished red brick, and surrounded by a moat, lined with hewn stone; the whole ornamented with gates and towers, and laid out in a diversified and elaborate manner.

The city, surrounding the imperial residence, is four miles long, and two and a half wide, encircled by walls, and entered by nine gates; which have given to it, the appellation of the " City of Nine Gates." This was the original capital; but since the occupancy of it, by the present dynasty, it has been increased by the addition of another city, larger than the former, and covering an area of fifteen square miles. These two cities are severally called the inner and outer, or the Tartar and Chinese city. In the former of these, directly to the north of the imperial palace, is an artificial mount, the summits of which are crowned with pavilions, and the sides ornamented with walks, and shaded with trees. Game of all kinds enliven the scene, and thousands of birds please the ear, with every variety of song. Corresponding with this mount, is a lake, about a mile and a half long, and one third of a mile broad, crossed by a bridge of nine arches, built of fine white marble. Its banks are ornamented with a variety of trees, and its bosom garnished with the flowers of the water lily; so that in the estimation of Father Hyacinth, "the infinite variety of beauties which the lake presents, constitute it one of the most enchanting spots on earth." In the midst of the lake, is a marble isle, adorned with temples, and surmounted by an obelisk; affording a delightful view of the surrounding gardens. A temple, dedicated to the discoverer of the silk-worm, stands near these gardens, where the empress, and the ladies of the court, attend to the cultivation of silk ; in order to encourage a branch of industry, on which China mainly depends for its wealth and elegance. In these gardens, the arrangement is such, that the whole seems the production of nature, rather than the effect of art; and affords a pleasing retreat for those who would retire from the symmetrical disposition of the imperial palace, to enjoy the mildness of natural scenery, in the midst of a dense and crowded capital.

In this division of the city, and nearly fronting the imperial palace, are the courts of the six grand tribunals of the empire, which have been before described; together with the office of the astronomical board, and the royal observatory. At the south-east corner of the northern division of the capital, is the grand

L

national college.   At a short distance, is the general
arena for literary controversy, where the public examinations, for the capital, are held.   The cells for the
candidates are numerously disposed round the arena;
where many an anxious heart beats high with expectation, and many an aspiring mind is plunged into deep
disappointment, when classed with those who fail.
Amongst the literary institutions of this great city,
may be enumerated a college for the cultivation of the
Chinese and Mantchou languages, and one for the
study of the Thibetan tongue.   A Mahomedan mosque,
with a Russian church, and a Roman Catholic temple,
are all enclosed within the walls of the imperial city;
but all these edifices are surpassed in splendour by the
many shrines of idolatry which abound; among the
rest may be specified the " white pagoda temple," so
called, on account of a white obelisk, erected in honour
of the founder of Buddhism, the scab of whose forehead,
produced by frequent prostrations is still preserved and
venerated as a holy relic.

The southern division of the city, where the Chinese
principally reside, is the grand emporium of all the
merchandize that finds its way to the capital, and tends
to ornament and gratify the adherents of the court.
Here, relieved from the strict discipline that prevails in
the palace, the citizens give themselves up to business,
or dissipation; encouraged and led on by voluptuous
courtiers, who have nothing to do, but to display their
grandeur, or to please their appetites.   There is an
immense deal of business done in this southern city,
and the broad street which divides it from north to
south, is constantly thronged by passengers and tradesmen.   Chinese shopkeepers are in the habit of adver-

tising their wares, by long projecting signs, hung out in front of their houses, painted in the gayest colours; while the bustling crowd, perpetually thronging the principal avenues, contributes to enliven and animate the scene.   In the southern division of the city, is an enclosure about two miles in circumference, where the emperor, and his great officers, annually go through the ceremony of ploughing and sowing the seed; in order to set an example to the subjects of this vast empire, and to encourage agriculture, from which the greatest part of their support is derived.   Notwithstanding these vacant spaces in the city of Peking, the population is so dense where the citizens reside, that the number of inhabitants cannot be much less than two millions.   Such, then, is the seat of government, and such the palaces and buildings it contains; worthy the metropolis of a great and civilized country.

CHAPTER VII.

LANGUAGE AND LITERATURE.

ORIGIN OF LANGUAGE — HIEROGLYPHICS — PHONETIC CHARACTERS — CHINESE MODE OF RECORDING EVENTS — SIX CLASSES OF CHARACTERS — NUMBER OF SYMBOLS — REDUCIBLE TO FEW ELEMENTS — MODES OF WRITING — QUESTION ABOUT EGYPTIAN ORIGIN — PORCELAIN BOTTLE — INSCRIPTION EXPLAINED — DATE ASCERTAINED — CHINESE CLASSICS — AUTHORIZED COMMENTARIES — ESTEEMED WORKS — HETERODOX PRODUCTIONS — ORAL LANGUAGE — MONOSYLLABIC MODE OF SPELLING — INITIALS AND FINALS — VARIETY OF TONES — COLLOCATION OF PHRASES — CHINESE GRAMMAR — FIGURES OF SPEECH — POETRY — LITERARY EXAMINATIONS — HONORARY DEGREES — VILLAGE INSPECTION — FIRST — SECOND — THIRD — AND FOURTH EXAMINATIONS — EFFORT NECESSARY — ADVANTAGES AND DISADVANTAGES OF THE SYSTEM.

In the Chinese language, both the oral and written mediums are of the most primitive order. Their words are all monosyllabic, and their characters symbolic; while both continue as they most probably existed in the earliest ages of antiquity. The first invention of the written character was such an effort of genius, that the Chinese have hardly ventured to advance on the original discovery, and have contented themselves with imitating the ancients. Before, however, we discuss the nature of their figures, it will be necessary to trace the progress of the human mind, in the art of communicating and recording thoughts; and point out how the Chinese were led to the adoption of their present mode of writing.

That which constitutes the most striking superiority of the human over the brute creation, is the ability of the former to conceive and communicate ideas to their fellows, by articulate sounds. The first employment of human speech is referred to in Gen. ii. 19, 20. " And God brought every beast of the field, and every fowl of the air to Adam, to see what he would call them ; and whatsoever Adam called every living creature, that was the name thereof. And Adam gave names to all cattle, and to every fowl of the air, and to every beast of the field." Having once affixed a definite term to each object, that word continued to be the sign of the object referred to, and each called up the other to recollection, whenever presented to the mind. In communicating with their fellows, human beings soon found that the names of things were insufficient to express all they wished to say, and attributes and actions received appropriate appellations. The operations of the mind, next required designation and description ; and speech at first poor, became gradually enriched, until it answered all the purposes of human society.

But the ear is not the only inlet to the soul, and as men derived knowledge to themselves by the organs of sight, they soon found that it was possible to communicate information to others through the same medium. Hence, when language failed, external action was resorted to, and the eye as well as the ear, aided in the interchange of ideas. When both voice and gesture were insufficient for their purpose, delineation was employed ; and objects were rudely pictured for the inspection of the bye standers. The same method was used for sending intelligence to a distance, or recording events for the benefit of posterity. Hence originated pictorial writing, or what is generally termed hieroglyphics. As scenes and circumstances became complicated, abbreviation was found necessary; and the principal part of an event was substituted for the whole; which has been called a *curiologic hieroglyphic.* A second mode of abridgment was by putting the instrument for the thing itself; which has been termed a *tropical hieroglyphic.* A third method, borrowed from the use of metaphor in language, was to make one thing stand for another; which has been denominated the *symbolic hieroglyphic.* This pictorial mode of writing, abridged as it was in the way above described, being insufficient for all the purposes of human intercourse, a certain number of arbitrary marks were invented, to express, not only mental conceptions, but visible objects. These went on increasing, till they, in some measure, answered the purpose of a written medium.

The next step was the construction of Phonetic characters; which seems such a leap from the previous mode, that many have thought the human mind, unaided by Divine inspiration, incapable of discovering it. It consists in uniting, what has no connection in the nature of things, form and sound. Finding that vocables were numerous, and their component parts but few, it occurred to some remarkable genius, that the words in common use might be resolved into their elements, and that it would be easier to invent arbitrary marks to represent the few elementary sounds, than to construct new and different signs for the multitude of things. We cannot exactly say, what led to the adoption of the particular signs for the elementary sounds which are found in most ancient alphabets; but the presumption is, that selecting the names of some very common objects, in the beginning of which certain sounds occurred, they formed a rude representation of the object, and made it stand for the sound in question; thus *aleph*, " an ox;" *beth*, " a house;" *gimel*, " a camel;" and *daleth*, " a door;" were probably pictured something like those objects, and stood for the sounds a, b, g, and d. Pursuing this method, they soon obtained marks for all the elementary sounds; and combining them, formed words. This brought about an entire revolution in the written medium of the ancients; and certain combinations of characters became the representatives of audible words, instead of visible objects; by which the written medium was rendered as full, compact, and definite as a spoken tongue; and ideas were communicated to the distance of a thousand years, or as many miles, with certainty and precision.

We are now prepared to consider the origin and nature of the Chinese mode of writing. Their traditions tell us, that in the infancy of their empire, events were recorded by means of knotted cords, as among the Peruvians. These were soon found indistinct, and pictorial representations were resorted to, similar to those used by the Mexicans. The abridged plan of the Egyptians was then adopted; and curiologic, tropical, and symbolic hieroglyphics were used; till all these proving insufficient, arbitrary marks were invented, and increased, till the present written medium, with all its variety and multiplicity, was formed. The Chinese characters are not strictly hieroglyphic; as they were neither invented by nor confined to the priesthood. They were in the first instance, doubtless, pictorial, then symbolic, afterwards compounded, and finally arbitrary.

The invention is ascribed to Tsang-këĕ, who lived in the reign of Hwang-te, about 4500 years ago. This is of course an extravagant assumption. Still, from the simple and primitive nature of their words and characters, we may infer, that their origin was extremely ancient. It is evident, that writing was used by the Chinese long before the time of Wăn-wang and Woo-wang, B. C. 1120, from a number of odes composed by those monarchs, and arranged by Confucius ; besides which, several instances occur, in the previous history, of written messages having been sent, and events recorded, which could not have been done without a written medium. They assert, that the first suggestion of arbitrary signs, was derived from the tracing of birds' tracts in the snow, and the observation of the marks on the back of a tortoise.

Their characters are divided into six classes ; first, *pictorial ;* or those which bear some resemblance to the object ; such as sun, moon, mountain, river, field, house, boat, tortoise, fish, horse, sheep, swallow, bird, &c. which are really representations of the things referred to : second, *metaphorical ;* or those which derive a meaning from something else ; thus the character for " handle," signifies also " authority ;" that for " raw hides," means, likewise, " to strip ;" while that for " heart," signifies, also, " mind," &c.: third, *indicative ;* or those which indicate the sense by the formation of the character ; as a man above-ground, signifies " above," and one underneath, " below:" fourth, *constructive ;* or those which derive their signification from the component parts of the character; as the symbol for "fire," and that for " surround," mean together " to roast ;" and the symbol for " metal," with that for " distinguish," mean,

when united, " to refine in the furnace ;" with many
others : fifth, *derivative ;* or those which are formed
from other characters, with a slight variation; as the
character for " old," if turned a little to the right instead of the left, means " to examine ;" and that for
" great," with an additional dot, means " very great :"
sixth, *phonetic;* or those in which form and sound har-
monize together; as the characters for " river," and
" stream," in which three drops represent the water,
combined with other characters, whose sound is well
known, to give some clue to the pronunciation.

According to these six modes, all the Chinese characters have been formed; and thus they have arrived at
the construction of their written language. The principle on which it is based, is that of assigning a separate character for each word ; and, with the exception
of the sixth division, above enumerated, of establishing
no connection between form and sound. By this means
the symbols of the Chinese language have become very
numerous, and can hardly be learned without great
difficulty. The characters in the imperial dictionary,
exceed thirty thousand; but many of these are obsolete,
and of rare occurrence. By a careful collation of a
historical novel in twenty volumes, and of the Chinese
version of the sacred scriptures, it appears, that the
whole amount of characters used in both does not much
exceed three thousand different sorts ; which would all
be known and readily remembered, by reading the
whole twice through.

Chinese characters appear exceedingly complicated,
to an unpractised observer; but a minute inspection
and comparison, will remove much of the difficulty.
It will soon be perceived, that however involved the

characters appear, they are all composed of six kinds of
strokes ; which, variously combined and repeated, constitute the formidable emblem, which startles and confounds the beginner. These strokes are the horizontal,
the perpendicular, the dot, the oblique slanting to the
right, that to the left, and the hooked. On further
examination it will appear, that the characters are re-
solvable into elements as well as strokes, some of
which occur very frequently, and are frequently repeated several times in a single character. The whole
number of elements is two hundred and fourteen, but
only fifty of these enter into frequent composition with
other characters ; and about ten or a dozen may be
recognized, in some form or another, in every sentence.
Indeed the component parts of a character may be
familiar to the student, while both the sound and
meaning are unknown.

The elements, or radicals, of the Chinese language
refer generally to very simple and well known things,
such as the human species, man and woman ; the parts
of the body, head, mouth, ear, eye, face, heart, hand,
foot, flesh, bones, and hair; human actions, such as
speaking, walking, and eating ; things necessary to
man, such as silk, clothes, dwelling, door, and city ;
celestial objects, such as sun, moon, and rain ; the five
elements, such as wood, water, fire, metal, and earth ;
the vegetable kingdom, such as grass, grain, and
bamboo ; the animal kingdom, such as birds, beasts,
fishes, and insects ; with the mineral kingdom, such as
stones, gems, &c. Most of the words referrible to
these substances or subjects, are classed under them;
and though the arrangement may not appear to us
exactly philosophical, yet it evidences the inclination

of the Chinese, at a very early period, to classification and order.   The radical is generally discernible without much difficulty ; and by a calculation of the additional number of strokes, the position of the given character in the dictionary is ascertained, almost as readily as by the alphabetic mode.   Each character occupies an exact square, of whatever number of strokes it be composed, and the Chinese delight in writing it in such a uniform manner, that the page shall appear as though divided into an equal number of sections, as pleasing to the eye as instructive to the mind.   The whole is surrounded by a border, with the title of the book, and the number of the volume, section, or page, noted on the side, instead of the top of the leaf.   The Chinese read from top to bottom, and commence at the right hand, going regularly down each column till the end of the book.   Chinese paper being thin, they write and print only on one side ; and doubling each page, leave the folded part outside.   The edges are not cut in front ; but on the top, bottom, and back of the book, where it is stitched and fastened.   Their volumes contain about eighty pages or leaves, and are about half an inch in thickness.   The Chinese use no thick covers for their books ; but instead of these, make a sort of case or wrapper, in which about eight or ten volumes are inclosed, and placed flat on the shelf.   In some books, the typographical execution and binding are superior; but in most instances, they are turned out in a slovenly manner, and sold at as cheap a rate as possible.

The modes of writing to be met with in Chinese books are various, viz., the ancient form, the seal character, the grotesque, the regular, the written, and the running hand; assimilating to our uncial, black, Grecian, Roman, Italic, and manuscript forms of writing. The ancient form shews, in some measure, how the Chinese characters were constructed ; for in it we find various objects delineated as they appear in nature. The seal character, as it is called, because found engraven on seals, differs from the usual form in being entirely composed of horizontal and perpendicular strokes, without a single oblique or circular mark belonging to it ; resembling in some degree the arbitrary marks used among the Egyptians. The regular and exact form is that met with, in all Chinese books, from which the written form differs, as much as our Italic from our Roman letters. The running hand seems to have been invented for the purpose of expediting business ; and by the saving of strokes, and the blending of characters, enables the transcriber to get over a great deal of work in a little time. Such productions are not easily decyphered, and yet the Chinese are so fond of this ready, and, in their opinion, graceful mode of writing, that they frequently hang up specimens of penmanship in the most abbreviated form, as ornaments to their shops and parlours. The Chinese writers are generally so practised in the use of the pencil, that they run down a column with the utmost rapidity, and would transcribe any given quantity of matter as soon as the most skilful copyist in England.

It has been suggested, that the Chinese mode of writing has been derived from Egypt ; and considering that the Chinese and Egyptians proceeded from the same stock, were civilized at a very early period, and resembled each other in their wants and resources, it is not to be wondered at, that they should adopt the same

method of communicating ideas. The notion of some
connection between China and Egypt has been revived,
since two small porcelain bottles were brought from
Egypt to this country; on these, inscriptions have been
discovered, apparently in the Chinese character; and
the learned have been curious to know their identity
and import. A fac-simile of one was seen by the
author in China; and a picture of the other has appeared in Davis's Chinese, but without any translation. On examination it has been found, that the
inscriptions are in the Chinese running hand, and read
as follows: Chun lae yew yǐh nëen, " The returning
spring brings another year:" and Ming yuĕh sung
chung chaou, " The clear moon shines through the
midst of the fir tree." This latter sentence is part of a
well known couplet, composed by Wang Găn-shǐh, a
famous writer under the Sung dynasty, A. D. 1068;
and as there is a curious circumstance connected with
it, we shall here relate it. The original couplet ran
thus :—

> Ming yuĕh sung këen keaou ;
> Wang keuen hwa sin shwuy.

> " The clear moon sings in the middle of the fir-tree ;
> " The royal hound sleeps in the bosom of the flower ! "

Soo-tung-po, another famous writer, who flourished
about fifty years afterwards, found fault with this
couplet, and altered it to the following :—

> Ming yuĕh sung chung chaou
> Wang keuen hwa yin shwuy.

> " The clear moon shines through the midst of the fir-tree;
> " The royal hound sleeps under the shade of the flower !"

Travelling, afterwards, in the south of China, he
heard a bird singing in the woods : and, on enquiry,

found that they called it, Ming-yuĕh, " the clear moon";
and, observing a grub nestling in a beautiful flower, he
ascertained its name to be Wang keuen, " the royal
hound." It is unnecessary to add, that he now became
convinced of his mistake; but too late to repair the
evil; as the couplet, thus amended by him, had already
been inscribed on various vessels, and transmitted, as
we find, to distant Egypt. It will easily be seen, that
this by no means strengthens the supposition of an
early connection between China and Egypt; and so
far from the bottles being coeval with Psammeticus,
B. C. 658, as has been suggested; its date cannot be
older than A. D. 1130 Since the commencement of
the Christian era, Chinese history makes mention of
foreign merchants coming from India and Arabia, by
sea, to trade with China.   A. D. 850, two Arabian
travellers came to Canton, who have published their
itineraries; and, A. D. 1300, Ibn Batuta visited China:
so that an almost constant intercourse has been kept
up between China and Arabia, by which means the
bottles in question may have been transmitted to the
latter country, and from thence conveyed into Egypt.
It does not appear that these bottles were discovered
" in an Egyptian tomb, which had not been opened
since the days of the Pharaohs;" for the travellers purchased them of a Fellah, who offered them for sale, at
Coptos.   Indeed, the circumstance of the inscriptions
being in the running hand, which was not invented
until the Sung dynasty, would lead us to conclude, that
the bottles are of a late date; and were, in all probability, carried to the west by Ibn Batuta.

The most celebrated compositions, in the Chinese
language, are the " five classics," and the " four books,"

most of which were compiled by Confucius and his disciples. The five classics are the Yĭh king, " book of diagrams ; " the She king, " collection of odes ; " the Le ke, " record of ceremonies ; " the Shoo king, containing the history of the three first dynasties; and the Chun tsew, which is an account of the life and times of Confucius. The book of diagrams is ascribed to Wăn- wang, B. C. 1130; the book of odes contains several pieces, referrible to the same age, and is a selection from a larger number, extant in the time of Confucius, and by him collected and published; the book of ceremonies was, probably, compiled from previously existing documents, in the same manner. The history of the three dynasties commences with an account of Yaou and Shun, in the traditionary period, coeval with Noah; and describes the principal events of antiquity, down to the times of Wăn, and Woo-wang, B. C. 1120, and is probably the production of Chow-kung, the brother of those monarchs. The last of the ancient classics was written by Confucius himself, and having been commenced in spring and concluded in autumn, was called *chun chew*, " spring and autumn." Of the " four books," the two first, chung yung, " the happy medium ;" and ta-hëŏ, " the great doctrine ;" were written by Tsze-sze, the grandson and disciple of Confucius : the third, called the Lun-yu, " book of discourses," is the production of the different disciples of the sage, who recollected and recorded his words and deeds ; while the last of the four books was written by Măng-tsze, or Mencius, the disciple of Tsze-sze, and bears the name of its author.

These five classics, and four books, are highly prized by the Chinese, and constitute the class books in schools, and the ground work of the literary examinations. The first business of a Chinese student is, to commit the whole of these books and classics to memory; without which, he cannot have the least chance of succeeding. The text of these nine works, is equal in bulk to that of the New Testament; and it is not hazarding too much to say, that were every copy annihilated to-day, there are a million of people who could restore the whole to-morrow. Having been composed at a very early period, and somewhat mutilated in the time of Che Hwang-te, it necessarily follows, that there are several indistinct passages, unintelligible to the people of the present day. Hence commentaries have been found necessary, and a very celebrated writer, who flourished in the twelfth century, called Choo-foo-tsze, has composed an extensive exposition of the whole. This commentary, is likewise, committed to memory by the student, and his mind must be familiar with whatever has been written on the subject. The number and variety of explanatory works, designed to elucidate the Chinese classics, shew, in what estimation these writings are held, and what an extensive influence they exert over the mind of China. A Chinese author says, that the expositors of the four books are more than one thousand in number. The style and sentiment of all the moderns is greatly conformed to this ancient model; and the essays and exhortations of the present day, are chiefly reiterations of the sentiments of their great master, and an incessant ringing of the changes on the five constant virtues, and the five human relations, which form the basis of moral philosophy in China. Even the Buddhist priests, and the followers of Taou, teach their disciples the books of Confucius; and nothing is looked upon as learning, in China, which does not emanate from this authorized and infallible source.

In addition to their classical writings, they have a number of works of high antiquity and great estimation; such as the Chow-le and E-le, supposed to have been written by Chow-kung, eleven hundred years before Christ; and treating of the ceremonies of marriage, funerals, visiting, feasting, &c. the Kea-yu, or "sayings of Confucius," ascribed to his grandson, Tsze-sze; the Heaou king, treating of filial piety; the Yew-hĕ̆, and Seaou-hĕ̆, intended for young persons; together with the writings of later philosophers, celebrated, both for their elegant style and orthodox sentiments. The Koo-wăn, or "specimens of ancient literature," contains extracts from their most celebrated authors, and is highly prized and commonly read in China. In addition to these philosophical writings, they have very voluminous works on history and biography, together with piles of poems, in which the genius of Chinese versifiers has been displayed, from the days of Wăn-wang to the present age. The departments of philology and philosophy, natural history and botany, medicine and jurisprudence, have been attended to by numerous authors; and though much improvement has not been made, of late years, yet the early advancement made in these studies, is creditable to the genius of ancient China.

Besides the writers in the orthodox school, there have been a great number of authors, advocating the system of Laou-keun and Buddha. The Taou-tĭh-king, composed by the former, is coeval with the books of Confucius, and nearly as much esteemed by the fol-

M

lowers of Taou; while the charms and prayers of the Buddhist sect, fill numerous cases, in all the temples of Fŭh, and find their way, by gratuitous distribution, into the hands of millions. Plays and novels, with works of a light and questionable character, are still more extensively multiplied, and actually deluge the land. A Chinese bookseller issues his catalogue, in the same way with our English bibliopolists, and in the number of works, with the cheapness of the prices, would vie with any advertisers, on this side the globe. Many of their publications amount to two hundred and fifty or three hundred volumes ; and one has been met with, amounting to three thousand volumes, indicative either of the abundance of their matter, or their tedious prolixity.

We have hitherto alluded principally to the Chinese characters, and the method they have adopted, of transmitting and perpetuating their ideas. We shall now treat of their spoken language ; not that writing preceded speaking, but because the written character constitutes the universal medium, and has been, for centuries, unchanged ; while spoken sounds vary in every province of the empire, and through each succeeding age. It is scarcely possible to ascertain the original sounds of the letters, in alphabetic languages, where the arbitrary marks are few; and how much less can the enunciations appropriated to several thousand characters, be retained unimpaired, for successive ages, among hundreds of millions of people. The written medium, therefore, must be looked upon as the most stable part of the language ; while their vocal communications come next into consideration.

The Chinese language is monosyllabic, inasmuch

as the sound of each character is pronounced by a single emission of the voice, and is completed at one utterance: for though there are some Chinese words which appear to be dysillabic, and are written with a diaræsis, as këen, tëen, &c., yet they are as really monosyllabic, and sounded as much together, as our words, "beer" and "fear." The joining of two mono-syllables, to form a phrase for certain words, as făh-too, for "rule;" wang-ke, to express "forget," &c. does not militate against the assertion above made, for the two parts of the term are still distinct words, which are merely thrown together into a phrase, for the purpose of definiteness in conversation.

As the Chinese do not divide their words into elementary sounds, they know nothing of spelling; but they have a method of determining and describing particular enunciations, which nearly answers their purpose. The plan they adopt is, to divide each word into its initial and final; and then taking two other well-known characters, one of which has the given initial, and the other the final, they unite them together, and form the sound required. This they call splitting the sounds: and though, from ignorance of the principles of orthography, they sometimes divide the sounds improperly; while, from the various sounds attached to the characters adduced, the result is frequently undetermined; yet it is the best method they have, and is employed in all their dictionaries. A reference to the initials and finals of the mandarin dialect, will enable the reader to see what sounds it contains and what articulations the educated Chinese are capable of pronouncing.

The initials are sixteen simple, five aspirated, and one silent. The sixteen simple initials are as follows :—

ch, as in *church*.

f, as in *far*.

g, hard, as in *go:* sometimes gn, as in *singing*.

h, strongly aspirated.

j, as in French, *jamais*.

k, as in *kite*.

l, as in *lame*.

m, as in *main*.

n, as in *nun*.

p, as in *path*.

s, as in *send*.

sh, as in *ship*.

sz, as in *his zeal;* pronounced without

the vowels.

t, as in *top*.

ts, as in *heart's ease*, dropping all but the ts, and the succeeding vowel.

tsz, a peculiar sound followed by a short e.

The five aspirated initials are the ch, k, p, t, and ts, described above, pronounced with a strong aspirate between these consonants, and the following vowels.

The silent initials give no sound to the finals, which, therefore, when joined with this negative beginning, stand as they are ; but wherever the diaræsis e, i, and u, occur in the final, y is prefixed, when writing the sound in English orthography, as ya, for ëa, yae for ëae, &c.

The forty-three finals are as follows :—

a,
ae, } the a as in *father*.
an,

ăn, as in *woman*.

ang, as in *bang*.

ăng, as in *hung*.

aou, this sound is a combination of the a, in *father*, and the ow, in howl.

ay, as in *hay*.

e, as in *me*.

e, as the French in *je ;* — found only in combination with sh, sz, and tsz.

ëa, as in *meander*.

ëae, the a as in *father* the e as in *me*.

ëang, as *ang*, in anger, preceded by e.

ëaou, like the aou, preceded by e.

ëay, as the ay, in hay, preceded by e.

ëen, as en in pen, preceeded by e.

en, as the e'e in e'er.

ëo, as in geomancy.

eu, as in the French *peu*.

ëuen, as *yawn*, preceded by e.

ëun, as the u, in *bun*, preceded by e.

ëung, as in *young*.

ew, as in *few*.

in, as in *pin*.

ing, as in *king*.

o, as in *no*.

oo, as in *loo*.

ow, as in *cow*.

uen, as the final sound of *lawn*.

un, as in *bun*.

ung, as in *flung*.

urh, as in *viper*.

uy, as in *fluid*.

wa, as in *quaternion*.

wae, as the former, succeeded by e.

wan, as in *truant*.

wăn, as in *won*.

wang, as the a in *father*.

wăng, as the a in *woman*.

we, as in *we*.

wei, as in *wily*.

wo, as in *wo*.

woo, as in *woo*.

By this, it will be seen, that the b, and d, are wholly wanting in the mandarin dialect; that the r has no vibratory sound; and that n and ng, are the only consonants among the finals; while all the rest have vowel terminations.

The orthography employed above, is that of Dr. Morrison's Dictionary, which is preferred, not as entirely unexceptionable, but as being generally known, and, at present, the only one which we possess, in the English language.

Were all these initials to be joined with the several finals, they would produce by their union nine hundred and forty-six monosyllables. They are not, however, varied to their utmost extent; and three hundred and two different monosyllables are all that the Chinese really extract from these combinations. In attempting to pronounce the names of foreigners, or the words of another language they endeavour to express them by combining the monosyllables of their own tongue; and if these are not sufficient, they have no method of writing, and scarcely any of enunciating the given word. Thus they make sad havoc of the language of other nations, and missionaries, in aiming to write scripture names in the Chinese character, find considerable difficulty in expressing them sufficiently concise and clear.

But, it may be asked, how do the Chinese manage to make themselves intelligible to each other, with only three hundred monosyllables, and how can these be sufficient for all the purposes of oral language? To this it may be replied, that the Chinese have a method of increasing the number of their words by assigning to each a different tone, which, though scarcely discernible by an unpracticed ear, are as readily distinguished and imitated by Chinese organs, as differences of elementary sounds with us. Indeed they more easily discern a change of intonation than a discrepancy in orthography; while even infants among them learn to imitate the tones as soon as they begin to utter words. All the words in their pronouncing dictionaries are arranged according to these tones, and they are as necessary a part of the language as the sounds themselves. Besides which, the tones never vary, either through the lapse of time or the distance of place; for however much the ancients may differ from the moderns, and the inhabitants of Peking from those of Canton in the sounds they apply to the various characters, yet the tones are invariably the same, not only throughout every province of China, but even amongst the neighbouring nations of Cochin China, Corea, and Japan. This is evident, from the poetry of the Chinese, which is based upon the intonation, and which was the same a thousand years ago that it is now, and continues to be modulated in the same manner wherever the Chinese character is used.

The tones are substantially four, which the Chinese call the even, the high, the departing, and the entering tones; and which are thus described:—

"The even tone has an equal path, neither high nor low;
"The high tone is a loud sound, both shrill and strong;
"The departing tone is distinct, but seems to retreat to a distance;
"The entering tone is short, contracted, and hastily gathered up."

These four principal tones are increased by adding a lower " even " tone, making five in all. These may be distinguished in European books, by the employment of accents, such as the acute and grave, the long and

short, with the circumflex. The "entering" or contracted tone, however, sometimes requires a different
orthography ; the concluding nasal being omitted, and
the contracted vowel followed by the letter h, to shew
that it is to be pronounced short. This exhibits in our
Chinese dictionaries alphabetically arranged, an increase of about one hundred words, though in fact the
number of real Chinese sounds, unvaried by tones, is
little more than three hundred. These three hundred
words, if accentuated by the five tones, would give the
sum of fifteen hundred distinguishable utterances in the
mandarin dialect; but the Chinese do not avail themselves of all the advantages which their pronouncing
system affords, and one thousand variations are the
utmost actually in use. It necessarily follows, therefore, that they have many characters under one and the
same sound. This constitutes a great difficulty in the
communication of ideas, and renders mistakes both easy
and frequent. In order to prevent the confusion likely
to arise from this paucity of sounds, the Chinese are in
the habit of associating cognates and synonymes, and of
combining individual terms into set phrases, which are
as regularly used in the accustomed form, as compound
words in our own language. Hence the Chinese has
become a language of phrases; and it is necessary to
learn, not only the terms and the tones, but the system
of collocation also ; which in that country is the more
important, on account of the paucity of words, and
the number of terms resembling each other in sound,
though differing in sense.

In the science of grammar, the Chinese have made
no progress ; and among the host of their literati, no
one seems to have turned his attention to this subject.

They have not learned to distinguish the parts of
speech or to define and designate case, gender, number,
person, mood, or tense; they neither decline their
nouns, nor conjugate their verbs, while regimen and
concord are with them based on no written rules. Not
that the language is incapable of expressing these ideas,
or that a scheme of grammar could not be drawn up
for the Chinese tongue; but the natives themselves
have no notion of such distinctions, and could hardly
be made to comprehend them. They have treatises on
the art of speaking and writing, but these handle the
subject in a manner peculiar to themselves. They
divide their words into " living and dead," " real and
empty;" a " living word " is a verb, and " a dead word"
a substantive; while both of these are called " real,"
in distinction from particles, which are termed " empty."
They also distinguish words into " important" and
" unimportant." The chief aim of Chinese writers is
to dispose the particles aright, and he who can do this
is denominated a clever scholar. As for the distinction
between noun, pronoun, verb, and participle, they have
never thought of it; and use words occasionally in each
of these forms, without any other change than that of
position or intonation. They have terms for expressing
the manner and time of an action, with the number and
gender of individuals; but they more frequently leave
these things to be gathered from the context, imagining
that such auxiliary words disfigure rather than em-
bellish the sentence. To an European, their composition
appears indefinite, and sometimes unintelligible; but
to a native, this terse and sententious mode of writing,
is both elegant and intelligible. In conversation they
are sometimes more diffuse, but in composition they

are concise, and delight to express much in a few words. Moral apothegms and pithy sayings, are frequently indulged in; and so sententious are their books, that whole chapters may be met with, in which the sentences do not exceed four words each. It will be seen from this, that Chinese grammar is of a truly primitive character, just as we might expect to find it in the infancy of language, when men expressed themselves in short sentences and few words. The student of Chinese will not have to burthen his mind with many rules; but framing his speech according to the native model, will gradually acquire a mode of communicating his ideas at once perspicuous and acceptable.

It must not be thought, however, that the Chinese language is destitute of ornament. They employ various figures of speech, and in some they excel. Metaphor is frequently to be met with in their writings, and similies are abundant. They are fond of alliteration, and attention to rhythm is with them an essential part of composition. Gradation and climax are sometimes well sustained, while in description and dialogue they seem quite at home. But the most remarkable feature of Chinese composition, is the antithesis. Most of the principal words are classed in pairs, such as heaven and earth, beginning and end, day and night, hot and cold, &c. From antithetical words, they proceed to contrast phrases and sentences, and draw up whole paragraphs upon the same principle. In these antithetical sentences, the number of words, the class of expressions, the meaning and intonation, together with the whole sentiment, are nicely and exactly balanced, so that the one contributes to the perspicuity and effect of the other. Such a counting of words, and such a mechanical arrangement of sentences, would be intolerable in European composition, but are quite elegant and almost essential in Chinese. Tautology, which is justly repudiated with us, is much indulged in by them; and sentences are rendered emphatic and distinct by repeating words, and sometimes phrases, or by reiterating the same idea in other terms.

In ancient times the Chinese composed a number of odes, which were handed down to later ages. Out of three thousand of these poems, Confucius selected three hundred, which are still extant in the book of odes. The principal of these are on the usual subjects of love and war, and are replete with metaphor drawn from nature. In these compositions some little attention is paid to rhyme, but none to measure; the poetry consisting chiefly in the arrangement of the sentences, and the figurative character of the language.

During the Tang and the Sung dynasties, the art of poetry was much cultivated, and the present system of Chinese versification was then established. Their poetic effusions are of three kinds, odes, songs, and diffuse poems. In their modern odes, they observe both rhyme and measure, and are very particular about the antithesis. Their verses consist of four lines, with five or seven words in each; the first, second, and last line of the verse being made to rhyme. The measure consists in the right disposition of the accents, which have been above described as four. In poetry, however, they divide these into two, viz., the *even* and the *oblique;* which latter includes all besides the even. The rule is, that if the first two words are in the even, the next two must be in the oblique tone, and so the oblique and even tones must be diversified and contrasted, to the end of the verse. So essential are these tones to constitute good poetry, that the Chinese will not look at a verse, however well expressed, and neatly rhyming, in which accent is outraged. In addition to rhyme and measure, the Chinese require that the expressions should be bold, the thought vivid and striking, and every word in each line corresponding with its opposite, so as to form a chain of beautiful antitheses, mutually illustrating and setting forth their fellows. The most celebrated poets of China are Le-tae-pïh, and Too-foo, both of whom flourished about a thousand years ago; and who not only animated their contemporaries by inditing rhymes, but have handed down a number of elegant and pithy poems, which are still the admiration of the Chinese.

The number of individuals acquainted with letters in China, is amazingly great. One half of the male population are able to read; while some mount the " cloudy ladder" of literary fame, and far exceed their companions. The general prevalence of learning in China, may be ascribed to the system pursued at the literary examinations; by which none are admitted to office, but those who have passed the ordeal with success, while each individual is allowed to try his skill in the public hall. Wealth, patronage, friends, or favour are of no avail in procuring advancement; while talent, merit, diligence, and perseverance, even in the poorest and humblest individual, are almost sure of their appropriate reward. This is their principle, and their practice does not much vary from it. They have a proverb, that " while royalty is hereditary, office is not; and the plan adopted at the public examinations is an illustration of it.

In order to understand the theory of these examinations, it will be necessary, first, to allude to the general divisions of the country ; because the various degrees of literary rank correspond to the size and importance of the districts, where the enquiry is held.   China is divided into eighteen provinces, each containing about ten counties, or departments ; and each county about ten districts ; the districts do not exactly correspond to this number, but the aggregate throughout the empire is fifteen hundred and eighteen.   In the province of Canton, there are nine counties, ten departments, and seventy-two districts.   The degrees of literary honour are four; viz. sew tsae, " men of cultivated talent;" keu jin, " elevated persons ; " tsin sze, " advanced scholars ;" and han lin, " the forest of pencils," or national institute.   The first title is conferred in the county towns ; the second in the provincial cities ; the third in the capital; and the fourth in the emperor's palace.

The examinations commence in the districts, in each of which about a thousand persons try their skill ; averaging about two per cent. of the male adult population.   Twice in every three years, the presiding officer of each district assembles all the scholars under his jurisdiction in the place of examination, and there issues out themes on which they write an essay and an ode, to see whether they are suited for further trial ; he then affixes a notice to the walls of his office, on which are inscribed the names of all those recommended to the lieutenant of the county ; this officer again examines them, together with those residing in the county town ; and after repeated trials selects a few, who thus gain what is called " a name in the village."   This distinction is much coveted by the candidates, as affording the advantage of a good standing before the literary chancellor; the first name among them being almost sure of a degree.

After the magistrates have tried the capacities of the young men, they are subjected to a more rigorous examination before the chanceller, which determines their fate as to the first degree. The trial takes place in the county hall, which is divided into compartments, just sufficient for the accommodation of each student; they are searched on entering, to prevent their carrying with them any books or papers, that might assist them in their compositions; themes are given out, on which they write both in prose and poetry; their productions are marked instead of being signed, in order to prevent partiality; and the papers being laid before the chancellor, he selects the best, and confers on their authors the title of *sew tsae*, equivalent to our bachelor of arts; at the rate of one per cent. on all the candidates; averaging ten for each district, twenty for each department, and thirty for each county; and giving about twelve hundred for the province of Canton, at every examination. As these take place twice in every three years, there must be an annual increase of eight hundred graduates for Canton alone. On attaining the first step of literary rank, the individual is exempted from corporeal punishment, and cannot be chastised but by the chancellor himself.

The examination for the second degree, takes place once in every three years, at the provincial cities; and is attended by *sew tsaes* only. The 2400 newly made graduates, together with the unsuccessful ones of former years, now assemble, and form a body of about

10,000 aspirants for the rank of keu jin, or " elevated men." This is a most eventful and trying period, and many an anxious heart beats high with expectation of mounting another step of " the cloudy ladder." The imperial chancellor, and the chief officers of the province, unite together in examining the candidates. The literary arena is provided with several thousand small cells, into which the competitors are introduced, and guarded by soldiers, so as to prevent collusion or communication, till the trial is over. The examination takes place in the eighth month of the year, and the days of trial are the ninth, twelfth, and fifteenth ; on the first of these days the candidates enter, and three schedules are handed over to them, containing seven texts from the classical writings, and three themes ; upon each of the former they have to write a prose composition, and upon each of the latter a poetical effusion, for the inspection of the examiners : a scribe stands ready to copy their productions with red ink, and sets a mark on both the original and the transcript, in order that the officers may not discover to whom the pieces belong. After the completion of the essays, they are sent in for inspection, and if the slightest fault be committed, or a word improperly written or applied, the individual's mark is immediately stuck up at the office gate, by which he may understand that it is time to walk home, as he will not be permitted to proceed to the next trial.

The second day is like the first, and the defaulters are struck off as before ; so that the number is greatly reduced by the time the third trial comes. At the close of this, the papers are closely inspected, and a few selected as the most intelligent, whose names are pub-

lished for the information of the people. Seventy-two
" elevated men," equivalent to our masters of arts, are
chosen out of the ten thousand competitors in the province of Canton, and about as many for each of the
other provinces, making about thirteen hundred for the
whole empire. When the announcement of the successful candidates is published, the multitude rush
forward to gain the intelligence, and hand-bills are
printed and circulated far and wide; not only for the
information of the candidates themselves, but their
parents and kindred also, who receive titles and honours
in common with their favoured relations. Presents are
then made to the triumphant scholars, and splendid
apparel prepared for them, so that they soon become
rich and great. To-day they are dwelling in an humble
cottage, and to-morrow introduced to the palaces of the
great; riding in sedans, or on horseback, and every
where received with the greatest honour.

The third degree is the result of a still more rigorous
examination at the capital. The thirteen hundred new
masters of arts, together with those formerly graduated,
who have not risen higher, assemble once in three
years, at the capital, to try for the third literary degree.
Here also about ten thousand candidates enter the lists,
and after an examination similar to what has been
described, three hundred are chosen, who are dignified
with the title of tsin-sze, or " advanced scholars,"
equal to our doctors of law. On attaining this degree,
they are immediately elegible to office, and are generally appointed forthwith. The superintendency of a
district is the first post they occupy, and there is not a
magistrate throughout the empire who has not attained
the degree referred to. The whole number of civil

officers in China, of the rank of district magistrate, and upwards, is about three thousand; and the addition of one hundred per annum seems but just enough to fill up the vacancies occasioned by death or dismissal.

The fourth degree follows a very close examination in the presence of the emperor. The three hundred newly made doctors are summoned into the imperial palace, where they all compose essays on given themes. A small number of these are chosen to enter the Han-lin-yuen, " the court of the forest of pencils," or national institute: where they reside, most liberally supported and patronized by the emperor, to prepare public documents, draw up national papers, and deliberate on all questions regarding politics and literature. The members of this court are considered the cream of the country, and are frequently appointed to the highest offices in the state. The three principal candidates at this fourth examination, are forthwith mounted on horseback, and paraded for three days round the capital, signifying that " thus it shall be done to the man whom the king delighteth to honour." The chief of the first three is one of a million, occupying the most enviable post in the nation, and yet a post to which all are eligible, and to which all aspire.

In order to succeed at any of the literary examinations, it is necessary to put forth extraordinary exertions. Each candidate is expected to know by heart the whole of the four books, and five classics, as well as the authorized commentaries upon them. They must also be well acquainted with the most celebrated writers of the middle ages; and the history of China, from the earliest antiquity, must be fresh in their recollection, that they may allude to the circumstances of bye-gone days, and enrich their compositions with phrases from ancient authors, who, in the estimation of the Chinese, thought and wrote far better than the moderns. The chief excellency of their essays, consists in introducing as many quotations as possible, and the farther they go back, for recondite and unusual expressions, the better; but they are deprived of every scrap of writing, and are expected to carry their library, to use their own phrase, in their stomachs, that they may bring forth their literary stores as occasion requires.

All this can only be attained by great application and perseverance. The first five or six years at school are spent in committing the canonical books to memory; another six years are required to supply them with phrases for a good style; and an additional number of years, spent in incessant toil, are needed to ensure success. Long before the break of day, the Chinese student may be heard chaunting the sacred books; and till late at night, the same task is continued. Of one man it is related, that he tied his hair to a beam of the house, in order to prevent his nodding to sleep. Another, more resolute, was in the habit of driving an awl into his thigh, when inclined to slumber. One poor lad, suspended his book to the horns of the buffalo, that he might learn while following the plough; and another, bored a hole in the wainscot of his cottage, that he might steal a glimpse of his neighbour's light. They tell of one, who fearing that the task assigned him was too hard, gave up his books in despair; and was returning to a manual employment, when he saw an old woman rubbing a crow-bar on a stone; on asking

N

her the reason, she replied, that she was just in want of a needle, and thought she would rub down the crowbar, till she got it small enough.   The patience of the aged female provoked him to make another attempt, and he succeeded in attaining to the rank of the first three in the empire.

The advantage of this system will appear, in the even-handed justice which it deals out to all classes. Caste is by this means abolished; no privileged order is tolerated; wealth and rank are alike unavailing to procure advancement; and the poor are enabled, by determined exertion, to obtain the highest distinction. Instances are frequent, of the meanest working their way, until they become ministers of state, and sway the destinies of the empire.   These facts being trumpeted abroad, every individual strives for a prize, which is equally accessible to all.   They say, of Shun, who was raised to the throne, by his talents and virtues, " Shun was a man; I, also, am a man; if I do but exert myself, I may be as great as he."   The stimulus thus given to energetic perseverance, is immense; and the effect, in encouraging learning, incalculable. All persons acquire some knowledge of letters; and learning, such as it is, is more common in China, than in any other part of the world.   Six poor brethren will frequently agree to labour hard, to support the seventh at his books; with the hope, that should he succeed, and acquire office, he may throw a protecting influence over his family, and reward them for their toil.   Others persevere, to the decline of life, in the pursuit of literary fame; and old men, of eighty, have been known to die, of sheer excitement, and ex-

haustion, in the examination halls. In short, difficulties vanish before them, and they cheer each other
on, with verses like the following :—

"Men have dug through mountains, to cut a channel for the sea ;
"And have melted the very stones, to repair the southern skies;
"Under the whole heaven, there is nothing difficult ;
"It is only that men's minds are not determined."

Another advantage of the system is, that it ensures
the education of the magistrates. Before a single step
can be gained in the literary ladder, the memory must
be exercised ; and the scrutiny through which the candidates pass, ensures a habit of vigilance and assiduity,
which must be serviceable to them ever after. The
ancient classics contain many moral maxims ; and the
history of the empire, recording the causes of the rise
and fall of dynasties, affords some knowledge of political economy: thus the mind becomes informed as far
as information is attainable in China. The man who
would prevail, must exercise his thoughts, and a thinking
man is likely to prove a good magistrate. The system,
at any rate, is calculated to ensure a corps of learned
officers ; and it would not be much amiss, if some triple
examination of the kind were adopted, before our district magistrates, and lord-lieutenants, received their
commissions. The Chinese look upon the public examinations as the glory of their land, and think meanly
of those nations, where the same plan is not adopted.

The disadvantages of the system arise from the contracted range of their literature, and from their pertinacious attachment to the ancients, without fostering
the genius and invention of the moderns. The sacred
books are supposed to contain every thing necessary to

be known; and whatever lies beyond the range of the human relations and the cardinal virtues, is not worth attending to. Ethics and metaphysics being their prime study, nature, with all her stores, continues unexplored; geography, astronomy, chemistry, anatomy, and mechanics; with the laws of electricity, galvanism, and magnetism; the theory of light, heat, and sound; and all the results of the inductive philosophy, are quite neglected and unattended to. The ancients being considered more intelligent and virtuous than the moderns, the highest excellence consists in imitating them; and it is presumption to attempt to surpass them. Thus the human mind is fettered, and no advance is made in the walks of science.

Another disadvantage is ascribable to the occasional departures from the system. Notwithstanding the rigour of the laws, and the vigilance of the magistracy, ways and means are frequently discovered of bribing the police; and of inducing some candidates, more desirous of present advantage than of future fame, to make essays for their companions.

In addition to these underhand methods of getting forward, the government sometimes expose offices to public sale, in order to relieve their own necessities; but this practice is much reprobated by the imperial advisers, and seldom resorted to. If the course of study were improved and enlarged, and if all abuses were carefully guarded against, the system itself is truly admirable and worthy of imitation; and so far as it is maintained in its purity, constitutes the best institution in China.

View of the Mission Chapel, at Batavia.

CHAPTER VIII.

THE RELIGIONS OF CHINA.

THREE SYSTEMS OF RELIGION — CONFUCIUS — HIS LIFE — MORAL AND PO-
LITICAL OPINIONS — NOTIONS ABOUT HEAVEN — AND THE SUPREME —
HIS THEORY OF THE UNIVERSE — THE TWO POWERS OF NATURE — THE
DIAGRAMS — SCHEME OF MATAPHYSICS — MATERIAL TRINITY — IDEAS
OF SPIRITUAL BEINGS — OF THE FUTURE WORLD — AND OF HUMAN
NATURE — THE RELIGION OF TAOU — ETERNAL REASON — INCARNA-
TIONS OF IT — PHILOSOPHER'S STONE — GHOSTS AND CHARMS — TREAD-
ING ON FIRE — DEMONIACAL POSSESSIONS — MAGIC ARTS — RELIGION
OF BUDDHA — HISTORY OF ITS FOUNDER — ENTRANCE INTO CHINA —
BUDDHIST TEMPLES — MEDITATION ON BUDDHA — REPETITION OF HIS
NAME — ABSORPTION OF A BLACKSMITH — FORM OF PRAYER — COM-
PASSION TO ANIMALS — FEEDING HUNGRY GHOSTS — PAPER MONEY —
AND HOUSES — SCRAMBLING FOR HOLY FOOD — DOCTRINE OF ANNIHI-
LATION — DESPISED BY THE CONFUCIANS — RESEMBLANCE TO THE
CATHOLICS — REVIEW OF THE THREE SYSTEMS.

THE religions of China are three; viz. the systems of
Confucius, Laou-tsze, and Buddha. Of these, the first is
the most honoured, both by the government, and the
learned: the works of Confucius constitute the class
books of the schools, and the ground work of the public
examinations; hence all who make any pretensions to
literature, pride themselves in being considered the followers of that philosopher. The religion of Laou-tsze, is
equally ancient with the favoured sect, and has a great
hold on the minds of the people. It has now and
then been honoured with imperial patronage; and during those golden opportunities has exerted a wider

influence over the population; but during the present dynasty, it has been left mainly to its own resources. The religion of Buddha was introduced from India into China, about the beginning of the Christian era: its priests and its temples are now spread over the whole land; and the majority of the common people are decidedly in favour of this latter system. But, as both the Taouists and Buddhists consent to accord the precedence to Confucius, and aim to combine the moral code of that philosopher with their own superstitious dogmas, they are commonly tolerated by the ruling sect. Now and then, the Confucians exclaim against the celibacy of the Buddhist priests, and indulge themselves in a few jeering observations on the demonolatry of Taou; but, generally speaking, the sceptics do not trouble themselves about the superstitious; and systems directly opposed, being both in the extreme of error, consent to let each other pretty much alone.

Some idea of the different religions may be afforded, by a slight sketch of their respective founders, and of the doctrines promulgated by them. To begin with Confucius; he was born, as has been before observed, in the twenty-first year of Chow Ling-wang, B. C. 549, in the state of Loo, now the province of Shantung. His mother had prayed to the hill Ne for a son, and on bringing forth the sage called his name Chung-ne. Fable says, that on this occasion, two dragons encircled the house, while sweet music was heard in the air. Confucius was left an orphan at an early age; and during his youth amused himself with marshalling the sacrificial vessels, as opposing armies or as princes and ministers. As he grew up, he studied the art of ruling; and at the age of fifty was employed by the sovereign of his native state, as magistrate of a small district. Here he instructed the people to nourish their parents while living, and to inter them suitably when dead; he directed the elder and younger to eat separately, and men and women to take different sides of the road; no one picked up what was dropped in the street, and all needless ornament was abolished. Three or four years afterwards Confucius was raised to the rank of prime minister of Loo. Some improvements took place under his rule; when the prince of a neighbouring state, fearing lest Confucius should acquire too great an influence, sent a band of female musicians to the Loo country, on the acceptance of which by his sovereign, the sage resigned, and left his native province. From this period he wandered from one petty kingdom to another, frequently exposed to the secret machinations and open attacks of foes, During these peregrinations, he taught his disciples under the shade of some tree; and, hurrying about from place to place, was sometimes deprived of the necessaries of life. At length the prince of Tsoo, a southern state, hearing that Confucius was in the neighbourhood, wished to engage him; but one of his own officers remonstrated, saying, that Confucius would never sanction their ambitious views; and that, therefore, it was not for the interests of Tsoo, that he should be retained. The prince listened to him, and declined the services of the sage. From thence Confucius retired to his native state, where he did not again solicit office, but employed himself in discoursing on ceremonies, correcting the odes, and adjusting music. He finally turned his attention to the diagrams, and read the book of changes so frequently, that he thrice renewed the leathern thong with which the tablets or leaves were strung together. His disciples amounted to three thousand, amongst whom seventy-two were most distinguished. His last work was, the history of his own times, wherein he gave his opinion so decidedly on the conduct of different rulers, that he made sycophants and tyrants tremble. About this time his countrymen discovered an unicorn in the woods, which Confucius considered as indicative of his speedy removal; and wiping away the tears, he exclaimed, " My teaching is at an end!" In the forty-first year of King-wang, B. C. 477, Confucius died; when the prince of Loo composed an elegy on his memory, praising his genius, and lamenting his end. His disciples said, " whilst he was alive you did not employ him, and now that he is dead you lament him ; how inconsistent!"

Thus it appears, that Confucius, during the greatest part of his life, was engaged in political affairs ; and only in his declining years, devoted himself to the establishment of a school of philosophy ; his system will therefore be more likely to refer to politics than religion, and the pursuit of temporal, rather than eternal good. In fact, it is a misnomer to call his system a religion, as it has little or nothing to do with theology, and is merely a scheme of ethics and politics, from which things spiritual and divine are uniformly excluded. In treating of the government of a country, Confucius compares it to the management of a family, and grounds the whole on the due controul of one's self, and the right management of the heart. He expressly lays down the golden rule, of doing to others as we would they should do unto us ; and lays the foundation of moral conduct in the principle of excusing and feeling for others, as we would for ourselves. The five cardinal virtues, according to his school, are benevolence, righteousness, politeness, wisdom, and truth; and the duties of the human relations, those which should subsist between parents and children, elder and younger brethren, princes and ministers, husbands and wives, friends and companions. Of all these, filial piety stands first and foremost; reverence to parents is required, not only in youth, when children are dependent on, and necessarily subject to, their natural protectors; but even to the latest period, parents are to be treated with honour, and after death to be raised to the rank of gods. Without filial piety, they say, it is useless to expect fidelity to one's prince affection to one's brethren, kindness to one's domestics, or sincerity among friends. Filial piety is the foundation of benevolence, rectitude, propriety, wisdom, and truth. This feeling, if conceived in the heart, and embodied in the life, will lead to the performance of every duty, the subjugation of every passion, and the entire renovation of the whole man. It is not to be confined to time and place, but is to be maintained, whether the objects of our respect be present or absent, alive or dead; and thousands of years after their departure, ancestors are still to be exalted in the liveliest apprehensions, and undiminished affections of their descendants.

It is strange, however, that while Confucius recommends such an excessive veneration for parents, he should have overlooked the reverence due to the Father of our spirits; and while he traced up the series from parents to ancestors, requiring the highest degree of honour to be paid to our first progenitors, that he should not have considered Him from whom all beings spring, and who is entitled to our first and chief regard. But it is a lamentable proof of the depravity of the human heart, that so acute, intelligent, vigorous, and independent a mind, should not have traced the generations of men up to the great Former of all, and left his followers in the dark as to the being, attributes, and perfections, of the one living and true God.

There are, in the works of this philosopher, some allusions to heaven, as the presiding power of nature; and to fate, as the determiner of all things; but he does not appear to attribute originality to the one, or rationality to the other: and thus his system remains destitute of the main truth, which lays at the basis of all truth, viz., the being of a self-existent, eternal all-wise God. On one occasion, Confucius exclaimed, " Unless it be heaven's design, that my cause should fail, what can the people of Kwang do to me?" Again, when one asked him, whether it were best to worship this or that deity, he said, " You are mistaken; he that offends against heaven, has no one to whom he can pray." Another passage runs thus: " Imperial heaven has no kindred to serve, and will only assist virtue." The glorious heavens are said to be " bright, accompanying us wherever we go." " When heaven sent down the inferior people, it constituted princes and instructors, directing them to assist the Supreme ruler, in manifesting kindness throughout all regions." " Life and death are decreed by fate; riches and poverty rest with heaven."

There are, besides these occasional allusions to heaven, various references to a Supreme ruler; which would seem to imply, that in the infancy of their empire, ere they were spoiled by philosophy and vain

conceit, they had derived by tradition from the patriarchal age, some notion of an universal sovereign, who
exercises unlimited control, and to whom all honour
is due. The book of odes, part of which was written
B. C. 1120, speaks of the imperial supreme, as " majestic
in his descending, surveying the inhabitants of the
world, and promoting their tranquillity ;" who is to be
worshipped and served with abstinence and lustrations ;
while he takes cognizance of the affairs of men, and
rewards or punishes them according to their deeds.

Chinese philosophers have also spoken much of a
" principle of order," by which the universe is regulated,
and which is accounted by them the soul of the world.
The heavens and earth, together with all animate and
inanimate things are, according to them, but one principle; which is as universally diffused through nature,
as water through the ocean. To this principle they
attribute the power of retribution; and say of the
wicked, that " though they may escape the meshes of
terrestrial law, the celestial principle certainly will not
endure them."

From these expressions, about " heaven," the " Supreme ruler," and the " principle of order," we might
infer, that the Chinese had some knowledge of the
Ruler of the universe, and honoured him as such; were
we not baffled by the very incoherent manner in which
they express themselves, and shocked at the propensity
to materialism which they constantly exhibit.

When describing the origin of the world, they talk
in the following strain : " Before heaven and earth were
divided, there existed one universal chaos; when the
two energies of nature were gradually distinguished, and
the yin and yang, or the male and female principles

established. Then the purer influences ascended, and became the expansive heavens ; while the grosser particles descended, and constituted the subjacent earth. From the combination of these two, all things were produced ; and thus heaven is the father, and earth the mother of nature."

The principle of the Chinese cosmogony seems to be founded on a sexual system of the universe. That which Linnæus found to exist in plants, the Chinese conceive, pervades universal nature. Heaven and earth, being the grandest objects cognizable to human senses, have been considered by them as the parents of all things, or the superior and inferior principles of being. These they trace to an extreme limit, which possessed in itself the two powers combined. They say, that one produced two, two begat four, and four increased to eight ; and thus, by spontaneous multiplication, the production of all things followed. To all these existences, whether animate or inanimate, they attach the idea of sex ; thus every thing superior presiding, luminous, hard, and unyielding, is of the masculine ; while every thing of an opposite quality is ascribed to the feminine gender. Numerals are thus divided, and every odd number is arranged under the former, and every even number under the latter sex. This theory of the sexes was adopted by the ancient Egyptians, and appears in some of the fragments ascribed to Orpheus ; while the doctrine of numbers taught by the Confucian school, resembles in some degree the monad and duad of Pythagoras, of which some have spoken as the archetype of the world.

The Chinese system of cosmogony is connected with their scheme of the diagrams, which they say was brought on the back of a tortoise, coming up out of a river. These diagrams consist of a magic square, in which the figures are so disposed into parallel and equal ranks, as that the sums of each row, as well diagonally as laterally, shall be equal; according to the following form:—

4	9	2
3	5	7
8	1	6

Of these, every odd number represents heaven, or the superior principle; and every even number, earth, or the inferior principle: the odd numbers combined make 25, and the even ones, with the decade, 30; and by these 55 numbers, they fancy that all transformations are perfected, and the spirits act.

Their diagrams are arranged thus:—

the extreme point, or nullity, which is a mere speck, carried out, produces a line; that line, extended and separated, produces two; represented severally by a whole and a divided line: these lines, doubled and interchanged, produce four; and trebled, eight; which are the eight diagrams. When carried out to six lines, they constitute 64; and, increased to twenty-four lines, placed over each other, they make 16,777,216 changes. Finding that such extensive results could be produced, by a few combinations, they have been led to imagine, that all the manifold changes of nature, and the secrets of providence, are arranged according to, and may be discovered by, these numbers. Hence, their belief in " intelligible numbers," as the foundation of their cosmogony; and the employment of these numbers to calculate destinies, by which unprincipled fortune tellers make a market of the simple hearted people.

In all bodies, the Chinese imagine that three things exist: first chïh, tangible substance, which is the gross and sensible part of things; secondly, ke, primary matter, or the substratum on which figure, and other qualities of bodies, are reared; and thirdly, le, an universal principle, which is present with every existence, inhering or adhering to it; but how or where attached, cannot be determined. This last, they call the principle of fitness, which corresponds nearly, to what some Europeans denominate the eternal fitness of things, or the internal and essential forms. It is immaterial and incorporeal, without figure; but is a kind of principle of organization, inherent in material bodies, and considered as their root and origin. Le is almost uniformly believed to be an independent principle, not under the controul of any superior being; while it regulates and remunerates the good and evil actions of men. After conversing long with the Chinese on the origin and superintendence of all things, and shewing them, that the material heavens cannot rule, nor senseless numbers originate the animate and rational creation, they exclaim, " It is all to be resolved into this one principle of order." And yet they attach no personality to this principle; they do not speak of it, as willing, or acting, according to choice; nor do they pay divine honours to, or expect eternal favours from it; it is, after all, essentially connected with matter, and inse-

parable from body; and if considered as the basis of
the Chinese cosmogony, shews that their whole system
is founded in materialism.

Thus, whether the Chinese speak of heaven and earth,
the extreme limit, or the universal principle, they still
connect the idea of matter, whether high or low, gross
or subtle, with what they say; and do not seem to have
any definite conceptions of a pure, underived, independent, and self-existent spirit, originating, supporting,
arranging, and governing all things.

The term, Shang-te, supreme ruler, as used in the
ancient classics, corresponds, in some measure, to the
Christian notion of God, exhibiting his supremacy,
authority, and majesty; but it is much to be feared,
that they connect with the expression, the ideas of state
and pomp, and the service of ministers, such as earthly
monarchs maintain and require.   Some of the Confucians, also, are in the habit of considering the Supreme
ruler, as synonymous with heaven and earth; and
thus confound the creator with his creatures.   If these
mistakes could be guarded against, it is likely that the
Chinese will get as definite an idea of God, by the use
of the term, Shang-te, as by the employment of any
other.

The followers of Confucius, now and then, talk about
fate, which is a blind and irreversible decree, to which
both gods and men are subject; but, by whom the
decree is established, they do not inform us.   Sometimes, they talk of the decrees of heaven; but if heaven
be mere matter, how can it form decrees?

This sect acknowledges a material trinity, called
heaven, earth, and man; meaning by the latter, the
sages only.   Heaven and earth, they say, produced

human beings ; but without communicating instruction, their work was incomplete.   Now, as heaven and earth could not speak, it was necessary for the sages to come to their assistance ; who, settling the form of government, and teaching the principles of right conduct, aid nature in the management of the world, and thus form a triad of equal powers and importance.   These sages are supposed to possess intuitive perception of all truth ; to know the nature of things, instantly, and to be able to explain every principle.   The following is a description of them, from one of the Four Books : " It is only the thoroughly sincere, who can perfect his own nature ; he who can perfect his own nature, can perfect the nature of other men ; he who can perfect the nature of men, can perfect the nature of things ; he who can perfect the nature of things, can assist heaven and earth in renovating and nourishing the world ; and he who thus assists heaven and earth, forms a trinity with the powers of nature."   Of this class, they reckon but few ; the most distinguished, are the first emperors Yaou and Shun ; the celebrated Wăn-wang, and his brother Chow-kung, with Confucius.   The latter is described by one of his disciples, in the following extravagant terms : " His fame overflowed China, like a deluge, and extended to the barbarians ; wherever ships or carriages reach—wherever human strength penetrates—wherever the heavens cover, and the earth sustains — wherever the sun and moon shed their light, —wherever frost or dew falls—wherever there is blood and breath—there were none who did not approach and honour him ; therefore, he is equal to heaven." This expression " equal to heaven," is oft repeated by the Chinese, with reference to Confucius ; and there can be no doubt that they mean, thereby, to place their favourite sage on a level with the powers of nature, and, in fact, to deify him. They even go the length of paying him divine honours; for it appears by reference to a native work, that there are upwards of 1560 temples dedicated to Confucius; and, at the spring and autumnal sacrifices, there are offered to him, six bullocks, 27,000 pigs, 5,800 sheep, 2,800 deer, and 27,000 rabbits; making a total of 62,606 animals, immolated annually to the manes of Confucius, besides 27,600 pieces of silk; all provided by the government; in addition to the numerous offerings presented to him by private individuals. Thus, have these atheistical people deified the man, who taught them that matter was eternal, and that all existences originated in a mere principle.

But it may be asked, have the Confucians no idea of a spirit, and do they not pay divine honours to invisible beings? To this we may reply, that the learned in China talk largely of spirits and demons, but assign them a very inferior place in the scale of existence. Instead of teaching that the Great Spirit was the former of all things; they hold that spirits are far inferior to the visible and material heavens, and even rank below ancient sages and modern rulers. Confucius confessed he did not know much about them, and therefore preferred speaking on other subjects. When one of his disciples asked him how he was to serve spiritual beings, he replied, " Not being able to serve men, how can you serve spirits?" And when the disciple continued to enquire about the dead, the sage replied, " Not knowing the state of the living, how can you know the state of the dead?" His universal maxim was, " Respect the gods, but keep them at a distance ;" that is, shew them all due honour, but have as little to do with them as possible. It is customary with the Chinese, to attach a presiding spirit to each dynasty and kingdom, to the land and grain, to hills and rivers, wind and fire ; while the four corners of the house, with the shop, parlour, and kitchen, of every dwelling, are supposed to be under the influence of some tutelary divinity. To these the sage considered it necessary to pay the accustomed honours, but was decidedly averse to what he called flattering the gods by constant services. Dr. Milne says, that " the word shin should very rarely, if ever, be rendered *god*, in translating from Chinese books; but rather æon, gods, a spirit, and intelligence, &c. How far it can be proper to express the Christian idea of God by the same term, when writing for the Chinese, remains a question, which has long been agitated, and is yet undecided.

With regard to a future state of being, the Chinese are as much in the dark, as in what relates to the deity. They speak of the intellectual principle, as distinct from the animal soul ; but do not say anything definitely about its existence after death. The sentence quoted above, shews how the philosopher evaded the question. Some of his followers have talked of three intellectual souls, and seven animal spirits, as attached to each individual; at death, the latter disperse ; and of the former, one resides in the grave, the other follows the parental tablet, and the third wanders about like the genii over the mountains ; but whether in a state of happiness or misery, the Chinese do not say. In fact, the Confucians do not connect the idea of retribution with the soul, or the invisible world at all : they imagine that all the rewards of virtue and vice, are confined to the present state ; and if not dealt out during the life-time of the individual, will be visited on his children and grandchildren to the latest generation. The attachment of parents to their offspring, and the desire of perpetuating one's name and estate to future ages, are thus appealed to ; but these feelings are far from influencing men to a suitable extent.   When, therefore, a Confucian can calculate on escaping imme- diate infliction, and can harden himself against his posterity, he has nothing to allure him to goodness, but the principle of pursuing virtue for its own sake ; which in a corrupt heart, will not carry the individual far.

Thus then, we find the far-famed school of Confucius deficient in two important points, the existence of a God, and the interests of the world to come ; teaching a lifeless, cold-hearted, uninfluential system, which is powerless in the present, and hopeless for the future world.   Of what avail is the parade about the five cardinal virtues, and the human relations ; when the foundation of all virtue, and the most interesting of all relations, is unknown and neglected?   The love of God, is a principle which Confucius never broached, and which his disciples, until taught by a better master, cannot understand ; while the employments and enjoyments of heaven never entered into their heads to conceive, nor into their hearts to appreciate. Surely, if ever any needed the teaching of the divine Saviour, the sages of China do ; and the first lesson they would have to learn in Immanuel's school is, humility.

Before quitting the system of Confucius, it may be

well just to allude to the opinion of his followers, regarding human nature. The orthodox sentiment on this subject is, that human nature is originally virtuous, and that each individual is born into the world with a good disposition; by intercourse with others, and through the force of example, men become vicious; but the sages, by their instructions, awaken and renovate mankind; when they revert to their original purity. This doctrine has, however, met with its opponents; among the rest, one Kaou-tsze contended, that human nature was neither inclined to evil nor good, but might be turned either one way or the other. A conversation between him and a disciple of Confucius is recorded in the Four Books, of which the following is the substance.

Kaou-tsze said, " Human nature is like the wood of the willow tree, and righteousness is like a bowl; the getting men to be good, is like working up the wood into bowls." Măng-tsze replied, " Can you turn wood at once into bowls? must you not cut and hack it, in order to form a bowl? and if it be necessary to cut and hack wood to make a bowl, do you mean to say, that we must cut and hack men, in order to render them good? This system of yours is calculated to make men abhor goodness, as contrary to their nature." Kaoutsze, not baffled by this reply, renewed his statement under another form, saying, " Human nature is like water gushing forth; if you turn it to the east, it will flow to the east; and if to the west, it will flow to the west; human nature has no preference for good or evil, just as water has no preference between east and west." Măng-tsze replied, " Water has indeed no preference between east and west; but do you mean to say, that it has no choice between up and down? Human nature is good, just as water has a tendency to flow downwards. Men are universally inclined to virtue, just as water invariably flows downwards." Feeling, however, that he had made rather a starling declaration, he qualified it by saying, " Water, by beating may be made to splash over your head, and by forcing may be made to pass over a mountain; but who would ever say that this is the natural tendency of water? It is because violence is applied to it. Thus men can be made vicious ; but it is by no means their nature."

This curious dialogue shews at the same time the sentiments of the Confucian school, and their inconclusive mode of reasoning. From this we see also, that similes are not arguments ; for here is a man employing the very same simile to prove men virtuous, which has been frequently used in the west to illustrate their vicious tendencies.

The next of the three sects, into which the Chinese are divided, is called Taou. This word means, originally, a way or path, a principle, and the principle from which heaven, earth, man, and nature emanate. *Le* is the latent principle, and *Taou* is the principle in action. It also means a word, to speak, and to say ; and is very like the *Logos*, or the " Eternal Reason" of the Greeks. The founder of this sect was Laou-tan, commonly called Laou-tsze, who was contemporary with Confucius ; but the Taou, or Reason itself, they say, is uncreated and underived. Some idea of it may be gained from the following stanza :—

> " How luminous is Eternal Reason !
> " Uncreated and self-derived :
> " The beginning and end of all the kalpas ;*
> " Before heaven and before earth ;
> " United brilliancy splendidly illuminated,
> " For endless kalpas without interruption.
> " On the east it instructed Father Confucius,
> " On the west it renovated the golden Buddha :
> " Hundreds of kings have received this law,
> " The host of sages have followed this master :
> " It is the first of all religions,
> " Majestic beyond all majesty."

---

* Kalpa is a Hindoo term for time, denoting about one thousand ages.

The doctors of Eternal Reason speak of it in a most rapturous strain.   They say—

" What is there superior to heaven, and from which heaven and earth sprang ? nay, what is there superior to space, and which moves in space ?   The great Taou is the parent of space, and space is the parent of heaven and earth ; and heaven and earth produced men and things."

" The venerable prince (Taou) arose prior to the great original, standing at the commencement of the mighty wonderful, and floating in the ocean of deep obscurity.   He is spontaneous and self-existing, produced before the beginning of emptiness, commencing prior to uncaused existencies, pervading all heaven and earth, whose beginning and end no years can circumscribe."

" Before heaven and earth were divided, ere the great principles of nature were distinguished, amid the ocean of vast obscurity and universal stillness, there was a spontaneous concretion, out of which came a thousand million particles of primary matter, which produced ' emptiness.'   Then, after nine hundred and ninety-nine billions of kalpas had passed away, the thousand million particles of primary matter again concreted, and produced ' space :' after another period of equal length, the particles of primary matter again concreted, and produced ' chaos.'   After chaos was settled, heaven and earth divided, and human beings were born."

The founder of the Taou sect, called Laou-tsze, " the venerable philosopher," and Laou-keun, " the venerable prince," though coeval with Confucius, is said to have existed from eternity, and to him they ascribe the creation of the world, as in the following paragraph :—

" The venerable prince, the origin of primary matter, the root of heaven and earth, the occupier of infinite space, the commencement and beginning of all things, farther back than the utmost stretch of numbers can reach, created the universe."

One of the fabled incarnations of Laou-keun is thus described :—" The venerable prince existed before the creation, but was incarnate in the time Yang-këǎ, of

the Shang dynasty, B. C. 1407; when from the regions
of great purity and eternal reason, a subtle fluid descended, from the superior principle of nature, and was
transformed into a dark yellow substance, about the
size of a pill; which, rolling into the mouth of a pearly
damsel, while she was asleep, caused her to conceive:
the child was not born till eighty-one years afterwards,
and on his appearance was grey headed: hence he was
called Laou-tsze, the venerable one. The second appearance of this wonderful individual was in the person
of Laou-tan, who was visited by Confucius, B. C. 500.
A third appearance occurred in the third year of Kaou-
tsoo, of the Tang dynasty, A. D. 623, when a man of
Shan-se province reported, that on a certain hill he had
seen an old man in white raiment, who said, " Go and
tell the emperor, that I am Laou-keun, his ancestor."
Upon which the emperor ordered a temple to be built
for him.

The votaries of this sect talk a great deal about
virtue, and profess to promote it by abstraction from
the world, and the repression of desire: this latter they
imagine is to be effected by eating their spirits, or
stifling their breath, for a length of time. They say,
that all depends on the subjection of the heart; and
therefore mortify every feeling, in order to attain perfect virtue, which is insensibility. Hence some of
them wander away to the tops of mountains to cultivate reason, and renounce all intercourse with men,
that their studies may not be interrupted. They affect
to despise wealth, fame, and posterity; urging, that at
death all these distinctions and advantages terminate
and the labour bestowed upon them is thrown away.

Much of their attention is taken up with the study

of alchymy; and they fancy that, by the transmutation of metals, and the combination of various elements, they can produce the philosopher's stone, and the elixir of immortality. Some of them affect to have discovered an antidote against death; and when the powerful ingredients of this angelic potion sometimes produce the very effect which they wish to avoid, they say that the victims of their experiments are only gone to ramble among the genii, and enjoy that immortality above, which is not to be found below. Several of the Chinese emperors, deceived by the fair promises of these alchymists, have taken the draught, and paid the penalty. One of them, having procured the elixir at an immense expense, ordered it to be brought before him; when one of his officers courageously drank off the full contents of the cup, in its way from the compounder to the throne: the enraged autocrat ordered the offender to be put to death; but he coolly replied, that all their efforts to terminate his existence would be vain; as, having drunk the elixir, his immortality was secure; or, the whole system was founded in error. This opened the emperor's eyes, the minister was pardoned, and the pretender driven from court.

The followers of Taou, like the Athenians of old, are "in all things too superstitious." While the Confucians have scarcely determined whether spirits exist or not, the advocates of eternal reason profess to have constant intercourse with, and control over, the demons of the invisible world. Chang Tëen-sze, the principal of the Taou sect, in China, who like the Lama of Thibet, is supposed to be immortal, or rather whose place is supplied by a successor as soon as the old one dies, assumes an authority over Hades. He appoints and removes the deities of various districts, just as the emperor does his officers; and no tutelary divinity can be worshipped, or is supposed capable of protecting his votaries, until the warrant goes forth under the hand and seal of this demon ruler, authorizing him to exercise his functions in a given region.

From the power which this individual is supposed to possess, his hand-writing is considered efficacious in expelling all noxious influences; and charms written by him are sold at a high price to those afraid of ghostly visits or unlucky accidents. In the absence of these autographs from the prince of the devils, each priest of Taou issues amulets, and large sums of money are realized by the disposal of small scraps of yellow paper, with enigmatical characters upon them. Having induced the belief, that this year's imps are not to be terrified by last year's charms, they are particularly busy every new year, in writing out fresh amulets for the people; who would not rest securely in their habitations, unless fully assured that the devil was kept away by these infallible preventatives.

Death is with them peculiarly unclean; and, wherever it occurs, brings a number of evil influences into the dwelling, which are only to be expelled by the sacrifices and prayers of the priest of Taou. This is what they call cleansing the house; and, as it is attended with some expense, many prefer turning lodgers and strangers in dying circumstances out of doors, rather than have the house haunted with ghosts for years afterwards.

As it is necessary to purify houses, so it is important to preserve districts from contagion; and with this view public sacrifices are offered, to which the inhabitants generally subscribe. One of these solemnities is cele-

brated on the third day of the third moon, when the
votaries of Taou go bare foot over ignited charcoal, by
which they fancy that they triumph over the demons
they dread, and please the gods they adore. On the
anniversary of the birth of the " high emperor of the
sombre heavens," they assemble together before the
temple of this imaginary being, and having made a
great fire, about fifteen or twenty feet in diameter, they
go over it bare foot, preceded by the priests, and bearing
the gods in their arms. The previous ceremonies consist of the chanting of prayers, the ringing of bells, the
sprinkling of holy water, the blowing of horns, and the
brandishing of swords, with which they strike the fire,
in order to subdue the demon, and then dash through
the devouring element. Much earnestness is manifested by those who officiate on these occasions ; and
they firmly believe, that if they possess a sincere mind,
they will not be injured by the fire : but alas ! their
hearts must be very bad, as both priests and people get
miserably burnt on these occasions. Yet the benefit
supposed to accrue from the service is such, that the
public willingly contribute large sums to provide the
sacrifices, and to pay the performers. The surrounding
mob seem to take a great interest in this ceremony ;
and when they set up their boisterous shoutings, and
rush through the fire, seem to be literally mad upon
their idols.

The adherents of Taou believe firmly in demoniacal
possessions, and endeavour to avail themselves of the
ravings of a disturbed imagination to discover future or
hidden things. They imagine that the spirits of the
invisible world employ the mouths of the possessed to
declare audibly the mind of the demon. There are

some who are regularly possessed, and some who can induce possession, which they call, "dancing the god." The author happened once to be present when such a scene was exhibited; the house where it was enacted, was nearly full of spectators; and at the head of the room, near the altar piece, stood a priest performing various incantations, and now and then striking the floor with a rope which he held in his hand.   He then approached a bench, on which sat a native in a pensive mood, over whose head he blew a horn and rang a bell, and went through a few more ceremonies; when the man referred to, began to move his fingers, hands, and arms; then his knees and legs, till his whole body became convulsed, and he sprang up, and danced round the room like a madman.   Just as he was in the act of falling, he was caught by the bye-standers, who listened attentively to what he might have to say, and stood ready to record every expression.   The occasion of the ceremony was the dangerous illness of an inmate, for whom they wished to obtain an infallible prescription.   The possessed soon announced the requisite remedy, which was something about three skeins of red thread, and half an ounce of carpenter's chips, to be boiled down in a pint of water, and a teacupful given occasionally.   After the unfolding of this wonderful recipe, the individual sank down into a sort of swoon, and was carried out.

Magic arts are used, or said to be used, by this sect; by means of which they profess to work wonders; some of them go about with swords thrust through their cheeks; and ride in sedan chairs, stuck round with sharp knives, without appearing to sustain any permanent injury.   In the year 1819, an open boat, with an idol and offerings on board, drifted down the China sea, and was picked up at Malacca. The Chinese venerated it as a wondrous relic, and made it the occasion of many sacrifices and superstitions.

The Taou sect worship a variety of idols, some of which are imaginary incarnations of Eternal Reason; and others, rulers of the invisible world, or presiding divinities of various districts. Among the rest are the " three pure ones," who are first in dignity; the " pearly emperor, and Supreme ruler," the most honourable in heaven: the god of the north, the god of fire, with lares and penates, genii and inferior divinities without number.

We now come to the consideration of the third religion in China, namely, the sect of Buddha. The account given of the founder of this system is as follows; Sakya Muni Buddha was born in the twenty-fourth year of Chaou-wang, B. C. 1027, at Magadha, in South Bahar; in his nineteenth year, he thought of quitting his family connections, and becoming a recluse, but was at a loss whom to adopt for his spiritual guide. He attended the four schools, but was not satisfied with them, because by all their studies old age, sickness, and death could not be avoided; when one night, a celestial being appeared at the window, saying,— " Young prince! you have long talked of quitting your family: now is the time; come away!" The prince, hearing this, cheerfully passed over the city walls, and went to the hills to cultivate virtue. After sixteen years' probation, without following the directions of a master, he entirely repressed the vicious propensities, until he became without feeling, and completely perfect. After escaping the infirmities of age, and avoiding the metempsychosis, he was annihilated, B. C. 948. Before his absorption into nothing, he delivered the following stanza :—

" In his system of religion, Buddha followed no system :
" But his baseless system, still became a system :
" He now delivers you this unorganized plan,
" That, by imitating it, you may form a system."

In the eighth year of the reign of Ming-te, of the Han dynasty, A. D. 66, the religion of Buddha first entered China. The emperor hearing that there was a divine personage in the west, of the name of Buddha, sent messengers to India, to enquire into his doctrines, obtain his books, and bring some of his priests to China. The historian tells us, that " the general scope of these books was to exalt annihilation, and promote compassion, by not killing animals; affirming that when men die, their spirits do not scatter, but assuming another form, receive the recompence of all the good and evil they have ever committed ; hence they constantly aim to cultivate and improve their spirits, till they become amalgamated into Buddha."

The empire is now full of Buddhist temples, and the priests of this sect, actually swarm. They profess to renounce all family connexions—take a vow of celibacy—shave their heads—dwell in temples—abstain from animal food — and subsist on the voluntary contributions of the people. The gods they worship, are the three precious Buddhas—the past, present, and future ; Kwan-yin, the goddess of mercy, the goddess of the small-pox, the patroness of barren women, the god of wealth, &c. The three Buddhas are generally represented half-naked, with woolly hair, in a sitting

posture; one holding the mundane egg in his lap;
one adorned with the sacred thread; and one with his
finger upraised, as though engaged in instructing mankind.   In front of the three images, or in a separate
temple, is an image of the goddess of mercy; in a
niche, on one side, the god of war; and, on the other,
the protectress of seamen.   A high table, for candles
and incense, stands before the images; and in the centre of the temple, is a large iron caldron, for burning
gilt paper in: on either side the hall, are placed, a
bell and a drum, to arouse the attention of the god,
when important personages come to adore him; and a
few cushions and mats, on which the worshippers
kneel, make up the furniture of a Buddhist temple.
They have no sabbaths nor periodical seasons of rest;
but observe the new and full moon, with particular
solemnity; and keep, on the whole, one hundred and
sixty-two fast-days every year; besides the matins and
vespers of each day.

The daily service consists in the offering up of certain forms of prayer, in the Sanscrit language, which
few even of the priests understand; and the repetition of
the sacred name of Buddha, to which they attach great
merit.   In a Buddhistic work, we have an exhortation
to meditate on and recite the name of Buddha, a few
extracts from which, may serve to shew the extent to
which they carry their vain repetitions :—

" Why do we exhort men to fix the thoughts on Buddha ? but
because the most serious consequences are connected with the thoughts
of men.   That which draws forth the soul, renders fate favourable,
and life secure; all proceeds from this source.   If the thoughts are
good, you ascend to heaven; if bad, you descend to hell.   One correct thought will cause you, in the transmigration, to return to the
world in the shape of a man; and one cross thought, in that of a

beast. Why are there so many hungry ghosts in hell ? Merely because of wrong thoughts. Think of the devil, and you will become a devil ; think of Buddha, and you will be transformed into Buddha. Would you prevent the six grades of the metempsychosis ? There is no other method, but to think of Buddha. If you will not think of Buddha, you will lose a human body, and for ten thousand ages not be able to regain it. To think of Buddha, and yet not be delivered from alternate births and deaths—it is impossible. If men pray to Buddha, and yet do not become Buddhas, the error is not in Buddha; it is because the mouth prays, and not the mind. We must have Buddha, in the mouth, and Buddha, in the mind—neither of these can be dispensed with.

" But it may be said, there are thousands and myriads of Buddhas, why then repeat the name of Amida Buddha only ; The answer is, because he swore, that if any one, in all the ten worlds, should, after repeating his name, fail to attain life in his kingdom, he would cease to be a god.

" The land of his kingdom is yellow gold. Its gardens and palaces are all adorned with gems. It is encircled with rows of trees, and borders of network. There are lovely birds of sparkling plumage, and exquisite notes. The great god O-lo-han, the goddess of mercy, the unnumbered Buddhas, the host of demi-gods, and the sages of heaven and earth, will all be assembled in that sacred spot. But in that kingdom, there are no women, for the women who will live in that country are first changed into men. The inhabitants are produced from the lotus flower, and have pure and fragrant bodies, fair and well formed countenances, with hearts full of wisdom, and without vexation. They dress not, and yet are not cold ; they dress, and are not made hot. They eat not, and yet are not hungry ; they eat, and yet never know satiety. They are without pain and sickness, and never become old. Enjoying themselves, at ease, they follow Buddha, gaily frisking about without trouble. The felicity of that kingdom may be justly considered superlative, and the age of its inhabitants without measure. This is the paradise of the west, and the way to obtain it, is the most simple imaginable ; depending on one sentence, O-me-to Fŭh (Amida Buddha); yet the world will not take the trouble to seek this good so easily attained ; but put on their iron boots, and go in quest of another road.

" Swear, then, that you will henceforth repeat the name of Buddha, and seek to live in that western world of joy. Give up books and classics, for others to fag at; leave the thousand roads for others to toil in. Beyond this sentence, " O-me-to Fŭh," you need not a single word. Let each seek a retired room, and sweep it clean; place therein an image of Buddha; put incense and pure water, with a lighted lamp before it; whether painted on paper, or carved in wood, the figure is just the same as the true Buddha; love it as your father and mother—venerate it as your prince and ruler. Morning and evening, worship before it with reverence; on going out, inform it; and, on returning, do the same. Wherever you travel, act as in the presence of Buddha. Whether you eat or drink, offer it up first to Buddha. Raising the eye, or moving the lips, let all be for Buddha. Let not the rosary leave your hands, or O-me-to Fŭh, depart from your mouths. Repeat it with a loud voice, and with a low one; in lines of six words, and four words; quickly and slowly; audibly and silently; with clasped hands, and with bended knees; when fingering the rosary, and when walking in the road; when in a crowd, and when alone; whether at home or abroad; whether at leisure or in a bustle; whether sitting or lying; repeat it, even, in your dreams. Thus to repeat it, will move your feelings, and make your tears to flow; thus to repeat it, will inspire the celestial gods with awe, and the terrestrial demons with reverence; thus to repeat it, will make heaven rejoice, and the gods be glad. At the sound of Buddha's name, the palace of the king of devils moves and shakes. At the sound of Buddha's name, the wood of swords and the mountain of knives (in hell) will, for you, be beaten as small as dust. At the sound of Buddha's name, hundreds and thousands of miseries will all melt away. At the sound of Buddha's name, the debt of gratitude to parents, princes, superiors, and benefactors, will all be paid. The man who would squeeze out the oil, must grind the more forcibly: and the mariner, who would stem the swelling tide, must ply the oar more vigorously. If you realize, behind you, the boiling caldron of hell, and before you the lotus pools of heaven, though all the world should try to prevent your repeating the name of Buddha, their efforts would be entirely vain."

Such is the heaven of Buddha, and such the way to obtain it. Every morning, after dressing, the devotee is to turn his face to the west, stand upright, clasp his hands, and with a continued sound, say, " O-me-to Fŭh."

To exhaust one breath is called " a repetition:" these repetitions must be according to the length of one's breathing.   When the breath is quite out, that is the limit.   The sound should be modulated according to the due medium.   While repeating the name of Buddha, the worshipper is directed to be as serious, as if going to execution, as if fleeing from a mortal enemy, or as if surrounded with floods and flames.   The advantages said to accrue to the repeater, are the following: all the gods of heaven will protect him: all the demi-gods will attend him: all the Buddhas will think of him: no devil can harm him: nor calamities afflict him: all his former crimes shall melt away, and he shall be delivered even from the crime of murder: his dreams shall be pleasant, and his heart always glad: the world will respect him: and when he dies, he will see O-me-to Fŭh, and all the sacred ones, who will introduce him to the pure land.

During the Sung dynasty, they say, that one Hwang, a blacksmith, was in the habit of repeating the name of Buddha, with all his might, at every stroke of the hammer.   One day, whilst at his work, he repeated the following verse :—

> " Ting ting tang tang,
> " Like the iron's clang :
> " Peace has come to my breast,
> " I am bound for the west :

saying which, he was instantly transformed into Buddha ; and, as the story goes, flew away to heaven.

In addition to the name of Buddha, the adherents of this sect are in the habit of repeating prayers or charms, composed in some Indian language, the sounds of which

are expressed in the Chinese character, and rehearsed
by the worshippers, without their understanding a single
word. The following is a specimen:—

"Nan-mo o-me-to po-yay, to-ta-kĕä to yay, to-te-yay-ta, o-me-le-
too po-kwăn, o-me-le-to, seĕh-tan-po-kwăn, o-me-le-to, kwăn-kĕä-
lan-te, o-me-le-to, kwăn-kĕä-lan-te, kĕa-me-ne, kĕa-kĕa-na, chĕh-to-
kĕa-le, pʋ-po-ho."

This form is as unintelligible to the Chinese, as it is
to the English reader. A very few of the priests, only,
understand it: and yet it is supposed efficacious in removing all evil. The books of Buddha affirm, that the
god, O-me-to, rests on the head of those who repeat
this prayer When a person has repeated it 200,000
times, the intelligence of the deity begins to bud within
him: when he has repeated it 300,000 times, he is at
no great distance from a personal vision of the god,
O-me-to. During the dynasty Tsin, they say, that a
teacher of the name of Yuen, whilst repeating this
prayer, saw a divine person from the west, holding in
his hand a silver throne, who addressed him, saying,
" Celebrated teacher! thy days are ended; ascend this
throne, and be carried to yonder region of exquisite
delights." The people in the neighbourhood heard the
sound of harmonious music, in the air, and a marvellous fragrance was diffused all around.

The Buddhists talk a great deal about compassion,
and insist on its display by all their votaries: but their
kindness is only manifested towards brutes and ghosts;
while the miserable amongst men, are left to starve.
They consider it an act of merit to rescue animals from
the butcher's knife, and the cook's caldron, keeping in
the temples a number of fat hogs, and lazy dogs, who

are sustained until they die of obesity, or perish by scurvy. No persons are permitted to slay or eat these animals, lest the spirits of their ancestors should be residing in them, and the murderers be guilty of parricide, and the consumers of canniballism. Their mercy to the brute creation, however, is not so singular as their providing for hungry ghosts; we may, therefore, be excused for alluding to this practice, a little more fully.

According to the precepts of Confucius, children are bound to sacrifice to their deceased ancestors: and at the anniversary of their parent's death, as well as at the annual feast of the tombs, all persons must present offerings to the manes of their progenitors. These sacrifices are not offered as an atonement or propitiation; the pardon of sin or restoration to the divine favour, do not enter into the minds of the Chinese, whilst performing these duties; but merely the support of the departed individual. The ghosts are supposed to feed upon the provisions offered up; and, in consequence, forbear to annoy their descendants; or, it may be, exert some influence in their favour. As the food, however, does not decrease in bulk, after being feasted on by the spirits; the Chinese imagine, that the flavour only is taken away, while the substance remains. These ethereal beings, they think, content themselves with the more subtle and imperceptible parts of the food, leaving the grosser particles to be devoured by the worshippers; while the Chinese contend, that there is no more taste, in the sacrificial food, after the ceremony is over, than in the white of an egg. Thus, those who leave children and grandchildren, are well provided for by their descendants; but, alas! for those

poor wretches, who happen to die without posterity.
Deprived of all sustenance and relief, they wander
about in the invisible regions, cold, hungry, and destitute.

The Buddhists have taken advantage of this prevailing sentiment, and have grounded on it a variety of
superstitious services. In the first place, they induce
survivors to call in their aid, at almost every funeral;
that the souls of their deceased relatives may be released out of purgatory, and be enabled to avail themselves of the provisions presented. But, not content
with persuading private families to employ them, these
fellows have succeeded in getting up public services,
on behalf of the wretched ghosts, who have no posterity
to provide for them. This, they put forth, as entirely
a benevolent undertaking, and solicit subscriptions for
it on charitable grounds. The ceremony is generally
performed during the seventh moon; and as each district, tything, and street, has hungry ghosts of its own,
so each locality must have a separate sacrifice. A
committee is appointed for collecting the funds, and
laying in the necessary provisions. On the day fixed for
the ceremony, stages are erected; one for the priests,
and one for the provisions; flags and lanterns are displayed near, while gongs and drums are beaten, to
give notice to the forlorn ghosts, that a rich feast is
provided for them; and then the priests set to work to
repeat their prayers, and move their fingers in a peculiar way, by which means they believe the gates of hell
are opened, and the hungry ghosts come forth to receive the boon. Some of the spectators profess to be
able to see the opening portals, and the scampering
demons, pale and wan, with hair standing on end, and

every rib discernible ; hurrying up to the high table, and shouldering away the baskets of fruit and pots of rice, or whole hogs, and goats, as the case may be ; and returning with satisfied looks, as if they had enough to last them, till the next anniversary.

The world of spirits, according to the Chinese, is like the world of men : and as, in this life, it is impossible to live without eating, or to obtain comforts without money ; so, in the life to come, the same state of things prevails. Hence, those who wish to benefit the departed must not only feed them, once in the year, but supply them with cash, for unavoidable expenses. In order to remit money into the invisible world, they procure small pieces of paper, about four inches square, in the middle of which are affixed patches of tin-foil, or gold leaf, which represent gold and silver money ; these, they set fire to, and believe that they are thus transformed into real bullion ; passing through the smoke into the invisible world. Large quantities of this material are provided, and sacrificial paper constitutes a great article of trade and manufacture, affording employment to many myriads of people.

Besides transmitting money to the distressed and indigent spirits, the Chinese think it necessary to provide their ghostly friends with clothes, and other articles, adapted for their use, in the shades below. With this view, they cause coats and garments to be delineated on paper, which pass through the fire, as certainly and as regularly as the paper money, into the abodes of spirits. Others construct paper houses, with furniture, cooking utensils, and domestic slaves, all ready for use on their arrival ; and, in order to certify the conveyance of the estate, they draw up writings, and have them signed and sealed in the presence of witnesses, stipulating that on the arrival of the property in Hades, it shall be duly made over to the individuals specified in the bond; which done, they burn it with the house; and, rest assured that their friends obtain the benefit of what they have sent them. Thus, they "make a covenant with the grave; and, with hell, they are at agreement."

When the priests have gone through their service, and the ghosts are supposed to have been satisfied, a signal is given, and the rabble rush forward to scramble for what the spirits have left, which is, all the material part of the food. It is amusing to see, the eagerness and agility with which the mob seize on these leavings; for, although the stage is generally twenty feet high, with the boards projecting about two or three feet beyond the head of the poles, the more expert manage to mount the high table, and engrossing what they can for themselves, bear it off, imagining that food over which so many prayers have been said, must be attended with a blessing. It is curious, however, to observe, how hypocrisy creeps into a religious service of so anomalous a character. The provisions consist of fruit and confectionary, with rice and vegetables, piled up in basins and baskets, which, to the eye, appear full to overflowing; but in reality, the hollow of each vessel is filled with coarse paper or plantain stalk, and the provisions are only thinly scattered over the top. On being remonstrated with, for thus deceiving the ghosts, the worshippers reply, that the spirits who are invited to the feast know no better, and by this means they make a little go a great way.

One cannot but turn with disgust from this system

of feeding, paying, and yet cheating spiritual beings; and ask, with surprise, is this the mode of worship adopted by a great, civilized, and learned people like the Chinese? After all the teaching of their boasted sages, their pratings about eternal reason, and the incarnations of the divine Buddha, is it come to this, that the wise Celestials display a silliness and absurdity in their religious practices, which children would scarcely practice? It is true, we do not find in their ceremonious observances, any of that impurity or cruelty, which disgraces the religion of India; but we do find a childishness, which we should hardly have expected from a people, in many other respects so shrewd and intelligent. So true is it, that the world by wisdom knew not God; and so necessary do we find divine revelation, in order to guide man in the way to heaven. It is comparatively easy for deists in Europe, who derive, though they will not acknowledge it, much assistance from the sacred scriptures, to draw up a system of natural theology, which shall look well, and sound pleasingly; but let them go to China, where little or no assistance has been derived from supernatural discoveries, and they will then see, how the wisest drivel in divine and eternal things, and how far they fall short of even children in Christianity.

One of the most favourite doctrines of Buddha is, that all things originated in nothing, and will revert to nothing again. Hence, annihilation is the summit of bliss; and *nirupan, nirvana,* or nonentity, the grand and ultimate anticipation of all. Contemplation and abstractedness of mind, with a gradual obliteration of all sense and feeling, are considered the nearest approaches to bliss, attainable on earth; and the devotees of this system aim and affect to have no joys or sorrows, hopes or fears, sense or emotion, either of body or mind; living without looking, speaking, hearing, smelling, or feeling; yea, without eating, and without breathing, until they approach to that enviable state of perfection, annihilation. Buddha is nothing, and to escape the various transmigrations, to rise above the happiness of heaven, and to be absorbed into Buddha, is to be amalgamated into nothing. Those who have attained the greatest nearness to this perfect abstraction, are considered the most holy; and if they can manage to sustain life, without appearing to live, they are denominated present Buddhas, and worshipped accordingly. The world-renouncing priest, with vacant stare and emaciated look, not deigning to regard any thing in heaven or on earth, receives divine honours from the wondering by-standers, who think him something more than mortal, because fast approaching to nonentity.

The Buddhist priests, though honoured by their immediate adherents, are treated with the utmost scorn by the literati of China. The indolent lives they lead, and their profession of celibacy, are both odious to the Confucians; not aiding the productiveness of nature, they are looked upon as drones in society, who do nothing towards the improvement of the world, or the benefit of posterity. Hence to be called "a shaven-headed priest," is a term of reproach, which a Chinese gentleman would ill brook. These cloistered monks subsist principally by begging, take a vow of poverty, and from their destitute and abject condition, get into habits of sly deceit and cringing meanness, which render them still more the objects of contempt. They seldom cultivate learning, and are content with being able to read their prayers, without understanding them. They are not allowed to attend the public examinations, as long as they continue priests; and thus every avenue to advancement is closed against them. Their numbers prevent them from making much profit by their profession; and most of them are obliged, whether they will or not, to carry out their vow of poverty. The degraded state of the Buddhist priesthood, and the dilapidated condition of their temples, would intimate the speedy downfal of the system, and should encourage Christians to undermine, what is already tottering to ruin.

We cannot conclude our account of the Buddhistic religion, without noticing the similarity of its ceremonies to those of the church of Rome. The points of coincidence are many and striking. The celibacy, tonsure, professed poverty, secluded abodes, and peculiar dress of the priests: the use of the rosary, candles, incense, holy water, bells, images, and relics, in their worship; their belief in purgatory, with the possibility of praying souls out of its fires; the offering up of prayers in a strange language, with their incessant repetition; the pretension to miracles; the similarity of their altar pieces; and the very titles of their intercessors, such as " goddess of mercy," " holy mother," " queen of heaven," with the image of a virgin, having a child in her arms, holding a cross, are all such striking coincidences, that the catholic missionaries were greatly stumbled at the resemblance between the Chinese worship and their own, when they came over to convert the natives to Christianity; and some of them thought, that the author of evil had induced these pagans to imitate the manners of holy mother church, in order to expose her ceremonies to shame.

On reviewing the three systems, we find that Confucius taught his disciples nothing definite concerning God or the future world; his scheme of cosmogony is irrational and unsatisfactory; and his compliance with the common superstitions, inconsistent and time-serving. The doctors of Eternal Reason make use of some expressions respecting an underived and all-pervading principle; but they have mixed up so much superstitious nonsense with their system, and are such gross idolaters in practice, that we must pronounce them as far from the truth, as the philosophic sect. While the religion of Buddha, imported from the west, though it talks about the retributions of a future life, and professes to manifest much compassion; yet in denying a first principle, and a last end; in contradicting the existence of an everlasting God, and eternal retribution; in deriving all things from nothing, and in making all things revert to nihility again, as the essence of being and the summit of bliss; has deluded the inhabitants of China, still more than their indigenous systems, and left them to the blackness of darkness for ever.

It is very remarkable, however, that all the sects in China acknowledge a trinity. The Confucians speak of the three powers of nature—heaven, earth, and man; the Taouists have some references to the "three pure ones," who combine in themselves the essence of eternal reason; and the Buddhists speak of the "three precious ones," viz., the past, present, and future Buddhas. In whatever these notions originated, the coincidence is striking, and deserves to be noted by those who think that they can find the doctrine of a trinity in all religious creeds, and who suppose, that the idea was derived by traditions from the early progenitors of mankind.

Another circumstance, in which the three religions of China resemble each other, is their atheism. The Confucians derive their diagrams, or mystic numbers, from the extreme point, or nullity; the Taouists talk of myriads of concretions, producing emptiness; and the Buddhist system is founded in nonentity. "No first cause" characterizes all the sects; and the Supreme self-existent God is scarcely traceable through the entire range of their metaphysics; and yet, the Chinese manage to combine, the apparently irreconcileable principles of atheism and polytheism. "Gods many, and lords many," are adopted by every sect, and it is more easy to find a god than a man in China. Though they account no divinity to be eternal, yet they discover a god in every thing. Their temples, houses, streets, roads, hills, rivers, carriages, and ships, are full of idols: every room, niche, corner, door, and window, is plastered with charms, amulets, and emblems of idolatry: so that while they acknowledge no god, they are overrun with gods; and find it their greatest burthen to support and worship their numerous pantheon.

CHAPTER IX.

CATHOLIC MISSIONS IN CHINA.

THE GOSPEL DESIGNED FOR THE WORLD — EARLY DIFFUSION IN INDIA AND CHINA — ANCIENT INTERCOURSE — THE MARBLE TABLET — ITS CONTENTS — ITS AUTHENTICITY—EFFORTS OF THE NESTORIANS—AND OF THE CATHOLICS — MISSION OF XAVIER — ARRIVAL OF RICCI — HIS JOURNEY TO THE CAPITAL — HIS SUCCESS — CHRISTIAN MANDARIN — HIS DAUGHTER CANDIDA — DEATH OF RICCI — ARRIVAL OF SCHAAL— ILLUSTRIOUS CONVERTS — ARRIVAL OF VERBIEST — PERSECUTIONS — REVIVAL — CANNON CAST BY THE MISSIONARIES — PATRONAGE OF THE FRENCH KING — DEATH OF VERBIEST — NEW PERSECUTIONS — AGAIN ALLAYED — DISPUTES AMONG THE MISSIONARIES — PAPAL BULLS — ROMISH LEGATES — FAILURE OF NEGOCIATIONS — EXPULSION OF THE MISSIONARIES — NEW EFFORTS — PRESENT STATE — NUMBER OF CONVERTS—MODE OF OPERATIONS—CHARACTER OF THE CATHOLIC MISSIONARIES — AND THEIR ADHERENTS — CONCLUSION.

THE Gospel is a revelation from God, designed for the instruction and salvation of fallen man. The darkness and misery of the human race being general, the remedy was designed to be general also. " Go ye," said the ascending Saviour to his disciples, " into all the world, and preach the Gospel to every creature." When the Spirit was vouchsafed from on high, there were assembled at Jerusalem, devout men out of every nation under heaven. Representatives from Europe, Asia, and Africa, were then present, who, hearing in their own tongues the wonderful works of God, returned, rightly informed themselves, and desirous of instructing their countrymen. According to the Syrian and Chaldean writers, Thaddeus, one of the seventy, was sent into Mesopotamia, and preached in the land of Shinar; where he established three hundred and sixty churches, and died in a city called Badaraja. Thomas, the apostle, however, is celebrated by the eastern Christians, as having been the first to preach the Gospel in India: all the Syrian churches in Malabar claim him as their founder, and his sepulchre is shown on the Coromandel coas t to this day.

Considering the extent, population, and civilization of China, it can hardly be supposed that so important a region was entirely neglected by the first propagators of the Gospel; and Assemannus assures us, that Thomas, the apostle, having done much for the establishment of the Christian faith in India, passed over to a country on the east, called China; where he preached the Gospel and founded a church, in the city of Cambalu (Peking): after which he returned to Malabar. In the Chaldee ritual, there is an office for the celebration of St. Thomas, which says, that " by him the Persians, Hindoos, and Chinese were converted to the Christian faith."

In confirmation of this tradition, it may be observed, that according to Chinese history, a very early intercourse subsisted between China and the west. Arabia and Judea are called in the native books, Ta-tsin; and Pan-chaou, a Chinese general, who flourished before the close of the first century, is said to have extended his conquests as far as Ta-tsin. It is also related, that in that early age, a veneration for the cross existed in China; while the famous Kwan Yun-chang, has left, in writing, an account of the birth, death, resurrection, and ascension of a Saviour, which must have been derived from some indistinct traditions of Gospel history. In the time of Han Hwan-te, A. D. 147, " the people of India, Arabia, and other parts, came by the southern sea to China, with tribute; and from this time trade was carried on with foreigners at Canton." Chinese history further mentions, that, about the same period, an extraordinary person arrived in China, who taught a doctrine purely spiritual; and drew the admiration of all, by the virtues he possessed and the miracles he wrought.

The next intimation of the introduction of Christianity into China, is given us in the famous marble tablet, which was dug up, at Se-gnăn-foo, in the year 1625. This tablet is ten feet long, and five broad, surmounted by a cross, resembling that used by the Syrians, in Malabar. It contains an inscription in the Chinese and Syriac languages, describing the principal doctrines of the Gospel, and the history of its introduction into China. The Chinese inscription is entitled, " a tablet recording the introduction of the religion of the Ta-tsin country into China." It commences with stating the existence of the living and true God—the creation of the world—the fall of man—and the mission of Jesus Christ. The miraculous birth, and excellent teaching of the Saviour, are briefly described. His ascension is spoken of; the institution of baptism, mentioned; and the cross declared to be effectual for the salvation of all mankind. The inscription goes on to state, that in the reign of Tang Tae-tsung, A. D. 636, a Christian teacher came from Ta-tsin to China; where the emperor, after examining his doctrines, published an edict, authorizing the preaching of Christianity among the people. The next emperor continued his patronage, but the Buddhist priests, apprehensive lest the new sect should eclipse and prejudice their own, endeavoured to stop its course; a persecution followed, which, at first, diminished the number of the faithful ; but, after a time, two able advocates were raised up, who brought the new religion again into notice. The emperor Sŭh-tsung founded several Christian churches; and, in order to perpetuate the memory of his good deeds, the tablet, in question, was erected, A. D. 782,

Some have affected to doubt the authenticity of this inscription, imagining it to be a mere trick of the Jesuits, to get the Chinese to credit the Christian religion. That this was not the case, we may infer from the fact, that the Chinese were the first to discover the stone, and that neither they nor the Jesuits understood the Syrian part of the inscription, till it was translated in Malabar. Besides, were it a pious fraud, the Jesuits would have been more likely to ascribe the introduction of Christianity, to the efforts of the Latin, rather than the Syrian church; and, had they made any pretensions of the kind, the other orders of the Romish clergy would have exposed their hypocrisy. We conclude, therefore, that the inscription is a genuine record of the labours of the Syrian Christians, during the seventh and eighth centuries, in China. A fac-simile of it may be seen in the library of the Vatican at Rome, and a full translation in Kicherer's China Illustrata.

Mosheim informs us, that in the end of the seventh century, the nestorians penetrated into China, where they established several churches ; and that A. D. 820,*

* In the year 846, the Syrian priests were included in the prohibition of heterodox systems, in the proclamation of Tang Woo-tsung.

David was appointed to be the metropolitan of China. In the time of Genghis-khan, numerous bodies of Nestorian Christians were scattered over Tartary; and the famous Prester John, in the twelfth century, exerted an extensive influence over central Asia. When the Mongul princes ascended the throne of China, A. D. 1280, they afforded toleration to all religions; which enabled the Nestorians to spread themselves, and to establish a flourishing church in the north of China. This continued to exist, according to Mosheim, till the beginning of the fifteenth century; but shortly afterwards, Nestorianism appears to have dwindled away in that country.

The efforts of the Roman catholics, in behalf of China, commenced in the beginning of the fourteenth century, when Nicholas IV. sent Corvino on an embassy, to Coblai, the first emperor of the Mongul dynasty; and, in 1307, Clement V. constituted him bishop of Cambalu, or Peking. Benedict VI. A. D. 1338, sent new agents into China and Tartary; and during the whole of the Yuen dynasty, both the Latin and Nestorian Christians had a fine opportunity for propagating their religion in eastern Asia; but, quarrelling amongst themselves, they hindered each others' success; and, towards the close of the century, the Mahomedans, gaining the ascendancy, drove the Christians from those regions.

No thing more is heard of efforts for the conversion of the Chinese, until the Portuguese rounded the Cape of Good Hope, and established themselves at Goa. In 1511, Alphonso took Malacca; and, eight years afterwards, Andrade sailed for China. The first acts of Europeans, in those parts, consisted mainly of plunder and piracy, which excited the jealousy of the Chinese

government, and rendered their attempts unsuccessful.
A second embassy was dispatched to China, A. D.
1552, accompanied by Francis Xavier, who ardently
desired the gaining of so vast an empire to the Christian religion ; and reckoned that he had done nothing,
in converting the nations of India, while China was
still unattempted.   On his arrival at the mouth of the
Canton river, he was told, that strangers were debarred
from entering the country ; and, that if he attempted to
land he would be imprisoned, or put to death.   Persist-
ing in his resolution, he induced a Chinese to convey him
on shore, during the night at the island of Sancion, or
St. John.   He was not permitted, however, to do more
than just to land, and die on the shore ; where his
tomb still remains, with the following inscription in
Chinese: " The monument of St. Francis Xavier, of
the Society of Jesus, in the great west, who ascended
to glory, in the winter of the thirty-first year of Ming
Kea-tsing, A. D. 1553."

The zeal of Xavier animated his brethren, but for
thirty years they could make no impression on China.
During this period, Valignani resided at Macao, and
cast many a longing look towards the celestial empire,
crying out in the fervency of his desire, " Oh rock!
rock! when wilt thou open?"   Not discouraged by
difficulties, he looked out for the fittest instruments ;
who, dead to themselves, and breathing nothing but
resignation and martyrdom, should by their skill in
the sciences be able to recommend themselves to the
Chinese.   In 1579, M. Rogier, an Italian Jesuit,
arrived in China, where he was soon joined by Matthew
Ricci.   These devoted themselves to the study of the
Chinese language, and made some proficiency in it.

A dispute having arisen between the Chinese and the Portuguese, Rugiero was sent to negotiate, when he requested to be allowed to settle in Canton; and, after some delay, he and his fellow missionary got introduced to Chaou-king-foo, then the capital city of the province. Here they were obliged to act with great caution; as the Chinese, having heard of the conquests of the Spaniards and Portuguese, were exceedingly jealous of strangers. The affability and talents of Ricci, however, soon gained them friends. The literati admired their doctrines, so far as they agreed with Confucius, and admitted the propriety of worshipping the Lord of Heaven, but objected to the mysteries of the Christian faith; while the prohibition of polygamy, and the vow of celibacy, were still more offensive to them. They accused the strangers of neglecting their deceased parents, and of not worshipping Confucius, while they paid too much deference to Jesus. The arguments and ridicule of their opponents, however, did not dishearten these zealous men; who, by their knowledge of the sciences, were enabled to instruct and interest the people. Converts were soon made, and a church formed, over which Ricci presided for about seven years; when he was obliged to quit the provincial city, and repair to Chaou-chow-foo, about one hundred miles to the north of Canton. Here he changed his dress, from that of a Buddhist priest, which he had formerly assumed, to that of the literati, which brought him more respect and consideration.

Having been successful in various parts of the Canton province, he burned with a desire to preach the Gospel in the capital: and, attaching himself to the retinue of a mandarin, travelled with him to Nanking. He soon

attracted attention by his discoures on science and
religion, and even gained the favour of the superior
authorities. Encouraged by this reception, and having
received some valuable presents from Europe, he resolved to make his way to the emperor. At court, his
presents were received, and his person honoured; a
house was assigned him, and he was taken into the
service of the state, A. D. 1601. Ricci was no sooner
settled, than he began to diffuse his doctrines; and in
a few years succeeded in converting several persons of
distinction. The number of Christians continued to
increase, and the new doctrine soon spread from the
capital, to distant cities; particularly Nan-chang and
Shang-hae; at the latter of which, a mandarin, of great
talents and influence, professed himself a follower of
Christ. This man, on his baptism, took the name of
Paul; as he wished to be the apostle of his countrymen.
His exertions and example did much to promote the
cause of Ricci, and his accurate knowledge of the language enabled him to throw the publications of his
instructor into a neat and elegant style, which contributed to their acceptability with the higher classes of
the people. He apologized for the Christian faith in a
learned manner, and defended the cause in the presence
of the emperor: in short, his zeal, his wealth, his
talents, and his influence, contributed much to the
extension of the Romish faith in China; and his posterity trod in his footsteps.

His youngest daughter, Candida, was a remarkable
woman. Having been left a widow at an early age,
she devoted herself to the promotion of the cause of
Christianity; and, reserving enough for her eight
children, she consecrated the rest of her fortune to the

founding of churches, and the printing of Christian books, for the instruction of the surrounding heathen. Having heard that the pagans, in several of the provinces, were accustomed to abandon their children as soon as born, she established a foundling hospital for infants ; and seeing many blind people, telling idle stories in the streets for the sake of gain, she got them instructed and sent forth, to relate the different events of Gospel history. A few years before her death, the emperor conferred on her the title of the " virtuous woman," and presented her with a rich dress, covered with plates of silver, which she disposed of, in order to apply the proceeds to acts of charity. She is said to have received the last sacrament, with a lively faith of being united to that God whom she had so zealously loved and served. Her loss was bewailed by the poor as their mother, by the converts as their pattern, and by the missionaries as their best friend.

In the mean time Ricci was joined by several devoted brethren, whom he established at the various places which he had visited on his way. At Peking the number of converts increased daily ; some of their neophytes were men of influence, and the good will of the great was purchased by liberal gifts.

At length, Ricci, worn down by excessive fatigue, died in 1610. During the reign of the emperor Wan-leïh, the mission continued to be patronized ; till the year 1615, when a persecution was raised against the missionaries, some of whom were beaten, and others imprisoned, while those at court were compelled to retire to Macao. Under the next emperor, the Tartars threatened the capital ; and the Chinese, alarmed for their safety, called in the Portuguese to their assistance.

At this juncture, Paul, the Christian mandarin, advised the recal of the missionaries also ; to which the emperor acceded, and the work went on again.

When the last ruler of the Ming dynasty ascended the throne, A. D. 1628, Adam Schaal found his way to court; and, by his skill in the mathematics, gained a fame equal to that of Ricci. Soon after this, the Dominicans and Franciscans entered China, and took their share with the Jesuits in the labour of converting so great a nation. Their operations were, however, soon interrupted by the wars and commotions which began to prevail. Two rebel chiefs raised an army of malcontents, and besieged the emperor in his capital; who, to avoid falling into their hands, committed suicide. Woo San-kwei, a Chinese general, then called in the Tartars to his assistance, who soon dispersed the rebels, and entered Peking in triumph ; but, instead of restoring it to the Chinese, took it to themselves, and with it, the throne of China. The Tartar prince dying, his son, a boy of six years old, was proclaimed sovereign; and, by the wisdom and energy of his uncle, was in eight years put in possession of the whole empire. In the southern provinces, however, the people still inclined to favour the fortunes of the Ming dynasty, and two Christian Chinese generals made head against, and on one occasion, routed the Tartar army ; the victorious Chinese immediately declared Tung-lëĕ emperor, and fixed his capital at Chaou-king, in the province of Canton. In the Chinese court were fifty ladies, who had been converted by an eunuch ; and the mother, wife, and eldest son of the new sovereign, were induced to receive the ordinance of baptism. These illustrious proselytes corresponded with the pope,

who rejoiced in the hope of seeing the whole of that
great empire follow the example of their mistress;
but the arms of the conquering Tartar soon subdued
the southern provinces, and the imperial race of Ming
became extinct.

In the mean time, Adam Schaal retained his place at
court, and stood high in the favour of the Tartar-
Chinese monarch, who appointed him superintendent
of the astronomical board, and conferred upon him
many marks of his approbation.   During the lifetime
of Shun-che, the Jesuits were in favour at Peking;
permission was granted to build new churches, great
accessions were made to the number of missionaries,
and Verbiest became the coadjutor of Schaal, in presiding over the tribunal of mathematics.   The emperor
frequently entered into conversation with these fathers,
on the subject of religion, read the Christian books,
and admired the morality of the Gospel; amongst the
rest, the seventh commandment, saying, " That is
indeed a holy law."   The sovereign, however, far from
giving a practical testimony in its favour, fell into a
crime similar to that which tarnished the reign of
David, and was led by the blandishments of his
favourite, to disregard the missionaries.   The death of
his idol so wrought upon the offending sovereign, that
he died of grief, in the twenty-fourth year of his age :
sending for Schaal in his last moments, and hearing
his advice with seeming humility, but not seeking the
rite of baptism.

The next emperor, Kang-he, was a minor, under
four guardians. His education was entrusted to Schaal,
who by that means obtained so much influence at court,
that he procured the exemption of Macao from de-

struction, when all the towns on the sea coast were broken up, in order to prevent the pirate Coxinga from sheltering himself in them.

About this time a learned man, mamed Yang Kwang-sëen, published a book against the missionaries. He accused them of forming a conspiracy to overturn the government; in order to which, he said, they had introduced a great number of strangers into the empire, and had secured to themselves whole hosts of adherents, who were prepared to aid them in their sinister designs. " In teaching," continued he, " that all mankind descended from Adam, they wish to infer that our princes came originally from Europe, and, their countrymen, as the elder born, have a right to our monarchy." And then, producing the sign of the cross, he exclaimed, " Behold the God of the Europeans, nailed to a cross, for having attempted to make himself king of the Jews; and this is the God they invoke, to favour their design of making themselves masters of China." These sage reasonings had the desired effect with the four regents, who ordered the missionaries to be loaded with chains, and dragged before the tribunals, A. D. 1665. The members of these tribunals declared, " that Schaal and his associates merited the punishment of seducers, who announce to the people a false and pernicious doctrine." After having been threatened with death, they were set at liberty; but the venerable Schaal sunk under his trials, and died A. D. 1666, in the seventy-eighth year of his age.

In addition to these troubles at Peking, the missionaries throughout the provinces were arrested, and three Dominicans, one Franciscan, and twenty-one Jesuits were banished to Canton. Four were still retained at court, who kept together the flock of professing Christians; until Kang-he, coming of age, found the calendar in such disorder, that he recommitted it to the hands of Verbiest, and reinstated him in his former office; thereby affording him an opportunity of promoting the interests of his church at Peking. Finding that the emperor was disposed to redress any grievances which had occurred during his minority, Verbiest presented a memorial, praying for the recal of his brethren; which, after some difficulty, was acceded to.

In 1671, the missionaries were put in possession of their churches, but were prohibited from making converts from among the natives. Notwithstanding this interdict, however, they baptized in that year 20,000 Chinese. The year following, the emperor's maternal uncle was added to the number; and the cause of the missionaries again flourished. The emperor himself studied the elements of Euclid, under Verbiest; and while the father was engaged in communicating some knowledge of the mathematics, he did not fail to inform his illustrious pupil on the doctrines and duties of Christianity. The mind of the monarch thus became more favourably inclined to the religion of his preceptor, and though he did not embrace, he desired that no one should vilify, the Gospel.

In the tenth year of Kang-he, an extensive revolt broke out in China. Woo San-kwei, who had assisted the Tartars in ascending the throne; and who, during the reign of Shun-che, had fought in their defence, now rebelled, and made himself master of the southern and western provinces. This revolt was so serious, that all the energies of the government were called forth to repress it. At this juncture Verbiest was applied to, to cast some brass cannon, with which to operate among the hills. The missionary at first excused himself; but when his unwillingness to aid the government was interpreted into a disposition to favour the rebels, he complied; and, by the assistance of these light pieces, the imperial arms were successful.

Verbiest now rose in favour of the emperor, and accompanied him in his journies to Tartary. The mandarins, also, encouraged by the example of the court, favoured the missionaries in all parts of the empire; and nothing seemed wanting, but an accession of labourers, to bring both China, Corea, and Tartary to the profession of Christianity: in conformity with Xavier's observation, that " if China embraced the Gospel, all the neighbouring nations, would soon demolish their idols, and adopt the Christian religion."

Encouraged by the openings which presented themselves, Louis XIV. king of France, resolved to send a mission to China ; and having selected a number of Jesuits, well skilled in the mathematics, he sent them with honours and pensions on this important mission. Among the rest, was De Fontaney, professor of mathematics in the king's college ; with Gerbillon, Bouvet, and Le Comte, afterwards celebrated for their labours in the east. They went first to Siam, and from thence proceeded, in a Chinese junk, to Ning-po, on the coast of China. The mandarins at that port received them with politeness; but the viceroy declared it unlawful for native vessels to bring Europeans to China, and threatened to send the missionaries back, and confiscate both ship and cargo. Verbiest, on hearing of this, memorialized the emperor, representing that they were men skilled in the sciences, and his brethren.

To which the emperor replied, " Men of that character must not be expelled my dominions. Let them all come to my court: those who understand the mathematics, shall remain about my person: the others may dispose of themselves in the provinces, as they think fit." On the receipt of this order, the viceroy was obliged to send those men to the capital with honour, whom he had intended to expel with disgrace.

At this juncture, Verbiest died, A. D. 1688, regretted by the Chinese, but still more so by the missionaries, who expected to derive great advantage from his counsel and assistance. His character, for humility and modesty, was only equalled by his well known application and industry. He seemed insensible to everything, but the promotion of science and religion: he abstained from idle visits, the reading of curious books, and even the perusal of European newspapers: while he incessantly employed himself, either in mathematical calculations, in instructing proselytes, in corresponding with the grandees of the empire on the interests of the mission, or in writing to the learned of Europe, inviting them to repair to China. His private papers are indicative of the depth of his devotion, the rigour of his austerities, his watchfulness over his heart amid the crowd of business, and the ardour with which he served religion. His sincerity was attested, by the endurance of sufferings in the cause he had espoused; and his disinterestedness and liberality, by the profusion of his gifts to others, and the renunciation of indulgences to himself.

Two of the missionaries were soon after this employed on an embassy to the Russian government, by which the boundary line was settled, and a war between the two countries prevented. The brethren were highly complimented on their success; and Gerbillon was, in consequence, treated with particular esteem. The kindness of the emperor to the missionaries at court, seemed to augur well for the interests of the mission; but the same laws against proselyting continued in force; and unfriendly governors of provinces had frequent opportunities of annoying the missionaries.

It was not long before a persecution against the Christians was commenced by the governor of Chĕkëang, who, depending on the letter of the law against proselyting, and the disposition of the tribunals to oppose all innovations, seized on several churches, broke the crosses, profaned the altars, and dragged the Christians before the judicial courts—imprisoning some, and torturing others. Among the rest, a physician endured the bastinado with great constancy, and presented himself afterwards in the church, as a sacrifice to the Lord, grieving that he had not shed his last drop of blood for his holy name. The missionaries at Peking, applied to the emperor for his interference, when his majesty observed, that " he was surprised to see them so much infatuated with their religion; and so busied about a world, where they had never been." He advised them to " enjoy the present life; being persuaded that their God was powerful enough to do himself justice, though they concerned themselves nothing about his matters." Not satisfied with this reply, they petitioned again; when the emperor referred it to their own choice, whether they would depend on his favour, or appeal to the tribunals. They chose the latter; and, the answer was unfavourable; which disappointed the monarch, as much as it grieved the missionaries; for the emperor was secretly desirous of aiding the foreigners, though he wished to throw the responsibility on his ministers. In order, however, to bring the tribunals to terms, Kang-he addressed to them a message, enumerating the merits of the missionaries, in arranging the calendar, casting cannon, and negociating treaties; stating his confidence in the goodness of their religion, and concluding with his wish, that all who felt inclined to embrace the Christian faith, might do so, without hindrance.

The result of this message was a reply favourable to Christianity, which the emperor immediately confirmed, A. D. 1692. In consequence of this, a fresh accession of missionaries soon flocked to China; and Louis XIV. appointed the sum of 9,200 livres, as a pension to twenty missionaries to China and the east; which was continued by his successor, Louis XV.

A new occasion soon presented itself for the missionaries to ingratiate themselves still further with the emperor. His majesty was seized with a fever, which threatened his life. Remedies were sought from all quarters; which proving ineffectual, the missionaries tried the celebrated Jesuits' bark, and the emperor recovered. Grateful for the benefit, he gave them a house within the precincts of the palace, ground whereon to build a church, and contributions in money, and materials, towards the completion of the building. Notwithstanding some remonstrances from the public censorate, against the magnificence of this edifice, it was opened in 1702.

The prospects of the mission were now favourable, and success appeared near; had not the work been interrupted by the disputes which broke out among the labourers. In order to understand these controversies, it will be necessary to retrace, in some degree the history of the mission. The questions most agitated were, whether the words Tëen, " heaven," and Shang-te, " supreme ruler," meant the true God, or the material heavens; and, whether the ceremonies performed at the tombs of ancestors, and in honour of Confucius, were civil or religious rites. The Jesuits maintained the former, and the Dominicans and Franciscans the latter parts of these propositions.

With regard to the terms employed to designate the Deity, difficulties always have been, and still are felt, which have been already alluded to; but as it respects the observances in honour of ancestors and Confucius, all who know anything about Christianity must see, that as sacrifices are offered, and temples erected to both, with incense and prostrations before them, the ceremonies in question must be accounted religious, and therefore idolatrous. At the commencement of the mission, Ricci had drawn up a set of regulations for the conduct of future labourers, in which he considered the rites referred to as merely secular; others, however, differed from him; and in 1645, Morales, a Dominican, procured a bull from pope Innocent X., denouncing them as superstitious and abominable. The Jesuits, on their part, were not idle, and made such representations on the subject, as induced pope Alexander VII., A. D. 1656, to declare, that these were merely political ceremonies, and that the toleration of them was both prudent and charitable. Thus there were two infallible decrees, in direct contradiction to each other; and two zealous bodies of labourers pursuing opposite plans for the accomplishment of the same object.

When the missionaries were banished to Canton, A. D. 1665, they began to think of settling their differences ; and three and twenty of them met to discuss the disputed points. Forty-two articles were then agreed to, as principles on which the mission was to be in future conducted. These stipulations were based on the decree of Alexander VII. sanctioning the cere- monies ; in order, as they said, not to shut the door of salvation against innumerable Chinese, who would otherwise abandon the new religion. Soon after this, Navarette, who had joined in the agreement, renewed his reprobation of the indulgences, in which he was joined by many others ; and in 1693, Maigrot, the apostolic vicar of China, issued a mandate, contrary to the bull of Alexander VII., declaring, that Tëen signified nothing more than the material heavens, and that the Chinese customs referred to were idolatrous. The opinion of Kang-he was now called for, and in 1700, that monarch declared, that Tëen meant the true God, and that the customs of China were merely political. Yet the decision of Maigrot was confirmed at Rome, by a decree of Clement XI., A. D. 1704. Thus the papal see again revoked its former opinion, and plunged itself into a contest with the emperor of China.

To settle this dispute, M. Tournon was appointed papal legate to China. The good intentions and zeal of this gentleman were unquestionable ; but he was ig- norant of Chinese etiquette and was influenced by a rooted antipathy to the Jesuits. He arrived in China, A. D. 1705, and promulgated the decree of Clement, prohibiting all Christian Chinese from practising the ceremonies which had been interdicted by the pope.

But Kang-he was not likely to resign the right to legislate for his own people into the hands of a foreign potentate; hence he issued, in 1706, a declaration, that " he would countenance those missionaries only who preached the doctrine of Ricci, and persecute those who followed the opinion of Maigrot." He then directed an examiner to enquire what missionaries were disposed to comply with the imperial will, whom he permitted to remain; but ordered the rest to depart within five days to Canton. Things now came to an extremity; the papal legate issued two decrees in 1706 and 1707, commanding the missionaries not to submit to the investigation of the examiner, on the controverted points. The emperor could not brook the contravening of his authority, and commanded Tournon to leave the capital; he was compelled therefore to return to Macao, where his circumstances were not much improved; for having offended the king of Portugal, by proceeding to the Indies, without embarking at Lisbon, he found the authorities of Macao arrayed against him, who deprived him of his liberty, and surrounded him with guards. Tournon now resorted to ecclesiastical censures, but they were laughed at by his enemies; and the bishop of Macao admonished him, under pain of excommunication, to withdraw them. Having been created a cardinal by Clement XI. he could ill brook this indignity, and in 1710, sunk under his insults and disappointments.

The pope now sent another legate to China, the patriarch Mezzabarba, who arrived in 1720, with the approbation of the court of Portugal. The purport of his message was, to request permission, to remain in China, as superior to the missions; and that the

Chinese Christians might be allowed to conform themselves to the decrees of the pope, on the subject of ceremonies. The emperor replied, that the papal decrees being contrary to the usages of the empire, the Christian religion could not subsist there ; and that the legate and all the missionaries, must immediately return to Canton. Mezzabarba now made some concessions, intimating that those ceremonies which were of a merely civil nature, would be allowed to the native converts. In conformity with which he proclaimed " eight permissions," as the length to which the Chinese Christians might go ; but these were far from satisfying the emperor, and were afterwards abrogated and condemned at Rome. No prospect of reconciliation appearing, the legate requested permission to return to the pope for further powers, hoping that things would remain as they were till his return.

In the mean time, Kang-he died, A. D. 1722, and Yung-ching, his successor, was no sooner seated on the throne, than he was pestered with petitions from the literati, containing bitter invectives against the missionaries, as perverting the fundamental laws, and disturbing the peace of the empire.

About the same time a literary graduate of Fŭhkëen, who had apostatized from Christianity, sent in a memorial, complaining that the missionaries immured young girls in nunneries, paid no honours to the dead, confounded the distinctions of families, and sought to turn the Chinese into Europeans. The matter having been brought before the tribunal of rites, representing the danger of allowing Europeans to remain in the provinces, the board decided, that the Europeans who were useful for reforming the calendar might be retained at court, while those in the provinces were of no manner of use, and must therefore be sent to Macao. The emperor confirmed this representation, A. D. 1723. Thus, all the missionaries were driven from their stations, three hundred churches were destroyed, or converted to a profane use, and three hundred thousand Christians at once deprived of their pastors.

Some of the priests still contrived to remain in the provinces, or re-entered China by stealth; while a number of native catechists, dispersed through the country, managed to keep the converts together. Ignatius Koegler was appointed president of the astronomical board, and the name and profession of Romanism were still maintained in the empire.

When Këen-lung ascended the throne, in 1736, a new search was made for the proscribed priests; and the emperor, finding that they returned after expatriation, made an example of Peter Sans, by putting him to death. Many others were seized and tortured, while churches were plundered, and property confiscated. New preachers, however, flocked to Canton, and were clandestinely forwarded to the provinces. On one of these occasions, a faithless adherent betrayed his trust, and four Europeans were apprehended in Hoo-kwang, and conveyed to Peking. This involved some of the native converts, who, at the sight of the instruments of torture, apostatized, and discovered the plans of the missionaries. A stricter investigation followed; more European priests were detected and imprisoned; while three of their assistants were put to death. Much interest was made at Peking, by the few missionaries in the service of the emperor, to mitigate the punishment that awaited the remainder; when a decree was issued, on the ninth of November, 1785, by which twelve Europeans were released from gaol, and allowed either to remain in Peking, or return to Europe: three of them preferred the former, and nine, the latter alternative.

During the present century, the mission has been persevered in, and thrice drawn forth the animadversion of government: in the years 1805, 1811, and 1815.

In June, 1815, a persecution was carried on against the Roman catholics of Sze-chuen. The viceroy of that province in reporting the matter, said, "That the religion of the west, denominated the Lord of Heaven's religion, was a depraved, or irregular system, particularly injurious to the manners and hearts of men." That five years previously, two thousand families had recanted, and since upwards of two hundred families. He had recently apprehended seventy-two persons, seized fifty-three books, and taken six hundred and twenty crosses, three strings of beads, two dresses, and two religious caps. In the books seized, however, there was not a single expression that could be construed into an opposition to government." He closed his report by stating, that "he suspected some Europeans were still lurking among the mountains of Sze-chuen, though he had not been able to apprehend them." His majesty in reply, noticed "the blind obstinacy of men, that, when once a notion of ascending to heaven takes possession of the mind, makes them regardless of death." Two leaders, who would not recant, were ordered to be strangled; and thirty-eight others were banished to Tartary, amongst whom were several women, and an old man of eighty. The latter, and a few others, who seemed more culpable than the rest, were condemned to wear the wooden collar *for ever*.

In 1817, a Tartar secretary, and his coachman, were apprehended, and delivered over to the board of punishments, on the charge of being Christians. The secretary acknowledged, that his grandfather had been a Christian, but that he himself had recanted ten years ago. The prosecutors argued, however, that as he had neglected to send for the Chinese priests during his mother's illness, and had not performed certain ceremonies at her death, therefore his plea of recantation was insincere. The reply of the emperor was, that as he had trampled on the cross, his recantation must be accepted. Fifteen others were implicated with him, most of whom held offices under government.

In 1819, an imperial censor, complaining of the existence of the Roman catholic religion in the capital, recommended that every house rented by catholics should be seized and confiscated; to which the emperor replied, that the existing laws ought to be rigorously enforced, but that the measure suggested would only create a disturbance.

In 1820, a French missionary was strangled in the province of Hoo-pih, by order of the government; and L'Amiot, who had been twenty-seven years in Peking, was banished to Macao.

The French monks of the order of St. Lazarus have, however, continued to labour secretly for the maintenance of the Romish religion in China. For some years, they have annually sent two or three young priests to that country, who quietly proceed to the head-quarters of the mission in the interior. They have now catholic communities in all the provinces, and in many there are public chapels, where service is performed by native priests. The mission has two seminaries; one at Macao, and the other in Tartary, beyond the wall of China. They have in Peking a catholic community, amounting to no less than twenty-six thousand members, over whom two French priests preside. In the province of Sze-chuen, Christians are interred in the churchyard; and over their graves, crosses are erected. When the rulers do not suspect the presence of Europeans, they are very indulgent toward the native Christians; and the local authorities having once tolerated them, are interested in preventing their detection in higher quarters; lest they should be called to account for their previous want of vigilance. When, therefore, a community is once formed, it incurs very little risk of being molested. Should the catholics succeed in forming a native clergy, competent to discharge the duties of their office, their cause may rally; for the government seeks to repress it, not on religious grounds, but because it is an instrument of European influence.

It is difficult to determine the precise number of adherents still claimed by the Romanists in China; the following, however, is from Marchini's map of the missions presented to the bishop of Macao, in 1810:—

Bishoprics.	Provinces.	Bishops.	Coad-jutors.	Mission-aries.	Native Agents.	Chinese Christians.
Macao ..	Canton, Kwang-se, and Hae-nan . .	1			5	7,000
Peking .	Pïh-chïh-le, Shan-tung, and eastern Tartary . . .	1		11	18	40,000
Nanking	Keang-nan&Ho-nan	1			6	33,000
		3		11	29	80,000

Vicarages.	Provinces.	Bishops.	Coad-jutors.	Mission-aries.	Native Agents.	Native Christians.
Fŭh-këen	Brought forward Fŭh-këen, Chĕ-këang, Keang-se, and Formosa . .	3 1	1	11 4	29 8	80,000 30,000
Sze-chuen	Sze-chuen, Kwei-chow, & Yun-nan	1	1	2	25	70,000
Shan-se .	Shan-se, Shen-se, Kan-sŭh, Hoo-kwang, and west-ern Tartary . .	1		6	18	35,000
		6	2	23	80	215,000

In 1833, the Chinese Christians, in the bishopric of Macao, amounted to 13,090, under the care of seven native priests, situated as follows :—

Macao, including Patane, Mongha, and Lapa . . 7,000
Shun-tïh 1,250
Hae-nan (the island of) 855
Shaou-chow, to the north of Canton 750
Shaou-king, to the west of ditto 730
Nan-hae, in the city of ditto 1,850
Nan-chow 655
_____
13,090

The salary of each native priest is eighty-two dollars yearly; travelling expenses, estimated at from forty to fifty dollars, are allowed; besides the pay of catechists, and other charges.

The college of St. Joseph, in Macao, is intended for the purpose of raising up native teachers, for China. It was founded, by the Jesuits, in 1730; transferred to the Propaganda, in 1784; and, in 1800, provided for by regular allowances from the senate of Macao. The college contains six European priests, of whom, one is the superior. The number of Chinese students is limited to twelve, who are clothed, boarded, and educated, at the expense of the institution; if they desire it, they are trained for the priesthood, and it generally requires ten years before they can attain the first order. Instruction is given in Portuguese, Latin, arithmetic, rhetoric, philosophy, theology, &c. The Chinese language is, also, taught; and the college possesses a Chinese library, moveable types, and conveniences for printing. A Portuguese and Chinese dictionary has been published by the Superior, besides other works, tending to illustrate the language and opinions of the natives. In 1831, the number of students was, seven young Chinese, two Manilla youths, and thirteen Portuguese; besides those who attended for daily instruction. A large stock of Christian books, in the Chinese language, is kept on hand, and missionaries are frequently despatched from thence, to the provinces. The Superior is in correspondence with the agents of the missions, in various parts of China, and can convey and procure intelligence, to and from the interior with the greatest regularity.

Besides the Lazarites and the agents of the Propaganda, the Spaniards have an establishment, at Macao, for receiving Missionary candidates from Europe, instructing them in the language, and conveying them into the country. Scarcely a month passes, without some new arrivals, or departures; and the vacant posts in the interior, are thus kept constantly supplied with pastors. They all wear the European habit in Macao, but adopt the native dress on entering the field. When Euro-

peans are to be introduced into the provinces, information is previously sent to the places appointed, where
adherents are prepared to receive and conceal them.
On arriving at the place of destination, the missionaries generally retire to some secret dwelling, known
only to the Christians, and seldom appear abroad;
while all who desire instruction, or the administration
of the sacraments, go to them.   Some remain, fifteen or
twenty years, in their secluded retreats, and thus keep
up the number of their followers, without attracting the
notice of government.   The allowance to an European
missionary, in the interior, is about one hundred and
forty dollars a year; considerable sums are, however,
required for travelling expenses—for ensuring secrecy
—for supporting the poor—and for carrying on the
other business of the mission: and a commercial gentleman, connected with Canton, informed the author, that
the different superiors of the missions, in Macao, negotiate bills on Europe, to the amount of £40,000 annually.

The character of the first catholic missionaries, may
be partly deduced from the preceding sketch of their
history.   In referring to their labours, Dr. Milne remarks, " The learning, personal virtues, and ardent zeal
of some of them, deserve to be imitated by all future missionaries; will be equalled by few, and, perhaps, rarely
exceeded by any.   Their steadfastness and triumph in
the midst of persecutions, even to blood and death, in
all imaginable forms, shew that the questionable Christianity which they taught, is to be ascribed to the
effect of education, not design; and afford good reason
to believe, that they have long since joined the army of
martyrs, and are now wearing the crown of those who
spared not their lives unto the death, but overcame by

the blood of the lamb, and the word of his testimony. It is not to be doubted that many sinners, were, through their labours, turned from sin to holiness ; and they will finally have due praise from God, as fellow-workers in his kingdom."

Some idea of their doctrines may be gathered from the books which they have published in the Chinese language.   Many of these are written in a lucid and elegant style, and discuss the points at issue, between Christians and Confucians, in a masterly and conclusive manner.   Their doctrinal and devotional works are clear, on the trinity and the incarnation ; while the perfections of the deity, the corruption of human nature, and redemption by Christ, are fully stated ; and though some unscriptural notions are now and then introduced, yet, all things considered it is quite possible for humble and patient learners to discover, by such teaching, their sinful condition, and trace out the way of salvation through a Redeemer.   It must not be forgotten, also, that the catholics translated the major part of the New Testament into Chinese ; and though there is no evidence of this having been published, yet large portions of the Gospels and Epistles were inserted in the lessons, printed for the use of the congregations.   As it regards the sciences, the catholics have done much to develope them to the Chinese ; and a native, who had been instructed by them, lately published a treatise on astronomy and geography, which has been highly esteemed and widely circulated.

The Romish missionaries have not been remiss in preparing works, for the elucidation of the Chinese language to Europeans.   A manuscript Latin and Chinese dictionary has long existed, while the work of

Premare, entitled " Notitia Linguæ Sinicæ," is above all praise. It embraces, within small compass, all that can be said on Chinese grammar; while, others attempting to reduce it to European models, have failed.

The present race of adherents to the catholic missions in China, whatever the original converts may have been, are, it is to be feared, sadly deficient, both in knowledge and practice. Deprived, for the most part of intelligent instructors ; left generally to the care of the native catechists, who are not much better than themselves; and adopting the Christian profession mainly as the result of education or connection, it is hardly to be expected that they would excel, either in grace or zeal. The modern missionaries, in admitting members, merely require an outward profession, without insisting on a change of heart, or scarcely a reformation of life; the Scriptures are not placed in the hands of the people; religious services are conducted in a language which the generality do not understand; ceremonies are frequent, and public preaching rare ; while, from the laxity of morals too common in their communities, we much fear, that the catholic converts, in the present day, are very little better than the surrounding heathen.

On the whole we may conclude, that the Romish missionaries, from first to last, have been rather solicitous about the quantity, than the quality, of their success ; while they have displayed a spirit of time-serving compliance with the prejudices of the heathen, and failed to exhibit Christianity in its most inviting form to the nations. Had they succeeded in establishing their religion throughout China, we question whether, from their known bigotry, they would not have presented insurmountable obstacles to the efforts of protestant labourers. If anything earthly could have contributed to success, they had certainly the fairest opportunity of realizing their object; the power of numbers, the influence of wealth, the patronage of Christian kings, the attractions of a showy worship, and high scientific attainments, all promised fair for the accomplishment of their design. They have, however, partially failed; and, in their failure, read us a lesson, not to make flesh our arm, but to trust in the living God, who worketh all things according to the counsel of his own will. At the same time, we are not to be discouraged by their repulse: the laws which proscribe them, do not necessarily affect us: some of their practices, against which the Chinese excepted, we shall not imitate; such as the celibacy of the clergy, and the cloistering of women; the interference of a foreign potentate, with the authority of the emperor, will not be promoted by us; the Scriptures will be made the standard of judgment, and reason and conscience alone appealed to. Instead of beginning from the top of society, we propose commencing from the bottom; and aim to influence, first, the extremities, and then the heart of the empire. With the love of Christ for our motive, and the salvation of souls for our end; employing Christian benevolence, and Christian intelligence, as the means; and depending simply and solely on God for his blessing, we hope and believe, that though slow, our work will be sure, and finally effectual.

CHAPTER X.

PROTESTANT MISSIONS TO CANTON.

MISSION PROJECTED—WANT OF INFORMATION—MORRISON APPOINTED—
SAILS FOR CANTON—MODE OF LIVING THERE—PIOUS BREATHINGS—
EXTREME CAUTION—MARRIAGE AND APPOINTMENT—RELIGIOUS SER-
VICES—PRINTING COMMENCED—ADVERSE EDICT—ARRIVAL OF MILNE
—VOYAGE TO JAVA—NEW TESTAMENT COMPLETED—BAPTISM OF A
CONVERT — GENESIS PRINTED — REMOVAL OF MILNE — EMBASSY TO
PEKING—OLD TESTAMENT COMPLETED—CHARACTER OF THE TRANS-
LATION—DICTIONARY FINISHED—MORRISON VISITS ENGLAND— PRE-
SENTED TO THE KING — RECEPTION BY THE SOCIETY — RETURNS TO
CHINA—LABOURS OF AFAH——HIS LETTER—BAPTISM OF TEEN CHING
—A-GANG—AND CHOO TSING — DEATH OF MORRISON— PERSECUTION
OF AFAH—PROCLAMATION OF THE MAGISTRATE—AFAH'S ACCOUNT—
CONCLUSION.

FROM the era of the reformation to the commencement
of the present century, protestant Christians attempted
nothing for the evangelization of China. A work of
such magnitude, called for a variety of talent and a
length of labour, which could not have been supplied
by individuals ; and the energies of an associate body
were necessary to grapple with difficulties so vast, and
to carry on operations so protracted.

The London Missionary Society, was the first protestant institution that considered the wants and claims
of China. In the year 1805, the directors turned their
thoughts toward that empire, and came to a resolution
to attempt a translation of the Holy Scriptures into the
Chinese language. The immense population of China,

and the deplorable darkness in which they were involved, led the fathers of the society to arrange a plan,
for bringing the light of divine truth to shine upon the
moral gloom ; but they felt satisfied, that in order to
do the work effectually, the individual undertaking it
should be well grounded in evangelical doctrine, and
thoroughly acquainted with the language of the country.
Their views were at first directed to Penang, which
being a free port, and having a colony of Chinese emigrants settled on it, afforded a good opportunity for
cultivating the language, and for labouring among the
people.   If a blessing should attend the design, native
agents might be raised up, and the Gospel extended
by their instrumentality into the heart of the celestial
empire.   As a collateral object, the Malay nations might
be attended to, and religious tracts prepared and circulated, for their benefit.   It is singular, that at that early
period, the plan should have been suggested, which has
in a great measure formed the basis of the Society's
operations ever since.   The scheme was, however, at
that time, only in embryo ; and little was done towards
the accomplishment of the design.

The difficulties in the way, were great : and among
the foremost was, the want of information.   The country
and its inhabitants were, in a great measure, unknown ;
and though the Romish missionaries had sent home
voluminous accounts of that region, yet their statements
had not obtained much circulation, or credence with the
British public.   The wondering style in which some of
them wrote, and the very wonderful things they related,
—unsupported by the collateral evidence of our own
countrymen, led many to doubt their judgment, and
some their veracity ; so that their accounts made but

little impression. The gentlemen connected with Lord Macartney's embassy, were none of them acquainted with the Chinese language; and were therefore unable to add much to what the Jesuits had communicated. Indeed, many doubted, whether the native tongue ever could be attained by foreigners : not considering that the catholic mission to that country had been carried on for more than two hundred years; during which time, the language had not only been acquired, but many treatises on religion and science composed, which had been understood and esteemed by the natives.

In the year 1806, two missionaries, Messrs. Brown and Morrison were appointed; and directed to turn their attention to the study of the language, assisted by Yong-sam-tak, a native of China, then in England. Some acquaintance with the mathematics, and with the medical art, was also thought necessary; and, as age is venerable in China, it was judged adviseable to request Dr. Vanderkemp, then in South Africa, to join his younger brethren, in this important undertaking. Mr. Brown, soon declined the mission; and Dr. Vander-kemp, "could not feel it his duty to leave Africa, till God should call him out of it, as evidently as he had called him into it." Thus, the devoted Morrison was left to undertake the work alone; and, considering his character and talents, it was well that the task of com-mencing so delicate and difficult an enterprize devolved on so pious, persevering, and prudent a labourer. "His talents," says Dr. Milne, "were rather of the solid than the showy kind; fitted more for continued labour than to astonish by sudden bursts of genius; and his well-known caution fitted him for a station, where one false step, at the beginning, might have delayed the work for ages."

About this time, it was discovered that there existed in the British Museum a Harmony of the Gospels and the Pauline Epistles, translated into Chinese, by some catholic missionary; this assisted the young student in acquiring the language, and was of some service, in preparing his subsequent translations. A manuscript Latin and Chinese dictionary was, likewise, obtained, from the Royal Asiatic Society; and thus every facility afforded for the prosecution of the undertaking.

Whilst these movements were going on in England, a simultaneous effort was made, in Bengal, for the attainment of the same object. Mr. Johannes Lassar, an Armenian gentleman, born and educated in Macao, had been appointed professor of the Chinese language, in the college of Fort William, in Calcutta, and engaged in the preparation of a version of the Scriptures from the Armenian into the Chinese. This production was distinguished more for its native style, than for its accuracy; indeed, it was hardly to be expected, that a person, ignorant of the original Scriptures, and destitute of biblical learning, should be able to produce a version, at once faithful and idiomatic.

In the month of January, 1807, Mr. Morrison was sent forth, not to Penang, as was at first intended, but to Canton, by way of America. In the instructions afforded him, the directors expressed their satisfaction at the zeal he had displayed in acquiring the rudiments of the language, and ventured to hope that he would succeed better under superior advantages. They suggested, that he might make himself useful, as a mathematician, and a teacher of English, whilst employed in acquiring the Chinese tongue; after which it was intended, that he should form a dictionary, and attempt a translation of the sacred Scriptures.

On his arrival at New York, our missionary soon found a vessel proceeding to Canton. During his short residence in the United States, however, the object he had in view, so recommended itself to Mr. Maddison, American Secretary of State, that that gentleman gave him a letter of introduction to the then consul at Canton, which afterwards proved of great service to him.

He arrived in China, September the 4th, 1807, and had no sooner landed in Macao, than his object was discovered by the Romish clergy. Proceeding to Canton, he lived in a lower room, in a very retired and economical manner. A lamp of earthenware afforded him light, screened by a volume of Matthew Henry. He adopted the dress and manners of the natives; allowing his nails and hair to grow, eating with the chopsticks, and walking about the factory in thick Chinese shoes. In this, as he afterwards acknowledged, he meant well, but he judged ill; for, in the first place, the confinement and hard fare injured his health; then, his singular habits deprived him of the associations of his countrymen; and lastly, his intercourse with the natives was hindered rather than promoted by it. Had he been residing entirely among the Chinese, far separated from Europeans, the adoption of the native costume might have prevented immediate observation, and conduced to permanent settlement; but in Canton, where there is a marked difference between the Chinese and Europeans, the attempt to unite such opposite classes, only excited the animadversions and suspicions of both. The catholics, in Macao, dress all their priests and catechists in the European costume, which is a sort of protection against native interference; but when they send agents into the interior, they clothe them after the Chinese fashion, in order to avoid the gaze of the populace, and the annoyance of the police.

Mr. Morrison, however, soon altered his opinion and his practice; he thought it wise not to distinguish himself from other foreigners, and therefore hired a factory, which was more convenient and conducive to health. He was now introduced by Sir George Staunton to Mr. Roberts, the chief of the Company's factory at Canton, who greatly furthered his views. Mr. R., on his death-bed, advised our missionary to avow his intention of translating the Scriptures, on the ground that it was a book which Christians highly esteemed, while the acceptance or rejection of the work would still rest with the Chinese.

His letters and journals of this period breathe a most delightful spirit of ardent piety, and persevering zeal; and we make no apology for affording our readers a slight specimen:—

"Allow me, in the fulness of my heart, to say, that on a review of what the Lord's people have done for this distant land, I am overcome with the most grateful emotions. I am grateful to you, dear brethren, on behalf of the heathen; but my regard rises to my Lord, and your Lord. It was Jesus, who on Calvary died upon the cross, that put it into your hearts, and I trust into the heart of your feeble sinful brother, who fills this page, to pity the nations. The spirit of Jesus moved on the face of the church, and excited the present concern for perishing millions. The same spirit must continue to operate, or the effort will decline to cold indifference. Allusions to self are here unsuitable; but permit me, in the simplicity of my heart, to request of you, with much affection, frequent supplications in behalf of him, who, in his voluntary exile to the land of Sinim, can

scarcely bear up under the multiplicity of cares and duties which
devolve upon him.

" But the voice of thanksgiving, not of complaint, should be ours.
Hitherto the Lord hath helped us. He has done great things for us,
whereof we are glad. We take not in the wide range of his benefits, which exceed the ken of angels, but we speak of his gracious
countenance afforded the mission to China. Your missionary sits
here to-day, on the confines of the empire, learning the language of
the heathen; and would go onward, believing that it is the cause
of Him, who can and will overturn every mountainous difficulty, that
may oppose the progress of the glorious Gospel."

Well might the directors say, on perusing these communications, " The spirit of perseverance, fortitude,
diligence, and fervent piety, manifested by our missionary, affords us great satisfaction ; and we trust is a
happy presage of the accomplishment of that great
work to which he is devoted."

In 1808, a misunderstanding between the British
and Chinese authorities, compelled Mr. Morrison, with
all other Englishmen, to repair to Macao. Here he
was employed in studying the Mandarin and Canton
dialects. His helps were imperfect, and his progress
unequal to his labour; but he plodded on, even offering
up his secret prayers in Chinese, that he might become
more accustomed to the language. Many civilities
were received, but he seldom went abroad. The first
time he ventured out in Macao, was on a moonlight
night, under an escort of two Chinese. There was,
indeed, great need of caution; as he had to guard against
the jealousies of the Chinese government on the one
hand, and the bigotry of the catholic priesthood on
the other: while it was equally necessary to secure the
good opinion of the British authorities, as they had the
power of deportation, whenever they judged his pre-

sence in China unnecessary or improper.   As Dr.
Milne has justly observed, " The patience that refuses
to be conquered, the diligence that never tires, the
caution that always trembles, and the studious habit
that spontaneously seeks retirement, were best adapted
for the first protestant missionary to China."

In the close of 1808, Mr. Morrison was married to
Miss Morton, daughter of John Morton, Esq., then on
a visit to Macao; and on the same day, received an
appointment as translator to the Company's factory at
Canton, on a salary which rendered him independent
of the Society's funds.   On the news of this appoint
ment reaching England, many thought that Mr. M.'s
attention had been diverted from the primary object of
his mission; and while they rejoiced in the relief
afforded to the funds of the institution, they feared that
a faithful labourer was thereby lost to the cause.   This
was, however, by no means the case.   One of the
objects for which Mr. M. left his native land, viz. the
acquisition of the Chinese language, and the preparation of a dictionary, could be better secured in the
service of the Company, than in that of the Society;
while sufficient leisure was left for evangelizing the
heathen.

Though preaching was not the main object of his
mission, yet Mr. M. could not be satisfied without
communicating religious truth orally to the natives.
As this could not be done openly, he endeavoured te
effect it by holding secret meetings, with a few natives,
in his own room; where, with locked doors, he read
and explained the Gospels, every Sabbath day.   Such
services, though not sufficient to gratify the ardent
missionary, who longs to address his listening thou-

sands, might yet be owned and blessed of God, to the awakening of a few; and these few might influence others, until with ever enlarging, and still increasing circles, the movement might spread, till it affected the whole surface of society.

This year a grammar was prepared for the press, and the manuscript of the New Testament was partly fit to be printed; but the publication of both were deferred, till a more extensive knowledge of the language should inspire the missionary with more confidence in his productions.

In 1810, Mr. Morrison, having satisfied himself that the Acts of the Apostles, brought out with him, would, if amended and revised, be useful, made an effort to get it printed. The expense was great, amounting to about half-a-crown per copy; which was about ten times as much as ought to have been charged for this business. But the book was ranked among prohibited works; and the printers, having to run some risk in getting it through the press, took advantage of this circumstance, and charged accordingly. On presenting a copy of the Acts to the Bible Society, the committee of that institution were pleased to vote Mr. Morrison the sum of five hundred pounds, to aid in promoting the circulation of the Chinese scriptures.

In 1811, Mr. M. transmitted his Chinese grammar to Bengal, for the purpose of being printed; but the publication was delayed till the year 1815, when it was printed at Serampore, at the expense of the East India Company.

In the same year a small tract on redemption was drawn up by Mr. Morrison, which has been widely circulated, and highly esteemed. The Assembly's shorter catechism was also rendered into Chinese; but being a translation, it was necessarily more stiff and unidiomatic than the former. It was used, however, in the mission schools, and has been of some service in training catechumens in the knowledge of Christianity.

In 1812, the Gospel of Luke was printed in Chinese, which having been presented to the Bible Society, a second donation of five hundred pounds was made. About the same time, the missionaries at Serampore printed the Gospels of Matthew and Mark, to which that of John was afterwards added, encouraged by grants of the Bible Society.

About this period, the Chinese government published an edict against Christianity, whereby printing religious books, and preaching the Gospel, were made capital offences. The Romish missionaries at Peking were silenced, and some of them imprisoned, till they could be transported to Europe. Mr. Morrison, however, proceeded in his work undismayed, resolved to persevere in spite of imperial decrees, though careful not to invite the notice of government. The directors of the missionary society, as little discouraged as their agent, sent out the same year Mr. Milne, to the aid of Mr. Morrison, who proved a very acceptable fellow-labourer.

In the month of July, 1813, Mr. Milne reached Macao; but was ordered, at the instigation of the Romish clergy, to quit the settlement within ten days. Having no resource, he proceeded to Canton, where he spent five months in studying the language; and at the close of the season, set sail for Java, with a large cargo of New Testaments and tracts, which were just ready for distribution. Thus the bigotry of the catholics turned out rather to the furtherance of the Gospel. The government of Macao have since become more liberal, and it is not likely that protestant missionaries will again be disturbed in their residence there.

Mr. Milne was furnished for his journey through the archipelago with two thousand testaments, ten thousand tracts, and five thousand catechisms; which, considering the jealousy of the Chinese government, were carried through the press without much difficulty. Having committed to memory Dr. Morrison's dialogues, and transcribed his grammar, Mr. Milne set out on this important tour. He touched at Banca, where many books were distributed; and on the tenth of March arrived in Batavia. The Hon. Sir Stamford Raffles, lieutenant-governor of Java, furnished him with the means of travelling, at the expense of government, over the whole island; whereby abundant opportunities were afforded for distributing books, and great interest excited amongst the Chinese settlers. During the course of his journey, he printed about eighteen hundred copies of the first chapter of Genesis, with three hundred tracts, and a thousand hand-bills; the latter his own composition.

In the mean time, Mr. Morrison continued his unobtrusive labours in Canton, expounding the Scriptures, and praying with his domestics. Some of whom appeared to profit by the word, and expressed a desire to be baptized.

On announcing the completion of the Chinese New Testament to the Bible Society, Mr. Morrison writes, January 11, 1814:—

" I beg to inform the society, that the translation of the New Testament into Chinese, has been completed, and I hourly expect the last sheet from the press. Allow me to notice, that I give this to the world, not as a perfect translation. That some sentences are obscure, and that some might be better rendered, I suppose to be matter of course in every translation made by a foreigner. I have done my best; it only remains that I commit it by prayer to the Divine blessing. The Gospels, the closing epistles, and the book of Revelations, are entirely my own translating. The middle part of the volume is founded on the work of some unknown individual, whose pious labours were deposited in the British Museum. I took the liberty of altering and supplying what appeared to me requisite; and I feel great pleasure in recording the benefit which I first derived from the labours of my unknown predecessor."

During this year, the East India Company, fully impressed with a sense of the value of the dictionary compiled by Mr. Morrison, sent out an experienced printer, with the necessary apparatus, to carry the work through the press. Much difficulty was at first experienced in getting the Chinese characters engraved, but by the talent and perseverance of Mr. P. P. Thoms, these difficulties were overcome, and the work made encouraging progress.

In 1814, a small tract was drawn up by Mr. Morrison, on Old Testament History, with a Chinese hymn book; another edition of the New Testament was also published, in the 12mo. form. The engraving of the blocks cost five hundred dollars, or eleven-pence for every hundred characters; and the printing and binding were done at half a dollar each copy. The Committee of the Bible Society, on receiving the first complete copy of the Chinese New Testament, voted the sum of one thousand pounds, towards furthering the undertaking. This year, the missionaries were encouraged by the baptism of the first Chinese convert. His name was Tsae A-ko, aged twenty-seven, who, after long

instruction and trial, came forward, and confessed his
faith in the Lord Jesus, in the following terms :—

" Jesus making atonement for us, is the blessed sound. Language
and thought, are both inadequate to exhaust the gracious and admirable goodness of Jesus. I now believe in him, and rely on his
merits for the remission of sins. I have many defects, and without
faith in Jesus, should be eternally miserable. Now, that we have
heard of the forgiveness of sins, through Jesus, we ought with all our
hearts, to rely on his goodness. When I reflect, and question myself,
I perceive that, from childhood till now, I have had no strength—no
merit—no learning. Hitherto, I have done nothing to answer to the
goodness of God, in giving me existence in the world, as a human
being. I have not recompensed the kindness of my parents, my relations, my friends. Shall I repine ? Shall I hope in my good deeds ?
No. I entirely cast myself upon Jesus, for the remission of sins, and
pray to God to confer upon me his Holy Spirit."

Dr. Morrison's account of him, is as follows :—

" When Tsae A-ko first came to me, he did not well understand
what I meant. Three years afterwards, when I could speak better,
he comprehended a little more ; and being employed in superintending
the printing of the New Testament, he began to see that the merits
of Jesus were sufficient for the salvation of all mankind, and hence
believed in him. His natural temper was not good, and I thought
it better that he should retire from my service. He continued, however, to come and worship with us on sabbath days. He prayed earnestly, and read our Christian books ; from the perusal of which he
became convinced of his errors, saw that his nature was evil, and that
he had not fulfilled his duty to his friends and brethren. His knowledge is, of course, limited ; but, I hope, that his faith is sincere.
Taking the conduct of Philip, therefore, for my guide, at a spring of
water, issuing from the foot of a lofty hill, by the sea side, away from
human observation, I baptized, in the name of the Father, Son, and
Holy Spirit, Tsae A-ko, whose character and confession have been
above given. May he be the first fruits of a great harvest ; one of
millions, who shall believe, and be saved from the wrath to come."

Tsae A-ko adhered to the profession of the Gospel,
until his death, which took place in 1818. He died of

a consumption; but having been removed to a distance from his instructor, there was no means of ascertaining his actual state of mind, whilst exchanging worlds.

During the winter of this year, the sum of one thousand dollars was paid to Mr. Morrison by the executors of the late W. Parry, Esq. for the purpose of diffusing the knowledge of our holy religion; the principal part was appropriated to the printing of the New Testament.

In 1815, the book of Genesis, and the Psalms of David, were printed; and the Bible Society assisted the work, by a further grant of one thousand pounds. The missionaries at Serampore were, also, encouraged by grants, in aid of their translations.

Finding that the public preaching of the Gospel, and free intercourse with the natives, were difficult in China, Mr. Milne suggested the propriety of establishing a mission in the Malayan archipelago, where no restrictions would be laid upon missionary exertions, and where pious young men might be trained for future labour.   He accordingly removed to Malacca, and commenced the mission there.

During the summer of 1815, the indiscretion of a native, who was engaged in cutting metal types for the dictionary, attracted the attention of the local government; and the person, in whose possession the blocks of the New Testament were, fearing lest he might be involved, suddenly destroyed the chief part of them; which cost the mission five hundred dollars to repair.

In the year 1816, another grant of one thousand pounds was received from the Bible Society, towards the printing of the Scriptures; and grants of three and four hundred pounds from the Tract Society for the purpose of printing religious tracts in the Chinese language. A few friends, in America, likewise contributed four hundred pounds.

On the 7th of July, 1816, Mr. Morrison accompanied Lord Amherst to Peking. They arrived at the capital, on the 14th of August, and the ambassador having refused to perform the ceremony of prostration before the emperor, they returned, by land, to Canton. Considerable information was acquired by this tour, both of the various provinces, and of the different dialects spoken in them.

In the year 1817, the Senatus Academicus of the University of Glasgow, conferred upon Mr. Morrison, the degree of Doctor in Divinity.

This year, Dr. Morrison published " A view of China, for Philological Purposes," in English; and a translation of the " Morning and Evening Prayers of the Church of England," in Chinese. At the same time, Dr. Morrison and Mr. Milne arranged between them, the portion each should take of the translation of the Old Testament; Dr. M. choosing the Pentateuch, with the Psalms and Prophetical Books, while the rest devolved on Mr. Milne. Considerable portions of both these divisions were, however, already prepared. This year, also, the Bible Society granted another thousand pounds, for the printing of the Chinese Scriptures.

During the year 1818, the direct labours of Dr. Morrison, to diffuse the blessings of Christianity in China, were confined to the narrow sphere of his own household, and a few others, who came to hear him, with closed doors. The earnestness with which he prosecuted his sedentary labours, in the compilation of the dictionary, and the further translation of the Scriptures, greatly encroached on his general health, and he began to suffer from severe attacks of indisposition.

In 1818, Dr. Morrison's health revived; the Chinese dictionary was in a state of forwardness, and the alphabetic portion brought to a conclusion. A few natives continued their attendance on his ministry, who manifested attention and reverence. In the month of November of this year, the translation of the Bible was completed by Morrison and Milne, and another thousand pounds was granted by the Bible Society. In reference to the principles and character of his translation, Dr. Morrison writes :—

" By the mercy of God, an entire version of the Scriptures, into Chinese, has been brought to a conclusion. Mr. Milne translated Job, and the historical books; the rest of the Old Testament, was wholly my own translation. Of the New, I translated the four Gospels, and from Hebrews, to the end. The other books of the New Testament, I edited, with such alterations, as in my conscience, and with the degree of knowledge of the Chinese language which I then possessed, I thought necessary.

" I always stated, explicitly, that the Chinese manuscript, in the British Museum, a copy of which I procured, was the foundation of the New Testament in Chinese, which I completed and edited.

" As to opinions which natives may give of the work, the following things should also be considered. China possesses much ancient literature, which has, for many centuries, been the constant study of the learned, who have wrought up the language to a high degree of elegant conciseness and classical allusion. In consequence of this, they are extremely fastidious in respect of style, and loathe whatever is not classical Chinese. The " vulgar talk" of the Chinese, which the literati despise, does not mean, " low vulgar expressions," but common language, in distinction from an elevated, classical, and recondite style, intelligible only to persons of education. The learned of China think, that every respectable book ought to be written in a sort of Latin, not in the vulgar tongue. Choo-foo-tsze, indeed, departed from this practice, in his Philosophical Essays; for new ideas cannot be communicated so well, as by the simplest language. To put the book of

God into such a language, either out of compliment to the learned, or to exhibit one's own classical attainments, seems to be acting over again the usage of the Egyptian priests, who expressed their doctrines by hieroglyphics, intelligible only to the initiated : or as other priests did, in the Rhemish translation, who introduced so many difficult expressions, that they contrived to render it unintelligible to the common people.*

" The duty of a translator is, first, to comprehend the sense, and feel the spirit of the original ; and then, to express it faithfully, perspicuously, idiomatically, and, if he can, elegantly. For the first, a Christian student will be more competent than a heathen translator ; for the second, one who translates into his mother tongue, will excel. I think the first to be of most importance ; for, no elegance of composition can atone for a misunderstanding of the meaning ; whereas uncouthness in style, destroys not the sense. By this, I mean, that a less pure and idiomatic translation, made by a Christian missionary, is better than a translation made by the most accomplished pagan scholar. Any of the Chinese, I have ever seen, would slur the work over in any way, or affect to *amend* the sense of the original, when it did not comport with their previous opinions.

" In my translation, I have studied *fidelity*, *perspicuity*, and *simplicity ;* I have preferred common words to classical ones ; and would rather be demed inelegant, than hard to be understood. To the task I have brought patient endurance of labour and seclusion from society, a calm and unprejudiced judgment, and, I hope, an accurate mode of thinking, with a reverential sense of the awful responsibility of misrepresenting God's word.

" I have made no departure, in any sensible degree, from the sense of the English version ; and have not affected to make a *new translation*, or an *improved version*, immediately and solely, from the original."

In the summer of 1820, Dr. Morrison opened a dispensary for the Chinese poor, at Macao, which was gratuitously attended by Dr. Livingstone, till the close of the season. It became very popular, but time and funds were inadequate to its continuance. Dr. M. also

* See D'Oyly and Mant's Bible.

delivered a lecture, in English, every Sabbath day, while a course of theological instruction was kept up with the few natives who attended.

In 1821, Dr. Morrison was suddenly deprived of his first wife, by the cholera; she departed in the assured hope of reaching the haven of eternal rest. In addition to his domestic affliction, Dr. M. was much concerned at the small effect produced by his labours, for with the exception of one or two, all remained dark.

In the beginning of 1822, a dispute occurred between the Chinese and English, when the gentlemen of the factory were obliged to remove. On this occasion Dr. Morrison's acquaintance with the Chinese language, was of considerable importance, and tended much to the pacification which afterwards took place.

The same year, Dr. Morrison brought his Chinese dictionary to a close, which has been printed by the East India Company, at the expense of £15,000. By this means, valuable facilities are furnished for the use of English students, in attaining a most difficult language, spoken by a people comprising one-third of the population of the globe. His own studies, however, were prosecuted with few of those helps; hence, a much larger portion of time was occupied, by him, in the acquisition of the language, than will be necessary for future labourers.

In the beginning of 1823, Dr. Morrison arrived at Malacca, where he found the missionaries in tolerable health; but sighed for his faithful fellow-servant, William Milne, who, though short the number of his years, lived much in a little time. He expressed himself highly satisfied with the college house and library;

the printers, unawed by mandarins, printing the word of God ; and the Chinese youths singing, in their own language, the high praises of Jehovah.

On the twentieth of March, 1824, Dr. Morrison arrived in England, and the following month was introduced at court by Sir George Staunton, Bart., and presented to the king by the president of the board of controul. Dr. M. laid before his majesty a copy of the Chinese scriptures, and an account of the Anglo-Chinese college ; when his majesty was pleased to convey, through the medium of the secretary of state, the expression of his marked approbation of that gentleman's distinguished and useful labours.

At the public meeting of the society the same year, Dr. Morrison presented a copy of the sacred scriptures in Chinese, and of his English and Chinese dictionary; which were received with the warmest expressions of satisfaction; when a resolution was passed to the following effect :—

"That this meeting contemplates with sacred delight, the completion of a translation of the Holy Scriptures into the Chinese language, by Drs. Morrison and Milne; and considers this event a most powerful call upon the Christian world to promote, by every practical method, the diffusion of the Divine treasure now provided, and the accomplishment of the general purposes of the mission, long established for that extensive and interesting country."

On seconding this motion, Mr. Butterworth said, that " nearly twenty years before, when passing through the British Museum, he had observed a young man poring over some Chinese manuscripts, and supposed it would prove a waste of time, considering the language of China almost unattainable ; but now the table is loaded with his honourable labours, and the Christian world is deeply indebted to him." At this anniversary another thousand pounds was given by the Bible Society

Before he left China, Dr. Morrison ordained Lëang Afäh, converted through the instrumentality of Dr. Milne, to the work of an evangelist; and thus sanctioned his endeavours to promote Christianity among his countrymen in China.

During the following year, Dr. M. endeavoured to promote the cultivation of Chinese literature in this country, by forming a language institution, in aid of the propagation of Christianity; designed to afford missionaries of every class the facilities for acquiring the rudiments of the native language, before proceeding to their stations. A few students commenced the study of Chinese on this principle.

In the month of May, 1826, Dr. Morrison, having been previously united in marriage to Miss Armstrong, of Liverpool, embarked on board the Orwell, for China, to devote himself again to the evangelization of that country; and on the nineteenth of September, arrived safe at Macao.

During Dr. Morrison's absence, Leang Afäh composed a small volume in Chinese, explanatory of the epistle to the Hebrews, of which Dr. M. spoke favourable: also an essay on the Christian religion; in which he pointed out the necessity of a Saviour; and directed his countrymen to the Bible, which had been translated for their use. He also drew up an account of his experience which has since been printed.

Of Afäh's conversations with his countrymen, the following is a specimen. Afäh, whilst in a passage boat, was reading the Gospel of Mark, when a fellow passenger cast his eyes on the expression " till the Son of Man be risen from the dead," and asked what it meant? Afäh told him of the death and resurrection of Jesus, to make atonement for sin, confessed his own faith, and preached to him the Gospel. Speaking of the miracles of Jesus, the man asked him, if he had seen them? His answer was, "No: but they are related in the Sacred Books." "Have you never read," said his opponent, "what Măng-tsze has said, ' It would be better to have no books than to believe every book?' although the western nations believe these writings, it is not necessary for us to credit them." To this Afäh replied, "that he believed the things recorded in the Bible, because he felt that he was a sinner, and that without a Saviour, he could not escape punishment." Then, quoting Măng-tsze again, he said, "A good man may be deceived by a distorted representation of facts, but cannot be deluded so as to believe things absolutely absurd."

Another conversation occurred with a literary graduate, who taking up a volume read in the epistles for an hour; when being asked his opinion, he said, "Some parts are easily understood; in some sentences there is an inverted collocation of words; and there are paragraphs of which I cannot understand the subject spoken of." To this Afäh replied, "This book, being translated by persons from the western world, contains expressions, that are a little rugged. In some parts, foreign customs and allusions are introduced, and therefore those passages are difficult to be understood." The man then expressed his desirableness of notes, to explain ancient usages and allusions; "otherwise," said he, "the book is liable to be despised."

During the summer of 1827, Dr. Morrison performed

public worship, once every sabbath day. Leang Afäh was with him all that time, reading the Scriptures, and hearing them explained. Afäh drew up a paraphrase on the Romans; and Dr. Morrison composed two volumes, introductory to the reading of the Scriptures, in Chinese.

Leang Afäh lamented, with tears, his want of success in converting souls to Christ, and resolved to write short tracts, and put them into people's hands, as the most practicable method of disseminating divine truth.

In a letter to the directors, he thus expresses himself:—

" I thank the Lord for his wondrous mercy, in converting my whole family. Having been made a partaker of this great grace, my chief happiness consists in obeying the precepts of the Lord, and in loving others as myself; the greatest expression of which is to teach them to know the true God, and the grace of our Lord Jesus, in redeeming the world. The men of my country are bigotted to the worship of idols, ignorant of the true God, and of the preciousness of the soul : hence, my heart is stirred up to learn the true way, that I may teach it to them, and thus, not render nugatory the grace of God, in preserving me, and providing a salvation for all mankind.

" I have a partial knowledge of the Gospel, but the field of enquiry is unlimited ; the more thought that is bestowed upon it, the more profound it appears. I therefore entreat the Lord, by his Holy Spirit, to open the perceptions of my mind, if perhaps I may learn the art of repressing passion, diminishing excesses, correcting self, and admonishing others.

" But, although learning the principles be easy, carrying them into practice is difficult ; therefore, I entreat all the teachers, in your honoured country, to pray for me, a simple disciple, that the Lord may increase my knowledge, and help me to instruct others.

" But the people of the middle country (China) are divided into many sects, and pride occupies their hearts; so that their speedy conversion will not, I fear, be accomplished. I can only study the truth, practice it, and set an example, that will move men's hearts, praying the Most High Lord to convert them. The Chinese are glued fast to ten thousand forms of idols : the root is deep, and the stem strong ; to eradicate it suddenly, will not be easy.   Therefore, I hope, that all believers in the Lord Jesus, in your honoured country, will increase in benevolence, till all nations become one family, and the Gospel be spread throughout the whole world.

In the beginning of 1828, a Chinese convert was baptized by Leang Afăh ; his name was Keu Teën-ching ; a young man, brought up to the learned profession, residing in a country village, about eighty miles from Canton.   Afăh's letter to Dr. Morrison, contains the following account of his baptism :—

" On the fourth day of the present month, being the day of worship, Keu-Tëen-ching received the rite of baptism, and entered into the family of God.   He and I dwell in a small house, where with united hearts we study the true doctrine.   We are desirous of writing a catechism of the truth, for the use of children ; and propose opening a charity school.   Next full moon we intend to begin."

We subjoin a letter from the convert to Dr. Morrison :—

" The moral disease of man in this world, is ignorance of his true condition, and too great a compliance with the customs of the world, During the last few months, I have fallen in with my religious elder brother, and have been with him morning and evening, listening to the truth.   He says, the great source of truth is from heaven ; that ancient doctrines, though diverging through many channels, all revert to one God.   On hearing this, I was suddenly awakened, and began to think of my former sins, stains, and pollutions ; I desired to seek the gate of pardon, and knew not the way thither.   Happily I found the hand of my religious brother pointing the way.   He said ' though your sins be as heavy as the great mountains, if you truly repent, reform, and trust in Jesus, the saviour of the world, you will obtain the obliteration of all your sins, and acquire everlasting life.'   I therefore poured out my heart, reverently believed, and received the rite of baptism, to cleanse away the filth of sin ; hoping for the grace of the Holy Spirit, to implant in my heart a root of holiness, and assist me in bringing forth the fruit of holy virtues."

T

Afäh has recorded some of the conversations he had with his idolatrous countrymen in 1830. Ignorant and atheistical objections were made by some, while others were deterred by the fear of man, from confessing Jesus. Afäh's father was so far softened, as to worship Jehovah, though he continued to adore the idols of the country, not venturing to think himself wiser than the emperor and his mandarins.

The same year another Christian was added to the number, named Keŭh Agang. This man had been connected with the mission, as a printer, from its first establishment; and during the life time of Dr. Milne, displayed some anxiety to become a Christian. He is remarkable for his honest simplicity, and firm attachment to the cause. In the beginning of 1830, he went to live with Afäh, and studied the truths of the Gospel, with a desire to improve. After prayer for the Spirit's aid, and grace to persevere to the end, Agang was baptized by Afäh; and then went home, to exhort his wife to desist from worshipping false gods, and to trust in Jesus for the remission of sins. When he knelt down to pray, she wondered that he did not use incense matches and crackers, after the manner of the Chinese; and reproached him for worshipping the god of foreigners; while she declared her determination to adhere to the religion of her forefathers. She complained to a neighbour, that her husband had forsaken the gods of his own people, and refused to eat things offered to idols. She proceeded even to rail him, and mock at his morning prayers, saying that they brought her no luck, as it had rained for two days, while she was washing.

This summer, Afäh, accompanied by one of the

new converts, went to Kaou-chow-foo, about one hundred and fifty miles W. S. W. of Canton on the occasion of a literary examination. Here he distributed tracts throughout the city; and posting himself in front of the examination hall, before the literary chancellor, supplied the students with books, to the number of seven hundred volumes.

In the year 1832, Dr. Morrison writes, " I have been twenty-five years in China, and am now beginning to see the work prosper. By the press, we have been able to scatter knowledge, far and wide. Agang has been engaged with the lithographic press, and Afäh, in printing nine tracts of his own composition; besides teaching his countrymen daily, three of whom he has baptized during the year."

The following year Dr. Morrison laboured, with his assistants, Afäh and Agang, to scatter the word of life; the former embracing the opportunity of distributing tracts among the students, at the literary examination. These candidates had repaired, to the provincial city, from a circuit of one hundred miles; when Afäh, in the most public manner, presented them with religious books, which they received with avidity; and many, after reading came back for more. Afäh's mind was made up for all consequences and he felt excited to work, " while it was called to-day." This year, 60,000 sheet tracts, chiefly selections from the Scriptures, were printed; with 10,000 copies of prayers and hymns. Afäh was occupied in circulating these, and printing more; he, and his fellow disciples, having had their spirits stirred to unusual boldness, in tract distribution. The rulers had not molested them, for which they thanked God, and took courage. Dr. M. though much indisposed, continued the usual religious services; while Mrs. M., and the children, embarked for England, for health and education.

A Chinese teacher named Choo Tsing, who had been formerly employed in the college, at Malacca, returned this year to China. On the voyage, they fell in with a heavy gale, which carried away the masts, and caused the vessel to spring a leak. Every one expected a watery grave, and while consternation spread through every breast, the teacher lifted up his heart to heaven, and recollecting that he had heard the Gospel preached without giving his heart to its cordial recebtion, he determined, that, if God would forgive his sins, and save him from the impending calamity, he would spend his life, in obedience to his will. After a time, the storm abated, and they reached China in safety; when the heathen began to collect money, to buy victims, incense, and candles, to offer in the idol temples. Choo Tsing refused to contribute to this object, but aided some shipwrecked sufferers, who stood in need of his charity. After his arrival at Canton, he was engaged in the service of the Company, and having been tried for some time, was baptized by Dr. Morrison. He then commenced reading the Scriptures, and prayer in his family, at which his pagan wife laughed. He persevered, however, in this duty; and on Sundays, his neighbours joined him, when they had a service of an hour's length, with ten or a dozen persons to hear.

About this time, Afäh writes,—

"Several persons have obeyed the truth, and entered the church of the holy religion. There are upwards of ten of us, who with one heart, serve the Lord, and learn the doctrines of the Gospel. Every

Sabbath day, we assemble together to praise the Saviour for the mighty grace of redemption. Hitherto, the Lord has protected us; so that we enjoy tranquility; therefore, I praise our heavenly Father, for converting us by his grace. Further, I hope, that me may persevere in persuading men to serve the Lord; and, finally, ascend to the heavenly regions, to praise the self-existent God, throughout eternal ages."

In the beginning of 1834, Afäh, and one of his disciples made a short tour, to distribute books among the people in the country, which were generally well received. One schoolmaster requested copies of the Scripture lessons, for the use of his pupils in the school.

On the 1st of August, of the same year, the beloved Morrison was called away by death. He had been indisposed for some time; but his removal, at last, was sudden. He had composed, about forty days before his death, a sermon in English, from the first three verses of the fourteenth of John, which he entitled, " Heaven, the believer's home;" but increasing debility prevented his preaching it. His services in Chinese, with his domestics and dependents were, however, continued to the close of his life. On the last of his earthly sabbaths, about a dozen were assembled in an upper room, for prayer. During the service, the Spirit of God seemed to be present. They sang the Redeemer's praises, in Chinese, with unusual ardour; and the venerable missionary, notwithstanding his extreme weakness, exhorted them, with affectionate warmth, to flee from the wrath to come. He declined soon afterwards; and on the 1st of August, his weakness and pain were extreme. They then prepared to send him to Macao, but it was his corpse only that went; for on that night, about ten o'clock, he peacefully fell asleep in Jesus.

Previous to his death, Dr. Morrison had recived an

appointment from the King, similar to that which he had held under the Company : this new office he was allowed to hold only a few days, when he was called away, to fill a higher situation, conferred upon him by the King of kings, in the courts above. His esteemed son, Mr. J. R. Morrison, now occupies the post of translator.

In his last letter to the Directors, Dr. Morrison writes :

" I wait patiently, the events to be developed in the course of Divine Providence. The Lord reigneth. If the kingdom of God our Saviour prosper in China, all will be well : other matters are comparatively of small importance. May the Lord bless and prosper the London Missionary Society, and may we all be prepared for that day which is fast approaching. Farewell."

Thus he died as he lived, full of the spirit of piety, and panting after the salvation of China.

Not a month after Dr. Morrison's death, a new calamity befel the mission. The devoted Afah, anxious to make the best of every opportunity, had, according to his previous practice, been engaged in distributing books among the literary candidates at Canton ; and in order to this, took up his station in front of the examination hall. Both the motive and action were good, but the effort was ill-timed. It was just at the period, when the native authorities were in a ferment, about the affair of Lord Napier ; the British trade was stopped, and every thing connected with foreigners fell under suspicion.

On the first day, a petty officer ordered Afah not to distribute books, and took some away ; but, as they were not disapproved of by the magistrate, he continued to distribute them. On the following day, the petty officer again interfered, and took one or two of the distributors before the magistrate. They were, however, dismissed; and here the matter might have rested, but for political affairs. About this time Lord Napier, finding that the Chinese government had stopped the trade, and declined all direct communication with the British authorities, resorted to the extraordinary measure of publishing " an official document," in the Chinese language, exhibiting " the present state of the relations between China and Great Britain;" which he had lithographed, and placarded in the neighbourhood of the factories. This new step, appealing to the public sentiment, in a county where no one had hitherto been allowed to think, independently of the government, roused the ire of the viceroy; who issued a new edict, interdicting all trade with the English, and denouncing, as traitors, all natives that might enter the factories. Upon this, the servants of the foreigners fled in a panic, and consternation spread among the Chinese in every direction.

The next step was, to ascertain who had drawn up and printed the offensive document. As the native rulers never would believe, that foreigners could write, still less print Chinese, they imagined that some of their own subjects had done it for them; and as Afäh's companions had been recently before the magistrates, charged with circulating foreign books, they were suspected of aiding Lord Napier in printing his circular. Of this, however, Afäh and his brethren were perfectly innocent; but, as they had been engaged in distributing foreign books, they were held responsible for the offence.

The following proclamation was issued on the occasion; and in it, the enmity of the human heart against the Gospel, will be sufficiently apparent, in the epithets bestowed on our Christian publications:—

" Proclamation by the magistrate of Nan-hae (one of the divisions of the city of Canton) for the purpose of strict prohibition. Whereas the printing of obscene and idle tales by booksellers, has long been a matter of legal prohibition:—it having now been discovered, that there are persons who fraudulently make depraved and obscene books of the outside barbarians, and falsely assuming the pretence of admonishing to virtue, print and distribute them, which is in a high degree contrary to law; orders are therefore hereby given to the police runners, to make strict examination for them; to ascertain correctly the shop where the books have been printed; and to burn and destroy the blocks used. If any rashly presume to print and distribute such books, they shall assuredly be seized, and punished with the utmost rigour of the law. Decidedly no indulgence shall be shewn."

Here it may be observed, that the Chinese are in the habit of designating every publication that differs from the Confucian, or orthodox school, as depraved and obscene; though it may not contain a single expression offensive to modesty, or injurious to morals. They are anxious, at the same time, to make all their proceedings wear the appearance of justice; hence they affect to be the firm opponents of every thing that may deprave and delude the mind. Their standard, however, being incorrect, their boastings are vain, and their vituperations unfounded; while the only purpose such documents serve, is to blind a people already misled to their own ruin.

Afăh's account of the affair is as follows:—

" Leang Afăh respectfully writes to all those who love and believe in Jesus, wishing them happiness.

" For three or four years I have been in the habit of circulating the scripture lessons, which have been joyfully received by many. This year the triennial examination of literary candidates was held in

Canton, and I desired to distribute books among the candidates. On the twentieth of August, therefore, accompanied by Woo Achang, Chow Asan, and Leang Asan, I distributed more than five thousand volumes, which were gladly received, without the least disturbance. The next day we distributed five thousand more. On the third day, after several hundreds had been circulated, a police officer seized Woo Achang, with a set of books, and took him before the magistrate of Nan-hae; who, after examining them, bade the officer not interfere with a matter of such little importance. On the fourth day, we proceeded with our work, when the police officer again seized ten sets, while the distributor happily escaped, and returned. The next day, I heard that the police officer had taken the books to the chief magistrate of the city; and apprehending a search, we put the rest of our books into boxes, and removed to another place. On the twenty-fifth, the chief magistrate sent officers to my house, and seized Chow Asan, with his partner Akae, and brought them up for trial. Akae refused to afford any information, when the magistrate commanded the attendants to give him forty blows on the face, which rendered him unable to speak. When Chow Asan was examined, he disclosed every thing. The next day, the magistrate sent a number of men in pursuit of me, but being unsuccessful in their search, they seized three of the printers, with four hundred copies of the scripture lessons, and the blocks, which were taken to the office of the chief magistrate.

" On the eighth of September, I fled with my wife and daughter to Keang-mun, a large town west of Macao. The next day, the magistrate sent two government boats, and a hundred men to my residence, to seize all my family, male and female; but not finding us, they seized three of my kindred, and sealed the doors of my house. On hearing this, I fled to Chïh-kan (a more secluded sea port in the same direction) where I remained several days.

" At length, my money was all expended, and I dared not return to Canton, lest I should fall into the hands of the police officers. I therefore made an effort to go to Macao, which, by the gracious protection of God, I reached in safety. When I met Mr. Bridgeman, the sorrow of my heart was so extreme, that I could not refrain from weeping bitterly. He told me, however, that Mr. J. R. Morrison had made arrangements with the chief magistrate, and for the consideration of eight hundred dollars, had obtained the liberation of the printers, and the cessation of the prosecution; but the lieutenant-governor insisted on my being apprehended; upon which Mr. Bridgman took me in a fast boat on board the English ships at Lintin, where I was kindly entertained.

" Thus situated, I call to mind that all who preach the Gospel of our Lord Jesus, must suffer persecution ; and though I cannot equal the patience of Paul or Job, I desire to imitate the ancient saints, and keep my heart in peace."

Mr. Bridgman writes on this occasion, " Had Afäh fallen into the hands of his pursuers, his life, for aught we can see, would have been taken away. But our heavenly Father has kept both him and us in safety."

The little flock were now scattered, as sheep without a shepherd ; Afäh was obliged to leave for Singapore, where he might diffuse the Gospel among the emigrants, without fear of persecution. Agang, however, remained in Canton, and was the medium of communication between the missionaries and the native converts, who were unable to come to the foreign factories.

CHAPTER XI.

MISSION TO CANTON, CONTINUED.

SITUATION OF FOREIGNERS IN CANTON — SURVEILLANCE OF THE HONG-
MERCHANTS — AND COMPRADORES — CONFINEMENT — AND INSULT —
RESTRICTIONS ON MISSIONARIES — STUDY OF THE NATIVE LANGUAGE
PROHIBITED — DIFFICULTIES OF PRINTING NATIVE BOOKS — MODE OF
OBVIATING THEM — STATE OF MACAO — HOW FAR OPEN TO MISSION-
ARY OPERATIONS — ENQUIRY AFTER NATIVE CONVERTS — THE LITE-
RARY GRADUATE — THE PRINTERS — THE FAMILY OF AFAH — AGANG
AND HIS SON — EDICT OF THE EMPEROR — COMMISSION OF ENQUIRY —
ITS FATE — MISSIONARIES NOT INVOLVED — NEED OF CAUTION — LITTLE
INTEREST IN BEHALF OF CANTON — RECOMMENDATIONS.

On the twenty-first of July, 1835, the author arrived
in Canton, for the purpose of enquiring after the little
flock of native Christians, gathered by Dr. Morrison;
and of undertaking a voyage along the coast to distribute Christian books among the Chinese. His observations on the aspect of missions and the native
church in Canton will be most suitable here; reserving
the account of his voyage to a future chapter.

It will be necessary, first, to advert to the situation
of foreigners in Canton. All persons who visit that
city are supposed to go thither for the purpose of trade,
and are expected to reside only so long as their commercial engagements require. Military officers, and
travellers, if they wish to proceed by the inner passage from Macao, must represent themselves as merchants, ere they can be allowed to embark. When they

go in European packets, however, the native authorities take no cognizance of their arrival, and ask no questions.

The barbarians are considered by the Chinese, turbulent and crafty; and so far out of the pale of civilization, as not to be controlled by the laws of the celestial empire. It has been found necessary, therefore, to make natives observant of their conduct, and responsible for their good behaviour. With this view, hong, or security merchants are appointed; who, while they monopolize the trade, are required to instruct foreigners in their duty, and to see to the doing of it. In order to the fulfilment of this difficult task, the foreigners, without being consulted on the subject, are placed under the surveillance of the securities, who are made acquainted with every thing done by the barbarians, and who report it, if necessary to the native authorities. The way in which they acquire the requisite information, is the following. No foreigner, except a Parsee,* is allowed to purchase provisions in the markets: and no unauthorized Chinese is at liberty to sell eatables to a foreigner. Again, all the buildings of the foreign factories, belong to the security merchants, who let them out to such persons, and for such purposes, as they choose. Thus a foreigner cannot procure food or shelter, without employing an authorized purveyor, and hiring a factory from the hong-merchants. This purveyor is called a compradore, and must be furnished with a license from the security merchants, ere he can

---

* The Parsees are a class of wealthy and industrious merchants, who trade between China and Bombay; and who, for economy's sake, bring their own servants with them. These being Asiatics, and peaceably disposed, are allowed to purchase their own provisions.

fill that office. In fact, he is the agent of the priviliged trader, placed as a spy upon the proceedings of the foreigner; who, paying him high wages, and allowing him a large profit upon all his purchases, supposes him devoted to his interests; but the security merchant has a stronger hold upon him, being empowered to fleece him of his property, and to get him bambooed and banished, if he does not in all things study the interest of the native merchant, to the prejudice of the foreigner.

There are besides, a set of men called linguists, between the security merchant and the compradore; but they are only a link in the chain, and are as much devoted to the security merchants, as the purveyors are.

When a compradore is once fixed for an individual or firm, he has the control of all the Chinese business; and if the parties insist on doing any thing against his advice or interest, he throws up his office; and another purveyor not being procurable, except on harder terms, the foreigner must comply, or the business stop. The interference of the compradore, extends to the hiring of native servants; and if they are not such as he can depend upon, or will approve of, he objects, and threatens his employers with resignation, unless his wishes be complied with. Thus every one about the premises of a foreigner, even to the servant at his table, or in his bedroom, is a spy upon his conduct, and carries every thing of importance to his superiors; in default of which, compradores have been stripped of their all, linguists sent to the cold countries, and hong-merchants ruined.

Confinement is another evil, which foreigners, in Canton are obliged to bear. The factories comprise a pile of buildings, about a quarter of a mile square, through which they may range, without molestation. In front of these is an open space, not more than a hundred yards long, and fifty wide, where they may take the air; but this esplanade is generally so choked up with barbers and fortune-tellers, venders of dogs and cats, quack medicines, and trinkets, with a host of strangers, come to gaze at the foreigners, that it is difficult to move. Adjoining the factories, are two rows of native houses, called new and old China street, where foreigners may ramble, and purchase trinkets; and, if they can endure crowds and confusion, with the chance of being pushed down, they may stroll through the narrow streets of the suburbs, but never without much offence to the olfactory nerves, or the finer feelings. Another mode of recreation, is the pleasure of rowing European boats up and down a crowded river, where the stranger is in continual danger of being upset by large Chinese barges bearing down upon him, without warning; while no one makes the smallest effort to save those who may be precipitated into the water. Should he land at any given spot, up or down the river, he is always liable to be stoned or bambooed by the natives, when they are strong or mischievous enough to attempt it. The government does, indeed, allow foreigners to take a trip, in parties of eight or ten, about once a month, to the flower gardens, which lie three miles up the river; but this indulgence is so pompously given, and of such little worth, that few avail themselves of it.

Insult is another evil which foreigners are obliged to endure, whilst resident in Canton. In addition to the word " barbarian," which is liberally bestowed on all without the pale of Chinese civilization, a more offensive epithet is not unfrequently employed. On passing through the suburbs of Canton, or up and down the river, the cry of "foreign devil," salutes the ear on every side; even mothers may be seen, teaching their infants to point, and shout the offensive epithet, as the stranger passes by. Some will even go out of their way, or desist from their work, to gratify their railing propensities. Even the government stoops to the mean practice of abusing Europeans; and "devil ship," was, until lately, the title given by the superintendent of customs, in official papers, to square-rigged vessels.

Those who understand these abusive epithets, feel them the more keenly; and it requires no little forbearance to restrain the temper, and pass the assailants unnoticed. It has been urged, that the people of Canton, have been so long accustomed to call foreigners "devils," that they scarcely know when they do it; but this excuse, which has often been vainly urged in defence of profane swearing, is, by no means, tenable; for the Chinese employ the term with a zest and emphasis, indicative of an intention to annoy. They even accompany it with a chirping noise, which they suppose to be the cry of devils, and vary the epithet, so as to leave no doubt of their real meaning. They never employ the term to their own countrymen, except when highly offended and disgusted; but apply it to strangers, as a matter of course, and appear surprized when any question the propriety of the appellation.

Foreigners, who come to China, to carry on a regular trade, have not much to fear from the system of espionage; while the confinement and abuse are tolerated, for the sake of gain, with the hope that they may soon escape from the scene of restriction and insult, to enjoy the fruits of their patience in their native land.

But with missionaries, the case is different. Their very residence, and the whole of their proceedings, as far as respects the conversion of the Chinese, is an offence in the eye of the law. They may come as chaplains, to instruct their fellow-countrymen, in which capacity they are called "story-telling devils;" but were they to announce themselves, as proselyters, aiming to bring over the natives to Christianity, there is no Chinese authority that would tolerate them a single day. If content to pursue their labours unobserved, they may remain unmolested, for years; and their real object would be winked at, only to be brought forward, when money is to be squeezed out of "traitorous natives," for permitting such things to exist, without informing their superiors.

In the next place, the study of the Chinese language, so far as the assistance of the natives is concerned, is contrary to law. What foreigners can effect by their own unassisted efforts, the government has nothing to do with; but woe to the native who shall be known to assist barbarians in acquiring the language of the "flowery nation." The softest term by which such men are designated, is that of "Chinese rascals," whose crime consists in holding intercourse with foreigners, and in revealing the secrets of the celestial empire to its avowed enemies. They are, therefore, by virtue of their office, offenders against the law; and though they pursue their vocation year after year, yet they do it at their own peril; and the compradores who wink at it, are liable to be seized and punished for their neglect of duty. Now and then, a hue and cry is raised about " traitorous natives," and these teachers are obliged to absent themselves for a time; while their pupils are requested not to speak Chinese in the streets, or to stand looking at native handbills; lest some police officer observing it, should trace them to their factory, and procure the arrest of the compradores who permitted, or of the teachers who assisted them in acquiring the language. The fears of the compradores on such occasions, are exactly in proportion to the amount of property they possess, and are consequently liable to lose; and thus the more respectable and trustworthy a purveyor may be, the greater the probability of his being robbed of all.

The Chinese do not, or will not, perceive their own inconsistency in these proceedings; for, if foreigners are expected to obey the laws, they ought to be able to peruse them; but, if they are kept in ignorance of the imperial will, they can hardly be blamed for opposing it. The native rulers, however, consider that the security merchants have a sufficient knowledge of the English language, to instruct foreigners in their duty, and sufficient influence over them to secure their doing of it, without the barbarian's busying himself with the Chinese tongue. Thus the study of the native dialect is prohibited to merchants, and much more to missionaries; who have sometimes found it very difficult to get a teacher, and at other times have had their studies interrupted for months together. They have, therefore, preferred locating themselves in the Malayan archipelago, where they might learn the language from the Chinese colonists without restriction.

Another difficulty in the way of missionary opera-

U

ations in China is, that the printing of native books, by foreigners, is strictly prohibited. The English press is free in Canton; so that two newspapers, and one magazine are published there, without interference or molestation. But while foreigners are permitted to " corrupt one another," as much as they please; they are not allowed to poison the minds of the natives, by their " depraved productions." This does not refer to Christian books merely, but to all books constructed by foreigners in the native language; and it applies with equal force to the Society for promoting Useful Knowledge, and the chamber of commerce, as it does to missionary institutions. All that is attempted in this department, therefore, must be done outside the factories.

Again, when foreigners wish to engage type cutters, they cannot stop in the streets and negotiate with them; for nothing could be done in such situations without attracting the attention of bye-standers, who do not fail to report all that is done by strangers. Even in China-street, where foreigners usually buy their trinkets, the door is shut, immediately a customer enters a shop, lest some police officer passing by should notice and squeeze the native dealer; how much less could secret transactions be carried on in the streets devoted to native trade, where all would see and hear, what it is wished that no one should know.

The only way, therefore, is to employ a Chinese broker, in whom confidence can be placed; who will come privately to the rooms of the foreigner, receive his orders for work, and get them executed in some distant village. But even then, the arrangement must be made under great disadvantages; for large advances must be made before the work is commenced; a higher

price must be given than what is really required : and
the business must be carried on entirely at the leisure
and convenience of the workmen ; added to which, the
undertaking is sometimes brought to a long stop,
owing to the real or alledged enquiries made by the
native authorities ; and sometimes a whole edition is
destroyed to elude the vigilance of the police. Finally,
when the work is done, the contractor must convey his
books secretly out of the port, and cannot consider himself safe till the whole investment is beyond the Bogue.

The difficulty of printing Chinese books, however,
does not interfere with a missionary's usefulness in
other particulars. He may, if already acquainted with
the rudiments of the language, greatly increase his acquaintance with the literature and religion, manners
and customs of the Chinese. He would be in the way
of attaining the earliest information as to what is passing in the interior of the empire, and be ready to avail
himself of any change that might take place in the
political condition of the people. He might continue
to watch over, instruct, and increase the native church
existing there ; and every day he might sally forth and
converse with the people in the suburbs, where a word
spoken in due season, might leave a salutary impression on the bye-standers, without exciting the animadversion of government. Tracts might also be distributed, in small quantities, and with some caution, till
the ferment lately occasioned has subsided, when efforts
more extensive and effectual for the conversion of the
heathen might be made.

With regard to missionary operations, Macao is
somewhat different from Canton. This settlement is
built on a promontory, jutting out from the south end

of the island of Heang-shan, from which it is separated by a small isthmus, defended by a barrier. Macao is inhabited partly by Portuguese, and partly by Chinese, severally under the authority of their respective governments. It is difficult to determine to whom the settlement really belongs. The Portuguese conceive that it is theirs; having been ceded to their ancestors by the former emperors of China, in consideration of important services rendered by them to the state. They have a governor appointed by the queen of Portugal, and a senate chosen from amongst the inhabitants of Macao. They are under Portuguese laws; a small military force is kept up, and a European custom-house is established. A century and a half ago they excluded all the Chinese inhabitants, except a few artisans and tradesmen; but in 1793, they began to let their houses to the natives; and now they have at least thirty thousand Chinese within the barrier, while the Portuguese citizens do not amount to five thousand. The Chinese thus introduced, have had a magistrate placed over them, who holds his court in the native part of the settlement; while a Chinese custom-house is established on the beach, and Macao may be said to be under two sets of rulers, both independent of each other.

In 1802, the English sent an armed force to take possession of Macao, in order to prevent its falling into the hands of the French; and in 1808, the attempt was renewed. In both cases, however, the Chinese resented the aggression, and stopped the trade, till the English troops had disembarked, on the ground of Macao being a part of the celestial empire. This claim they have continued to maintain, and now the Portuguese cannot build a new house, or even alter an old one without the permission of the Chinese authorities; while the governor was lately hindered in making a new pathway over a hill, by the mandarin driving away the Chinese workmen employed.

The houses, however, all belong to the Portuguese; into the dwellings of Europeans, the Chinese authorities never enter, not even to apprehend offenders of their own nation; but as soon as the delinquent shews his face outside, the mandarin runners lay hold of him. Thus, a foreigner has only to rent a dwelling of a Portuguese citizen, and that house is his castle; where he may print books, in any quantities, without danger of interference from the mandarins: he may even have a Chinese school, and retain a number of writers and teachers about him, so long as these do not put themselves in the way of the native police. A missionary however, who intends carrying on Chinese printing, in Macao, should be somewhat acquainted with the language, and employ principally foreign servants, so that no natives may be implicated in vexatious proceedings, on his account. He may then open his doors to any poor or enquiring Chinese, who may come to him for relief or advice, while he shuts them against all police officers, who are, in China, the least respectable part of the population.

It was found, on the author's arrival in Canton, both a delicate and difficult task, to institute an enquiry into the circumstances of the native converts; as a single question, proposed by a stranger, might bring them under suspicion, and the mere mention of their names involve them in difficulties. The persecutions of the previous year, had scattered them abroad, and driven most of them into an obscurity, from which they dared not emerge. In the best of times, the intercourse of missionaries with their disciples, in Canton, is necessarily limited, and must be conducted with caution: how much more when the few adherents of the mission have been denounced by name, some obliged to flee the country and the rest to hide themselves for a while, until the "indignation be overpast." Missionaries in Canton, cannot go to the houses of the native converts, who reside generally within the walls of the city, or in the surrounding villages, from which foreigners are excluded.   Did the converts, however, dwell in the suburbs, to which Europeans have access, they could not be visited, without attracting attention, and involving the native Christians in difficulties with their own government.   Propagators of the Gospel, therefore, must be content to wait until their disciples come to them, in some unfrequented part of the factories, where they may discourse together, with closed doors ; taking care to admit those only who can be confided in ; and conducting their meeting without noise.

No sooner, therefore, are a few enquiries made, than notice is taken of the fact, and people begin to wonder, why such investigations are instituted.   Questions, instead of bringing people near, only drive them farther away ; and no more effectual method could be taken of preventing the approach of an individual, than asking others if they had seen him.   It was extremely difficult, on these accounts, to ascertain fully the state of the Christian church in Canton, but a few hints have been gathered.

One of the number, Lew Tse-chuen, a literary graduate, came to the author, in Mr. Morrison's room, in Canton ; this man was baptized by Afăh, about a year before, and living near, was induced to attend. He appeared an intelligent man, but afflicted with an impediment in his speech, so that it was difficult to comprehend him. Resorting to the pencil, however, he soon made himself intelligible. He said, that he first heard the Gospel from Afäh, about two years previously. He had been engaged in transcribing some Christian books, and being frequently at the house of our evangelist, heard him discourse morning and evening, on the Scriptures. Beginning to dispute, he found Afäh ready to answer all his objections: and as he was a man of letters, Afäh gave him a number of books to examine, in order to correct the style. Having attended to this business, for several months, his mind was suddenly awakened, as if from a dream; and he requested baptism. Afäh did not refuse it; and since that time, by the gracious influences of the Saviour, he had been easy and comfortable. Before he had seen the Christian Scriptures, he said, he did not know the Supreme Being, and was carried away with the example of the many, stupidly worshipping false gods. This he felt to be a great evil. He had also disobeyed his mother, by persevering in literary pursuits, notwithstanding his poverty, and the difficulty he experienced in obtaining support for her and himself. He found, further, that he could not keep his mind free from defilement; evil thoughts would spring up, though he endeavoured to repress them, and did not allow them to proceed to sinful compliances. "To prevent the rising up of evil thoughts," he continued, " and to maintain purity of heart, requires our utmost exertions; and after all, it is necessary to rely on God's help, to keep us from evil. Having no power to renew ourselves, we should depend on Jesus for aid. Once, I frequently offended, but latterly, through the grace of Christ, such thoughts have been few, and I pray that they may be entirely obliterated, and, for his sake, forgiven."

By the above hints, it will appear, that his knowledge of himself, and the Saviour is still imperfect; though his mind is doubtless sincere. He is exceedingly humble, quite willing to learn, and thankful for instruction. He is employed in copying for the missionaries, and by his perfect acquaintance with the native language, is able to suggest many idiomatical improvements in their productions, which have been, for the most part, adopted; while he himself professes to have been much benefited by the perusal of what has passed through his hands. He is passionately addicted to the study of the Chinese classics, for the purpose of attaining literary fame, and consequently, rank and office; for this, he sacrifices time, health, and comfort; cheerfully putting up with poverty, and sitting up whole, nights to commit portions of the classics to memory; but whether he will succeed, is a great question, particularly as there are so many competitors, and as his religious profession, if known, would stand in the way of his advancement. The same amount of ardour and perseverance, bestowed in studying the doctrines of Christianity, and real science, would, doubtless, be crowned with the happiest results. However, few can do what he does; and, should he gain the accomplishment of his wishes, retaining his love for the Gospel, he might help our cause, in a quarter where the interference of every other would be unavailing. His present situation is unfavourable to religious advancement, as he enjoys none of the means of grace, and can hardly communicate with the missionaries, without great risk to himself. The only means of improvement which he possesses, are the Scriptures and tracts; but by the teaching of the Holy Spirit, he may still attain a proficiency in Divine knowledge, greater than that which sometimes results from superior advantages elsewhere.

Among the number of the baptized, we find the name of Choo Asan, who, it may be remembered, was apprehended when the stir was made about Christian books, in 1834. Akae, who was arrested with him, refused to give any account of these transactions; and though a heathen, submitted to forty blows on the face, by which he was altogether deprived of utterance, rather than reveal his accomplices. Choo Asan, however, told everything he knew, and assisted in guiding the police officers to Afäh's house, in the country; by which means some of our evangelist's relations were apprehended, and his property destroyed. Had Afäh himself been there, he would most likely have paid, with his life, for the indiscretion, to say the least of it, of Choo Asan, in discovering his abode. This man was one of the first baptized by Afäh, though he never afforded any satisfaction to his master. From the beginning, his aim appears to have been, the obtaining of money on account of his profession; and when told, that money was never given, except for work done, or goods delivered, he became indifferent, and is now, we fear, gone back.

Woo Achang, another of the baptized, after his release from confinement, fled to Singapore; where he has since been employed, by the American missionaries, in their printing-office, and has proved both useful and faithful.

Leang Ataou and Leang Asun, relatives of Afäh,

were employed by him in printing and circulating books; but since the persecution, have been scattered, and are making, it is to be feared, little progress in good things. Le Asid, a bricklayer, is in the same condition, afraid to come near the foreigners, until the vigilance of the police is a little relaxed.

Of Choo Tsing, who was formerly a teacher at Malacca, and who, on his return to China, was baptized by Dr. Morrison, some account has already been given. When the persecution broke out, he immediately withdrew himself from intercourse with Europeans; and, having been denounced by name, as a traitorous native, was glad to secrete himself in some distant part of the country, where he is not to be discovered by friend or foe.

Le-she is the wife of Afǎh, who, with her daughter, continues still to reside in the interior, and has only once been seen by the missionaries. Her situation, in the midst of a heathen population, deprived of Christian instruction, is both perilous and ensnaring. Afǎh has often wished her to emigrate to Malacca, where she would be safe from persecution, and enjoy the counsels and solace of her natural protector; but attachment to her native soil, connected with the fear of undertaking a sea-voyage, has hitherto prevented her from complying with his request. It is, therefore, difficult to ascertain the state of Le-she's mind, but the presumption is, that persecutions have combined with the instructions of her husband, to enlighten her understanding, and to deepen in her heart an attachment to the truth.

Leang Atǐh is the son of Afǎh, a lad of seventeen, now studying with Mr. Bridgman, in Canton. He has acquired a tolerable knowledge of the English language, while he pursues at the same time his Chinese studies. He is quiet, attentive, and obedient; and was baptized in his infancy. Should he happily become the subject of serious impressions, and be endowed with a missionary spirit, he will be of much service to the cause, and may one day prove a valuable assistant in revising the Chinese version of the Scriptures. With this view, Mr. B. is already teaching him Hebrew, and will continue to afford him a thorough classical education. At present his situation is by no means comfortable, being confined entirely to the house; for should he appear in the streets, his known connection with Afäh, and his profession of Christianity, would expose him to immediate apprehension and punishment.

Of Keŭh Agang, we are all disposed to think favourably; his firm attachment to the cause for several years, notwithstanding the persecutions which have scattered the rest, shews that he has adopted his profession from principle, and is not unwilling to suffer, if called to it. He is endowed with a good share of common sense, connected with a feeling mind, though his knowledge of Christianity is neither deep nor extensive, and his ability to instruct others rather circumscribed. Having unwittingly offended one of his fellow countrymen, he was, in 1835, reported to the police, as having had connection with foreigners, and a warrant was issued for his apprehension. Timely notice having been given him, he fled to the English ships at Lintin, and afterwards proceeded to Malacca. In the mean time, his son, Ahe, having been decoyed out of Mr. Morrison's house at Macao, was apprehended and brought before the magistrate; where he readily confessed that he had been employed in arranging the metal types for Dr.

Morrison's dictionary. The chief magistrate finding him such a ready informant, instead of punishing, gave him money, in order to induce him to tell more. He has, however, been kept in confinement, notwithstanding various efforts have been made to release him.

The case of this young man was reported to the emperor; and in an edict published in 1836, we find a reference to his name. In that document, after descanting on the efforts made by the catholics for the last two centuries to penetrate into the interior, and preach Christianity; and after stating, that fifty years ago, three Europeans, and twenty years ago, two, had been put to death, or driven away; he says, that lately English ships have passed along the coast of China, and distributed European books, which, as they exhort to believe in, and venerate the chief of that religion, named Jesus, must be intended for diffusing the same faith that was formerly persecuted and banished. The emperor, conceiving that Macao and Canton are the only places where the Europeans and Chinese associate together; and that traitorous natives must have assisted the barbarians in composing and printing the above treatises, sent down, in 1835, a commission to those places, and seized one Keŭh Ahe, a printer, together with eight European books, which were laid before the imperial tribunal. The edict concludes, by ordering all persons to deliver up the Christian books in their possession, within the space of six months, under the threat of severe punishment, declaring, that if any (native) should continue to preach and profess the Christian religion, he shall be prosecuted with the utmost rigour of the law.

The author happened to be in Canton when this

commission arrived. Enquiries were immediately set on foot, to discover the culprits, and the whole assembly of teachers and printers were placed in jeopardy. Not only were the works in hand immediately stopped, but the printers were obliged to bury and conceal the blocks, in order to escape detection. The teachers of the language, also, begged to stay away for a time; and the missionaries found it necessary to be careful, lest they should involve others in trouble, and retard future operations. On enquiry, it appeared, that Mr. Bridgman had formerly ordered books to be printed, in consequence of which, they wished to know by what ship he came to China (though he had been five years in Canton), in order to make the security merchant, who had become bound for the good conduct of all on board, responsible for Mr. B's delinquencies.

Soon after this, the principal security merchant in Canton was deputed by the native government to call on Mr. B. to enquire after native books, and the blocks from which they were printed. Of course he was politely received, but gained no information. Failing in his object, he requested an American merchant to ask, if Mr. B. had any blocks, and to solicit the loan of them. This method proving ineffectual, an English merchant applied to the author, wishing to know where certain native books had been printed; but the requisite information was respectfully declined. The gentlemen referred to, were perhaps little aware how much they would have prejudiced the cause of truth, and gratified its enemies, had they succeeded in obtaining and communicating the intelligence sought; for not only would their countrymen have been disturbed in their benevolent attempts, but various innocent natives would have been involved in difficulty, and perhaps ruin.

The security merchant was now puzzled to know what to do; for having been deputed to investigate the business, he was obliged to return an answer of some kind. He finally discovered, however, that many Chinese books came from Malacca, and that the people in foreign parts were able to make Chinese characters. The case of the author was also adduced, as being able to speak the native tongue fluently, though only a few months in Canton; from which it was seen, that foreigners could acquire the Chinese language, and print native books abroad, without having any intercourse with the acknowledged subjects of the native government. This satisfied the enquirers for the time; and the deputation having been subsequently wrecked in a typhoon, between Macao and Canton, the investigation was given up.

Since that time, the persecution has been relaxed, and Afäh has returned to his native village, to visit his family, after which he again embarked for Malacca.

From all that has been hitherto observed, it will be seen, that foreign agents run no risk in carrying on missionary labours either at Canton or Macao. The Chinese authorities cautiously avoid interfering with the subject of any foreign state, and the European habit is a protection against magisterial visitations. Thus personal liberty and life are quite secure, while the foreigner keeps within a moderate distance of the ships and factories. Barbarians are considered out of the pale of civilization, and not to be controlled by the principles which usually influence mankind; while they possess such power and resources, that it is thought dangerous to provoke their governments.   But though foreigners are left to pursue their wayward courses, uninterrupted by the authorities, the natives are made responsible for them; and there is not one of them who has not a security for his good conduct in the person of hong-merchant, linguist, compradore, or servant, set to watch over his proceedings.   When an offence is committed by a stranger, the ship by which he came is ascertained, and the linguist of that vessel made answerable for his good conduct for years afterwards.   Or the factory where he resides is found out, and the compradore of that factory seized upon; and if no trace of his connection be discoverable, then the whole body of hong-merchants are made to answer with their fortunes or their lives for what the stranger has done amiss. During the disturbances which occurred about the affair of Lord Napier, a hong-merchant was imprisoned, and a linguist banished to Tartary, because his lordship came up from Whampoa to Canton in the boat of the Fort William, for which ship they were securities, and therefore responsible for all his lordship's actions.

To a rightly constituted mind, it is equally, if not more grievous, to be the means of involving others in calamities, than to endure those calamities one's self. Proceedings, therefore, will not be rashly entered into, because the individual, engaging in them, is exempt from personal harm; but great caution will be exercised, in order not to involve innocent persons in transactions, with which they have no share.   If the object be to attract natives to our cause, it will be adviseable not to jeopardize them more than necessity requires, and to conduct operations as quietly as possible.   It is generally agreed, that it will not be prudent to attempt the printing of Chinese books in Canton.   They can be made fast enough elsewhere; while a sufficient number can be introduced from abroad, in sealed parcels, to supply the demand in Canton. This caution being taken, conversations may be carried on with the inhabitants of the suburbs, and meetings held in the foreign factories, entirely free from observation and interference, without risking either the heathen securities, or the Christian converts. Thus Canton may still be considered a most useful missionary station; and Macao, form the field of exertion to several active missionaries.

We cannot conclude this chapter, without remarking on the little interest taken, in Canton, by the British churches. It is true, that so early as 1807, they sent an agent to that city, which was then denominated, " the most important station upon earth;" but, it is also true, that since the year 1808, the Christians of Britain have not maintained a missionary there; and though they were relieved from the principal expense, by Dr. Morrison's supporting himself, yet they have not afforded him a single assistant in China, and have left his station vacant, four years after his death, without appointing an agent to gather the scattered church, console the persecuted disciples, or endeavour to spread the little leaven, till it leavened the whole lump. This conduct is the more inexplicable, as contrasted with the zeal at first displayed in the cause, and the earnestness with which the British churches have been excited to pray that the barriers might be removed, and a wide and effectual door opened before God's servants. China has been denominated the object of faith, hope, and supplication; but we humbly submit that prayer, without corresponding exertion is, to say the least, inconsistent; and that, if we want the barriers removed, and the door opened, the mere sitting still, and wishing it, is not the way to get the one or the other speedily accomplished.

The American churches, though late in the field, have maintained several agents in Canton, since the period of their first occupying it, in 1830; and notwithstanding their limited resources, have come nobly forward with men and money, in this important undertaking.

The state of things in Canton would seem to indicate that, in the future appointment of missionaries to that station, such should be selected as possess a previous knowledge of the language, and some experience in the work of missions among the Chinese. They should be persons of ardent zeal, and, at the same time, of great prudence, so as to avoid, if possible, the recurrence of events, similar to those which were witnessed in 1834. It may be very well, for a man to risk all for the Gospel, and to stake his life for the truth; but he should consider, whether by awakening the suspicions of a hostile government, and arraying a host of foes against his object, he would not retard more by his imprudence, than advance by his martyrdom, the spread of Christianity. Besides, there are others concerned; and though he may be willing to offer up himself " upon the sacrifice and service of the faith," yet he is not authorized to bring the same calamity upon his brethren. Zeal, connected with prudence, therefore, combining a previous acquaintance with the language and habits of the people, should unite in the individuals who occupy so difficult and important a post, as the key to the largest empire in the world.

CHAPTER XII.

THE MISSION TO MALACCA.

RESOLUTIONS REGARDING MALACCA — OCCUPATION OF THE STATION BY MR. MILNE — BAPTISM OF AFAH — HIS EXPERIENCE — ARRIVAL OF THE AUTHOR AND OTHER BRETHREN — SCHOOLS — TRACTS — AND TRANSLATIONS — ANGLO-CHINESE COLLEGE — VARIOUS LABOURS — RESCUE OF A MALAY FAMILY — DEATH OF MILNE — MORRISON VISITS MALACCA — ARRIVAL OF KIDD — VISIT OF THE DEPUTATION — DEATH OF COLLIE — BAPTISM OF A MALAY SLAVE — AND A CHINESE YOUTH — TOMLIN'S SUPERINTENDENCE — ARRIVAL OF EVANS — FRESH BAPTISMS — DYER JOINS THE MISSION — MORE ENCOURAGEMENT — TWENTY INDIVIDUALS BAPTIZED — TEN MORE ADDED — THEIR EXPERIENCE — MISSION TO PENANG — STATION AT JAMES TOWN — LABOURS OF DYER — MISSION TO SINGAPORE — JOINED BY THE AMERICAN MISSIONARIES.

MALACCA, situated on the east side of the strait of that name, was one of the earliest European settlements in the east, and now contains about 25,000 inhabitants; of whom 4000 are Chinese, 2000 Portuguese, about the same number of Malabars, and the rest Malays.

Mr. Milne first visited this place in 1814, on his way from Java to China. During the following year, it was resolved to occupy Malacca, as being nearer to China than any of the neighbouring settlements, and as commanding a ready intercourse with other parts of the archipelago. The station was intended with a view to the Chinese principally, though not exclusively; and as the inhabitants of the neighbouring nations were included in the object, the undertaking assumed the general name of the Ultra-Ganges Missions.

In the spring of 1815, Mr. Milne left Canton, accompanied by a Chinese teacher, printers, and materials for publishing books. The Resident received him with great kindness, and proposed that he should take charge of the Dutch reformed church, established there; which Mr. M. consented to do, as far as his missionary engagements would allow.

Soon after his arrival, Mr. Milne established a Chinese school, into which fifteen children were admitted. A Christian catechism was introduced, and a catechetical exercise maintained every Sabbath afternoon. A public service in Chinese was commenced, and family worship conducted daily, to which the adherents of the mission paid serious attention.

A periodical publication in the native language, having been considered advisable for a reading people, the first number of the Chinese Magazine left the press in the month of August, 1815. The promotion of Christianity was its primary object; yet knowledge and science were called in to the aid of religion; and instructive anecdotes, with occasional notices of political events, gave a pleasing variety to the work.

The same year, Mr. Milne was joined by Mr. Thomsen, who came out to establish a Malay mission in Malacca; and for that purpose devoted himself to the study of the language.

In the summer of 1816, a more than usual attention to the truth was paid by one of the Chinese printers, who professed his determination to take up the cross, and follow the Saviour. The following extract from Mr. Milne's journal refers to this individual :—

" Nov. 3.—At twelve o'clock this day, I baptized, in the name of the adorable Trinity, Leang Kung-fah, commonly called Leang Afăh, The service was performed in a room of the mission house. Care had been taken, by previous conversation and prayer, to prepare him for this sacred ordinance; and finding him still steadfast in the faith, I baptised him. The change produced in his sentiments and conduct is, I hope, the effect of Christian truth,— yet who of mortals can know the heart? Several searching questions were proposed to him, and an exercise suited to a candidate for baptism composed and given to him to meditate on. He belongs to the province of Canton, is about thirty-three years of age, can read a plain book with ease, and is of a steady character and frugal habits. His temper is not so sociable as that of many other Chinese: he was formerly obstinate, and occasionally troublesome, but of late there has been scarcely anything of this kind to complain of. With respect to his former life, he observed, ' I rarely went to excess in sin; yet I have been occasionally guilty of drunkenness and other kindred vices. Before I came hither, I knew not God; but now I desire to serve him.' He wished to be baptized exactly at twelve o'clock, when, to use his own words, ' the shadow inclines neither one way nor the other.'

" At baptism, the following questions were proposed to him, to which he answered as follows ,—Q. Have you truly turned from idols, to serve the living and true God, the creator of heaven and earth? A. This is my heart's desire. Q. Do you know and feel, that you are a sinful creature, totally unable to save yourself? A. I know it. Q. Do you really believe that Jesus Christ is the Son of God, and the Saviour of the world; and do you trust in him alone for salvation? A. This is my hearts's desire. Q. Do you expect any worldly advantage, profit, or gain, by your becoming a Christian? A. None: I receive baptism because it is my duty. Q. Do you resolve from this day till the day of your death, to live in obedience to all the commandments and ordinances of God; and in justice and righteousness before men? A. This is my determination; but I fear my strength is not equal to it.

" On my part, the ordinance was dispensed with mingled affection, hope, and fear. May he be made faithful unto death; and as he is the first fruits of this branch of the mission, may an abundant harvest follow, to the joy of the church, and the honour of Christ."

His account of his own experience, is as follows :—

" Before I believed in the Saviour, though I knew myself to be a sinner, I did not know how to obtain pardon. I used to go every new and full moon to the temple, and prayed to the gods to protect me; but though my body worshipped the gods, my heart still cherished evil thoughts and desires, together with designs of cheating and lying, which never departed from my mind. After a time, I was brought to Malacca, in the family of a missionary, who used to preach to his domestics the doctrine of salvation through Jesus. I attended his ministrations, but my heart was not engaged. Sometimes I looked at the Scriptures, and heard them explained, but I did not fully comprehend the meaning. Hearing the missionary exhort men not to go and worship the gods, I used to say, ' this is a strange kind of doctrine. According to this, gilt paper and sacrificiel candles, gold flowers and paper money, must be useless and sinful. I fear that Buddha will soon bring punishment and death on such an opponent of the gods, and then we shall see whether he will continue to preach these doctrines.'

" A few months afterwards, a priest of Buddha came from China, and lived in the temple of Kwan-yin, hard by. He visited me frequently, and I asked him how I was to obtain the pardon of sins ? He answered, ' Daily recite the true forms of devotion, and Buddha, who resides in the western heavens, will remit the sins of your whole family. If a person give a little money to the priest, to chaunt the prayers for him, he will, in the next life, be born into a rich family, and will not be sent to hell to suffer misery. When I heard this, I desired to become a follower of Buddha. The priest immediately sent me a volume of prayers, and desired me to repeat them ; saying, that if I recited them a thousand times, I should cancel all the debts of my former life. I accordingly began to repeat the prayers; but one evening, while sitting alone, it came into my mind, that I had committed many real sins, and could hardly expect by reciting prayers without performing a single virtuous action, to obtain forgiveness.

" In the mean while, I heard the missionary preach the doctrine of atonement through Jesus, and at my leisure, I examined the Scriptures, which forbad uncleanness, deceit, and idolatry. Then I thought, ' these are good books, exhorting men to depart from iniquity: moreover, the doctrines are attested by the miracles of Jesus, therefore this book must certainly be true.' I then listened to the explanation of the Scriptures, and on the Sabbath day read the Bible more attentively requesting the missionary to explain it to me. I asked what was meant by Jesus making atonement for sin. The missionary told me, that Jesus was the Son of God, sent into the world to suffer for the sins of men, in order that all who believe in Him might obtain salvation. Feeling myself to be a sinner, I asked how I was to obtain pardon ? The missionary said, ' If you believe in Jesus, God will receive you as his adopted son, and in the world to come, bestow on you everlasting life.'

" On returning to my room, I thought within myself, ' I am a great sinner, and if I do not depend on the merits of Christ, how can God forgive me ?' I then determined to become a disciple of Jesus, and requested baptism.

" After receiving this rite, I employed my mind diligently in guarding my life and actions, and became more and more fond of reading the Scriptures. I prayed to God, to drive all evil thoughts out of my mind, and cherish good desires within me.

" I now not only refrained from worshipping images myself, but pitied those who did, and sought to instruct them in the way of salvation. With this view, I made a small book, exhorting men to worship God, and believe in Jesus; and on my return to my native village in China, I printed a hundred copies, for the purpose of distribution; when one day I was suddenly apprehended by the police, who brought me before the mandarin. He said, that my believing in Jesus, and printing Christian books, were both violations of the law, and ordered me into confinement. While there, I thought with myself, ' this book contains the true doctrine of Jesus, the Saviour of the world, who exhorted men to become good—why then should I be persecuted for printing it ? I suppose it is because my sins have provoked God to punish me.' Therefore I heartily repented, and prayed that God would pity and pardon me. The missionary afterwards interested some persons to speak to the mandarin on my behalf; who, after giving me thirty blows with the bamboo, on the soles of my feet, till the blood flowed, liberated me. The police officers also extorted from me seventy dollars. After I had suffered this persecution and loss of property, I did not dare to turn my back on the Lord Jesus, but accounted that I suffered the just punishment due for my sins."

In 1817, an English periodical, called the " Indo-Chinese Gleaner," was begun. It contained the most recent information from China, notices about the literature and religion of the Ultra-Ganges nations, with the best method of evangelizing them ; but it was never adequately supported, and after three or four years' trial was given up.

This year, the weight of the establishment pressed very heavily on Mr. Milne, who was almost sinking under a load of cares, when the author arrived, June, 1817, to his assistance. The number of works passing through the press, both in the Chinese, Malay, and English languages, at Malacca, required the special attention of one individual, and it was for the purpose of superintending this department that he was originally destined. In order to this, it was necessary that the Chinese and Malay languages should be learned; and this agreed with a previous desire, to connect with secular duties the more important occupation of imparting direct religious instruction to the natives. About a month afterwards, Mr. Milne visited China for the benefit of his health, leaving the whole care of the mission including preaching, schools, printing, and tract distribution, to his newly arrived coadjutor. This, together with the acquisition of the language, became a heavy burthen for a young beginner, but by God's help, the machine was kept in motion; while the demands on ingenuity, to render himself intelligible, soon forced the inexperienced labourer into a tolerable acquaintance with the vernacular tongue.

At the close of 1817, the mission was joined by Mr. Slater, who devoted himself to the study of the Chinese language, and, after a year's residence went to revive the mission in Batavia.

In the beginning of 1818, Mr. Milne returned from China, much improved in health; and towards the close of the same year, the mission was strengthened by the arrival of three additional labourers, Messrs. Beighton,

Ince, and Milton, the former of whom applied to the study of the Malay, and the two latter to the Chinese language.

Whilst the newly arrived brethren were occupied in studying the rudiments of the different tongues, the author took charge of the Chinese schools, which were three in number. By devoting more attention to this department, some improvements were introduced. Mr. Milne's Youth's Catechism was explained weekly, in the colloquial dialect, by which means the scholars soon knew more of Christianity than they did of Confucianism.

In the distribution of tracts, frequent opportunities of usefulness occurred. Several strangers from Siam and Cochin China manifested a great desire to obtain copies of the New Testament and tracts, and came to the mission house requesting to be supplied.

Mr. Milne, in the mean time, pursued the work of translation; and contemplated drawing up commentaries on various parts of the Bible. For Mr. M. felt convinced, that we must direct the attention of the heathen to the Scriptures, if we would furnish them with ever new and saving truth. The Bible is the only book that can long keep up the attention; and to make solid and rational Christians, to lay the foundation of extensive and permanent usefulness, and to fix the religion of the Redeemer in a pagan country, so as to defy the possibility of extermination, no means are equal to those which lead the heathen directly to the Holy Scriptures.

In the month of November, 1818, the foundation stone of the Anglo-Chinese College was laid. This institution was intended for the cultivation of English and Chinese literature, with the diffusion of Christianity.

It owed its origin to Dr. Morrison, who devoted the sum of one thousand pounds to the erection of the house, and five hundred pounds for the instruction of one European, and one Chinese student for the first five years. The college was designed to afford to Europeans the means of acquiring the Chinese language, and to Chinese an opportunity of becoming acquainted with the science and religion of the west. The directors of the Missionary Society were of opinion that the proposed college was likely to advance Christianity in the east, and therefore voted five hundred pounds towards the institution; suggesting at the same time, the importance of giving a paramount attention to missionary objects, while they advised that no young man, whose piety was in the smallest degree questionable, should be admitted into the college.

Dr. Morrison, in writing on the subject, says,—

" Let me beseech you, by the tender mercies of God our Saviour, to continue your parental care of these missions, and particularly to deal kindly with the infant seminary, the Anglo-Chinese College. It is the offspring of the Missionary Society; and like that, is devoted to the cause of our common Christianity. Literature is the means, not the end. God grant that it may prosper, be an honour to my country, and a blessing to China; and thus unite in its name and in its benefits, the west and the east, and finally blend in peaceful intercourse the extremities of the earth, Britain and Japan."

During the year 1819, the distribution of tracts was carried on with activity; almost every house in the town was visited, for the purpose of conversing with the inhabitants, and supplying them with the means of instruction. Two New Testaments and several tracts were conveyed, by Capt. P. Gordon, to Japan, and left in the hands of the natives of Jeddo. The raging of the cholera through the settlement was improved by the missionaries, to press eternal things more seriously on the attention of the natives. Religious exercises were conducted daily in Chinese and Malay, at the mission house; while the author commenced preaching in the Fŭh-këen dialect four times a week, in different parts of the town. This year, four of the brethren left for the various stations in the archipelago, and the concerns of the mission devolved on the three labourers who first arrived.

The following year the Malacca mission was strengthened by the arrival of two labourers; Mr. Fleming, for the Chinese department; and Mr. Huttman, to take charge of the printing, instead of the author, who removed to Penang. Mr. Thomsen's labours in the English and Malay school, were rewarded by the gratifying progress of the children, and their willingness to instruct others. Mr. T. succeeded also in rescuing a Malay family from slavery, whom he regularly instructed, and was happy to see them renounce Mahomedanism and embrace Christianity.

Mr. (now Dr.) Milne composed an essay on the nature, immortality, and salvation of the soul, in two volumes, 12mo., calculated to meet the sceptical objections and metaphysical reasonings of the Confucians, and to give them just views on so important and essential a theme.

In the year 1821, Mr. Humphreys joined the station; and the following year the mission was strengthened by the arrival of Mr. Collie; but it sustained a severe loss in the death of Dr. Milne. He had for several years been declining in health, and was advised to visit Europe for its re-establishment; but his anxiety

to complete the translation of the Old Testament, and
to watch over the infant college, induced him to prolong his stay in India, till disease had made such progress, as to baffle the utmost efforts of medical skill.
In the beginning of the year, his disorder became so
violent as to compel him to remove to Singapore, and
from thence to Penang. But growing worse, he signified his wish to return to Malacca; and there being
no vessel sailing for that place, the governor of Penang
ordered the Company's cruiser, Nautilus, to proceed
thither with him, accompanied by Mr. Beighton. He
was just spared to land at Malacca, where on the
second of June, he calmly resigned his happy spirit
into the hands of the Redeemer. In him, the Christian
church sustained no ordinary loss; but if his course
was short, his labours were abundant, and he lived
long enough to see his plans consolidated, and in a
great measure carried into vigorous operation.

The same year Mr. Thomsen quitted Malacca, to
establish a Malay mission at Singapore.

Afäh, the converted Chinese, arrived from Malacca
this year, with three new workmen, to expedite the
printing of the Chinese Scriptures, which he was honoured to commence and to bring to a conclusion. By
the decease of Dr. Milne, however, the Chinese Magazine and the Indo-Chinese Gleaner, were discontinued;
while preaching in the native language was suspended.
Dr. Milne, before his death, baptized a Chinese woman;
and Mr. Thomsen, two Malays, all of whom appeared
to be sincere converts to Christianity.

In the beginning of 1823, Dr. Morrison visited Malacca, and one of his first acts was to erect a monument to the memory of his late friend, with appropriate

inscriptions in Hebrew and Chinese. The Chinese services were resumed by Dr. Morrison, the attendance on which amounted to sixty persons; after his departure, Mr. Collie continued this exercise. Some strangers from Cochin China applied for a fresh supply of Scriptures and tracts, and said, that some Roman catholics in their country had got more rational and satisfactory views of the eucharist, from reading some of our tracts, than they had before possessed.

The number of students, in the college, was fifteen; these youths approved of Christianity, and generally entered, with cheerfulness, into the religious exercises of the mission: and, although none of them manifested any decisive evidence of conversion, yet they had entirely given up idol-worship, and abstained from joining in heathen ceremonies.

In the year 1824, Mr. Kidd joined the Malacca mission, and commenced the study of the Fŭh-këen dialect. In the college, the number of inmates amounted to twenty-six, who were diligent in their studies, and frequently accompanied the brethren in their missionary excursions; whilst in the heathen temple they raised the tune, and assisted in conducting the worship of the true God. Respect and affection towards their teachers, was manifest in these young men, and their knowledge of religion increased daily.

During the year 1825, the mission books were more sought after than formerly; many applied for particular works, and expressed a wish to have larger treatises on the Christian religion. Many tracts had been sent to the neighbouring colonies and to China; while the missionaries continued to itinerate in the surrounding villages.

In the following year, the mission was strengthened by the arrival of Mr. Smith; while the brethren were cheered and encouraged by the visit of the deputation from the Parent Society, consisting of Messrs. Tyerman and Bennet. The Chinese schools contained two hundred and fifty children, and the deputation expressed themselves satisfied with the progress of the boys, and the principles on which the schools were conducted. The local government engaged to support two of these establishments, and a free school, containing one hundred and seventy boys, was maintained by the inhabitants. The deputation thought that a prominent object in schools, established in heathen countries should be, to train up the elder boys as schoolmasters; it being reasonable to suppose, that persons thus educated, would be less attached to idolatry, and better fitted both morally and intellectually, for promoting the object of missionaries, than the present race of heathen schoolmasters.

The number of students in the college was twenty; one of whom, a native of China, had in little more than a year, acquired such a knowledge of English, as to enable him to translate Keith's Treatise on the Globes, into Chinese. No instances of conversion had occurred among the native students, but a considerable degree of important information was acquired, and the youthful mind stored with those great truths, which are able to make wise unto salvation. At an examination held by the deputation, when the students were questioned on subjects relating to geography, arithmetic, grammar, theology, &c., several of them acquitted themselves much to the satisfaction of their examiners.

During the year 1827, the mission chapel was opened

for public worship, when sermons were preached in the various languages spoken in the settlement; the college students attended the service, and the congregations were good.

The following year, the mission was deprived of one of its most valued labourers by death, David Collie. Mr. C. enjoyed excellent health, during the whole of his residence in India, with the exception of the year in which he died. His exertions in behalf of the heathen, were unremitting; he rose early and sat up late, redeeming his time for the one great object in view. He was taken ill in January, and became so much worse in the following month, that the medical men advised his proceeding to a colder climate : with this view, he embarked for Singapore, intending to go on to the Cape, or England ; but rapidly sinking, he died on the following day, surrounded by strangers and foreigners, without a Christian friend to impart the least consolation or assistance. His remains were committed to the deep, with the hope, that one day, the " sea would give up the dead that were in it."

The Chinese branch of the mission now devolved on Messrs. Kidd and Smith ; while Mr. Humphrey's preached in Malay, and had the gratification to baptize a Malay female slave, with her children, who had regularly attended at the mission chapel, and given evidence of conversion to God. On being asked why she wished to be baptized, she said that she felt herself a great sinner, and knew of no other Saviour but Jesus.

Messrs. Humphreys and Smith returned, in 1829, to England, and Mr. Hughes was sent out to strengthen the Malay mission. In April of this year, Mr. Kidd baptized a Chinese youth, named Tsze-hëa, who had been educated in the college. The boys in the Chinese schools amounted to two hundred. Miss Newell, who had been sent out in 1827, for the purpose of promoting native female education, succeeded in establishing five girl's schools in Malacca. The number of students in the college was thirty. One of them, a native of China, had translated Stockii Clavis, into Chinese; and on leaving the institution, proceeded to Peking, where he was employed as imperial interpreter of western languages.

In the year 1831, the aspect of the mission became more favourable; knowledge was increasing, distrust gave place to confidence, and a spirit of enquiry succeeded to the previous apathy. A Malay man, who had formerly enjoyed the benefit of Mr. Collie's instruction, was baptized by Mr. Kidd. Three Malay schools were opened by Mr. Hughes, which contained eighty children, of both sexes. Miss Wallace, who succeeded Miss Newell, in the superintendence of native female education had ten schools under her care; viz. eight Chinese, one Tamul, and one Malay school. containing two hundred girls.

Mr. Kidd returned to England in 1832, when Mr. Tomlin took charge of the station; Chinese preaching was continued, and the whole number of children educated in the schools, exceeded five hundred.

During the year 1833, Mr. Tomlin continued his superintendence of the mission and college. Into the latter, he introduced, what he called, a radical reform. This consisted in abolishing the monthly stipend allowed to the students, which, in the infancy of the institution, was deemed necessary; but as the benefits of the college became apparent, it was thought that this might gradually be dispensed with.   In the beginning of 1833, all fresh applicants were informed, that no allowances would be made as formerly, and that all who entered must expect no pay.   Twenty volunteers appeared on this system; and at the close of the year, there were fifteen pensioners, and seventeen free boys. A Bible class was commenced, at which the schoolmasters and senior scholars, with some young professing Christians in the town, attended.

With the commencement of 1834, Mr. Evans took charge, and on the 4th of May, delivered his first sermon in Chinese, after having been only nine months in Malacca.   " I have thus found," says he, " all the difficulties of this hard language vanish away before perseverance; and cannot be sufficiently thankful to the Lord, for thus enabling me to engage in every duty connected with my department, in eight months after my arrival!"   His son, in the same space of time, spoke the Malay, with the fluency of a native, and has since applied to the Chinese language.   The mission, also, wore a favourable aspect; one Chinese and two Malay females, with one Malay man, had been baptized.

A few months afterwards, a Tamul man was baptized, who gave satisfactory proofs of his sincerity, by renouncing caste, in spite of persecution.   His conduct since his baptism, has been highly praiseworthy.   There were also several Chinese candidates for baptism; some of them, frequently engaged in prayer, and began to understand the scriptures.   The religious services were all well attended, and the thirst of the Chinese for books, increased daily, so that they could not be printed fast enough.

In his report of the college, for 1834, Mr. Evans calls it the *Alma Mater* of China, and speaks of it as having been the instrument, either directly or indirectly, of converting every Chinese, who has embraced the Christian faith. The total number of students who had finished their education, since the commencement of the institution, was forty: part of these are sincere Christians, and all respectable members of society.

Anxious to promote the efficiency of this station, the Directors instructed Mr. Dyer, to remove thither, from Penang, in 1835. Preaching was continued in the different languages, while the Chinese congregations amounted to two hundred and fifty Three Tamul men had been baptized, besides three Chinese, two of whom were students in the college; the entire number of baptized during the year, being eight adults and two children. One of the Chinese converts was very useful among his countrymen, conversing with the children of the schools, besides labouring among the adults. Mr. Evans writes, " the whole number of Chinese Christians is now nearly thirty; those whom I have baptized, adorn the doctrine of our God and Saviour. They are now ready to go forth, as preachers of the Gospel, to their countrymen. Their knowledge of Scripture is extraordinary.

In the year 1836, the native Christians, who had been compelled to quit China, by persecution, found an asylum in Malacca. Amongst the rest, Leang Afäh, who availed himself of the opportunity to spread religious knowledge amongst the emigrants preaching both in the Füh-këen and Canton dialects. The usual services in English, Chinese, and Portuguese, were continued.

Mr. Hughes having quitted the service of the Society, the Malay department was this year but partially attended to. Mr Dyer was actively employed in preparing Chinese metal types, in which he was aided by liberal donations from India, England, and America. The students in the college amounted to seventy, and their pursuits were divided between Chinese and English literature. Six of the senior students having renounced idolatry, were supported by the London Missionary Society. Four of these, together with one Siamese, were baptized during the year, after having publicly abjured heathenism. Mr. Dyer wrote, that he never viewed the Ultra-Gangetic missions in a more favourable light than at the time referred to; the gloom he said was passing away, and the light springing up.

Subjoined is the substance of the questions proposed to the candidates, at the time of their baptism:—

"Why do you wish to receive Christian baptism? Because I feel myself to be a great sinner: and now desire to repent of my sins, that I may obtain forgiveness.

"Do you think that baptism alone is able to save your soul? No: but I believe that Jesus Christ, who commanded believers to be baptized, is able to save me.

"What has Jesus Christ done for you? He suffered and died, to atone for my sins, and procure my salvation.

"Do you wish to follow the doctrine of Christ, in preference to that of the Chinese sages? I do: because I believe, that Christ alone can guide me to happiness and heaven.

"Can you truly say, that you have forsaken the vain superstitions of your countrymen? I have hitherto foolishly worshipped idols, but now I desire to worship the living and true God, only

"Do you feel that you are a great sinner, and deserving of eternal punishment? I know that I am a sinner, and that I ought to suffer the punishment due to sin.

"Do you think that any good performance of your own will be sufficient to save you? All I can do will be wholly insufficient to save me, and I pray for salvation, through the merits of Christ alone.

"Is it with the view of advancing your worldly interests, that you wish to be baptized? No: my sole reason for desiring baptism, is that I may become a disciple of Jesus Christ."

In the year 1837, the brethren at Malacca transmitted accounts surpassing any that had previously been sent from that station. Divine service was continued in the various languages, as usual, with a regular attendance, particularly at the Chinese service, when the mission chapel was crowded. The number of children receiving education in the schools, was, four hundred and ninety-five. Mr. Lay, the agent of the Bible Society, had been liberally supplied with Chinese Bibles and Testaments. In the month of April, 1837, twenty individuals were admitted to the Christian church, by baptism, viz. four Chinese families, consisting of four men, with their wives and five children; besides six young Chinese and one Siamese. These all adorned the doctrine of God their Saviour, and their whole conduct comported with the principles of Christianity. The renunciation of idolatry, by one of these persons, is remarkable. He came to the college one day, expressing a wish to embrace Christianity. This was objected to, on the ground of his house being still furnished with an idol; when he immediately went home, tore down every vestige of idolatry, and committed all to the flames, in the presence of his family: "Here," say the brethren, "are the first fruits of 350,000,000 of the human race."

In the month of May, of the same year, ten more individuals were baptized: one of them was a venerable man, with a long white beard, about sixty-five years of age. He was formerly a schoolmaster, and a most rigid idolater; perhaps one of the last persons, humanly speaking, upon whom religion seemed likely to make an impression; and, yet, he said, the things which he read in the Christian books, caused him to see the folly of idolatry. The truth seemed to have been working in his mind, for many months; and, at last, he came forward, with a degree of courage, quite surprising in so old a man, and exclaimed before his idolatrous countrymen, " I have served idols, but I will serve them no more."

Two of the baptized, a man and his wife, were somewhat dependant on the person with whom they resided; their patron threatened, that if they were baptized, they should quit his house, with nothing but the clothes they had on. This threat deterred them, for some time; but at length the husband remembering the words of the Saviour, " If any man will come after me, let him deny himself, take up his cross, and follow me;" determined to sacrifice all for Jesus. On this determination being made known, the opponent's heart relented, and he not only recalled his former threat, but promised, that if they would remain with him, he would take down his idol. The man was true to his word, for when they returned home, after baptism, every vestige of idolatry was removed.

Another family, baptized at the same time, consisted of a man, his wife, and two children. The man carried on the business of a shoe-maker in the town, in the midst of idolaters. Having been present at the former baptism, his mind became so deeply impressed with the solemnity of the service, and the truths of Christianity, that he borrowed some Christian books, and continued to peruse them for a considerable time, without communicating his opinion and determination to any one. At length, the change in his conduct became so manifest, that his acquaintance began to ridicule him. Being thus called upon to confess Jesus, before men, he was not ashamed to do so: and has since continued a firm and consistent follower of that Saviour, whom he has been spiritually taught to serve.

The other individuals consisted of one man, about thirty, and two young men, who are preparing in the college to enter on the Christian ministry. The conduct of all is most commendable: their attendance on the means of grace is punctual and regular, whilst they conduct family worship, morning and evening, in their own dwellings. They seem not only desirous of walking worthy of their profession themselves, but of inducing others to come with them, that they may do them good; whilst the order and consistency of those young men studying for the office of evangelists, is such as to afford much comfort to those under whose charge they are placed.

As the missions to Penang and Singapore were intimately connected with that to Malacca, we shall here introduce a brief notice of them.

Though Penang was pointed out as the most eligible spot, on which to commence a mission; yet it was not till Canton and Malacca had both been occupied, that the brethren turned their attention to Prince of Wales' island. Mr. Milne did, indeed, take a journey thither, in 1816, to solicit a grant of land for the Malacca station; but in 1819, the first efforts were made to evangelize the inhabitants of that settlement. In the spring of the latter year, the author proceeded thither, to distribute tracts, and establish schools, for which the support of government was obtained, and then made way for Messrs. Beighton and Ince, who occupied the station as resident missionaries.

Towards the close of the following year, however, the author again visited the island, and settled at James Town, in the midst of a rural population, having charge of a native orphan school, consisting of about twenty individuals, who resided in the missionary's house, and under his own eye. A dispensary was likewise opened for the sick poor, and visits paid to the heathen in their dwellings, while divine worship was regularly conducted with the inmates of the mission family and a few neighbours. During the author's residence there, a Chinese catholic applied for instruction. He retained a general knowledge of the Christian history, but lamented that he had lost his crucifix and missal. With the view of keeping him near the missionary's residence, a pepper garden was purchased for him; but he made off with the proceeds, and was never heard of more. The catholics possess a seminary in Penang, for the purpose of training up young Chinese as preachers to their own countrymen. The principal had been fifteen years in China, and there were about twenty inmates in the establishment. After spending a year in Penang, the author removed to Batavia.

In the year 1824, a neat and commodious chapel was built for the use of the mission, towards which the inhabitants of the settlement subscribed very liberally. The chapel had scarcely been erected a year, however, when the mission sustained a severe loss in the death of Mr. Ince. After a delay of two years, Mr. Dyer arrived to occupy his place.

Soon after his arrival, Mr. Dyer commenced the

work of casting moveable metallic types for the Chinese language, and attempted to establish schools on the British system. His chief employment consisted in going about from house to house, and preaching the Gospel to every creature. In order to be more completely amongst them, he purchased a small house in the centre of the Chinese town, where he received all who came for religious instruction and medical advice, while the intense breathing of his inmost soul was to be made a blessing to that heathen land.

In 1832, a Malay female was baptized, whose profession appeared to be scriptural and sincere. Two or three years afterwards the number of baptized amounted to thirteen, and the communicants from among the English congregation to twenty.

In the close of 1835, Mr. Dyer was appointed to Malacca, and his place supplied by Mr. Davies. During all the intervening years, from the establishment of the mission, two or three Chinese, and half a dozen Malay schools have been kept up, some of them supported by government. In these, the brethren have laboured to impress religious truth upon the minds of the young, with varied success. In the Malay schools, some of the young people have become familiar with the Scriptures, and some have been trained up to be teachers to others. In the Chinese schools, however, owing to the peculiarity of the language, and the obstinacy of the teachers, little good has been done.

No sooner was the British flag hoisted at Singapore, than a grant of land was obtained for the mission there; and Mr. Milton proceeded, in 1819, to commence operations for the benefit of the Chinese in that island. In 1822, Mr. Thomsen removed thither from Malacca, for the purpose of instructing the Malays.   Two years afterwards, the mission chapel was built, and in the course of time, three natives were baptized, who gave pleasing evidence of their sincerity.   The mission was strengthened in 1827, by the arrival of Messrs. Smith and Tomlin, who established schools, and distributed Chinese tracts throughout the settlement, and amongst the native vessels in the harbour.   The following year, Mr. Tomlin paid a visit to Siam, in company with Mr. Gutzlaff, where they distributed twenty-three boxes full of Chinese books among the people.   The medical aid afforded to the natives attracted multitudes to the dwelling of the missionaries, and something was done towards their instruction; while one Chinese was baptized by Mr. Gutzlaff, as the first fruits of the mission to Siam.   A rough translation of the Gospel of Matthew, was drawn up, and a Christian tract was printed in the language of that country.

Both Messrs. Smith and Tomlin having afterwards removed to Malacca, and Mr. Thomsen being compelled to return to Europe, on account of ill health, the mission at Singapore was but feebly supported. In 1835, Mr. Wolfe was sent thither, but in two years was called away by death.   The station is now occupied by the Messrs. Stronachs, who have just arrived.

Our American brethren have occupied this station for the last four years, and intend making it the seat of their printing establishment, and a point from which to operate on the nations beyond.   Their efforts have been blessed for the conversion of several individuals, and the energy with which they are carrying on their labours, promises, at no distant period, a happy result.

Buddhist Priests on a Stage.

Adoration of a Celebrated Devotee.

Service in a Chinese Temple.

CHAPTER XIII.

MISSION TO BATAVIA.

FIRST THREE MISSIONARIES — SUPPER'S LABOURS — SLATER'S MISFOR-
TUNES—THE AUTHOR'S ARRIVAL — SCHOOLS—PRINTING — AND OTHER
EXERTIONS — CHRISTIAN VILLAGE — CONVERSATIONS WITH HEATHEN
—MALAY JUDGE — NAPOLEON'S PICTURE — VISIT OF THE DEPUTATION
— DESULTORY LABOURS — TRACT AGAINST THE MISSIONARY — JOUR-
NEY TO SOERABAYA — THE TANGGAR MOUNTAINS — JAPANESE BOOKS
— CHINESE PREACHING — IRONICAL ARGUMENTS — COMMUNICATION
OF THE GOSPEL — WORK ON CHRONOLOGY — JAVANESE TYPES—JOUR-
NEY TO PAHANG — TRINGANO — KLINTAN — PATANI — AND SONGORA —
VOYAGE TO PONTIANAK — STATE OF BORNEO — CHINESE UNDER CON-
VICTIONS — ANOTHER INCENSED — VISIT TO BALI — ERECTION OF THE
CHAPEL — PREACHING TO CONVICTS — ACCESSIONS TO THE CHURCH —
BAPTISM OF SOLDIERS — COVENANT WITH THE DYAKS — BAPTISM OF
A CHINESE.

THE visit of Mr. Milne to the island of Java, has been noticed in a former chapter. In the year 1814, Messrs. Kam, Supper, and Bruckner, arrived at Batavia, to commence permanent missions in the Malayan archipelago. The former of these, proceeded to Amboyna, where he laboured faithfully for twenty years, in reviving and extending the native church, in that and the surrounding islands. Mr. Bruckner went to Samarang, where he took charge of a Dutch congregation; but changing his views on the subject of baptism, he joined the Baptist Missionary Society, and has continued ever since a faithful labourer among the Javanese. Mr. Supper remained in Batavia, where he preached to the native Christians. He likewise employed himself in the distribution of Chinese scriptures and tracts, which were received with gratitude, while the heathen asked for some teacher to explain the truths which they contained.

Mr. Supper writes, " I have often found Chinese parents reading the New Testament to their families, and requesting instruction about some passages. One merchant delayed his departure from Batavia for some days, in order to read a bible which he had received, with tranquillity and reflection ; he promised to recommend it to his countrymen, and implored a thousand blessings on the Bible." One of the most opulent Chinese observed, " I have read the New Testament with pleasure ; it is very fine ; and it would be well, if every one led such a life as Jesus Christ has taught us to lead." This Chinese on his return home, tore down all the painted images from the walls, and threw them into the fire.

In three short years the useful labours of this promising missionary were terminated by death.

In the year 1819, Mr. Slater proceeded from Malacca to Batavia. On his voyage, he touched at Singapore, Rhio, Lingin, and Banca, as well as at Pontianak, and Sambas, in Borneo ; and having been provided with about fifteen thousand Chinese and Malay books, he distributed them liberally among the people. At many of these places no protestant missionary had previously been ; the books, therefore, excited the greater attention. A copy of the divine word, had however, reached Pontianak before Mr. S. arrived, from the perusal of which one Chinese had obtained a knowledge of his own depravity, and the undertaking of Jesus Christ. He approved of the work of missionaries, and promised that if one came to settle in Pontianak, he would give him a house for nothing.

Arrived at Batavia, Mr. S. had scarcely provided himself with a house, before it was burnt to the ground; perhaps by some dishonest servant, as he had been twice robbed previously. Part of his property was saved, but a quantity of Testaments and tracts were consumed.

The subscriptions of the inhabitants enabled Mr. S. to repair his damage; and in the year 1821, a small bamboo chapel was built for the use of the mission, at the cost of two hundred pounds, which was principally raised by the English inhabitants.

In the beginning of 1822, the author arrived from Penang, to strengthen this mission; Chinese preaching was immediately commenced in four different places, the attendance at which was small. In Malay and English preaching, the brethren engaged alternately; but Mr. Slater's health failing, he was obliged to undertake a voyage to sea.

On his return in 1823, he dissolved his connection with the society, and the whole weight of the mission fell on the author. Into the Chinese schools a plan was introduced of getting the parents to pay half the expense, in order to lead them to take an interest in the education of their children, and relieve the funds of the society. This was found to work well, and has been continued ever since. A house was likewise engaged in the centre of the Chinese town, where a number of Christian books were deposited, and where the missionary spent the greatest part of each day, in exhorting all who came, to embrace the Gospel.

Having procured printers from China, books were published in the native language; among the rest, the Chinese magazine, which, having been discontinued at

Malacca by the early removal of Dr. Milne, was resumed in Batavia. Of this work one thousand copies were published monthly.

During this and the following year, Mr. Diering, a baptist brother, rendered great assistance to the mission, by preaching occasionally in Malay. A European gentleman also built a small bungalow for the accommodation of the natives on his ground, which was visited weekly by the missionary. The people, most of them natives of Bali, paid much attention, and expressed themselves delighted by the service. Whatever their real sentiments were, it was a pleasing spectacle to see Mahomedans attending to the preaching of the Gospel.

Two adjacent villages, called Tugoe and Depok, inhabited by native Christians, were also visited, and the attendance was encouraging. The origin of the latter of these villages, is worthy of record. More than a century ago, a Dutch gentleman, named Chasterling, having an estate about six miles long, by two wide, cultivated entirely by slaves, proposed to liberate them and make them a present of the land, if they would consent to be instructed, and on a profession of their faith, baptized. In compliance with his part of the proposition, he made over the whole of his estate to his former bondmen, built a church for them, established a schoolmaster over them, subject to the pastoral oversight of the Dutch clergy, and left them and their families FREE. In the beginning of the present century, the inhabitants of Depok amounted to about two hundred souls. Never was there a more quiet village, or a more inoffensive people ; and though the majority may be attached by interest or education to Christianity, a few appear to be lovers of the Saviour, and some have already found their way to the haven of rest. This village was visited by the author, almost monthly, for several successive years. Latterly, a Dutch missionary has been settled there, whose labours have been blessed to the good of the people. There are about seventy members of the church, and upwards of fifty children in the school.

About this time, some of the books published at Batavia were sent home to England, and Dr. Morrison, on looking over them, was much gratified to see this medium of conveying Christian knowledge in operation in Java. He said of them, " The tracts for children are formed on the model of Chinese school-books, only substituting Christian for pagan sentiments. One of these comprising three words in each sentence, and hence called the ' Three character classic,' is well calculated to instil into the tender mind of Chinese children correct ideas of the true God, and the Saviour of men. The Chinese magazine contains miscellaneous subjects blended with Christian truths, designed to disseminate religious and general knowledge in that quarter of the world."

That the Chinese read the books put into their hands, the missionary had frequent proofs. The method adopted to excite attention was the following :— The distributor would sometimes go, with a few tracts in his hand, and sitting down in a public place, would read to those who happened to be near ; more would soon gather round, and look on, to whom the missionary would address himself on the subject of the tract, and at the conclusion present the bye-standers with a few copies, which were in general well received. Thus the Chinese town was visited almost daily, and the opportunity embraced of addressing all who were at leisure. For this purpose, every passing circumstance was improved, and the most convenient places chosen for engaging persons in conversation. At their religious feasts, the visiting of the tombs, or sacrifices to the dead, there was no want of hearers; as on these occasions the Chinese seemed to relax their wonted eagerness for business, and listened willingly to religious discourse.

A part of this year was spent at a neighbouring town called Buitenzorg, where the Mahomedan judge of the district manifested some concern about his eternal interests. Struck with the serious manner, and humble spirit of this individual, the author entered into conversation with him; when the depravity of man was pointed out, and the question proposed, how a sinner could be saved. The Mahomedan acknowledged, that he knew no satisfactory answer to this enquiry, and stated his earnest desire to hear of some plan, by which he might obtain peace with God. He was gladly referred to the words of the apostle, " Believe on the Lord Jesus Christ, and thou shalt be saved." The next day, the Mahomedan affirmed that he had had no rest all night thinking of those words, to which he clung as a drowning man grasps a plank in the midst of the ocean. Whilst proceeding to explain these things more fully, the Mahomedan took out pen and ink, in order to write down what was said. He was told, however, that he could be furnished with books containing all these things in detail, which he might peruse at leisure. One tract written by Mr. Robinson, of Bencoolen, which contains as clear a statement of the all-important doctrine as was ever penned in any language, was read over with him, and seemed to be the very thing he wanted. This, with a Malay Bible, and a number of other tracts, were left in his hands, with the prayer that he might be guided into all truth, and enabled to find the path of heaven.

The Chinese captain of this town, was the very opposite of the Malay judge, being much taken up with the " wind and water system" of his countrymen, according to which they believe, that the fortunes of the living are greatly influenced by the position of the graves of the dead. In one of the houses, a Chinese had set up over his altar piece, a picture of Napoleon Buonaparte, in a gilt frame, to which he offered the accustomed meed of incense. Probably, in the height of his ambition, the French emperor little dreamt of being worshipped as a god.

In the year 1825, the deputation from the society, consisting of Messrs. Tyerman and Bennett, visited Java, and accompanied the author on a tour to the eastern parts of the island. The object of this journey on the part of the deputation, was to ascertain the spiritual condition of the people, and the openings that appeared for the further spread of Christianity. The design of the missionary in undertaking the tour, was to distribute Chinese books and tracts, which were very extensively circulated through every town and village along the coast, as well as in the populous cities of Samarang and Solo.

This year the cause of religion in Batavia sustained a serious loss in the decease of Mr. Diering, whose character stood singularly and deservedly high for integrity, benevolence, and piety. Though incessantly engaged in worldly business during the week, he spent his evenings and his Sabbaths in unceasing exertions to spread the Gospel, and to benefit his fellow-men; doing as much in direct labour as most missionaries, while he contributed liberally to the support of the mission. His end was remarkably peaceful and happy.

An exposition of the Ten Commandments, which had been previously delivered in the form of lectures, was drawn up and printed in Chinese. Two new tracts were also prepared, " On the New Year," and " On the Feast of the Tombs;" which having reference to the native festivals, were more attentively perused than any tracts previously circulated.

In the Chinese town, the missionary still continued his rounds, for the purpose of tract distribution and religious conversation. In these walks, persons of different tempers were met with; some utterly indifferent, careless alike whether their gods were abused or praised; while others contended for the propriety of idol-worship, in voice and gesture of no very gentle kind; urging the practice of antiquity, the doctrine of the sages, and the miracles wrought by their fabled deities. The expense to which they go, in the service of idolatry, is astonishing; all classes spending a tenth of their income in public and private sacrifices, while the funeral of a superior relative increases their outlay in a fourfold degree. A coffin of solid oak, six inches thick, the purchase of a lucky site, for a grave, frequent sacrifices to the names of the departed, and the burning of gilt paper, to serve for money in the other world, all involve an expenditure which nearly ruins a poor man. In fact, the Chinese, though the most covetous nation upon earth, are, in matters of religion, lavish in the extreme. Would that we could see such profusion in a better cause; or that Christians, who have higher motives, did not allow themselves to be outdone by heathen, in religious generosity.

When Jesus and his sufferings become the theme, the missionary is generally left to pursue his observations undisturbed, as they have seldom anything to urge against the Gospel plan of salvation.   This is, because they cannot see themselves sinners, or, at least, such sinners as stand in need of eternal redemption; and thus when the undertaking of a Saviour is alluded to, they say, " It matters not where these men begin, they are sure to end in Jesus and his salvation."   Sometimes, they affect to recognize a resemblance between Christ's merits, and the virtues of the goddess Kwan-yin, who by her fasting and austerities, rescued her family, for several generations, from the pains of hell.   At other times they observe, that their ancient sages did but tell them to be good, and there left them; but the deliverer of the west, gave up himself for the salvation of the world; by which means pardon may be extended to the guilty, and the evil be made good.   Most of them, however, pass over the subject in silence; or in the midst of a solemn discourse, interrupt the speaker, with some irrevalent question about his age, travels, or family, evidently showing that they have no heart to the doctrine propounded.   It has no charm, no interest, with them; and they say, with Esau, " What good shall this birth-right do to me ?"

In 1826, the missionary had still to complain of the difficulty of forming a Chinese congregation.   Not having been accustomed to meet, for the purpose of social worship and mutual edification, in their own country, they could hardly be induced to attend the stated ministry of foreigners, to hear doctrines that were disagreeable, and opposed to all their previous inclinations. Finding, however, that the heathen would not come to the missionary, the missionary was compelled to go to the heathen ; and what could not be effected by preaching to large assemblies, was made up by frequent addresses to small auditories.

The tracts on the feasts of the Chinese, bearing so directly on their superstitions, had awakened all the wrath of the advocates of idolatry, and one of them sat down to write a tract against the missionary.   In this, he argued, that it was monstrous in barbarians to attempt to improve the inhabitants of the celestial empire, when they were so miserably deficient themselves. Thus, introducing among the Chinese the poisonous drug, opium, for their own benefit, to the injury of others, they were deficient in benevolence : sending their fleets and armies, to rob other nations of their possessions, they could make no pretensions to rectitude ; allowing men and women to mix in society, and walk arm in arm through the streets, they shewed that they had not the least sense of propriety ; and, rejecting the doctrines of the ancient kings, they were far from displaying wisdom : indeed truth was the only good quality to which they could lay the least claim. Deficient, therefore, in four out of five of the cardinal virtues, how could they expect to renovate others.   Then, while foreigners lavished much money in circulating books for the renovation of the age, they made no scruple of trampling printed paper under foot, by which they shewed their disrespect for the inventors of letters. Further, these would-be exhorters of the world, were themselves deficient in filial piety, forgetting their parents as soon as dead, putting them off with deal coffins, only an inch thick, and never so much as once sacrificing to their manes, or burning the smallest trifle of gilt paper, for their support in the future world. And, lastly, they allowed the rich and noble to enter office, without passing through the literary examinations, and did not throw open the road to advancement to the poorest and meanest in the land; by all which it appeared, that foreigners were inferior to the Chinese, and, therefore, the most unfit to instruct them.

Some of these arguments had peculiar force, and all of them weighed much with the Chinese. It was, therefore, necessary for the missionary to defend himself, by publishing a few familiar dialogues, in which these objections were introduced, with the most conclusive answers that could be found. The justice of their remarks, respecting European aggressions and corruptions, was, of course, admitted, while the connection of missionaries with those evils was utterly denied. The other pleas were met by such reasonings, as would suggest themselves to any cursory observer; but it would be impossible for a stranger to conceive what a hold these apparently absurd scruples have upon the Chinese mind. The answer, however, was attentively read, and frequently formed the subject of discussion.

This year, a tour was performed along the eastern coast of Java, touching at Tagal, Samarang, and Soerabaya. The Chinese, at the latter place, appeared to be a more intelligent class of men, than on other parts of Java; and had more leisure, as well as inclination, for religious enquiry. One Chinese family, of considerable influence, has, for six generations, abstained from the worship of images; and an aged gentleman, of that nation, listened to the missionary, with great attention, expressing himself in a way which was hardly to be expected from one who had been brought up a heathen. A small body of Dutch Christians, in Soerabaya, had formed themselves into a missionary society, holding regular meetings for business and prayer, and making every effort to disseminate religious truth amongst the heathen. For this purpose, they had composed a number of evangelical tracts, in the Malay and Javanese languages. They had even translated the New Testament into low Malay, and raised funds for the printing of it. The author, in conjunction with the Dutch minister at Batavia, gave this version a thorough revision; and, having obtained the use of the government printing-office, carried an edition of it through the press.

During this journey, a visit was paid to the Tengger mountains, in the neighbourhood of Passerwang. These consist of a range of hills, about 6,000 feet above the level of the sea, inhabited by an aboriginal race, who, when the Mussulman arms prevailed in Java, fled to the hills, and refused, either through fear or persuasion, to embrace Mahomedanism. These people amount to several thousands, governed by laws and customs of their own. Their religion consists of a sort of Hindooism, mixed up with a peculiar veneration for fire, manifested by their regard to the domestic stove, the erection of altars towards the rising sun, and their reverence for a volcanic mountain, which towers above their range of hills, and is always in slow, but terrific action. The author ascended to the edge of the crater, with some of the awe-struck villagers, and saw the effect which the universal stillness, the entire absence of all animal or vegetable life, and the deep roaring of the volcano, produced over the savage mind. The crater was designated Bromo, to which they addressed a prayer, throwing various offerings into the vast orifice, and entreating preservation from its half-smothered fires. Around the peak of Bromo, and still at an immense elevation, was an extensive flat of sand, which the wind had formed into gentle undulations, resembling precisely a sheet of water, but as hard as the solid ground. The natives call it the " sand sea."

The governor-general, Baron Van der Capellan, pointed out these villages, as the most eligible field for missionary exertions on the island of Java; the inhabitants were exempted from Mahomedan prejudices, and their Hindoo superstitions were merely traditional reminiscencies; they were far removed from the contamination which foreign intercourse engenders; and already possessed a simplicity of manners quite favourable to the introduction of the Gospel; while the extreme salubrity of the climate, and the splendour of the surrounding scenery, were sufficient to invite and reward the residence of a missionary. But, alas! this fertile, peaceful, beauteous region is left, to this day, without a single effort to evangelize its inhabitants, beyond the distribution of a few tracts in the Javanese language, and a transitory annunciation of the Gospel.

In the year 1827, the author was obligingly furnished with the loan of some Japanese books, calculated to throw light on that important language. Both Drs. Morrison and Milne had long desired to get some acquaintance with the Japanese tongue, in order to ascertain whether the present version of the Chinese Scriptures would do for that people. As the owner of the books gave full permission to copy them, the author devoted his whole attention to this subject, besides employing a dozen Chinese to assist him in the undertaking. The most important of the works, appeared to be those on philology; comprising a Dutch, Chinese, and Japanese dictionary, drawn up by the Japanese themselves; a Japanese, Chinese and Dutch dictionary, arranged according to the Japanese alphabet; two or three Chinese and Japanese dictionaries, classed according to the Chinese radicals; and, lastly, a Japanese and Chinese dictionary, arranged according to the native alphabet, appended to which were numerous graphical representations of arms and implements, manners and customs, history and adventures, geography and astronomy, plates, maps, and charts; in short, a complete encyclopœdia. In addition to the dictionaries, were the " Four Books" of Confucius, in Chinese, interlined with a Japanese translation. This work was of incalculable importance, as shewing, that Chinese books, as they stand, are not intelligible to the mass of the Japanese, and need some addition, in order to general circulation. Some original works in the Japanese language, were also transcribed; such as historical novels, and several works on the medicine, botany, mineralogy, history, and statistics of Japan.

It appeared from a comparison of these, that the Chinese character was not in general use, in Japan, except when interlined with Japanese. That the latter language differed from the former, in being alphabetic and polysyllabic; and that the Japanese alphabet consisted of forty-seven letters, of which there were two forms, like our printed letters and running hand; the former most frequently used in connection with Chinese characters, and the latter generally standing alone. It was thought a good omen, that books began to be brought from a country which had been hitherto sealed against the Gospel—no missionary was allowed to approach its shores, neither could any native come from thence. Little was known of their language, by the propagators of Christianity, and little did the Japanese know of our religion, as it really is. But this looked like a harbinger of better days. The travelling westward of Japanese books, seemed to invite the travelling eastward of missionaries. The word Japan, in the native language, means " the rising of the sun," and reminds us of the prophecy of Isaiah, " men shall fear Jehovah from the west, and his glory from the rising of the sun."

After copying these works, the author proceeded to the compilation of an English and Japanese vocabulary, which was afterwards printed. This little work does not profess to present a full and extensive developement of the language, and enters very little into its structure or character : it is hoped, however, that it may afford some assistance to future labourers, endeavouring to investigate that rich and copious tongue, with a view to convey the treasures of divine inspiration into it. Without intercourse and conversation with the people, however, it was impossible to proceed further in the acquisition of the Japanese language, and the study of it gave way to more immediate and imperious claims on time and attention.

An effort was made, this year, to raise a Chinese congregation, by attending, statedly, at a little building by the roadside. Of the multitudes that passed by, some were induced to step in, till the place became full. They were generally stragglers, however, who sat down for a few minutes, and then went away, to have their places supplied by others; while few stopped to hear the service out, or came a second time.

Seeing the Chinese engaged in an idol feast, the missionary tried the effect of irony upon them. He pointed out the folly of providing a feast for hungry ghosts, without knowing whether they were hungry, or might be permitted to partake of it, or would be benefited by it. He told them first to ascertain the wants of the spiritual world; then to send invitations to each separate individual; and, finally, to provide an allowance of ethereal food, such as their ghostly friends might be able to digest; but not to go to work in the dark, as they were then doing. On hearing this, they were confused; some endeavoured to frame an answer; but the major part advised to leave the matter alone, lest they should be too clearly convinced of their error.

During the year 1829, the missionary still continued to testify, that there was none other name given under heaven, whereby men could be saved, but the name of Christ Jesus. His chief effort, in dependance on divine aid, was to convince the people of sin, and point them to the Saviour; for he found, that though he might bring them to laugh, or to cry, at the absurdities and extravagances of their idolatry, yet, unless they could be led to see the exceeding sinfulness of sin, all other admissions were of little avail. In the regular preaching of the Gospel, there was an increased seriousness, and a growing acquaintance with Christianity. Some of the Amboynese, who attended the mission chapel, became sedulous in instructing their children, and in recommending religion to their neighbours.

This year the art of lithography was called in to aid the diffusion of Gospel truth, which rendered the missionaries independent of native type-cutters, and was found to be much cheaper than the former mode of printing by means of wooden blocks.

Among the rest of the chinese works published by this means, was a system of comparative chronology, with the Chinese and European accounts exhibited in parallel columns. The similarity between the more authentic records of the Chinese, and the Scripture history, is remarkable. According to both, the human race sprang from one individual, the flood occurred about the same time, preceded by the discovery of metals, and followed by that of wine. The seven years' famine of Egypt nearly synchronize with those of China; and Sampson's strength and fall have their counterpart in the east. This work was drawn up to correct the vain boasting of the Chinese, and to shew them that we possess records four thousand years earlier that the Christian era.

A fount of Javanese types were this year cast by the author, who had to superintend the cutting of the punches, the striking of the matrices, the reduction and composition of the metal, and the adjustment of the whole; and considering the few facilities existing in a foreign colony, for executing works of art and utility, the want of proper instruments and materials, together with the inexperience of those engaged, it will easily be seen, that the undertaking must have been attended with immense trouble.

In the month of August, this year, the author set sail with a large cargo of books, intending to accompany Messrs. Tomlin and Gutzlaff to Siam, but arrived at Singapore two days after their departure. Finding it impossible to follow them, a passage was taken in a

Chinese praw, without deck, or shelter, for the east coast of the Malayan peninsula. The shore, from Point Romania northward, is covered with an impenetrable jungle, off which lie the islands of Pulo Tinggi and Pulo Timoan, inhabited for the most part, by pirates. The entrance to the river of Pahang is picturesque, but the town has a miserable appearance. The Chinese houses stretch themselves along the southern bank of the river, and the Malay cottages skirt the northern. The Chinese are the only labourers and shopkeepers, while the Malays strut about in silken breeches and glazed cloths, as if they were never born for work. The residence of the rajah is situated in the midst of the Malay huts, and, covered with plate tin, glitters splendidly under a burning sun. Extensive rice fields occupy the attention of the peasantry, and mining operations employ the energies of the Chinese settlers. The tin mines are at the distance of several days' journey in the interior, where that metal is found both plentiful and pure, about seventy-five tons of which are exported monthly. From the tin to the gold mines, the journey occupies twenty days more; at the back of which is a chain of mountains, skirting the colony of Malacca. There cannot be less than five thousand Chinese in the territory of Pahang, who are all given up to the smoking of opium, wasting at the same time their gains and their constitution. The Malay rajah oppresses them, in every possible way, and demands about twelve pounds sterling from every individual on his return to his native land.

Between Pahang and Tringano, the Chinese boat, in which the author sailed, was attacked by two pirate praws. They advanced during a calm, by means of double banks of oars, and were each provided with a battery, mounting a six-pounder, with which they kept up a smart fire. The Chinese were very cool on the occasion, plying their oars with the utmost steadiness, while the master and mate returned the fire of the enemy. A desperate conflict was expected, as the Chinese, knowing that no quarter would be given, were prepared to fight for their property and their lives. A merciful providence, however, interfered; and a breeze springing up, the Chinese caught the favouring gale, and were soon out of sight of their opponents.

The town of Tringano is more populous and busy than Pahang, though its territory is much smaller, and possesses no gold mines. It has, however, some plantations of pepper, and yields a few tons of buffalo butter; while dried fish and tortoise-shell help to increase their list of exports. Situated half way between Malacca and Siam, it was formerly a place of great trade, but since the establishment of Singapore, Tringano is sinking into insignificance. The present rajah has raised himself to the throne, to the exclusion of his elder brother's children; but having obtained the sanction of the Siamese government, no one presumes to dispute his usurped possession. There appears to be no court of justice, but causes are settled according to the will of the ruler, and vengeance falls instantly on the supposed criminals, dictated chiefly by the pride or passion of the royal judge. Murder, of all other crimes, seems to be most leniently dealt with; hence daily assassinations occur, which are frequently passed over, as proofs of the courage of the perpetrators, or of the demerits of the victims. Such is the insecurity of person and property, that every individual carries half a dozen weapons about him; and no man dares make known the extent of his possessions, for fear of losing them.   The Chinese are especially oppressed by their Malayan chiefs, who take their choicest goods, and fairest daughters, without the least chance of redress; but the abject colonists tamely submit to this, with the hope of making up by deceit what they lose by violence. The shops in Tringano are provided with railings, like prison bars, through which the purchaser throws his money, previous to receiving his goods; and every article is hastily removed to the inner apartments, immediately a follower of the rajah appears, as these harpies insist on purchasing all that is valuable, without the slightest intention of paying for it.

Northward of Tringano, lies the rich and populous country of Klintan, which owing to its extensive gold mines, has lately risen to great importance.   Its gold is reckoned the best on the coast; but the rajah levies a duty of fifty dollars on all Chinese vessels, great and small, with the view, it is said, of discouraging the introduction of opium, which would prove the bane of his rising state.

Patani, the next state to the northward, was once an important settlement, having had an English and Dutch factory there, which carried on an extensive trade with China; its grandeur is, however, fled, and its trade annihilated.   Repeated attacks from the Siamese have impoverished the country.   The old town is a heap of ruins, and the natives have taken up their residence on the banks of a small river, deeply imbedded in the jungle.   The country is rich and fertile, and the precious metals easily procurable; yet

owing to war and anarchy, all is wildness and confusion. The people of Patani are so intolerably lazy,
that it is impossible to procure labourers of any sort,
while the Chinese are the only workers of the mines.

Songŏra, is the first regular Siamese town on the
coast, the approach to which is exceedingly romantic ;
pagodas gild the tops of the hills, and files of Siamese
junks moored along the shores, present a lively and
interesting appearance. There is no regular custom
house, but a present is expected on the arrival of a
vessel, and the first offer of the cargo must be made
to the ruler. The town consists of substantial houses,
laid out in regular streets, and was once surrounded
by a wooden palisade. Several Chinese temples stand
at the head of the different ways ; and large Siamese
pagodas peep through the groves : the adherents of
both are worshippers of Buddha. The Siamese priests
swarm ; every morning the street is yellow with them,
going about to beg for their daily alms. They are
of all ages and ranks, living together in cloisters and
idleness. No business must occupy the attention of
the holy brotherhood, lest their minds should be taken
off from the repetition of the name of Buddha, which
elevates them to the highest pinnacle of holiness and
felicity.

Leaving the peninsula, the author proceeded to the
west coast of Borneo, and landed at Pontianak. This
settlement was first established by an enterprising
Arab, who, after cutting off a French ship, fixed his
residence at the confluence of two mighty rivers, coming
from Landak and Sangow, yielding gold and diamonds.
Here he soon attracted, by his liberality, a number of

followers, and took the title of sultan of Pontianak. The ruler of Landak, alarmed at his encroachments, made a grant of the land, on which the new town was built, to the sultan of Bantam, who surrendered it to the Dutch; and it has ever since been occupied as an European settlement. The Dutch fort stands on the south side of the Sangow river, flanked by the Chinese town; while the sultan's palace is built on the tongue of land which separates the two streams, surrounded by native huts built on poles or rafts, which float on the surface of the water and rise and fall with the tide. The Malay population is about twenty thousand; the Bugguese, five; and the Chinese, two. The interior of the country is peopled with a race of cannibals, called Dayaks, who are generally tyrannized over by the Malays; hence they detest the Mahomedan religion; and, being tired of their own, have in some instances adopted that of the Chinese. These people present a most inviting field for missionary operations, and our German and American brethren have already begun to labour among them.

The Dayaks, in the residency of Pontianak alone, amount to 240,000, besides those which are to be found in the north and south-eastern parts of the island. They are a wild race, wearing no clothes, and utterly destitute of civilization. Their institutions are so sanguinary, that no young man can marry, unless he bring two or three human heads as a dowry. These trophies are received by the women with triumph, who suck the blood that may be yet dripping from them, and adorn their houses with the skulls, and their necks with the teeth of the slaughtered victims. They are, however, desirous of instruction, and were missionary efforts for their benefit persevered in, the result might be as favourable, and the success as glorious, as among the inhabitants of the South Sea islands.

The Chinese having discovered that the precious metals abound in Borneo, have been attracted thither in great numbers. Their principal settlements are at Mandoor and Montrado, but they have established themselves at Landak and Sangow. The author visited Mandoor, which he found a flourishing town, inhabited wholly by Chinese, under a government and laws of their own choosing. The people employ themselves in collecting gold dust from the neighbourhood, which lies a few fathoms beneath the surface, in a strata of sand, under a bed of yellow clay. The Chinese commence by removing all the superincumbent earth, and carrying out the sand in baskets, deposit it in an inclined trough, subjected to a rapid stream of water, which carries away the sand, and allows the gold to sink to the bottom. When all the sand is thus taken out, and washed away, they collect the gold and carry it to market. It is generally found in fine dust, sometimes in particles as large as a pea, and some pieces have been discovered about the size of a hen's egg. The gold is valued at nearly three pounds the ounce. Much of the ground in the neighbourhood of Mandoor, has been turned inside out, and exhausted of the precious metal, which the Chinese calculate will be expended in forty years' time. They have a superstitious notion, that the gold is capable of running away, if the gods be displeased, or their ancestors neglected; hence they send much money to China, to keep up the accustomed sacrifices, and will not carry an umbrella near the mines, lest the local deities should be displeased.

Montrado is more populous than Mandoor, and was the first Chinese settlement on the coast. The inhabitants are turbulent and intractable, having once waged war with the Dutch, when they invested the fort at Pontianak, and surprised the resident at Sankaowang; on both of which occasions they nearly annihilated the European power on the coast. Peace has since been concluded; but a bitter feeling is left, which breaks out into frequent expressions of distrust and revenge.

Sambas lies on the river of the same name, navigable for vessels of three hundred tons burthen, thirty miles from the mouth. This was formerly a nest of pirates, the sultan of which gloried in mastering as many vessels as he could. The Bengal government chastised him, a few years ago, by burning his whole settlement; since which time the Dutch have established themselves there. The state of morals in this place is wretched, and the Chinese inhabiting it are idle, voluptuous, and given to gaming.

To the northward of Sambas, barbarism and piracy prevail: hundreds of streams here empty themselves into the ocean, from which issue the marauding Dayaks, seeking only for iron and heads. Every human being they meet with is sacrificed to their fury, and the heads carried home in triumph, as testimonials of their valour.

The interior of Borneo swarms with independent rulers; in the residency of Pontianak alone there are about two hundred and fifty sovereign princes, whom the Europeans set up or put down at pleasure; each of them, however, pleading for the divine right of kings, and exercising the power of life and death in their petty dominions.

The Chinese in all these parts amount to twenty-five

thousand; who received the Scriptures and books with great cheerfulness and avidity. Their chiefs assisted the author in his journies, and entertained him hospitably in their dwellings. Some suspicion was at first excited, at the unusual appearance of a European in those parts : but immediately they were addressed in their own language, their apprehensions vanished, and the stranger became a friend. The Chinese captain of Mandoor placed the author at the head of his table, afforded him guides and protection through the mining district, and presented him with a gold ring on his departure. A New Testament was found entire in the interior of Borneo, presented ten years before, which bore evident marks of having been frequently perused.

Notwithstanding the wide circulation of religious truth, the missionary, on his return to his station, lamented his want of success, and sighed for more substantial evidence of usefulness. When one day sitting in his study, during the heat of the meridian sun, he observed a stranger enter, and sit down by his side. Having been frequently interrupted by stragglers, who came merely to waste time, no notice was taken of the visitor, and the usual studies were pursued. After waiting awhile, the stranger broke the silence, by asking, what he must do to obtain the salvation of his soul. The missionary laid down his pen, and thought of that passage, " When the Lord bringeth back the captivity of Zion, we were like them that dream:" it appeared so like a dream, to hear a sceptical Chinese enquire about the salvation of his soul. They seldom believe that they have a soul, and still less concern themselves about its destinies. He was of course directed to the right source for help, and pointed to the " Lamb of God,

which taketh away the sin of the world." He heard
with attention, and interest. His abode was discovered,
and frequently visited. His name was Lae San-tsoo.
He grew rapidly in spiritual knowledge; and drew up
a sketch of his views on religion. Speaking of trusting
to Christ, and not to our own merits, he said, " How
can a man think of trusting to his own righteousness?
why, it is like seeking shelter under one's own shadow; we may stoop to the very ground, and the lower
we bend, we find the shade still beneath us: but if a
man flee to the shadow of a great rock, or a wide spreading tree, he will find abundant shelter from the rays of
the noon-day sun. So human merits are unavailing,
and Christ alone able to save to the uttermost, those
who come unto God by Him." This man was early
removed by a stroke of apoplexy, which carried him so
suddenly away, that the missionary was not aware of
his illness, before he heard that he was gone.

A different effect was produced in the mind of another heathen, by the statement that Confucius knew
little or nothing of the unseen world, because, when
asked concerning it, he evaded the question, and bade
his disciples attend more particularly to the duties of
life. At the mention of this, the pagan's wrath was en-
kindled: he declared, that the inference was false; that
the missionary had slandered the memory of the sage,
and that if the latter were aware of it, he would immediately petition the king of Hades, to have the ca-
lumniator's tongue cut out, and himself consigned to
the lowest pit of Pandemonium, not to be born into the
world again for a thousand ages. Had the missionary
contented himself with studying the doctrines of the
philosopher in the language of China, he would have

benefited himself, and been applauded by others; but
now that he set himself up for a judge, and opposed the
sage, he was the veriest sinner upon the face of the
earth, who, if he fell into the hands of the rulers of
China, would be made to suffer the worst of deaths.
When the Christian denounced idolatry, and declared
his determination to worship the Supreme God alone,
the Confucian exclaimed, " I do not think that the
Supreme God would be worshipped by you, or accept
your services. You call upon heaven, but heaven is
high, and cannot hear you; you kneel before the Supreme, but the clouds are impenetrable, and he cannot
see you." At length, softening down, he said, " I see,
sir, that your anxiety to instruct the Chinese, originates
in a kind intention; but your books are filled with a
few cunning remarks on an obtruse subject, mixed up
with much that is unfounded. Our ancient philosophers taught the doctrine of filial piety, but left the
mysterious subject of spiritual beings alone as not
intimately connected with the happiness of the people.
In your books, every expression tends to this point;
while the duties of the human relations are seldom
referred to. This is neglecting the important, and
caring about the insignificant. Confucius cautioned
men against paying too much attention to religious ceremonies, and forbad their flattering the gods to procure
protection; but if ignorant people will busy themselves
in begging for blessings, they only squander their own
time and money, and do no harm to others; why
then trouble one's self about them? The religious
practices of men are as various as their minds; let
every one follow his own inclinations, and not interfere
with others."

2 A 2

In the close of 1829, the author visited Bali, accompanied by Mr. Tomlin. The people of that island were found in a state of great ignorance and barbarity. Their religion is Hindooism, and 'their priests, Brahmins. The island is divided into eight states, inhabited by nearly a million of people. There are several upland lakes, which supply the plains with an abundance of water, for the irrigation of the rice fields. These constitute the riches of Bali: and the kings of the island, establishing themselves on their borders, keep the inhabitants in complete order, by commanding their supply of water. The people of Bali are much given to opium-smoking and cock-fighting. The ground is so productive, that there is little poverty ; and yet the people are so indolent, that there is less wealth. The female sex is much oppressed, being obliged to do all the work of the house, the market, and the field; while the only reward they get for their toil, is the privilege of burning with the dead bodies of their husbands. This is sometimes done to an extent unequalled even in India; for on particular occasions, fifty or sixty women are sacrificed, at once, on the funeral pile. These are either stabbed and burnt, or leap alive into the flaming pit, from which there is no escape.

During this journey, great quantities of Chinese and Javanese tracts were circulated, which were all well received. The health of the author, however, suffered considerably on this tour, and a jungle fever was caught, which undermined his constitution, and, finally, compelled a return to Europe.

In the year 1831, a new and handsome chapel was erected at Batavia, which was opened, in the month of September, by a sermon from the Rev. Archdeacon

Scott. In this building, Episcopalians, Independents, and Baptists, have joined in the work of proclaiming a crucified Saviour; and Europeans and Asiatics combined in celebrating his love.

Besides preaching in the chapel, the missionary addressed several hundred Malay convicts on the Sunday afternoons. They assembled in their chains, under the shade of a few trees, and sitting on the ground, listened with remarkable eagerness to the news of salvation. They could not, at first, understand for what purpose they were congregated. When they heard their sins exposed, they thought the missionary was about to accuse them to the government, to get a protraction of their punishment; and when they were told of the liberty wherewith Christ makes us free, they imagined that their chains were to be knocked off, and they restored to liberty. They soon discovered, however, the object of the service, and paid the more serious attention. One of them, on his death-bed, declared his faith in that Saviour, whom he had heard preached under the trees; and when told by his companions that he ought to call upon Mahomed, he replied, " No ; Jesus is the only Saviour, and I desire to honour him alone."

This year Lukas Monton, a native of Menado, in the island of Celebes, applied for admission into the church. This young man is endowed with a fervent zeal for the diffusion of the Gospel, urging his countrymen to attend the means of grace, and distributing tracts among the Chinese and Malays, in great abundance. He sometimes travels to distant towns and villages, standing up in the streets and market-places, to exhort the multitude. His address is bold, and his gift in prayer, fluent. An elderly woman, of Dutch extraction, born in Samarang, joined the church at the same time, and has continued zealous and faithful ever since.

Malay tracts, about this time, came into great demand: sometimes, one hundred and fifty were put into the hands of the people, on a single market day. To those who know the deadly prejudices of the Mahomedans against Christianity, and who have been accustomed to see them shun a tract, as they would the plague, this appeared a great change. It was to be attributed, under God, to the practice of posting little hand-bills about the town, containing passages of Scripture, and brief exhortations; which, being perceived to be of a harmless character, induced the natives to take books the more readily; and, after a while, to grasp them eagerly on every occasion.

The Chinese were, with difficulty, brought to see the evil of sin. The word *sin*, in their language, being synonymous with crime, they seldom think that they are chargeable with sin, unless guilty of some crime against the state. Thus, murder, arson, theft, and adultery, are considered sinful; but lying, fornication, gaming, and covetousness, are seldom looked on as evils. They openly plead for the practice of cheating in business; and think that there is no harm in opium smoking, so long as they purchase it with their own money. The only evils, with which they charge themselves, are, quitting their native land, while their parents are alive, being without posterity, treading on an ant, abusing printed paper, eating beef, and leaving hungry ghosts to starve. Thus, not knowing the real nature of sin, they have no sense of the need of a Saviour, and hear of his dying love without emotion.

In the year 1833, six native soldiers, born in Menado, were baptized; and four more of those baptized in infancy, were admitted to church-fellowship. An orphan school was established for the descendants of Europeans, which has been liberally supported. Premises were purchased, buildings erected, and thirty children placed on the foundation, who have been boarded, clothed, and educated, without the least expense to the missionary society.

In 1834, one country-born was admitted to the church, and six natives of Menado, baptized. Another native soldier was baptized in the presence of the captain and the whole company, when the service was very solemn and impressive.

In the year 1835, two more of the native Christians joined the church; and one Mahomedan woman was baptized. During the same year, the author visited China, leaving the station under the charge of his assistant, Mr. W. Young, while Lukas Monton undertook a voyage to Benjarmasin, on the island of Borneo, accompanied by Mr. Barenstein, a German missionary. The town of Benjarmasin contains several hundred houses; but the chief population consists of Biajoos, a tribe of Dayaks, who live in the interior. After supplying the Chinese and Malays with books, the travellers visited the Dayaks, who were glad to receive them. Listening to their discourse on divine things, the Dayaks said, " This is the true doctrine, and suits us better than the teaching of the Mahomedans, which we do not understand." The Dayaks, how-

ever, were unwilling that the missionaries should come
and live amongst them, unless they would make a
covenant by blood; which consisted in drawing a few
drops of blood from the arms of the chiefs and missionaries, into four cups of water, which were drunk by
the respective parties, in the presence of great crowds.
When the agreement was thus ratified, the Dayaks
embraced the strangers, and said, " Let us be friends
for ever, and may God help the Dayaks to obtain the
knowledge of religion from the missionaries." After
this, the chiefs assured the brethren that they might
dwell with them without fear, promising to defend them
with their life's blood, and to die, themselves, sooner
than they would see the missionaries slain. This mission has since been vigorously prosecuted by our German brethren sent out by the Rhenish Missionary
Society.

A short time previous to the author's quitting Batavia, he was accosted by a respectable Chinese, requesting baptism. On being asked whence he came, and
why he desired admission to that ordinance, he replied,
that he was born in Amboyna, where he had enjoyed the
benefit of Mr. Kam's ministry. He was able to read
the Scriptures in the Malay language, and displayed a
very extensive acquaintance with religious truth. His
views of the all-sufficiency of Christ, and his deep feeling of anxiety to be intimately connected with the
Saviour and his people, induced the missionary to baptize him.

CHAPTER XIV.

VOYAGES UP THE COAST OF CHINA.

SUMMARY OF MISSIONARY ATTEMPTS IN THE COLONIES—DESIRE TO BENEFIT THE MOTHER COUNTRY — GUTZLAFF'S VOYAGES — DIFFERENT VIEWS — ANXIETY FOR MORE INFORMATION — AUTHOR'S ARRIVAL IN CANTON — DISCUSSION REGARDING OPIUM VESSELS — REASONS FOR NOT EMBARKING IN THEM — AS DISREPUTABLE, INCONVENIENT, AND INVOLVING THE MISSIONARY IN DIFFICULTY — THE PROPRIETY OF HIRING A VESSEL, OR PURCHASING A MISSIONARY SHIP — OFFER OF THE HURON — PREPARATIONS FOR DEPARTURE.

PROTESTANT missionaries in their attempts to operate on China limited their efforts, for a quarter of a century, to those parts where Europeans generally reside, or where the British and Dutch governments afforded protection. Considering themselves excluded from the interior of the empire and finding a host of Chinese emigrants in the various countries of the Malayan archipelago, they aimed first to enlighten these with the hope that, if properly instructed and influenced, they would, on their return to their native land, carry with them the Gospel they had learned, and spread it among their countrymen. With this view, our brethren established themselves in the various colonies around China, studied the language, set up schools and seminaries, wrote and printed books, conversed extensively with the people, and tried to collect congregations, to whom they might preach the word of life. Since the commencement of their missions, they have translated the holy Scriptures, and printed two thousand complete Bibles, ten thousand Testaments, thirty thousand separate books of Scripture, and upwards of half a million of tracts in the Chinese language; besides four thousand Testaments, and one hundred and fifty thousand tracts in the languages of the Malayan archipelago, comprising upwards of eight thousand leaves of new matter, and twenty millions of printed pages. About ten thousand children have passed through the mission schools; nearly one hundred persons have been baptized, and several native preachers raised up, one of whom has proclaimed the Gospel to his countrymen in the interior of the empire, and endured persecution for the sake of Jesus. Such a result cannot but be gratifying to the friends of missions, and on a review of it, the labourers employed would "thank God and take courage."

But all this is far from satisfying the desires of the ardent missionary, or from accomplishing the object for which he went forth. Whatever be done in the colonies, the friends of China cannot be content until some impression be made upon the mother country; and as the emigrants are but a sprinkling compared with the bulk of the population, so the converts from among the colonists bear but a small proportion to the salvation of the whole empire.

Whilst the rest of the brethren were employed in the more settled and sedentary part of missionary work, it pleased God to stir up one to attempt the hazardous enterprize of introducing the Gospel into China itself. Mr. Gutzlaff, a German missionary, sent out by the Netherlands Missionary Society, having first made his way to Siam, and laboured for two years in that kingdom with some evidence of success, took his passage in 1831, in a native vessel, for the port of Teën-tsin, within two days' journey of Peking. He had with him a large quantity of Christian books, and a small stock of European medicines. Clad occasionally in a Chinese dress, and adopting the name of one the native clans, he was recognized as a member of that great nation. Being in a weak state of health, exposed to the jealousy and treachery of the natives, and embarked in a frail vessel, unskilfully managed, he was frequently in imminent danger; but was graciously preserved from these and all other hazards, till he arrived at the destined port. Living on shore at the town of Teën-tsin, he was announced as a " a son of the western ocean," who had been subjected to the civilizing influence of the celestials, and who came to benefit them in return by his knowledge of medicine. He attracted so many visitors to the house where he was residing, that a person offered to purchase him of the captain of the junk for a large sum, with the view of drawing customers to his shop. He spent nearly a month at this place, and an equal period in Chinese Tartary, after which he returned to Macao.

In the following year, Mr. G. embarked in the Lord Amherst, a ship chartered by the East India Company, and under the charge of one of their supercargoes. The voyagers proceeded along the whole coast of China, Formosa, Corea, and Loo-Choo. They were invariably hailed with joy by the people, and flattered or feared by the mandarins, as interest or policy seemed to prompt; many books were distributed, but the attempt to open out a new channel for regular trade, completely failed. Another voyage was undertaken in

1833, in the Sylph; and subsequently, several others, during successive years; on all of which occasions books were distributed, in great numbers, to the high gratification of the people. The accounts of these voyages, which were published to the world, struck most of our English readers with amazement. It had long been supposed, that China was hermetically sealed against the propagators of divine truth; that it would be death to set foot on her shores; and madness to attempt to diffuse the Gospel in those regions. But here was a man, who had gone and returned unhurt; had maintained an extensive intercourse with the people; had resided, for months together, in their cities and provinces; had met the far-famed and much dreaded mandarins; and instead of being arrested, imprisoned, and sent back in a cage to Canton, had been, in every instance, treated with civility, and, sometimes, with respect. What knowledge of medicine and navigation he possessed, had won the confidence of multitudes, who saw and felt his superiority to their own pretenders to those sciences, and who were willing to harbour and protect him for the sake of his attainments. It was objected, on the other hand, however, that Mr. G. was a man of such an ardent temperament, enterprising spirit, and versatile genius, that he might safely venture where others dared not go, and throw himself into the midst of difficulties, from which his ingenuity might extricate him: while his perfect knowledge of the language, intimate acquaintance with the people, and somewhat similar cast of features with the Chinese, might enable him to do, what no one else could attempt. There were not a few, also, who insinuated that his lively imagination, and confident expectation, had led

him to give too high a colouring to things; while his
zeal had prompted him to state what he wished or contemplated, rather than what he actually experienced.
There were others, again, who mistook his language,
or improved upon his statements, and made him responsible for their misapprehensions and enlargements.

Further, the different state of things existing in
those parts, to which Europeans had lawful access,
compared with what was said to be the cause where
there were only interlopers, greatly perplexed the generality. When it was heard, that the missionaries in
Canton were subjected to surveillance, restriction, and
insult, while the native converts were obliged to flee
for their lives; the public could not understand how it
was, that Gutzlaff could wander, from place to place,
along the coasts of that empire, and distribute thousands of tracts, in the cities and towns of the north, in
defiance of imperial authority and magisterial interference. Judging of legislative enactments and judicial
processes, by what exists in our own country, English
readers could not conceive it possible that laws could
be broken, and its guardians set at nought, with impu-
nity. There was a difference of opinion, therefore, on
the subject; some contending, that China was, and
others that it was not, open to the efforts of missionaries to propagate the Gospel.

Anxious to set this question at rest, the directors of
the missionary society encouraged the author to undertake a voyage along the coast of China, to distribute
Scriptures and tracts, and to ascertain the openings
which existed, for the propagation of the Gospel, in
that empire. The Bible Society, also, authorized the
late Dr. Morrison, to go to the extent of two hundred

pounds, in promoting the circulation of the Scriptures; so that both those institutions concurred in patronizing the proposed undertaking. Not that either Committee imagined, that China was to be evangelized by such desultory labours, or dreamed of calculating the number of converts by the amount of Bible or tract distribution; but, because they imagined that barriers and restrictions would, by that means, be broken down, the minds of the people become gradually enlightened, and the government be led eventually to sanction what the mass of their subjects might be induced to adopt. More knowledge of the country might likewise be gained, and confidence inspired in the breasts of missionaries, who might advance, step by step, to more extensive and permanent efforts for the diffusion and establishment of the truth.

The catholic missionaries had once no knowledge of, or adherents in China; but went forth, in the first instance, unprotected; and gaining friends wherever they turned, were by them screened and supported, till they had secured a footing, and were with difficulty expelled. Further, when the decree went forth, to banish their agents, and destroy their churches, they still found means to work their way into the provinces, because they already knew the road, and had established an acquaintance with thousands of the inhabitants. It is possible, that the means they used to escape the notice of the government, and to ingratiate themselves with the people, were such as protestant missionaries could not employ; but the knowledge of the country, and familiarity with the inhabitants, was the main secret of their success; and, if we wish to stand on the same vantage ground, we must go thither frequently, and protract our stay, until we can at length sit down and cultivate the field. The first Romish missionaries recommended themselves by their scientific acquirements;—modern protestant labourers contemplate winning their way by benevolent efforts;—the healing of the sick and the instruction of the ignorant, may produce as deep an impression on the minds of the Chinese, as the calculation of eclipses, or the arrangement of the calendar; and seeking alone the glory of God, and the salvation of man, we may confidently look for a blessing on our endeavours.

On the author's arrival in Canton, in the summer of 1835, he was welcomed by the American missionaries, who had been labouring there for several years, and introduced, by them, to the acquaintance of D. W. C. Oliphant, Esq. an American merchant, of high respectability, and well-known benevolence, who took great interest in the propagation of the Gospel in China. The conversation immediately turned on the propriety of a voyage up the coast. There was no question about the importance of the undertaking, as it appeared almost the only mode of reaching the mass of the Chinese people; but great difficulties appeared in the way, the principal of which was the want of a suitable vessel, in which the voyage could be made. A passage in the opium ships, proceeding in that direction, appeared very objectionable; as the habits of such vessels. the nature of the intercourse carried on by them, and the class of the Chinese, with whom they came in contact, almost precluded the possibility of effecting any good by such means. A trading vessel, with a general cargo, intending to touch at the various ports, towards the north-east, would be more eligible; but the most suitable of all, would be a ship taken up for the purpose, which might be under the entire direction of the missionaries, go where they directed, stay as long as they pleased, and mix up nothing with the object, which might be likely to prejudice the cause in the estimation of the heathen.   As, however, no trading vessel, with an unexceptionable freight, was announced for sailing, and as no prospect offered itself for chartering a ship, for the purpose in view, the author was obliged to remain until some more favourable opportunity occurred.

A month had scarcely elapsed, before a vessel was put up for the northern ports, intending to touch at Ning-po, in the province of Chĕ-Keang, and to call at various other places, with the view of extending the trade in that direction.   The owners obligingly offered the author a passage in her; but it was ascertained that she carried, in conjunction with other merchandize, the prohibited drug, opium; and as it was necessary to come to a final decision upon the question, whether missionaries should avail themselves of such opportunities, or not, the whole case was looked into, and the supposed advantages or disadvantages of the undertaking fully canvassed.

In favour of the voyage, it was urged, that the vessel was going to a considerable distance, would touch at a number of places, and was likely to be employed in the expedition for a length of time; thereby affording abundant means for communicating with the natives, and for circulating tracts in all directions.   The experience of the commander, and his extensive acquaintance with the coast, and its inhabitants, were also stated, by which means many dangers in the navigation, and impediments in the intercourse with the people, would be avoided.   The time of her sailing was considered advantageous, as the winds were favourable for proceeding to the north-east, and the monsoon would just be on the turn, when the ship would have to steer homeward.   The probability of this being the only vessel was hinted; and the inference drawn, that if this opportunity were lost, it was not likely that another would soon occur.   A great number of books were lying ready, on board the receiving ships, at Lintin, and it was difficult to stow them elsewhere, in China: if means were not taken to circulate them, therefore, the patience of those kind friends, who gave them gratuitous ship-room, would soon be exhausted, and they must be sent back to Malacca or Singapore.   A strong desire was known to exist among the people of England, to ascertain the real state of things on the coast, and whether China were, or were not, open to the Gospel: while the visit of the author, to Canton, was mainly to discover the facilities for tract distribution, and free intercourse, which it would be impossible to find out without proceeding in that direction.   However unadvisable, therefore, the connection between missionary operations and opium speculations might be, as a general thing, yet, in the present instance, there were those who thought, that the opportunity ought not to be lost.

This appeared to be the utmost that could be said in favour of the voyage, while on the other hand, the objections against it were powerful and insurmountable. The simple circumstance of the vessel being engaged in the opium trade, was enough to deter the propagator of Christianity from connecting himself with her.   It was not meant to be argued, that there was anything morally wrong in the taking, and, consequently, in the vending of opium, when required or prescribed as a medicine: but when employed as a mere stimulant, and indulged in as a luxury, it was known to be injurious to the health and interests of those who habitually used it.   It not only involved a waste of property, time, and physical energies, but it prostrated the mental powers, and benumbed the conscience of every constant consumer; while the disgrace connected with it, induced a habit of deceit and concealment, which gradually obliterated all regard to truth and honesty. There could be no question, therefore, that every one who used opium, as a daily beverage, did wrong, and was highly culpable, as a self-destroyer.   In like manner, those who helped him to it, for such purposes, had some share in the guilt of hastening his ruin.   No one pretends that the opium sent to China, falls into the hands of the faculty, and is prescribed by them to allay the pain of their patients.   It is certain, that all of it is bought up by persons entirely ignorant of medicine, and is used solely as a means of stupifying and poisoning the people.   The quantities in which it is imported, and the class of persons to whom it is disposed of, sufficiently prove this.   With this full perception of the evils of the habit, while we readily admit that the opium consumer does wrong, we cannot deny that the opium dealer offends also; and that all connected with the trade in question, err in exact proportion to the extent in which they are mixed up with it.   The grower, the vender, and the carrier of opium, where it is raised, and disposed of, in large quantities, for the purpose of supplying an ignorant pagan people, who use it as a means of intoxication, must all be implicated in blame.   Were there only a chest or two of opium, on board a vessel proceeding from one European port to another, where it might fall into the hands of the apothecary, and be properly and discreetly used, no objection could be taken to the holiest and best of men embarking in the voyage; but where a vessel is loaded with it, and where the object is to extend the trade in this deleterious drug, beyond the confines of civilization, amongst a people who know not the proper use of it; then the expedition itself must be evil, and all who accompany it, knowing the object and its tendencies, must come in for their portion of blame.

The connection of a missionary with a regular opium ship was found to be disreputable. The opium merchants, themselves, though exceedingly friendly, and ready to lend every possible aid to persons wishing to explore the coast, yet conceive it quite out of character for missionaries to make opium vessels the vehicle for the diffusion of divine knowledge. All wise and good men, also, consider the cause of God contaminated by such connections. But the most serious objection is, that the Chinese bring it as the main argument against Christianity, that its professors vend opium; with how much greater force would they urge this objection, should a missionary embark in an opium ship, and carry out boxes of tracts in company with chests of opium? The Chinese authorities, and people, observing a missionary on board such a vessel, and not being able to discriminate, would recognize him as a real vender of the drug, and stigmatize his character and doctrines accordingly.

The nature of an opium voyage would greatly cramp the efforts of a missionary connected with it; for, supposing the captain and supercargo to be ever so friendly, and willing to afford every facility for the accomplishment of his plans, yet it is not always in their power to do so. The object of the opium smugglers being to elude the vigilance of the Chinese authorities, they frequently lie at a considerable distance from the shore, where a few lawless adventurers come off in boats and purchase opium. These transactions are carried on in the night, and always under the apprehension of a sudden surprise; should a government cruiser heave in sight, the boats of the contraband traders immediately decamp; and, by the dawn of day, nothing is seen of the native smugglers. Meanwhile the European continues in the offing, without sending a boat on shore for weeks together; and when the commanders have leisure and inclination so to do, they are not unfrequently deterred by the inclemency of the weather, and the rocky nature of the coast. Besides which, the character established by the vessels engaged in this trade, is not calculated to procure them a favourable reception when they do land, so that the communication with the shore is necessarily circumscribed.

Further, it would be difficult for a missionary to remain neutral on the opium question, whilst embarked on such an expedition. He would be frequently interrogated by the natives as to the existence of opium on board, and would now and then be asked as to its price. Should any misunderstanding arise between the foreign merchant and the native dealer, about the bargain, the missionary, as being best acquainted with both languages, would be most readily appealed to, when he would feel himself called upon to express an opinion.

Thus, he must either give some assistance to the trade, or he must denounce it: the former would be improper; the latter, in his circumstances, imprudent.

Again, a missionary embarked in an opium ship, must be in a certain sense dependent on those who manage the vessel. For, although he may pay for his passage, to and from the place of his destination, yet that would not entitle him to the use of the boat, or the boat's crew, on all occasions; or to the moving of the vessel from place to place, to suit his convenience. Should this ever be conceded, through the kindness of the captain or supercargo, the missionary would feel himself under an obligation to men, of whose course of conduct he could not approve, and yet could hardly bring himself, in such a situation, to condemn.

By means of the proposed voyage, the opium trade would most likely be extended to a province in which it had been before but partially known; and should the missionary's aid, in interpreting between the voyagers and the natives, be called in, he would be contributing in some measure to the further spread of a mischief which has been already too widely diffused.

Besides which, the evils connected with the disposal of opium on the projected voyage, were likely to be greater, more extensive, and more durable, than the good that might be accomplished by the distribution of books. In fact, the effects resulting from the one would be immediate, palpable, and certain; while the consequences of the other would be distant, partial, and to us unknown.

Every instance of the connection of missionary operations with opium speculations, strengthens the hands of those engaged in the trade, and weakens the force of those arguments that may be employed against it. Insignificant as missionaries may personally be, their character is of some weight; and men engaged in a questionable sort of traffic, would be glad of their countenance and example. Now the time is not far distant, when the opium trade, like the traffic in slaves, will be denounced by every friend to religion and morality; but the man who is connected with, and under obligations to, such dealers, in the transactions referred to, can hardly raise his voice against it; while the individual who has ever kept aloof from such associations, can go to the full extent, which conscience urges, in condemning the trade. Missionaries ought not, therefore, to deprive themselves of a powerful argument against a crying evil, by uniting their operations with the proceedings of those, whom they now inwardly, and must one day outwardly, condemn.

It not unfrequently happens, that the Chinese smuggling boats come in contact with the revenue cutters, when contests ensue, and blood is shed. The natives fit out, for such illicit transactions, some of the smartest and fleetest craft that ever cut the waves; and pulled by fifty men on a side, they dart through the water like a shot. The government officers have imitated them in this, and sometimes overtake and grapple with them. In this way, desperate fights occur, and numerous lives are lost. Besides what takes place afloat, the Chinese on shore are frequently taken up for engaging in the opium trade, and beheaded for their disobedience. While the author was in China, the heads of two native opium dealers were sent round the towns and villages, to strike terror into other offenders; and since the emperor has come to the resolution to put down the opium trade by main force, numbers have paid the forfeit of their lives for their connection with these lawless proceedings. Now, had these men fallen in a good cause, we should reprobate the sanguinary edicts which unjustly cut them off; but having been sacrificed at the shrine of lust and avarice, we must not only acquiesce in the deservedness of their punishment, but consider all engaged in the trade as in some way implicated in the guilt of their untimely and disgraceful end. How then could a missionary consistently unite himself with transactions of such an injurious tendency?

These considerations induced the author to decline the offer of a passage in the ship referred to; and rather forbear ever to set foot on the northern shores of China, or to distribute one book there, than to do so through the medium of opium vessels.

While such ships, however, are objectionable, regular trading vessels are not procurable. European commerce on the north-east coast of China, whether in opium, or in other commodities, is altogether contraband. The high price and small compass of opium, together with the prohibition of it in the regular port, and the insatiable desire of the Chinese to obtain it, render it a profitable speculation, even to the clandestine trader. But the precarious nature of illegal traffic would not answer for common goods, which might be disposed of at Canton; hence few merchants think of sending vessels slong the coast, for any other purpose than to vend opium. The Company's chartered ship, the Amherst, in which Mr. Gutzlaff made his second voyage, had no portion of the drug on board; but very few vessels trading in the same direction since, have been free from it. To wait for an opportunity, therefore, in an unexceptionable trader, would be an idle anticipation, destined not to be realized.

The only plan that suggested itself, was to hire a vessel for the purpose, carrying neither opium nor contraband commodities of any kind, and infringing no law, but that which forbids the introduction of the Gospel into a heathen country. In the further prosecution of these undertakings, it will doubtless be the cheapest and most convenient plan to purchase a vessel, to go when and where the missionaries direct, and to stay as long as any advantage is to be gained to the cause. A missionary or two, devoted to the undertaking, might take up their residence on board; and a printing establishment, by means of wooden blocks, or lithography, be kept in operation, whether the vessel be under weigh or at anchor. A pious physician might accompany the expedition, and landing daily, or residing on shore, while the ship remained at anchor in any port, he might secure for himself and coadjutors, the favour of the populace, and the countenance of the magistrates. Native converts, who are the objects of persecution, might take refuge in the missionary ship, where they would be as safe from the malice of the native government, as though they were in Europe; and be at the same time useful in printing, binding, copying, or interpreting for the missionaries. Thus the vessel would answer the manifold purpose of a missionary residence, asylum, church, dispensary, printing office, and depository of tracts; while it was employed in multiplying and dispersing the word of life, in all parts of the China sea; and gathering information, at once useful to the missionary, the mariner, and the merchant. When persecuted in one city, the voyagers

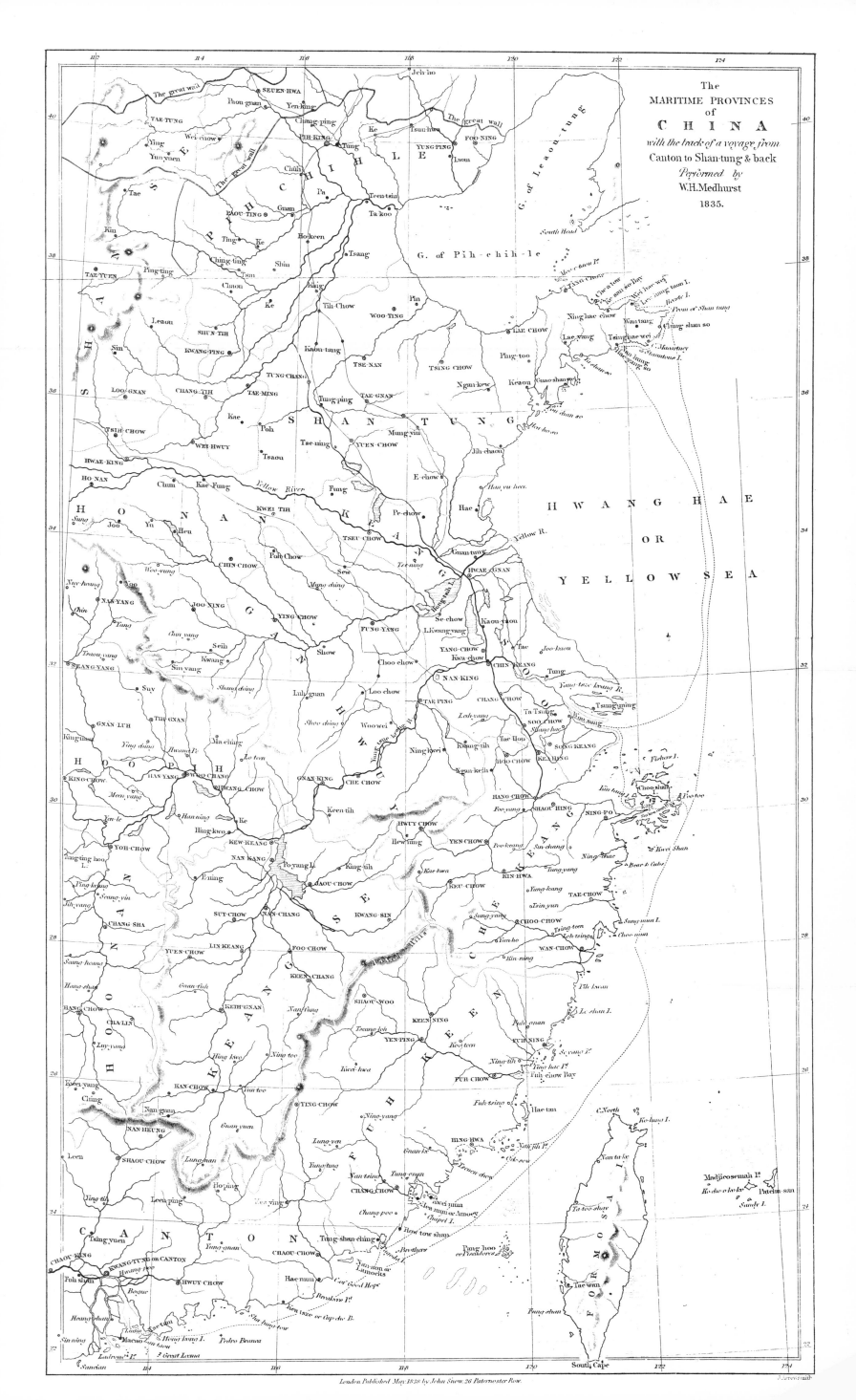

The
MARITIME PROVINCES
of
CHINA
with the track of a voyage from
Canton to Shan-tung & back
Performed by
W.H.Medhurst
1835.

London Published May 1838 by John Snow, 26 Paternoster Row.

might literally flee to another; no surveillance or espionage need be apprehended, and no native would be implicated in the conduct of those on board, as none would be security or responsible for them. Much new ground for missionary operations would be discovered, and great advances made in the work of spreading Bibles and tracts, superior to any that have yet been witnessed. When the vessel was not employed in prosecuting these voyages, she could be stationed at Lintin, where printing could be carried on, and missionaries reside, while divine service might be performed for the benefit of the crews of the numerous vessels lying there. In fact, considering the restriction on missionaries in Canton, and the openings afforded for extensive tract distribution on the coast, a vessel of the kind referred to, is the principal means of operating effectually among the Chinese. Should the commander and crew be well-disposed, their example would go a great way towards neutralizing the pernicious effect of a contrary course of conduct, so long and so plentifully exhibited before the natives of the east. Not only would such an enterprize bear essentially on the best interests of China, but mutual intercourse between that country and foreign nations would be promoted, commerce advanced, and navigation freed from dangers, by the discoveries made on that hitherto unexplored coast. The only objection against such an undertaking is the expense, which would be too great for a missionary society to bear, if drawn from their usual funds; but if raised by an extra effort, the objects of the friends of missions would be answered, without crippling the energies of the institution in other quarters. It is pleasing to reflect, that just as such an object became necessary, an association in aid of it has been formed ; and a number of pious and public-spirited merchants of America, have put down their names for the sum of ten thousand dollars, in order to procure a vessel for such purposes.   The Christians of Britain have not been behind their trans-atlantic brethren ; and a vessel has actually been purchased in England, and has already sailed, for the purpose of conveying missionaries from island to island, through the South Seas.   If, however, such a means of extending the truth, be necessary in the islands of the Pacific, it is much more needed in China, where the missionary's home and refuge must be afloat, till he can " find rest for the sole of his foot" ashore ; and where there is a much wider and more populous field, for the propagating and planting of Christianity, than in the whole world beside.

While thus deliberating and planning, an American brig, the Huron, Thomas Winsor, master, burthen two hundred and ten tons, arrived at Lintin, chartered by the house of Oliphant and Co. of Canton, at the rate of six hundred dollars monthly.   A cargo not being ready, the charterers generously offered the use of the brig, for several months, for a voyage up the coast, if the missionaries could come to an agreement with the captain, for his extra trouble, and for the additional expense of the expedition.   The captain being a stranger in China, and hearing that the coast was unsurveyed, and the navigation dangerous, felt unwilling to go ; preferring to proceed to Manilla or Singapore, in compliance with his original charter, rather than undertake the intended voyage, for as much again.   He complained, also, that his brig was too slightly manned, deficient in the necessary tackling for a coasting voyage, and had her copper much out of repair; so that if the missionaries went on the proposed expedition, they must ship six additional hands, provide another anchor, find themselves in provisions, and pay him, in addition to the sum specified in his charter-party, four hundred dollars monthly, for the increased wear and tear of his vessel, and for the additional trouble and care necessary in navigating an unknown coast; besides providing the requisite insurance. This would, altogether, amount to six hundred dollars monthly, beyond the original hire. On enquiry, however, it was found that both sums, put together, would not much exceed the usual terms at which vessels are hired for the north-east coast of China. It was thought better, therefore, to pay the sum demanded for the Huron, than much more for a vessel that would not answer half so well; particularly as the charterers so generously offered to relinquish the use of the vessel for the object specified.

It was not, however, without some difficulty that the captain could be induced to venture, even after his terms had been agreed to; and not before Mr. Gutzlaff had represented to him the ease with which the expedition might be made now, compared with the state of things when he first undertook his voyage. The bargain was at length struck, stores were laid in, new hands shipped, and the travellers prepared to embark immediately. With regard to charts, great difficulty was experienced; for, with the exception of Ross's chart, along the coast of Canton, and Ree's sketches of the entrance to Shang-hae, Ning-po, and Fŭh-chow, together with a description of two harbours on the northern coast of Shan-tung, we had to trust entirely to the old Dutch and French charts, or to the maps

constructed by the catholic missionaries.   The new
chart of the north east coast of China, published by
Horsburg in 1835, had not arrived in China, by the
time the expedition sailed. If that had been possessed,
much trouble and danger would have been spared, and
the voyage rendered more expeditious and effectual.
The late Rev. Mr. Stevens, seaman's chaplain, at
Whampoa, who had formerly accompanied Mr. Gutzlaff on one of his voyages, embarked with the author;
and though imperfectly acquainted with the language,
his counsel and experience proved of great assistance.
The vessel was not freighted with any cargo, as trade
was not the object of the voyage.   Several hundred
bags of rice were, however, put on board by the Christian merchant, who lent us the brig, with the view of
assisting the suffering natives, should a scarcity of provisions be found to prevail on the coast. Of this a small
portion was given away to a few starving fishermen;
and the rest, as much as could be saved from consumption and spillage, was returned to, and received by the
shippers.   The only disposable cargo, consisted of
books; about twenty boxes of which were stowed
away in the hold.   There were about six thousand
volumes of portions of Scripture, and the rest consisted
of books and tracts, printed at Batavia, Malacca, and
Canton, which had been lying some time at Lintin,
ready for distribution.

CHAPTER XV.

NARRATIVE OF THE VOYAGE.

EMBARKATION — APPREHENSION OF A STORM — WATER - SPOUTS — CHI-
NESE IDEAS OF THEM — VOYAGE UP THE YELLOW SEA — ARRIVAL AT
SHAN-TUNG AND WEI-HAE — FIRST LANDING — VISIT OF THE MANDA-
RINS ON BOARD — SECOND LANDING — DIFFICULTIES IN THE WAY —
DISCUSSIONS ON THE BEACH — ADJOURNMENT TO THE TEMPLE — EX-
CURSION INTO THE INTERIOR — AMICABLE CONFERENCE — EAGERNESS
FOR BOOKS — RAMBLE OVER THE ISLAND OF LEW-KUNG-TAOU — VISIT
TO A PEACEABLE VILLAGE — SECOND DAY'S OPERATIONS — A BURIAL
GROUND — DESCRIPTION OF THE VILLAGES — AND STATE OF THE
COUNTRY — CURIOSITY OF THE PEOPLE — QUIET DISTRIBUTION OF
BOOKS — ANXIETY FOR MORE — ATTENTION TO PREACHING — SECOND
VISIT OF THE MANDARINS ON BOARD — SUMMARY.

IN presenting the reader with a narrative of the voyage,
made by the author up the north-east coast of China,
the usual parade of courses and bearings, with other
uninteresting appendages, of a nautical expedition, will
be omitted; and only such events and circumstances alluded to, as may be likely to throw light on the country
and its inhabitants, and to represent the nature of the
intercourse which foreigners are enabled to hold with
the people of China.   The author will be compelled in
the narrative, to speak in the first person; and as the
description here given is the result of impressions made
on the spot, a liveliness of style may sometimes be met
with, which it is hoped the reader will kindly excuse.

Having shipped our additional hands, and laid in the

stores necessary for the expedition, we set sail on the 26th of August, 1835, from Kap-sing-moon, and dropped gently down the Canton river. Owing to calms and light winds, we made but little progress; while the heat was so intense, that we could hardly endure the suffocation below, or the broiling above. We reached the Lan-taou passage by the evening; and the next day, standing through the channel, we came to an anchor off the mouth of Tae-tam bay; intending, if it should blow a hurricane, which, by the falling of the barometer, we had reason to apprehend, to run into the bay for shelter. This bay affords a convenient retreat for vessels going out to the eastward, being sheltered from all winds except the south; and so secure, even in that direction, that there is little danger of a heavy sea in this quiet harbour. The typhoons or hurricanes, in these latitudes, are tremendous, and when vessels are overtaken by them off shore, without sea room or shelter, their destruction is almost inevitable. Even in the harbour of Kap-sing-moon, where the receiving ships anchor during the stormy season, vessels have been known to drift from their moorings, and have been found high and dry upon the beach, after one of these dreadful gales. An English ship, only a few weeks before we sailed, drove eight miles, with two anchors down, among rocks and islands, and was within a few yards of destruction, when the storm abated. A fine well-built coaster was also dismasted at the same time, in the very passage in which we lay; so that, considering the threatening aspect of the weather, there was every reason for the utmost caution.

A lowering calm continued the whole of the next day; but towards evening, a breeze springing up, we stood on for Pedro Branca. This is a white rock (as the name in Portuguese indicates), on the south side of the province of Canton, and serves as a mark for shipping proceeding along the coast.

On the 30th of August, we were in sight of Këä-tsze, or Cup-chee bay, with the wind a-head, and frequent squalls. About noon, several water-spouts were seen, which afforded us much interest; one of them formed within a hundred yards of the vessel, so that we could distinctly mark its operation: we were, however, in great consternation, lest it should break over our heads, particularly as it fell a dead calm just at the time, and we found our vessel drifting nearer and nearer to the aqueous phenomena; till at length, to our surprise and joy, it dispersed. The Chinese imagine these water-spouts to be occasioned by the ascent and descent of the " dragon king of the deep;" and indeed, they bear such a striking resemblance to a rising serpent, a foaming dragon, or a flying monster, that we can scarcely wonder at their having formed this superstitious idea. When the watery cylinder first rises, they say, the dragon is ascending to heaven; and when the spout is forming in the clouds, they imagine, they can trace his horns; while his head and tail they think never appear at the same moment. Representations may frequently be seen in Chinese houses, of the " divine dragon," the idea of which probably originated in these water-spouts. They have, however, carried their fancies of the dragon much farther than water-spouts would warrant, and have associated it with every thing that is imperial and divine; hence we find dragons depicted in their temples, rampant on the roof, twining round the pillars, or encircling the candles; while " the dragon throne," " the dragon eyes," and " the dragon pencil," are terms exclusively applied to the Chinese autocrat. It may be, that " the great red dragon, that old serpent the devil," has invented and fostered this idea, in order to get himself worshipped, in his own much-loved form, by one third of the human family.

Towards evening, we came in sight of Breaker's Point, which forms the boundary of the Canton province; and on the next day, passed the Lamocks, a few rocky islets, lying off the southern extremity of Fŭh-këen. On the second of September, we were opposite Amoey (or Hea-mun, in the mandarin dialect), when several fishing boats were seen, some of which we supplied with books. These boats were thirty miles from land, and one of them had been out six days without provisions: of course, our rice was very acceptable to the half-famished crew.

The next day, we came in sight of Hae-Tan, a large island on the east coast of Fŭh-këen, which we passed with a favourable breeze, going at the rate of five knots an hour, with scarcely any apparent motion : the air was pleasant and comparatively cool, and, altogether, the day was one of the most agreeable we had spent since leaving Canton. This was the more remarkable, as the Formosa channel, in which we then were, is celebrated for storms and rough weather.

On the next Lord's day, we were favoured with a prosperous breeze, which took us past Sampansan, and several other small islands, towards the Choo-san archipelago. We embraced this opportunity of having service on deck, when a sermon was preached, to which the people were very attentive. Having passed the Choo-san islands, without seeing them, we scudded

through the yellow sea, with a fair wind ; and, on the
10th of September, passed the Shan-tung promontory,
round which we intended to commence our operations.
There were a number of boats and junks in sight, the
crews of which were, doubtless, astonished to behold a
barbarian ship in those seas. After rounding the promontory, we steered for Wei-hae bay, but were kept
off, by baffling winds, for a whole day ; and in the
night, drifted back beyond Alceste Island, which is
remarkable for a hollow rock, through which the sky
is visible on the other side of the island. The next
morning, the breeze freshening, with the tide helping
us, we fetched into the harbour of Wei-hae, and cast
anchor, behind the island of Lew-kung-taou, on the
11th of September. Here we had gratefully to record
the goodness of our heavenly Father, in bringing us
safely to such a distance ; and prayed earnestly for
needful grace, to enable us to act on this important, and,
perhaps, hazardous mission, as became " the servants of
the most high God, come to shew unto men the way
of salvation."

Having observed the inhabitants of Lew-kung-taou
very busy, in sending off ten or a dozen boats towards
the town of Wei-hae, all of them full of people, and
apparently of valuables, as though they apprehended
us to be marauders or desperadoes, we thought it best
to undeceive them ; and, notwithstanding the heavy
rain, we went on shore in the afternoon. On arriving at the beach, most of the people ran up into the
village, but a few of the more robust and daring,
stood their ground. This was a critical moment, and
the feelings of both parties were, perhaps, a little agitated. Not having set foot on this part of China before,

2 c

we did not know how the natives would receive us. Much had been said about the hazard of landing at any other place except Canton; and insult, imprisonment, and death, were predicted as the consequences of such a step. The natives, on their part, did not know who or what we were; and apprehended the most fearful things, when they saw " the fierce barbarians" coming amongst them. Stepping ashore, however, we saluted them in their own tongue, to which they cheerfully responded, and a little acquaintance with each other, soon taught both parties to lay aside their suspicions.

After asking the name of the place, and introducing our object, we went forward, through some cultivated fields, to the village; at the entrance of which, men, women, and children stood to receive us. They returned our salutations in a cheerful manner, and led the way into a house. This was a poor, mean dwelling, half full of Barbadoes millet, which appeared to be, with them, the staff of life. One end of the chief apartment was occupied by a sort of raised platform, which served the inhabitants for table, chair, bed-place, and oven; upon this we sat down, to converse with the natives, who soon filled the house. On opening the basket of books, we found that few, if any, could read, and only one individual accepted of a volume. They were, however, very civil; and conversed familiarly, for some time. Among other things, they asked, whether our vessel were the same that had visited their island, twenty years ago, alluding to Lord Amherst's embassy; or whether we were connected with two vessels which had more recently entered their harbour, for the purpose of distributing books. They asked how many hands we had on board; and were surprised to hear, that the whole ship's company amounted to no more than fifteen persons, saying that we should never be able to get our anchor up with such a small complement of men. We invited them to come on board and see ; and, receiving a present of a few fresh vegetables, we returned to the ship.

The next day it continued to rain and blow, but in the afternoon a Chinese boat came off to us, from Weihae, with a naval captain, two lieutenants, and a train of followers. The captain was an elderly man, with an opaque white button on his cap, as his badge of office, while the lieutenants had gilt buttons.* They asked our names and surnames, whence we came, and whither we were going. To this we replied, that we came last from Canton, which place we had left about sixteen days before, but that our future course would be very much determined by the wind ; for if that blew from the north, we should go to the south : and if from the south, we should steer to the north. At the latter statement, they seemed rather amused, and asked us our object. We informed them that our design was to do good; that a number of pious persons in our own

* The Chinese divide their civil and military officers into nine ranks, which are severally distinguished by a button or ball, about the size of a walnut, on the top of their conical caps. The first rank includes ministers of state, and presidents of the tribunals, whose caps are adorned with a red gem. The second rank comprises viceroys and governers of provinces, who wear an inferior red gem. The third rank embraces the judges, treasurers, and salt superintendents, who are distinguished by a dark blue stone. The fourth rank comprehends the superintendents of circuits, and the lieutenants of counties, whose caps are surmounted by a light blue stone. The fifth rank refers to the rulers of departments who wear a chrystal globe. The sixth and seventh ranks include the magistrates of districts, whose appropriate badge is a white stone globe. The eighth rank respects the assistant magistrates of districts who are known by a flowered gilt globe. And in the ninth rank, are village magistrates and inferior officers, whose badge is a plain gilt globe. The military officers wear the same badges, but whatever, their rank, they always give place to civil officers, even of inferior dignity.

2 c 2

country, who feared God, and believed in Jesus, felt themselves exceedingly happy in their profession, and wished to extend the blessings of their religion to other parts of the world. They therefore caused books to be printed, and sent out agents to distribute them, to all who might be able and willing to read them. We further informed them, that our object was to instruct all who came to us in the knowledge of God, and to administer relief to the sick and miserable. They then asked to see the books, that they might know the nature of these instructions ; and on a basket full being handed up, they helped themselves plentifully. After this, they seemed to comprehend our object, and made no objection to it. They then enquired as to our cargo, and were informed that we had nothing but books, and rice, wherewith to supply the necessitous. They said, that the principal mandarin on shore would have paid his respects in person, but that he was prevented by the weather ; we made the same excuse for being detained on board, and proposed to visit the authorities on shore, as soon as the rain should cease. The old naval captain was very decrepid, and required to be supported into his boat ; but the lieutenants were robust men, though very unwarlike. They were all dirty in their appearance, and had it not been for their satin boots, and mandarin caps, we should not have distinguished them from the vulgar. The captain belonged to the naval station of Tăng-chow-foo, while the lieutenants came from the town of Wei-hae.

The day following being fine, we resolved to commence our missionary operations on shore, and communicate to the surrounding heathen the word of life. We therefore left the brig, about nine A. M., and made for the town of Wei-hae. Observing several vessels in the harbour, we stopped to supply them with books. They belonged to the province of Keang-soo, and differed from the junks of Canton and Fŭh-këen, in having large and commodious cabins abaft, well sheltered from the rain and cold. The master of the first junk was a respectable well-informed man, and received our books and advice, with much deference and attention. His crew seemed to be under great subjection to him, which is not the case with the sailors of the southern provinces; and all appeared desirous of seeing and hearing the foreigners. After calling at two or three vessels, we proceeded towards shore, passing by a small fort on a hill, in which we observed a few soldiers, waving a flag to induce us to return. But insensible to such signals, we kept on our way, and soon met a government boat, with a mandarin on board, whom we recognized to be one of the lieutenants who had visited us the day before. He raised his hands, on meeting us, in a complimentary way; and cried out, that the principal mandarin was gone on board one of the junks in the harbour, to await our arrival. We thought, however, that this was only a pretence to draw off our attention from the shore; and that if he got us on board the junk, he would raise objections against our landing, and probably defeat our object at the outset. We therefore told him, that we would go on shore first, and converse with the mandarin on our return. With that, giving orders to our sailors to pull stoutly, we soon left the native officer astern.

On approaching the shore, we found it lined with a dense crowd, into the midst of which we made our way, and began to distribute books. We had not proceeded

far with our work, before the same officious subaltern
was at our elbow, pressing us most earnestly to go on
board the junk, where the chief mandarin was waiting
for us. We replied, that we should first take a walk
round the town, and converse with the people, after
which it would be time enough to pay visits. So saying, we pushed through the crowd, the officer doing all
he could to prevent us; first, by urgent solicitations,
and then by holding our hands and arms. We resisted
all attempts at personal restraint, and a tumult was
excited by the contest; which we feared might proceed
to extremities, and induce the natives to assist their
officer in compelling us to return to the boat. In this,
however, we were mistaken; as the uniform experience
of all who have had anything to do with the Chinese
is, that the people have no sympathy with their officers,
and never assist them, unless compelled by force. The
oppressions and exactions of the mandarins, in every
part of the empire, have effectually destroyed all respect
for their person or office, and inevitably deter the populace from aiding or abetting them.

We pushed on in our course, till we came to a row of
houses which lined the beach, and had just proceeded
through one small street, when the arrival of the chief
mandarin and his retinue was announced; on looking
round, we saw the officers landing from the boat, and
found it necessary to halt, in order to receive them in a
proper manner. The police runners made way for
their superiors, by beating amongst the crowd, right
and left, in a most unceremonious manner; and then
we could perceive, three or four well-dressed, and well-
fed gentlemen, walking up the beach, with a dignified
air, towards us. The officer in attendance, pointed to

his superiors, and wished us to go down to the beach to meet them; but we thought it more suitable to stand where we were, and await their approach. On a nearer view, we found that one of them was adorned with a light blue button on his cap, while the rest wore flowered gold buttons, as the badges of their office. The first of these we ascertained to be a tsan-tseang, or sub-colonel; the second was a civil mandarin, from the district of Wăn-tăng, about twenty miles off: and the rest were subalterns.

When they approached, the civil mandarin became the chief speaker, and putting on a stern countenance, asked us, in an angry tone, from whence we came, and what was our business? We told him to what country we belonged, and said, that our object was to do good, by distributing books, and dispensing medicines. He suggested, that we should put off to one of the junks in the harbour, and hold a conference on the subject; which we promised to do after our books were distributed. Having said this, we made a move, and took a few steps in land. They then placed themselves between us and the town, and said that we could not be permitted to proceed in that direction. The ground on which we trod was the celestial empire, and the emperor who commanded all under heaven, had given strict orders that no foreigners should be allowed to go a single step into the interior. We said, if this were the celestial empire, and comprised all under heaven, then we, as dwelling under heaven, were subjects of the emperor, and entitled to his protection; we should therefore proceed but a little way and return.

Here they took hold of our hands, and said that they could not allow us to proceed, as it was absolutely forbidden by the laws. Upon which, we remonstrated against their rude behaviour, and said that those laws were made for lawless people and robbers, who would injure and destroy all they came near; but we were civil and gentle persons, who came to do no harm, and designed to effect as much good as possible. With this they softened their tone, and said that they were far from thinking ill of us, or our intentions; but such were the commands of their superiors, which they had no power to alter, and dared not disobey. Finding them a little pacified, we said, that the open beach, surrounded by a dense crowd, was not a proper place for gentlemen to converse on matters of business; and the least they could do would be, to invite us into a house, and present us with a little tea and confectionary, when we might talk over these affairs in a proper way. To this the colonel replied, that we might go to the temple hard by, and sit awhile. The civil officer, opposed this sternly, saying, that it would be very improper to allow us any indulgence. We, however, caught at the old gentleman's word, and said, " To the temple, to the temple;" and the crowd re-echoing the expression, made way for us to pass, while some of them shewed the way.

The temple was situated on a rising ground, a little above the village, and we proceeded with a quick pace towards it. On arriving, we found that we were considerably before the mandarins, and that a pathway lay before us, which led further up into the country; so, without appearing to notice the temple, or to heed the loud cries of the people, we stalked on, with stoical indifference, and rapid strides, till we left the mandarins, policemen, crowd, and all, far in the rear; and kept on, over fields and farms, to the foot of a hill; this we ascended, and nearly gained the summit, before we stopped to look round on the world below. One of the police-runners, with great difficulty, kept up with us, complaining of our rapid pace, and unusual course. By degrees, one and another of his brethren came in sight, out of breath, but not of patience; and sitting down by us, asked us very pleasantly and familiarly, if we liked the appearance of the country, and whether the prospect bore any resemblance to the scenery of our native land? They pointed out to us, the real position of the town of Wei-hae, which it seems we had missed, by landing at a small village further up the bay.

After resting a little while, we ascended higher, till we beheld the sea on the other side of the promontory; and then, marking the situation of the different towns and villages, through which we might itinerate, we thought it best to descend, and wait on the mandarins in the temple. At the foot of the hill, we met our old friend, the inferior officer, who first accosted us on the beach. With him we proceeded leisurely to the temple, which we found surrounded by crowds of people, with a few horses, miserably caparisoned, standing in front of the edifice. There was a paved causeway leading up to the shrine, and a number of small houses to the right and left, intended probably for priests or strangers. After the temple had been hastily cleared of the common people, who had crowded into it, we were invited to step into one of the adjoining buildings, where the mandarins were awaiting us.

In dealing with so ceremonious a people as the Chinese, it is necessary to be very particular in matters of etiquette; not so much out of regard to personal dignity, as the success of our undertaking. The Chinese authorities generally treat strangers with contempt, in order to degrade them in the eyes of their own people; the immediate effect of this is to prejudice the business of the foreigner, and, if not met by an uniform and steady resistance, it generally ensures the failure of his object. We had resolved, therefore, that should we find the mandarins seated, and no accommodation placed for us, we would decline the conference, rather than submit to the indignity of standing, while the rest were seated. To our surprise, however, we found the mandarins standing to receive us; and on our entrance we were invited to take the chief seat on the left, which, with the Chinese, is the post of honour. Tea was brought in, and we began the conversation by stating our object, and expatiating on the principle doctrines of the Gospel. We observed that, having seen in our own country the blessed effects of Christianity, we were anxious to impart the same benefits to others; and were, therefore, come to distribute good books, and preach salutary doctrines: besides which we were willing to relieve their bodily maladies, should any present themselves. They replied, that they were fully aware of our friendly intentions, but that the laws prohibited intercourse; and that the imperial decree had limited the foreign trade to the single port of Canton. We admitted, that Canton was the only place appointed for foreign trade, but as our object was the spread of religion, and not the promotion of commerce, this limitation did not affect us. We then asked the mandarin, whether he had perused our books, and what he thought of them? He answered, that he had read them, and found that, though somewhat different from the Chinese classics, they still contained many goods things, and he saw no objection to their circulation; but, that he could not allow of intercourse. If we wanted supplies, he continued, they were willing to furnish them gratuitously; or if we were short of water, they would bring it off to us themselves. We said, that we were not much in want of water, and, as for supplies, we needed none, but what we might be allowed to pay for. After some complimentary expressions, the conference broke up, and we took our leave.

On our arrival at the beach, we were anxious to distribute a few tracts before our departure; but the officer in attendance said, that as the mandarins had been supplied with books, it was not necessary to spread them among the people. We were, however, of a different opinion; and, opening our stores, we began to deal them out to the bye-standers. To our surprise, the moment a tract was held up a rush was made for it; and as quickly as we could take them out, they were snatched from our hands by the natives. This caused a tumult, and the officer, finding the people crowd around in such numbers, began, with the police runners, to beat them off with cudgels. The populace, however, returned to the charge, coming up on one side, as fast as they were driven off on the other: until, dissatisfied with our slow method of distribution, they thrust their hands into the basket, and helped themselves. It was in vain to remonstrate; they were determined to have the tracts, and in a few minutes every leaf disappeared: while we, with difficulty, maintained our standing. Had we been aware of their intention, we might have mounted some elevated place, or have pushed off, to some distance, from the land; but it was

as sudden, as to us it was new; and when once commenced, could not be resisted. No sooner were the
books in the hands of the crowd, than they were out of
sight of the officers; for the Chinese wear large loose
sleves instead of pockets, and immediately a tract was
obtained, it went up the sleeve, so that it was difficult
for the mandarins to find or recover one.

We now quitted the shore, and proceeded to the rest
of the junks, where we distributed a number of books,
which were willingly received. On board one of the
Fŭh-këen junks, was a man who had been hurt by a
fall, to whom we administered medicine.

After returning to the vessel, and obtaining refresh-
ments, with a new supply of tracts, we started again
for some of the villages on the island of Lew-kung-taou:
where we distributed books, without the least restraint
or contest, and held long conversations with the people.
We had discoursed for some time, before it occurred to
them that we were speaking in their own tongue;
when suddenly they exclaimed, " Why these strangers
speak Chinese, where have they acquired it?" They
then paid more attention, and assented to the truth of
what they heard; but could not belive, that the author
was a foreigner, frequently putting their hands behind
his head, to ascertain whether he wore his hair plaited
into a cue, like the Chinese. Their attention was then
taken up with our apparel, admiring the cloth of which
our coats were made; after which, they examined our
waistcoats, shirts, and cravats, and were more interested
about these appendages, than they were with our
doctrines.

Having passed through two or three villages, we took
to our boat, and stood over to the opposite side of the

bay, where we observed a hamlet, pleasantly situated among the trees. We were met, at the entrance, by a number of inhabitants, whom we supplied with books, and pressed with exhortations; after which we went from house to house, distributing our publications, and conversing as freely as we might have done in a village at home. The women appeared very shy, and, when they could, retreated into their houses.

One woman was observed driving an ass round a mill; in order to grind millet. The nether millstone consisted of a circular slab, about five feet in diameter, and a foot in thickness, with a hole in the centre, in which was fixed an upright piece of wood, with a horizontal beam attached. On this was fitted a large stone wheel, through which the beam passed, and reaching a little beyond the edge of the flat stone, was moved by the ass, which walked slowly round. The millet ground by this wheel, appeared very fine and clean, and was kept in its position by the individual who attended the mill. The woman, observing our approach, left the mill, and walked quietly into the house; while the ass being blindfolded, kept on his accustomed round, as though his mistress had been behind him.

Through this village ran a beautiful stream of water, which was as refreshing to the sight, as it was to the taste. A rude bridge thrown across, enabled us to pass to the other side of the hamlet, giving tracts to all who could read, or were inclined to accept of them. We met here two schoolmasters, both of whom accepted our books gladly; and one of the inhabitants endeavoured to testify his gratitude, by presenting us with a beautiful bunch of grapes, which we received as the first fruits of this land of promise. Beyond the village, we observed a white

tombstone, very much resembling those of our English
burial grounds, erected to the memory of a faithful wife,
by a sorrowing husband.   The pure whiteness of the
monument, the affecting inscription, the adjacent village,
the purling stream, and the silent evening, all conspired
to awaken sensations of the most pleasing kind; and to
enkindle anew the ardent longing, that these peaceful
villagers might be rendered still more happy by the
religion of the Gospel.

On the third day after our arrival, we felt inclined to
get under weigh, and steer to the westward, while the
fine weather lasted; but thinking that we might extend
our researches a little more, before we left the harbour,
we resolved to land at the east end of the bay, and
proceed from village to village, towards the western
side of it.   It may be observed here, that wherever we
saw a cluster of trees in Shan-tung, there also we found
a village; so that we had only to take the telescope, and
count the groves, from our vessel, to ascertain the number of hamlets in sight.   But it must not be supposed,
that the rising grounds of this hilly country, were naked
and rocky; on the contrary, many of them were cultivated, and nearly all were covered with a green sward.
After breakfast we left the ship, and landed at a spot
which gave little prospect of cultivation or inhabitants;
but on ascending the high bank, we discovered a pathway leading towards some corn fields; and passing
through these, we soon came in sight of a pleasant
looking village, at the bottom of a valley.   Thither we
proceeded, and were met at the entrance by a crowd of
persons, to whom we announced our object, and presented our publications.   Numbers came out to hear,
and to see this new thing; while they received our

books gladly, and invited us to smoke with them. Again we repeated the nature of our mission, and exhorted them to serve the living and true God, who sent his Son from heaven to save sinful men. After this we proceeded through the village, the houses of which were constructed of granite, and thatched with straw. The large rough stones, of all possible shapes and sizes, were placed very skilfully together, and joined to each other by a very strong cement, as hard as the rock itself. The walls were very thick, and the windows latticed, without glass. The ceiling of one, which we entered, was beautifully plastered, and looked as smooth and firm as marble. In the midst of the village was a temple, most plentifully stocked with idols, but apparently neglected and out of repair. One of the natives asked us to sit down on a plank, which appeared to have formed part of a shipwrecked junk, and here we reiterated our former statements. Having satisfied them as to our object, we rose to prosecute our journey.

The walk over the hill was pleasant, the air salubrious, and the scenery delightful; while the abundant cultivation shewed, how anxious these people were to extract the utmost benefit out of the scanty soil, in order to supply their own necessities. In a vale near the sea shore, we came to a burial place, differing in appearance from any which we had previously seen among the Chinese. The tombs were square, surmounted by a dome, built of granite, about eight feet high, and as many in diameter, finishing in a point at the top. They were strongly built, and calculated to last for ages, but they had no inscriptions on them, nor anything that could indicate the name, age, or sex of the persons interred; we counted fourteen of these mausoleums, besides a few other tombstones, and graves of different shapes and sizes. Near this cemetery, on a bluff head-land, was a small temple; as indeed there was on every projecting point of land, throughout the harbour; built, as we were told, by fishermen, to ensure success in their precarious occupation. Every person we passed in the fields suspended his labour, and was ready with a cheerful word to welcome us and direct us to another village. Some ran on before, and announced our approach, lest the females should be alarmed at our sudden appearance.

In the second village at which we arrived, the people seemed to hesitate about receiving our publications; but on our telling them that they would probably never have another opportunity of getting books, they gladly accepted them. They gave us in return a few pears, which were so hard, that we could with difficulty bite them. At a third hamlet, we found scarcely any one at home; and passed from house to house, meeting only a few old women, and one man, who was too much frightened to receive a book; at length, just as we were about to quit the place, an individual came out with a friendly aspect, who, after a little debate, accepted a book, and by his example, induced several others, who by this time had gathered round, to take some also. They then invited us into a house, one third of which was occupied by a raised platform, provided with stoves underneath, serving the double purpose of fire-place and bedstead. In the same dwelling, we observed a loom, and a piece of nankeen cloth, about half finished, attached to the machine. The people now crowded into the house, and took away all the books they could find in the basket, presenting us with fruit in return. We observed a pig in this village, but it was so miserably lean, that one of the sailors, willing to be facetious, called it a *hog-goblin.* The dogs also were poorly fed, and the only creatures that appeared to thrive were the asses, who browse on the common, and put up with the roughest fare.

In our way towards the next village, we had to cross a swamp, and perceiving no way of avoiding it, waded through, sometimes up to our knees in mud and water. Some Chinese, who stood by, looked on with the greatest indifference, and it was with difficulty we could get them to point out the shallowest part of the stream, which we had to ford.   On approaching the cluster of houses before us, we found the people busy, gathering in the produce of their fields, and threshing their corn upon the floors. Having only half a dozen books left, one of us went to the boat for more, while the other engaged the people in conversation.   At the head of one of the streets, a crowd gathered round, who were addressed on the most interesting of all topics ; which failed, however, to attract their attention.   They listened for a time, but instead of remarking on the preacher's discourse, proceeded to admire his habiliments.   The women and children, seeing a single stranger, came forward, without the least alarm, and gazed at him with the most stupid astonishment. The people, however, were little disposed to take our books, and having supplied their few wants, the author started in search of his companion ; but mistaking the road, soon found himself surrounded by bogs and swamps, which completely obstructed his progress.   Making for the rising

2 D

ground, and looking round, he observed his fellow-traveller approaching, with two sailors, and a large supply of books.

We then directed our course towards a distant village, which, on our approach, appeared to be in an uproar; we accosted an old man at the entrance, and gave him a book, when others came around, and received their portion. But as the principal part of the inhabitants seemed to be on the other side of a small stream, we waded through it, and called the people to us, under the shade of two large trees, in front of a temple. Here the crowd was so great, that we apprehended a rush for books. We therefore placed our basket on the ground, and told them that we would not give them one single volume, unless they behaved themselves in an orderly manner, and received the tracts in rotation. Having induced them to agree to this, we opened the basket, and took out half a dozen volumes, which we deliberately gave out; then half a dozen more; and so on, till the applicants were satisfied. As a proof that they understood and valued the books, several of them who had obtained the first or second volumes of the Harmony of the Gospels, came, requesting to be supplied with the corresponding volumes; and appeared highly delighted when they could make up a set. We then addressed them on the doctrines of the Gospel, and on the divine mission of our Saviour, to which they listened for some time attentively.

Having accomplished our task here, and distributed nearly two bundles of books, we proceeded over a high promontory to the beach, where the boat lay, which had been following our course, as we travelled along the shore. Here a crowd of people were assembled, clamorous for books; but they were so ravenous, and caught at them so eagerly, that we were obliged to restrain their avidity, and distribute them from the boat, while the applicants waded into the water to obtain a supply. Being now rather faint and hungry, we relished a little salt beef and biscuit; and with a supply of water from a neighbouring brook, we were enabled to proceed on our delightful tour.

With a fresh stock of books, we walked about two miles in land, to a large village, accompanied by a number of persons, who had begun to feel interested in our undertaking. Our heralds soon brought out the inhabitants, begging for books. " Give me one;" " and me another," was the cry, from a score of voices at the same time. We therefore took the volumes out of the bag, and supplied each outstretched arm, as fast as we possibly could. Still the hands were so numerous about the mouth of the bag, that we were obliged at length to hold the books on high, and let those have, who were best able to reach them. Finding that they were likely to overpower us, we removed to a threshing floor, at the entrance of the village, where there was a fresh set of people; who, in compliance with our earnest and frequent remonstrances, were a little more sedate and quiet, than on the previous occasion.

Their anxiety to obtain books, however, must not in the least be ascribed to any knowledge of, or relish for, their contents; but merely to an eager curiosity, to get possession of something that came from abroad, and an insatiable cupidity, to obtain what was to be had for nothing. After having supplied them liberally, we stood up in the midst of the threshing floor, and with a loud voice, proclaimed the news of salvation to

2 D 2

the listening throng. We told them of God's pity to mankind, in sending his own Son to save our sinful race, and detailed to them the relation of the birth, life, death, and resurrection of our blessed Saviour ; in obedience to whose commands we were come, to testify the glad tidings of great joy in their ears. One man, who had listened attentively, exclaimed, " Oh ! your are come to propagate religion ?" Just so, we replied, and happy will you be if you receive it.

After having spent some time with these people, we proceeded over hill and dale, through a most romantic country, the valleys of which were fed with limpid streams, and the heights covered with fruitful fields, till we arrived at another village, where the whole of our books were expended. While our attendant went down to the boat for a fresh supply, we pressed on, anxious to reach the end of the bay before sun-set. On the way we met a respectable man, who appeared to be a builder, to whom we gave a book ; on receiving it, he put his hand on his purse, and asked how much he had to pay ; but when told that it was a gift, he made a very low bow, and thanked us heartily. Coming to a stream of water, the inhabitants, who had now become friendly with us, voluntarily carried us on their backs to the other side.

The last cluster of houses we came to, consisted of two villages united, where we gave books to a number of healthy old men, one of whom followed us, to solicit medicine for his child. By the time we reached the boat, we were completely tired, having been travelling all day, through eight or nine villages. Blessing God for the favours of the day, we went on board, and reached the brig just as it began to grow dark.

On our arrival, we found that the mandarins had been to pay us a visit, in two junks, bringing with them about one hundred men. As there were only eight hands in the vessel, the mate was disinclined to receive them, and intimated that the captain was not on board; but they appeared so friendly, that he allowed them to come upon deck. They expressed their surprise at every thing they saw, went down into the cabin, and even looked into the hold at the books and rice. The mate then fired a six-pounder, to call us on board; they were unwilling, however, that he should make the signal and begged him not to fire, lest the gun should burst; while one of them, a naval captain, actually made haste over the side of the vessel, in order to avoid the explosion. Finding that books were to be procured, they asked for some, and took about fifty volumes away with them. After waiting for us hours, they departed, highly pleased with what they had seen.

Thus we were enabled, within two days, to distribute one thousand volumes, each containing one hundred pages, in a place where we expected to meet the most unwelcome reception; for which we thanked God, and took courage. We have been thus minute in describing this day's work on shore, because, with little variation, it may serve as a specimen of all the days which we spent in visiting the villages. Sometimes we found them more ravenous for books, and sometimes afraid to take any at all; but this is nearly a fair sample of the way in which we were treated by the people, when free from the influence of the officers of government.

On the 15th, we stood out to sea, but were becalmed all day; though towards night, a breeze sprang up, which enabled us to proceed to the westward.

CHAPTER XVI.

PROCEEDINGS AT KE-SAN-SO.

PROVIDENTIAL DELIVERANCE — EVENTS ON LANDING — SUSPICIONS OF
THE PEOPLE — ARRIVAL AT THE TOWN—EAGERNESS FOR BOOKS—DIS-
PUTE WITH AN OFFICER — A TEMPLE AND A STAGE — PERMISSION TO
PURCHASE PROVISIONS —TOUR THROUGH THE VILLAGES—OBJECTIONS
OF A CONFUCIAN — HOSPITALITY OF A PEASANT — RAPID DISTRIBU-
TION OF BOOKS — A CHINESE FORT — EXCURSION TO AN ADJOINING
BAY — EXHIBITION OF AN ARMED FORCE — INVITATION OF THE MAN-
DARINS—SECOND VISIT TO THE TOWN —ANXIETY TO SEE THE STRAN-
GERS — DISCUSSION ABOUT CEREMONIES — INTRODUCTION TO THE
PRINCIPAL MANDARINS — ETIQUETTE OBSERVED — QUESTIONS PRO-
POSED — OBJECTIONS TO OUR ENTERPRISE—ADVICE OF THE GENERAL
—DISCUSSION ABOUT PRESENTS—CONVERSATION ON POLITICS—MAGIS-
TERIAL DIGNITY AND MEANNESS—PRESENTS RECEIVED AND RETURN
MADE—DISTURBANCES ON BOARD.

On the 16th of September, 1835, we reached the harbour of Ke-san-so. This bay is defended by the high
and bold cape of Che-a-tow, and the Kung-kung group
of islands, on the north and west; while in a southerly
direction, it deeply indents the main land. It derives
its name from a village at the bottom of the bay, which
is a place of considerable business, where many trading
vessels touch on their way to the province of Peking.
On entering the harbour, we were not aware of a very
dangerous sand-bank, stretching from one of the islands
towards the main. It was towards evening, when we
arrived, the sails were taken in, and we were merely
going a-head by the force of the vessel's way, when
just as we were about to let go the anchor, the mate
observed some birds on the water, not half a cable's

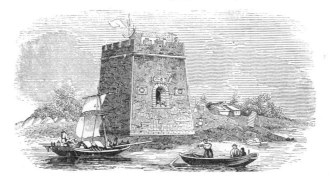

Chinese Fort.

Guard-room with Soldiers

Cluster of Temples

length from the vessel, and immediately discovered that they were perched on a sand bank : not a moment was lost in hoisting the fore-topsail, and we barely succeeded in bringing the brig's head round, in time to clear the edge of the bank, not half the ship's length from it. When the vessel rounded to, we had only half a foot water to spare ; the sea was, however, still, and the tide favoured us, so that we avoided the danger. We could not help noticing the near escape we had experienced, and blessed God for his gracious interposition. How small a circumstance sometimes interposes to prevent great perils ! Had those unconscious birds not been perched upon the bank, we should have gone straight on it, and sustained serious injury, if not total shipwreck. Truly, the hairs of our head are all numbered.

The next morning, the glass presented us an inviting prospect; the weather was fine and clear, the thermometer standing at seventy degrees, and the whole coast of the extensive bay, appeared dotted with those little groves, which indicate the presence of numerous villages, with their white-washed houses ; while the outskirts of the town of Ke-san-so discovered themselves, at the bottom of the inner harbour, just peeping from behind a hill, adorned with a white tower. We immediately landed, to commence our operations among the villages, before we went to the larger town, where we expected to have some difficulty with the mandarins. On reaching the beach, we were well received by the few natives there assembled, who took our books gladly. But they strongly opposed our going to the villages, lest we should alarm the women and children. We told one of them, therefore, to go forward, and give information, that the females might get out of the way. He had not been gone long, however, before a very officious man came down, and absolutely resisted our advancing a step further. We told him our object was to do good, without expecting anything in return. That might be very true, he said, but it was contrary to law for foreigners to enter their country, and further we should not go.

Finding that nothing was to be done with this man, and not liking to make the people angry at the first onset, we turned along the beach, and set off in the direction of another village. On our way thither, we met with some very civil people, who received our books thankfully. We also observed a well-dressed young lady on horseback, who did not seem much disconcerted at our presence. On approaching the next village, we were met at the entrance by a number of persons, who were very suspicious of us, and amongst the rest, one old man appeared apprehensive that we were come to take the country. He first wanted to know, how many ships we had? and when assured that we had only one, he asked how many men we had on board? On being told that there were only eighteen, he exclaimed, " A very likely story indeed! you come along here, to such a distance, with one ship and eighteen people, merely to distribute books, and to do good: and what is more, you expect us to give you credit for upright intentions. We want none of your books nor your goodness either." On his saying this, the few who had taken books gave them back, and nothing would induce a single individual to receive a volume in all that village. We were the more grieved at this, as the place was large and populous.

Thinking that their shyness arose from our not having first visited the town, we made the best of our way towards the boat, and steered for Ke-san-so. This town is situated at the bottom of a deep and spacious bay. On the beach is a sort of custom house, attended by an inferior officer, and a few policemen: at the back of this small building, is a market, and a large temple; a little beyond, are the suburbs, where the families of the inhabitants reside. On approaching the beach, we found the water too shallow to enable us to land, and we stood off to some rocks on the eastern side of the bay. This enabled the people of the town to get a good sight of us before we landed, and induced many of them to come down to meet us. Stepping on shore, we began to give away a few books, which were no sooner in their hands, than we were surrounded by numbers, begging for more. These being supplied, others came; and we found it necessary to get on the bottom of a boat, that was lying inverted on the beach. Here we told the sailor, who accompanied us, to open his basket; when the whole crowd rushed forward, and thrusting their hands, at once, among the books, tumbled both sailor and basket off the boat into the sand; the man however, recovered his position and his temper, but was again overturned; when, in another minute, the books were gone.

We then moved forward, surrounded by a dense crowd, while the sailor went back for more books. On the way, we observed a junk, hauled up on the beach, the deck of which was about eight feet high; this we mounted, and began to harangue the people, some of whom paid great attention, while others manifested a little noisy curiosity. From this elevation, we proceeded to distribute tracts to the crowd, but had scarcely given out one or two, when a number of eager applicants got up from behind, and, seizing the basket, divided its contents among themselves, without in the least consulting us, as to the most suitable persons to whom the books should be dealt out.

Seeing the crowd so outrageous, we judged it best to suspend the work of distribution, and proceeded to the custom-house, where we found the officer in charge, not a little displeased at the disturbance we had occasioned. One poor man had been seized by the police, for having had some share in the scramble, and firmly held by his cue of hair, he stood trembling before his superiors. Now it is a matter of policy, as well as principle with us, always to take the part of those natives who may be implicated in blame on our account; for unless we assist them out of their difficulties, we shall soon find them tire of taking our parts. Seeing this poor man in jeopardy, therefore, we went up to the officer, and asked him, in a friendly manner, to let the poor culprit go, as he had not been more noisy than the rest, and as it was quite excusable, to be a little excited on such an extraordinary occasion. To this he made no other reply, than that he should mind his business, and leave us to mind ours. We then told him, that it was our business to see that a poor fellow was not bambooed for what we had done; and that we should take it as a mark of disrespect to ourselves, if anything were done to him on account of this affair. Finding the officer deaf to our entreaties and remonstrances, we assumed a bolder tone, and told him that we were resolved not to move from the spot where we stood, till the poor man was released. Seeing us determined, the supposed culprit

was instantly let go, and the officer became exceedingly
civil.

We now told him that we were in want of fresh provisions, and should be glad if he would tell us where
to procure them.   He replied, that no provisions could
be obtained then, as it was past noon, and the market
people were all returned home.   This we were resolved to ascertain for ourselves, but had no sooner
entered the market, than every shop was shut, and the
goods put away ; while we could hear the policemen on
before, ordering the people not to sell anything to the
foreigners.   Of course we could obtain nothing.

Having passed through the village, we came to a
temple, in front of which was a stage, built of substantial materials, as though intended to last as long as the
temple, of which it was an inseparable appendage ; for
the Chinese invariably connect theatricals with religious worship, thinking them equally acceptable to the
gods, and amusing to the people.   This stage was
about ten feet high ; on mounting it we found ourselves
in the midst of the comedians, and began to discourse
from this elevation to the wondering bye-standers, who,
notwithstanding the height, climbed up on all sides, to
get a nearer view of the strangers.   After having been
heard and seen in this way for some time, the actors
began to be rather displeased at our intrusion, particularly as we drew such a crowd around us, and necessarily put a stop to their proceedings ; accordingly we
removed from the stage into the temple, where we
continued to discourse with the people.

Having gone round the village, we went again to the
officer, and remonstrated with him respecting the orders
which he had given.   We said we did not want to

trade, but we must eat, and were ready to pay for what we had; why then did he forbid the people to sell us provisions? At first he denied, that he had given any such orders, but we appealed to his own people in proof of the fact. Finding him still unwilling to accommodate us, we at length insisted on his complying with our reasonable suggestion, and declared that we would not leave the place till he had countermanded the previous order. After some further altercation, he did so; and it was surprising to see how, on our second tour through the market, every stall was open, and we were permitted to buy whatever we pleased. But now a new difficulty arose, as our only money was Spanish dollars, which the people would not take at any rate, not knowing the value of them. We were finally obliged to request the master of a Fŭh-këen junk, to buy what things were necessary, and bring them on board; which he promised to do.

On proceeding to the boat, we found that a number of books had already been given away, and that there were still many applicants; these we supplied, and were pleased to see how they clung to the rock, and waded up to their middle in water, while some came rowing with all their might from various parts of the bay, begging for books. After satisfying their demands, we went on board the principal junks lying in the harbour, where we were well received; and distributed altogether about five hundred books before we reached the vessel. One man seeing the medicine chest, applied for relief, but was rejected, as not being sick. He pleaded, that he might soon be indisposed, and desired to have some remedies ready. However, as he could neither foretell the kind of sickness he intended to have, nor the sort of medicine he should need, he was obliged reluctantly, to see the chest return to the vessel, without obtaining a supply.

The following morning, we went on shore at a more easterly part of the bay, travelling through half a dozen villages, in all of which we were received in a suspicious, though not in an unfriendly manner. The first village we came to, was walled round; but in many places, the defences were miserably out of repair. On the south side there was a large gateway, furnished with a watch-tower and ramparts. The people came out to us and received our books, while the women and children thronged the portals to see the strangers. Beyond this fortified position, was another village, in the valley, which we also visited and supplied with books.

Leaving this place, we went on to the next hamlet, on the side of a hill, and began to set forth our stores. One man, hearing that we had books for " the admonition of the age," asked, whether they were the exhortations of the goddess Kwan-yin? We said, that they were exhortations to believe in Jesus, who came to save mankind. On hearing this, some accepted of books, while we endeavoured to explain to them the way of salvation. Passing on, we came to a third collection of houses, near which, on an eminence, we observed two village elders, distinguished by immense straw hats, and large spectacles, dignified aspect, and portly stature. On going up to them we were beckoned off; and not wishing to offend, we passed on to the entrance of the village; when these worthies came down, and told us not to enter their hamlet, but to avoid it by taking another road. We said that we were come to distribute good books, and should do no harm to any one. " We have seen your books," said one of them, " and neither want nor approve of them, having abundance of instruction handed down from our great sages, which are far superior to any foreign doctrines that you can bring." " Your sage," we replied, " taught you the duties of the human relations, while he said nothing about the Supreme Being, or the life to come ; but Jesus, having descended from above, and risen from the dead, was able to give us every information about eternal and invisible things." " Nevertheless," said he, " we want not your books ; there is the road—go." " If you want them not," we continued, " others may ; and as they contain exhortations to goodness, they may benefit your neighbours, and make them better." " We want not to be made better," he rejoined ; and again pointing to the road, advised us to go. We said we should go when we pleased, without waiting for his advice. " Well then," said he, " be pleased to go now." " No," we replied, " it is now our pleasure to stay ; and as we are under the canopy of the universal heavens, and treading upon one common earth, we have a right to pass along the public way without impediment." Finding us determined, he left us, when another began. " You speak of this Jesus as a Saviour ; pray whom does he save ?" " All who believe," we replied. He resumed : " You talk of the forgiveness of sins ; shall I obtain the forgiveness of sins by reading this book ?" " If you follow its directions, and believe in the holy Saviour, you will." " What will this Saviour bestow on those who trust in Him ?" " He will take them to heaven." " Have you believed ?" " I hope I have." " Has he taken you to heaven ?" " I trust he will when I die." "Die! Oh, you have to wait till death for all this: give me present enjoyment; who cares what will happen after death, when consciousness ceases?" So saying, he turned away. Some who stood by however, took a few books; and we passed on to the other side of the village, where we made a halt, and again addressed the people, who received our tracts gladly; and when the rest were supplied, we were pleased to see our old Confucian opponent come forward and solicit books. The Sadducean objections of these village gentry, are a fair specimen of the sort of opposition we meet with from the Chinese literati. These, though painful to the feelings, we had rather encounter, than the violent and unreasonable resistance of those in authority, who oppose our efforts merely because they are innovations, without condescending to give a reason for their conduct, or allowing their subjects to think for themselves. With argument we may grapple, and enter the lists with the most hardened scepticism; but we know not how to deal with fire and sword, which may be aptly denominated the "ultima ratio regum."

Parting from them, we proceeded through two other villages, to the sea shore, where we saw a man eating his dinner: on our approach, he invited us to sit down with him, on the sand, and partake of his fare. Having assented, he helped us to a basin full of boiled millet, and a little salted fish-roe, which we relished much. When we had eaten, he offered us drink out of his own pot, which was supplied with a kind of porridge, strongly impregnated with garlic. This hospitality was the more highly prized, as it was unsolicited, and so much unlike what we had experienced from others, during the day.

Having gone through several other hamlets, we made our way across the bay, to some villages under the cape Che-a-tow, one of which was defended by a fort. The shore on our approach was lined with inhabitants, who eagerly seized our books, and one basketfull, after another, disappeared quickly amongst them. In fact, it was impossible to deal out the tracts with any regularity, for, so soon as the basket was opened, the people seized the contents, and, literally, helped themselves.

On our subsequent walk through the village, we looked into a shop, and observed some of our books, together with a number of native works, exposed for sale. From this, we concluded that the Chinese set a value on our publications; and instead of regretting that they were thus disposed of, we rather rejoiced that by this means, Christian treatises were likely to be more widely spread than otherwise. Having completed the work of tract distribution, we visited the fort on the hill, which we found to be small, and ill calculated for warlike operations; the whole garrison amounting only to five men, and, as far as we could see, without arms!

The next village we went to, was situated like the former, on the sea beach, and the inhabitants were just as eager to receive tracts, so that our whole stock was soon exhausted. One man had already obtained some acquaintance with a few facts of Gospel history, which he had gleaned from a hasty perusal of the tracts just given him. This encouraged us to hope that our labour

was not altogether in vain ; and it being now near
evening, we set out for the vessel, which we did not
reach before dark.

Finding that little more was to be done in the vicinity of our anchorage, we moved the ship on the 19th,
a few miles to the eastward, to enable us to visit the
villages lining the coast ; and coming to an anchor,
about ten o'clock, we set out in search of a bay, which
we thought might be the entrance to Ning-hae-chow.
On rounding a point of land, on which was erected a sort
of guard-house, we observed a village or two on the
beach, both of which we entered, and met with an
extensive demand for books, without demur or opposition.　The people here had just desire enough for the
tracts, to receive them quite eagerly, without being so
furious, as to tear them from our hands.　We asked
them respecting the road to Ning-hae-chow, and one
man was about to inform us, when his neighbours suddenly interrupted him, saying that it was unlawful to
give directions to foreigners, respecting the situation of
places in the interior.

Leaving these scrupulous people, we went to the
opposite shore, and had scarcely reached the middle of
the bay, when we observed a number of villages on the
side we had left, stretching along for several miles,
affording us a fine field for operation.　The bay being
very shallow, and the tide setting out, we were unable
to get the boat within half a mile of the beach.　The
only expedient left us, therefore, was to wade through
mud and water, up to our knees, for a considerable
distance, in order to reach the dry land.　The whole
flat was covered with people, in search of crabs, who

on seeing us, came and asked for books, which they
appeared glad to obtain.

On shore the inhabitants thronged about us as formerly, though some of the better class kept aloof.
This they did, probably, because they were better acquainted with the restrictive laws of China, and more
afraid of the consequences of holding intercourse with
foreigners. However, the books we intended for the
two villages, were all expended among them ; and one
man, opening a volume, pointed to the name of Jesus,
and asked whether he were not the deliverer of mankind. The walk through fertile fields and thriving
farms, here, quite repaid us, for the trouble of wading
through the mud, in order to reach them ; and the
health, respectability, and comfort of the villagers, assured us that peace and plenty were, with them, the
order of the day.

Quitting the villages on the east side of the bay, we
proceeded to the more distant ones on the west, wading
again through the water, for about half a mile, already
up to our knees, and now and then sinking into holes
up to the middle.

The evening coming on, we judged it prudent to return, and the sun set as we doubled the point of land,
leading out of the bay. At the guard-house, we observed about fifty people drawn up, with pikes and
matchlocks, waiting for us to pass. Remembering the
affair at the Min River, when a peaceful boat was fired
on as she passed, we thought, at first, it would be
better to give them a wide berth ; but not being able
to turn off without manifesting alarm, we determined
to stand on, and passed within a few yards of the walls,

in silence and in safety. After we had rounded the point, the armed force removed to the top of the hill, and kept observing us, till darkness and distance obscured us from their view.

On arriving at the vessel, we found that a number of mandarins had been on board, wishing to see us. The mate fired two six-pounders, to inform us of their presence, but we heard nothing of the matter; and, after waiting three hours, they took their departure, leaving the following notice in writing, " The civil and military mandarians of the celestial empire have come to pay their respects, and to say, that the general of the district waits at Ke-san-so, where he requests the strangers to go on shore and arrange matters." Their polite and friendly manners, connected with their civil message, induced us to comply with their invitation, and we resolved to return to Ke-san-so.

On the following day, we stood in for the harbour, in order to have a more favourable opportunity of conversing with the mandarins. We had scarcely anchored, however, before a boat-load of native officers came off, one with a light blue button, intimating that he belonged to the fourth rank, and about half a dozen with gilt buttons, who filled inferior situations. The first was a captain in the army, and one of the others was commander of a war junk. These were very hearty and cheerful men; and one of them, who wore a row of large lion buttons in front of his coat, was not a little pleased, when we told him, that some of our own naval officers wore the same. Tae-laou-yay was the chief speaker. He said, that he had been to pay us a visit the day before, but was disappointed at not finding us on board. He asked our names, country, and profes-

2 E 2

sion, together with our object in coming to the place. This gave us an opportunity of explaining the doctrines of the Gospel, to proclaim which was our chief errand, and of directing his attention to the books, which we had been spreading on the same subject.   He said, he had read our publications, and found many good things in them, though they differed, in some respects, from the Chinese classics.   He listened attentively, while we spoke of the true God, his worship and service ; and was surprised when we told him, that we worshipped none but the Supreme Being.   He asked us respecting our voyage, and wondered how we could come so far, without seeing any land, or touching for fresh supplies. We explained to him the system of our navigation ; and showed him how, by means of a sextant and chronometer, we managed to ascertain the exact latitude and longitude of any place where we might happen to be ; we further said, that we carried but few men, in consequence of which, our provisions occupied but little room.   He then wished us to furnish him with a list of the things we wanted, promising to take care and provide us with them ; upon which we made out a short list of such articles as were needed.   Having given us an invitation to see him on shore, Tae-laou-yay and his fellows returned to the town.

Immediately after their departure, we descended into our boat, and passing by them, got first to land. On our arrival, we were met by two native officers, who said that we must return on board, till the mandarins arrived from the vessel, when they would introduce us to the general of the district.   We objected, that we could not remain in the boat during the rain, and urged that the least they could do was to afford us a place of shelter.   So saying, we moved on towards the custom-house, accompanied by a dense crowd, who strove on all sides to get a sight of us.   Arrived at the office, we were invited to sit down, and the multitude pressed eagerly round to see the strangers.   As they increased in numbers and eagerness, the police officers became exceedingly free with brooms, sticks, and whips, which they laid most profusely on the heads and shoulders of the people; hallooing and scolding, and throwing handsful of sand in their eyes, in order to keep them at a moderate distance from the building. We observed, however, that they never offered to strike or push any of the Fŭh-këen sailors, who seemed to carry themselves with an air of independence, and would not be turned aside from the front of the door. Seeing this, we got up and spoke to them in their own dialect, and enlarged on the doctrines of the Gospel; to which they listened attentively, and by which they were induced to receive our publications.

Some inferior officers gathering round, we spoke to them as long as they would listen, and employed the time as profitably as we could, while the mandarins were making arrangements for our reception.

At length, after waiting for several hours, we informed Tae-laou-yay, that unless we were speedily introduced to the general, we must return on board, as the day was fast drawing to a close.   He said, that we might be introduced immediately, but he wished first to know, what ceremonies we meant to observe on seeing such a great officer.   Their custom, he continued, was to kneel down, and knock head against the ground, on coming into the presence of superiors, and he desired to be informed whether we would do the same.   We told him, that we were not in the habit of prostrating ourselves before our fellow mortals, but that we were willing to pay the same deference to Chinese mandarins of high rank, as we did to our own superior officers. " Well," said he, " I will speak to the general, and try to arrange that matter for you." " But further," we observed, " when the ceremony of introduction is over, we expect to be allowed to sit down in the presence of the general, otherwise we beg leave to decline the conference." " This also," said he, " shall be arranged to your satisfaction;" and with this assurance, we proceeded to the temple, where the great officers were sitting.

Much difficulty has ever been experienced, by all who have had any negotiations with the Chinese authorities, on the subject of ceremony; and these perplexities are felt as much by the ambassadors of Christ, as by the envoys of Cæsar. Two modes of arranging matters of etiquette have generally been adopted; the one is to maintain a determined resistance to all encroachments, and the other to manifest an unreserved compliance with the demands of the natives. English diplomatists have adhered to the former; and though they have sometimes failed in their object, they have never been despised. Dutch and Portuguese negotiators have adopted the opposite plan, and while they have been equally unsuccessful in their aims, have been frequently contemned, and compelled to go through the more burthensome ceremonies, just in proportion to the obsequiousness displayed in complying with former requisitions. For our own personal convenience, therefore, as well as from policy and principle, we judged it best to maintain the honour of our country, and the dignity of our office, by not paying adoration to our fellow men, though vested with a little brief authority.

Of the officers to whom we were introduced, the one was named Chow Ta-laou-yay, the tsung-chin, or military superintendent of the province of Shan-tung; he wore a red coral button, indicative of his belonging to the second rank, and was adorned with a peacock's feather, which is a distinguished mark of imperial favour. The other officer was a governor of the county of Tăng-chow, wearing a light blue button, which implied that he filled an office of the fourth rank. They were seated in the large temple before alluded to, which was fitted up for the occasion; a screen having been placed before the gods, and the principal hall left free for the mandarins to sit in state.

At the door of the temple stood two civil officers, who introduced us into the court yard, which was lined by about fifty men in uniform, arranged to the right and left, but without arms.

The two mandarins were seated behind a table, adorned with a red cloth hanging down in front, and surmounted with emblems of magisterial office. They sat, when we entered, assuming an air of great dignity and solemnity, without moving a muscle of their countenances, or turning their eyes to the right hand or the left. On each side of the mandarins stood about half a dozen inferior officers, and some lictors, all as still and silent as the grave.

On ascending the steps of the temple, we uncovered our heads, and bowed respectfully to the mandarins, which compliment was returned, first by the civil, and then by the military officer, lifting their folded hands as high as their breasts, and then slowly letting them down

again. One of the attendants then pointed to two chairs
and tables, provided with red cushions, and coverings,
a little to the left of the mandarins, on which we sat
down. The civil mandarin was the chief speaker, and
began the conference, by asking our names, and surnames, places of birth, date of leaving Canton, the ports
at which we had touched, and finally, our business.
To all these queries we gave suitable answers, adding,
that our object was to do good, by spreading religious
books, and exhorting men to repent and believe in
Jesus. The civilian then asked, who Jesus was, and
what was the meaning of the word Christ, which he
had met with in our books? This gave us an opportunity of explaining the work and undertaking of the
Saviour, whose benevolent doctrines we came to propagate, for the reformation and improvement of the
age. Here the general interposed, and asked, with a
gruff voice, how we could think of coming to China to
exhort people to be good; did we suppose that there
were no good people in China before? They had
already made arrangements to supply us with provisions; they had got sheep and pigs, fowls and ducks,
pulse and flour, to meet our necessities, and was that
not a proof of their goodness? We said, we had no
doubt that the people of China were good to a certain
extent, but they were far from perfect, and knew nothing of the way of salvation, which it was our business
to make known to them.

The civil mandarin then said, we have Confucius
and his doctrines, which have sufficed us for ages, and
what need we any further sage? We observed, that
Confucius merely enforced the duties of the social relations, but gave men no information on divine and eternal

subjects nor did he effect anything for the deliverance of mankind; wherefore, it was by no means superfluous to have a teacher and Saviour, such as the one now proposed to them. To this they replied, that in our opinion it might be good, but in theirs it was evil; that these doctrines, instead of benefiting, only corrupted the people, and therefore the dissemination of them could not be permitted. As for our books, they did not want them, and would not have them; and we ought by no means to be going from place to place, seeking to disseminate our publications, because such practices were contrary to law. We said that we had read the code of laws established under the present dynasty, but had never met with a single sentence against distributing good books, for the edification of the people. They said, that the code of laws forbad the preaching of strange doctrines, and ours being strange, were consequently prohibited.

Here they talked so fast, that we had not the least chance of getting in a word, unless by violent interruption; and on attempting to thrust in a remark, we were checked by the attendants, who told us that we ought to listen to the exhortations of the mandarins, without presuming to reply. We might, by acting with incivility, have talked as loud and as fast as they, but we did not see that the occasion called for it, or that it would have produced a good impression.

They then asked us about the vessel; to whom she belonged, and how we came to be in her; how much she cost, and whence we got the money; whether from private sources, or from government? We informed them, that the money was subscribed by benevolent individuals, who had formed themselves into a society for the diffusion of Christianity, and who had deputed us to make and distribute Chinese books, whilst they bore the expense of the undertaking. This society not only sent books to China, but extended their operations to all parts of the world, in obedience to the Saviour's command of preaching the Gospel to every creature. They then asked, where these books were made, and how we became acquainted with the Chinese language? We told them, that we had spent some time in the colonies beyond the limits of the empire, and associated much with the Chinese emigrants, by whose assistance we had learned the language and printed the books. They next enquired, from what provinces those emigrants went forth, and in what numbers they were to be found abroad? We told them, that they went principally from the provinces of Canton and Fŭh-këen, and settled in the colonies by myriads.

Here the old general interrupted the conversation, and advised us to return to our own country, as soon as possible, and tell those who had sent us, that it was all labour in vain to attempt to introduce religious books into China; for none, except a few emigrants abroad, or vagrants on the coast, could or would receive them. That their orders from court were, to treat foreigners with kindness and liberality, wherever and whenever they came, but by no means to allow them to stay and propagate their opinions. In conformity with this order, they had provided a liberal present for us, with which he hoped we would be content to depart, and by no means touch on any other part of the coast; for if we did, he was not sure that we should be treated so well elsewhere. They had now shewn us every mark of politeness, and hoped we would be equally polite in return, by getting immediately under weigh, and by touching nowhere else in the province of Shan-tung, all of which was under their jurisdiction.

We said, that we were very grateful for their kind treatment, and intended present, but should be still more obliged, if they would allow us to make them some remuneration: as we could not think of being under an obligation to any. They said, that they could receive nothing whatever from foreigners, and as to repaying the great emperor for his kindness, seeing that " all within the four seas " belonged to him, what present could we make, at all worthy of his acceptance. We said we hoped to be permitted, in return for their fresh provisions, to send some of the produce of foreign lands, such as a few bags of rice, on shore ; otherwise, instead of doing us a favour, they would be reducing us to the alternative of going without provisions, or of receiving a kindness without being permitted to reciprocate it. This latter, with some persons, might be of no moment, but with us, it was irksome in the extreme. They said, they could not help it, as they were strictly forbidden by the laws to accept of anything from strangers ; and as the present came not from them, but from the imperial treasury, it was out of the question to think of making any return.

In our own minds, we thought, that as we had bestowed on their people, books and medicines, of no small value, there could be nothing wrong in receiving presents from them in return ; but on the other hand, we considered, that as they would not acknowledge our gifts, but considered them so much time and money thrown away, calculated to do harm instead of good, the obligation, in their estimation, would be all on our

side, and none on theirs ; and as the report would go
up to the emperor, that they had been feeding these
" hungry barbarians" gratuitously ; we were resolved to
return them some rice for their provision, whether they
would accept it or not.

Amongst other enquiries, they wished to know
whence Mr. Stevens came; and, being told that he
belonged to New England, they enquired whether
there was a new, as well as an old England? which
led us to observe, that there was a new, as well as old
world, which was not known to the inhabitants of
Europe, till within the last four hundred years. After
the first discovery, we added, it was soon peopled ;
and England, at that time, having a surplus population,
multitudes emigrated, and formed the country of New
England. They then asked, under what sort of government this new country was, and who was king
over it? We said, " they had no king, but were ruled
by two great assemblies, at the head of which was a
president; all of them chosen by the people and re-
elected after a certain term." They asked, " what became of the old president, on his going out of office ?"
and, on being told that he became a common man they
wondered greatly ; and could not conceive how he could
be restrained from exciting rebellion, and employing
the power he so lately wielded, in raising up a party in
his own favour. In this, they reasoned from what frequently takes place in their own country, to what might
happen in other regions. With them, a man once in
power, aims to be always in power, and is never content with a private station, after having held the reins
of government. Hence, when an individual is deprived
of the supreme authority, his antagonist never con-

siders himself safe, till the previous ruler is put out of
the world, and his whole race extirpated ; lest some distant member of the fallen house, actuated by ambition
or revenge, should aim at the re-establishment of the
dynasty, or perish in the attempt to gratify his vengeful
feelings.   They then wanted to know, where the author
had met with Mr. Stevens, and how an old Englander
could so readily agree with a new Englander.   We said
that Christians were bound to each other by the peculiar tie of religion, irrespective of country ; and being
actuated by liberal views, were more likely to combine,
in the prosecution of a sacred object, than others, in
whom selfishness was the reigning principle.

The civil mandarin then made some allusion to Lord
Amherst's embassy, and described how the emperor
sent back the ambassador's presents, thereby proving
his indifference to their gifts, and his aversion to intercourse with foreigners.   He also asked if we knew one
Hoo-hea-me, (Hugh Hamilton Lindsay), and one Këa-le,
(Charles Gutzlaff;) and on our saying that we had seen
them, he asked, where and when ?   His next enquiry
was about one Gae-tun, (Gordon), and how many vessels were engaged in going along the coast of China.
These enquiries shewed, that the interrogator was generally acquainted with all the late attempts at negotiation
and intercourse made by our own countrymen with the
Chinese, whether of a public or a private nature ; and
the inference to be drawn from this fact is, that notwithstanding the paucity of public journals, information,
on such subjects, is more general throughout the country, than foreigners may at first imagine.

As it now began to grow dark, we rose and took our
leave, making the same salutation as on our entrance,

which was slowly and solemnly returned. On the whole, they treated us with civility and respect, but were far from being cordial; and the old general seemed sometimes disposed to be angry, while the civil mandarin assumed more of an authoritative tone. Accustomed to command, and usually receiving from all around them, nothing but servile and cringing obedience, they could not, of course, brook contradiction, or be expected to look favourably on foreigners; besides it was necessary, for them to put an appearance of dignity, in order to save their credit with their own people.

In the absence of mental and moral superiority, the rulers of the celestial empire contrive to invest themselves with a sort of mysterious solemnity, which is generally maintained by seclusion; and by manifesting a distant austerity when they do exhibit themselves to the vulgar gaze. A civil mandarin, on appearing abroad, is always preceded by lictors, who, in a loud and unearthly tone, proclaim the approach of the great man; and warn all persons to get out of the way, or to bow down in the dust before the representative of royalty. Dignity with them is manifested by immoveable stiffness, and the absence of all emotion; not a muscle of the face, or a member of the body must be moved unnecessarily; and a slow pace, undiverted eyes, and motionless arms, are essential to the state of a celestial mandarin. Curiosity, surprise, fear, joy, or admiration, would all be unworthy of such exalted beings; and terror, awe, and respect are the only feelings which they seek to engender in the breasts of others.

We could perceive the old general, however, when he supposed himself unnoticed by us, examining very curiously the various parts of our dress. The civil officer, also, condescended to send for our ever-pointed pencil; and Mr. S. seeing how much he was pleased with it, determined in his own mind to ask him to accept of it; but the sly fellow saved him that trouble, by putting it into his pocket. This unhandsome trick is quite characteristic of the Chinese mandarins, amongst whom we seldom meet with a truly respectable man. Delicacy of feeling, and uprightness of principle are unknown amongst them, and the highest officers of government make their way to their distinguished eminence, by a course of chicanery and deceit.

Returning to the boat, we were accompanied by the military and naval captains, and by Tae-laou-yay, who appeared very anxious to bring matters to an amicable settlement. He advised us by all means to accept of the present, otherwise the general would be displeased. We told him, that we could not think of it, unless they would receive something in return; in case of their refusal thus to exchange presents, as we were in want of provisions, we said we must buy from the people; and if they were resolved not to allow this, we must remain at anchor, till they would. On hearing this, he grasped our hands, and began to beg and pray that we would not delay our departure, as it would involve them all in trouble.

The evening having now closed in, we were constrained to depart, and leave them to act as they thought proper. A little after dark, we reached the vessel, and had scarcely taken some refreshment, when the presents arrived; and as the weather was stormy, we could do no less than allow them to be received on board. We now found, that instead of supplying a few necessaries, according to our list, they had provided a quantity far beyond what we required. We had asked for two pigs only, and they had sent ten; besides ten sheep, some bags of flour, two of peas, and two of millet, with a number of ducks and fowls.

The foolish people, however, had thrown the pigs and sheep altogether, with their legs tied, into the hold of the boat (the sheep being undermost), and had shut down the hatch; so that when they arrived alongside, seven sheep were dead, and the eighth required to be killed immediately, in order to render it fit for food. We therefore took seven pigs, and three sheep, with the other articles, and gave twelve bags of rice in return. The police officers who came with the presents, made some objection to this, but we soon overruled their scruples, and the boat returned to land.

The next morning the messenger came again saying, that the mandarins had received the sheep and pigs, but that the rice could on no account be accepted, and they had, therefore, brought it back. We observed, that they had probably returned the rice, on account of the smallness of the quantity, and that we would give them five or ten bags more. This put the old messenger into a fever; and he assured us, that the mandarins did not want any, much or little. We replied, that the rice had been once given, and it was disrespectful to take back presents. The messenger then said, that he had orders to throw the rice into the sea, if we would not take it. "Do as you please," we said, "but we cannot receive it on board." "I shall be beaten," continued he, "if I return without delivering the rice, so I beseech you to take it." We replied, that the great officers of his imperial majesty could never be so unreasonable, as to beat a man for what he could not help; we felt assured, therefore, that no evil would result from it. Finding every argument unavailing he returned on shore.

About two hours after, we observed the same boat approaching the ship, with a mandarin on board, bringing the rice; but before he could get alongside, we were already under weigh, and in a short time in full sail, bidding adieu to Ke-san-so, and the mandarins likewise. Having a good breeze, we sailed quickly along the coast, and arrived opposite Wei-hae before evening; where, as the weather was threatening, and the equinoctial gales expected, we thought it best to anchor.

Our stock of water being expended, we employed the crew, on the 22nd of September, in getting off a supply from the shore. In this work, we were assisted both by mandarins and people, who diligently exerted themselves, chiefly with the view of getting us away as soon as possible. At this place, and Ke-san-so together, we distributed about three thousand volumes.

Before leaving Ke-san-so, an unpleasant circumstance occurred on board, which may be adverted to, for the purpose of shewing how much inconvenience sometimes results from the fears and passions of one's fellow travellers. The chief mate of the vessel had, from the first, taken umbrage at not being allowed higher wages, when called upon to proceed on this unusual, and somewhat hazardous excursion. Being unacquainted with the coast, and the character of the people, he had greatly magnified the difficulties of the undertaking, in his own mind; and had even prejudiced the men against the expedition. Much unpleasant feeling was the result

2 F

and on the evening of the 20th, it came to an open rupture. It appeared, that during our absence on shore, in the morning, a number of mandarins had been on board, one of whom frightened the mate, by making signs of cutting throats and chopping off heads, which, added to his former apprehensions, made him think that our condition was by no means safe. Whilst at supper, therefore, he informed us of what had happened, and intimated his intention of taking the vessel out of the harbour the next morning. The captain asked him, how he would effect it? and he answered, that the men would very soon obey his commands, if he should direct them to weigh anchor. This was too much for the captain to bear, and an altercation ensued, which led to abuse, and would have ended in blows, had we not interfered, and told the mate that his conduct was quite mutinous, and would justify his being put in irons immediately. This remonstrance somewhat cooled him down, and he attempted to smooth over the affair, by saying that we must forget and forgive. Had he been allowed to proceed, however, the consequences would have been serious; and, as he had rendered the minds of the men disaffected, the whole object of the expedition might have been defeated, and the vessel placed in extreme jeopardy.

CHAPTER XVII.

PROCEEDINGS ON THE SOUTH OF SHAN-TUNG.

VOYAGE ROUND THE PROMONTORY—LANDING AT TSING-HAE—STATE OF
THE TOWN AND DEFENCES — INTERVIEWS WITH THE PEOPLE—AND
MANDARINS — EXCURSION THROUGH THE VILLAGES — SIMPLICITY OF
THE NATIVES—CALMNESS OF THE WOMEN — VOYAGE PROSECUTED—A
SECOND LANDING—ANNOYING INTERFERENCE—SUSPICIONS OF THE IN-
HABITANTS—SOLITARY JOURNEY—INTERESTING GROUP OF VILLAGERS
— VARIOUS ADVENTURES — A NEW HARBOUR DISCOVERED — VISIT TO
NAN-HUNG — ENQUIRIES AND ALARMS — A CHINESE FORT DESCRIBED—
GEOLOGICAL FORMATIONS — DISPOSITION OF THE NATIVES — AND RE-
CEPTION OF THE MISSIONARIES—DRESS AND HABITS OF THE MEN —
APPEARANCE OF THE WOMEN — THEIR DWELLINGS — TEMPLES AND
CEMETERIES — PRODUCTIONS OF THE SOIL — DOMESTIC ANIMALS —
STATE OF THE PEOPLE — REFLECTIONS.

On the 23rd of September, we got under weigh, and
stood for the promontory of Shan-tung, with a fine
breeze, which carried us clear round to the south side;
so that we came to an anchor to the westward of Staunton's Island, in the evening. We observed a number of
villages along the sea beach, on our way, but the shore
was so open to the north-east gales, which were to be
expected about that time, that we did not think it prudent to stop in a situation so much exposed.

The next day, we stood nearer in shore, under the
lee of cape Macartney ; but the weather was so rough,
that we could not land. An attempt was made in the
afternoon to reach the beach, but we carried away both
masts of the boat, and after several ineffectual efforts,
mere obliged to return.

The day following we went on shore, at Tsing-hae,
and were met, on our way, by a mandarin, in a boat,
who beckoned us to come to him ; but disregarding his
signs, we pulled towards land.   A number of people
were assembled on the beach, who received us in a
friendly manner ; and as soon as we had ascended the
cliff, the mandarin from the boat, approached us.   His
natural cheerfulness overcame his first alarm, and he
asked us in a very civil way, who we were, and whence
we came ?   We told him, that we came from the west,
to distribute good books, for the instruction of the age,
and with his leave, would give him one.   He took the
book, and said our object was good, but hoped that,
in prosecuting it, we would make no disturbance.   We
assured him, that we should not ; but, on the contrary,
endeavour to keep the peace.   We then gave out books
to the by-standers, who received them with eagerness,
but at the same time, with quietness ; awed, perhaps,
by the presence of the mandarin, and petrified with
amazement at the appearance of the strangers.   The
mandarin then said, that we were guests, and should
be treated with respect ; for which reason, he proposed
that we should repair to a temple hard by, where
the officers would assemble, and treat us with tea.
Upon this, we all proceeded thither, dealing out our
stores as we went along ; but, finding a path that led
directly to the town, we left the temple on the left,
and made towards the dwellings of the inhabitants.
This the mandarin strongly opposed, saying it would
lead to trouble ; but heedless of his remonstrances, we
pushed forward.   Arrived at the gate of the town, he
again attempted to dissuade us from our purpose, without success ; so that, after having passed through one

street, and finding us not to be wrought upon by his suggestions, in order to save his dignity in the eyes of the people, he left us and went away.

We had now time to look around us, and survey the town, which we found to have been originally surrounded with a mud wall, and provided with gateways, but now miserably out of repair. The ramparts were so low, and so sloping, that it was easy to walk up one side and down the other, while the portals were dilapidated and exposed. Only one-fourth of the space within the walls was occupied by houses, many of which were in ruins. All things marked decay rather than improvement, and the place must have sadly deteriorated within the last century, as the Jesuits have marked it down in their map, as an important military station. The same observation holds true of all parts of Shan-tung which we have seen. Every where there are watch-towers on the hills, fallen to ruins; forts dismantled, or nearly so; and long lines of mud fortifications, inclosing many acres of land, some of which are now turned into cultivated fields, without a building; while others still enclose a small hamlet, the miserable remnant of a fortress, where, perhaps, deeds of valour were once performed, and the enemies of their country withstood. This town was built, we were informed, in the Ming dynasty, and was intended as a defence against the incursions of the Japanese, who at that time were very enterprizing, and rather troublesome to their neighbours; but like other military preparations of the peaceful Chinese, the battlements have since fallen into decay for want of use.

While standing on the walls, the people gathered round us, and we spoke to them on religious topics, to which they paid some attention, and expressed, now and then, their assent and approbation. Having obtained another supply of books, we distributed them among the by-standers, and then set off to labour through the adjacent villages, that lay along the shore, where we were generally well received. At one place, we met with an old blind man, who had been a scholar in his youth, and still shewed considerable acquaintance with letters, writing them on his hand for our inspection. This man was quite interested in us, requesting to be allowed to feel and hear, though he could not see the strangers. He listened attentively to what was told him of the way of salvation, and appeared overjoyed at the opportunity of obtaining a book, which he said he would get some one, to read to him.

We had scarcely left this interesting group of villagers, before we saw a mandarin on horseback, coming to meet us. He addressed us in an angry tone, and said, " Since you have now seen what a poor country this is, you had better return, and go on board your vessel." We said, we were already on our way to the boat to which we were indeed going for a fresh supply of tracts, and would soon cease to be troublesome to him ; so saying, we went on, and having first ascended a rising ground, to get a view of the country, we proceeded to the sea shore, where we found the mandarin waiting to see us off. Getting on board, we set sail, and soon bid adieu to the mandarin and his train. After about an hour's sail, we landed on another part of the coast, where we were exempt from the interference of the officers, but where the people were more suspicious and less acquainted with letters. We here walked about eight miles, through five villages, but did not distribute many books. Our sudden appearance seemed to astonish the people. Most of them were not aware that a foreign vessel had arrived, and they did not know what to make of being offered books by such strange looking individuals as ourselves. No one here expressed any wonder to find that we spoke their language, for they had yet to learn that foreigners used another tongue. We found them generally very industrious, some ploughing and others reaping, some carrying out manure, and others fetching home produce; while numbers were collected on the corn-floors in the neighbourhood of each village, threshing, winnowing, sifting, and packing wheat, rice, millet, and peas, with the greatest diligence, and attention. Indeed, so busily were they engaged, that they would scarcely turn aside to look, as we passed along.

The ploughs they employed were simple, and easily wrought, but did not appear to make a very deep incision in the earth; while their teems were novel, and sometimes bordered on the ludicrous. Frequently four asses were seen yoked abreast; and again a cow with an ass on each side, or a cow, a horse, and an ass together; just as the fancy or the fortune of the owner dictated. The people were not fearful and even the females looked on as we walked through the villages, undismayed. Passing by one house, in front of which some women were assembled, and apprehensive lest our sudden appearance should alarm them, and induce them to arouse the villagers by their shrieks and cries, we told them not to be afraid as we did not intend to harm them. " Afraid of what?" they exclaimed, " why should we be afraid of you?" The women had all small feet, and hobbled about most awkwardly. The majority were poorly clad and ill-favoured, with a sallow aspect, and weakly frame, the consequence, doubtless of their confinement and privations; but we saw one young lady well dressed, in silks and satins, and riding by on horseback. After spending the day in going from place to place, we returned to the vessel in the evening. When arrived on board, we found that a mandarin had been off to the brig, who had remained two hours, and was much interested in all he saw, besides four or five boat-loads of people, who all took books and returned. On the 26th we weighed, and stood to the south-west with the wind against us, and the weather threatening and unfavourable. At night we came to an anchor, nearly in the same place where we lay the day before. The next day, being the Sabbath, we remained at our moorings, with the wind blowing very fresh ahead, and the sea rough; so that we were both discommoded and disheartened. All we could do was, to read and pray in the cabin, and long for more favourable weather.

On the Monday we got under weigh, but wind and tide failing us, we made little progress. In the afternoon, however, we had a light breeze, which carried us to the westerly side of the bay, where we came to an anchor, over a gravelly bottom, with many rocks and dangers on all sides of us.

The next morning we went on shore, opposite some villages, and commenced our operations among the people. On landing we were well received by a few stragglers on the beach, who took our books, and made no objection to our proceeding into the interior. At the first village to which we came, the inhabitants gathered round, listening to our story, and receiving our books without any demur, all concurring in kind and obliging behaviour. At the second hamlet, however, we found the people more backward, and one or two having refused books, the rest hesitated, and a few only accepted them. From this place we proceeded to some villages further inland. On the way thither, we were overtaken by a man who made us several low bows, and asked us to return with him to his house, as the place to which we were going, he said, was difficult of access, and skirted by a river, which could not easily be crossed. We told him, that we did not mind rivers, but that if he wanted a book we would give him one. Upon his making some demur, we packed up our treasures and passed on, with the man in our rear. When arrived at the side of the river, our companion soon found some one to carry him over on his back, while we had to wade through.

After crossing, we found our attendant seated by the road side, with a number of villagers around him. On his beckoning us to sit down by his side, we commenced a conversation on religious subjects, and dealt out our books, which were received by a few, while the man that followed us would not take any, unless we gave him a whole set, while he was particular in demanding one of each kind. We humoured him in this, and as we thought, satisfied him; after which we went farther into the village, and fell in with a few respectable old men, who approved of our object, and by their example, induced the by-standers to take our publications. Having supplied all that required our books, and left those who refused, to enjoy their own opinions, we passed on to the next hamlet, crossing the river again;

442

when we found that our new acquaintance was still
with us, evidently producing, by his presence, an unfavourable impression, and inducing the people to decline our publications, or to return them after having
accepted them.

Retracing our steps towards the sea shore, we came
to another large village, where we found the inhabitants willing to listen, and receive our books; but our
troublesome acquaintance was again at our side, on
seeing whom, the people shewed as much disinclination to intercourse as before.   We, however, canvassed
the village, and found some willing to accept of our
bounty; among the rest, a very interesting and intelligent youth appeared, who, having displayed a knowledge of, and a love to letters, was presented with a
book. After a brisk walk of a mile or two, we arrived at
another village, where we found our annoying acquaintance again, who had reached it before us by a shorter
route, and had so prejudiced or frightened the people,
that none of them would have anything to do with our
books. We began by this time to suspect that the individual who followed us, must have been some police
officer, or in some way accountable for the peace and
order of the villages, otherwise he would not have
taken so much trouble to prevent the success of our
undertaking.

Finding no way of escaping his officious intrusion by
land, and being now near the sea, we embarked, and
having a fair wind, proceeded to another cluster of villages, about six or eight miles further up the bay.
Here the author landed, with a basket of books, and
having made an appointment with Mr. Stevens, to meet
him at a distant village on a rising ground along shore,

he set off alone, in land. The travelling was, however, difficult; extensive flats of soft sand and mud had to be crossed, without any trace of a footpath; and every now and then a deep gully intervened, the bottom of which was choked up with thick mud. Into one of these, which was evidently knee-deep at the side, and much deeper in the centre, the author was about to descend, when some Chinese from behind warned him of the danger, and pointed out a more safe and commodious path: this he followed barefoot, over the sand and mud, till he came to a harder and firmer bottom, and soon made his way into the cultivated fields, through which a path led to the villages. Several persons on the way received books, but on approaching the first hamlet, the inhabitants were frightened, and would have nothing to say to the stranger, except ordering him off as quickly as possible. When about to depart, a respectable man came forward, and said, he had heard of our books, one of which he had purchased, and wanted some more. This encouraged others to approach, and not long afterwards two learned men came out of the village, and received our books with great civility and thankfulness.

Having a long journey to accomplish before sun-set, the author left this interesting group, to proceed on his way, which he found intercepted by a broad stream, about three feet deep, and skirted by extensive and treacherous quicksands. He managed, however, to wade through the water, and toil over the sand, with great difficulty; a labour which was ill repaid, by the partial success of his endeavours, in the village on the opposite side; for the greater part of the people fled at his approach, and the rest looked sullen and morose. A few books having been left among them, the traveller pressed on for the next village, and found, to his regret, the same ill will and sullen strangeness, as in the former.

Had there been time to remain among them, and remove their prejudices by friendly conversation, it is more than probable that the attempts would have been successful; but the day being far advanced, and the way to the place of rendezvous distant, the pilgrim was obliged to hurry on. The plain appeared highly cultivated, and, as far as the eye could reach, thickly studded with villages, to the number of eight or ten, within the circuit of a few miles. Finding the day at length gone, the author was compelled to make towards the sea shore; and Mr. Stevens having observed, from a distance, the signal made, soon joined the party; and we proceeded together on board, where we arrived a little after seven o'clock, much fatigued with the labours of the day.

The village on the rising ground, where Mr. Stevens went, had been observed by us the preceeding day, and appeared to have a great number of well-built houses; the windows of which, glistening in the setting sun, gave us a very favourable idea of its importance. It turned out, however, on nearer approach, to be but a small place, with few buildings inside the walls; being indebted for its appearance of magnitude, entirely to its position. It might have been a considerable town at some former period, but is now forsaken and in ruins. The name of the place, however, still conveys some idea of dignity, being called, Wan-kea-tan, "the village of ten thousand families."

On the 30th, we got under weigh, and stood to the

south-west, in search of Hae-yang; when finding a harbour at the head of the bay, which we thought might be near that town, we entered it,and came to an anchor. We had some difficulty in making our way into this harbour, which, having never before been visited by a European vessel, was, of course, unsurveyed. Whilst skirting along the shore, we discovered an opening between the islands, into which we thought it possible to steer the vessel, but were obliged to proceed with great caution, lest there might be sunken rocks in the way. Our navigator, however, deemed it safe to venture; and as we proceeded, we found the passage open out into a beautiful bay, carrying twelve and fourteen fathoms all the way. The harbour was sheltered from all winds, except the south, which in these latitudes is not much to be dreaded, and was capable of containing a whole fleet of merchantmen. About twelve o'clock we landed at the head of a small cove; and found that there were only a few villages in the neighbourhood, while Hae-yang was about thirty miles to the westward. The people in the first village were surprised at our appearance, and few ventured to take our books; but in the second, which was the largest, we had better success. This place was called Nan-hung, and contained several well-built houses, which displayed both the quality and the taste of their owners. Seeing some old men seated at the corner of a street, we approached them, and were invited to take a seat by their side. Our books, on being produced, were accepted without much demur, on the ground that they taught good moral lessons. When a number of people had been supplied, our attention was directed to a well-dressed young man, who was exciting some opposition. On approaching him, we found him apparently much displeased, and disposed to thwart our views. Upon this, we asked him, if he would receive a book ? " No," said he, " I cannot read." " Well," we said, " if you are so ignorant, that you cannot read, we cannot help you : but there are those who can, and who will ; why should you therefore, be envious of their superior attainments, and make others suffer for your deficiencies ?" To this he knew not what to reply ; as he evidently could read, and had only professed ignorance, in order to put off taking a book, and to give others an excuse for refusing our publications. The by-standers, however, were so far from being deterred by his opposition, that they enjoyed his confusion, and took the books with great readiness. This brought him at length into a better humour, and he accepted of a tract also. Passing now through the streets, we were civilly treated by the people, and asked to walk into a shop, and afterwards into a school-room, where the people listened attentively to what was advanced. Among other enquiries, they wanted to know how many ships we had got on the coast ; as they had heard that there was a very large vessel on the north side of the promontory, with two hundred men on board. We told them, that the large vessel of which they had heard, was none other than our small brig ; and instead of two hundred, she had not twenty men on board ; but that her size had been magnified by their fears.

Upon the whole we were well received by the villagers, and left them in good humour. Two more hamlets were visited, with various degrees of success, and we proceeded across an extensive mud flat, to the beach. On our arrival, we found our boat aground, through the carelessness of the mate, who had fallen fast asleep while the tide was ebbing, which left our little skiff high and dry upon the beach. We exerted ourselves to get the boat off, that we might visit another village on the opposite side of the cove : but failing in the attempt, we turned off to the eastward, to visit a Chinese fort, that stood on a hill at the head of the bay. This fort was about forty feet square, and twenty high, including the parapet, with a tower in front, which appeared to have been intended for the commanding officers. The gateway was under this tower, and as it was not provided with doors, there was no difficulty in obtaining an entrance. Inside the fort, we found three buildings, one of which was a stable, the other a cook-house, and the third a sleeping apartment, with bed places immediately over the oven ; but all very much out of repair, and apparently unoccupied for many months. A flight of steps led to the top of the wall, round which was a walk three feet wide defended by the parapet, only a brick thick. Over the tower, in front, was a level space, about ten feet wide, and on the right corner a flag staff. The fort was not calculated to resist cannon, but where fire-arms are scarce, a few men might defend such a post, against a great multitude.

On our return, we met the mandarin who had charge of the fortification, making, perhaps, his semi-annual visit to the position under his care; or to shew the " violent barbarians," that the " Sons of Han" could be fierce in their turn, when occasion required it. He was a fat, sleek well-fed gentleman, who did credit to his imperial majesty's maintenance ; and, mounted on a grey charger, about fourteen hands high, he made a respectable appearance in the turnip field, through which we were passing. On meeting us, he dismounted, and, without asking us a single question, began ordering us off. We told him our boat was aground, and that as soon as the tide made, we should be going, but in the mean-time we expected to be treated with civility. After a little while, he became more gentle and agreeable, and we parted good friends. He told us, that the harbour in which we had anchored, was a very unsafe place, having a sandy bottom, on which account vessels were apt to drive; and the bay being rocky, there was great danger of their being dashed to peices. Besides which, the waves sometimes rolled in with tremendous violence, and rendered the anchorage there insecure. This he said, merely to get us away as soon as possible; but as we knew that the bottom was soft mud, and that in the north-east monsoon, we had no occasion to be alarmed about a southerly swell, his warnings were quite thrown away upon us.

While lingering about the beach, we could not help observing the curious formation of the rocks which there presented themselves. In some instances, the strata ran in a horizontal, and in others, in a vertical direction. The different layers of rock were composed of black hornblende, mixed with white quartz, and now and then, a layer of gneiss intermingled. The whole seemed to be thrown together, by some violent convulsion; and the quartz had, in several instances, forced its way between the other rocks, pushing them aside, or making them project outwards, while some lines ran in an oblique direction, as thin as a man's hand. Numerous rocks of various kinds, lay scattered on the beach, and presented a most curious and fantastic scene. The operations of the waves dashing on the shore, had added not a little to the wildness and ruggedness of its appearance. Arriving on board in the evening, we considered that, as we had already spent a week to little purpose, on the south side of the promontory, and as the people were generally backward to receive our books, it would be better to proceed to a more favourable region: so we resolved, on the following morning to set sail, for the provinces of Këang-soo and Chĕ-këang.

On quitting Shan-tung, it may be proper to observe, that we have nowhere been roughly used or ill-treated, while the natives have been uniformly found harmless and peaceable. We seldom saw a weapon of any kind, beyond agricultural implements, and with the exception of one old man, in Ke-san-so, who had a rusty sword, and the few men drawn up at the guard-house, both soldiers and people, were without arms. We have sometimes been spoken to, in a surly manner; and, now and then, forbidden to proceed into the villages; but, when once on the high road, no one ever attempted to hinder or turn us back; and, for all that we could see, it would be no difficult matter to travel, from one side of the promontory to the other, if any object were to be gained by so doing.

The people, though inoffensive, were, by no means, forward to help or entertain us; we seldom had anything offered us, and, even with asking, could get little besides water. So that, had we depended on the charity of the people of Shan-tung, we should have been but ill supplied.

With regard to their reception of our message, this journal will speak for itself. On the north side, which was first visited, they were more willing to receive books, than on the south; while the further we went, the more disinclination was manifested. This may be attributed partly to the report of our arrival and operations having preceded us; and to the prohibitions which the mandarins had issued, against receiving our books, or holding any intercourse with us. We found, also, that the people on the sea shore, and in places of great concourse, were more greedy after books, so as even to rob us of them, while those in the retired hamlets were very shy. This may have resulted, in the former case, from the frequent communication kept up with strangers, while the villagers, being more secluded from the world, were naturally suspicious of foreigners. On the whole, the amount of books distributed in Shan-tung, considering the time occupied in the work, the extent of ground travelled over, and the number of persons met with, did not quite equal our expectations, or come up to what we hoped to experience in the south.

As to oral instruction, much cannot be said: for though the people, even to the youngest child, and the meanest clown, all spoke and understood the mandarin dialect, and thus could easily communicate with us; yet the time that we could afford to stay with them was so short, and the subject treated of so strange, that we could hardly expect the natives to be greatly interested or improved. Still something was attempted, at each place to which we came; enough to give them a general idea of the Gospel, and a clue to the better understanding of the books left among them; and who can tell, but in some future day, fruit will spring up to a good account, from the seed thus hastily sown. May the Lord, of his infinite mercy, be pleased to follow the distribution of three thousand books on the north, and of six hundred on the south side, of this promontory, with his blessing; and may the occasional conversations held with the people, be productive of great good, to His eternal glory.

The temporal condition of the natives of Shan-tung, seemed generally good. We witnessed nothing of that squalid poverty and deep distress, to be met with in other parts of the empire. The men were, for the most part, robust and well-fed, hearty and hard-working; while no want, so far as we could perceive, prevailed. We saw no beggars, and few ragged people; their clothing commonly consisted of cottons, sometimes doubled, and not unfrequently quilted; most of them wore shoes and stockings, and many had more jackets than one. Some had coats of skins, with the hair or wool inside, as a defence against the cold weather. A peculiar kind of cap was worn by the generality, made of white felt, fitting close to the head, and turned up on each side, with flaps which could be pulled down, if necessary, over the ears. Every individual was provided with a pipe, and a light kind of tobacco, which they smoked very frequently. They always carried a bit of steel about with them, and as the ground was covered with a kind of quartz, which by concussion emits sparks, they had only to stoop down and pick up a stone, and after striking a light, to throw it away again.

The women were not so good-looking as the men; some were ugly, almost all ordinary, and scarcely any handsome. They were pale-faced and sickly in general, and seldom exhibited the ruddy complexion observable in the other sex.

It is well known, that the Chinese have a method

2 G 2

of binding up the feet of their female offspring, from their earliest infancy. For this purpose, they use ligatures, wound very tight round the foot and instep, with the toes bent inwards, until they grow into the sole of the foot. Thus diminished and compressed, the foot is reduced to three or four inches in length, and as many in circumference, tapering towards a point at the end. Of course, the ankle bones become proportionably large, while the club feet thus produced are but ill-adapted for walking. Hence the gait of Chinese women is extremely awkward; they are obliged to throw themselves a little forward, in setting off, and to keep their bodies somewhat out of the perpendicular, or they would be in danger of falling backward: and as they have no spring in their toes, they are unable to urge on their journies with speed. Indeed, some of them are scarcely able to walk at all, and are obliged either to use sticks to support them, or to lean on a servant, in order to move along the streets. The poorer sort, however, may be seen working in the fields, and performing the most laborious employments. On our first arrival in a village, the women generally ran and hid themselves; but they speedily returned, crowding the doors of the houses, and the heads of the lanes, in order to see the strangers as they passed by, soon loosing all their timidity, in the eagerness of their curiosity.

The dwellings of the people in Shan-tung are mostly built of granite, but occasionally of mud; while the roofs are frequently tiled, but more generally thatched. Some are plastered and white-washed, and rather tastefully fitted up; the dwellings of the poorer sort, however, stand forth in all their native and rude simplicity.

The majority of the houses are about thirty feet long, ten wide, and eight high. A door occupies the centre of the front, and a window each side. Near the doorway, there are frequently seen two blocks of granite, projecting a little from the wall, with loopholes in them, which are used for tying up cattle, whilst feeding. Some houses are double, having a front and back range of buildings, but we saw few that were two stories high. The streets are from ten to twenty feet wide, running parallel to each other, crossed by narrow lanes.

Each considerable village is provided with a temple; but these are generally in bad repair, and the gods apparently much neglected. The idols worshipped are, either the phantom Buddha, or a martial hero, probably Kwan-foo-tsze, who flourished about the third century of the Christian era. Little shrines are also to be seen in the fields, with rude stone images in them; or a mere tablet, bearing a simple inscription. Tombs are scarce, but those which are met with, are for the most part upright, like head-stones in an English churchyard. These memorials for the dead are white, and sometimes polished, with the characters more or less neat, according to the wealth or skill of those who erect them: some tombs are round like domes, and others long, with a slanting roof of mason-work over the top. Still the receptacles of the dead are by no means so numerous, as the habitations of the living.

The ground is well cultivated, wherever it is capable of culture, and the sterility of the soil is improved by the attention that is paid to stercoration. Almost every person met with in the fields, is provided with a hand-basket and a rake, with which he collects the dung of all the cattle in the way, and carefully conveying it home, deposits it on the dung-hills, at the entrance of every village, where the manure is heaped up and ripened for use. The productions of the soil are, beans, in great quantities; millet, of various kinds; buckwheat, of a poor quality; rice, and wheat. The fields are not fenced off by hedges, but divided by small grassy ridges, sufficient to enable each man to know his own: and the houses are collected together in villages, either for defence or company. The cattle to be met with are, a small kind of oxen, horses of a diminutive size, asses in abundance, and some mules. Shaggy-haired goats were seen, but no sheep; though the mandarins managed to supply us with some at Ke-san-so. The domestic animals are never left to graze at pleasure, but tethered to a string, are removed from one place to another, when the grass is consumed. No venomous or wild beasts, of any kind, were seen, neither did we hear of any; but birds were espied, in great numbers, some of which being very tame, allowed us to come near them, without flying away.

The poor people who pursue, from youth to old age, the same monotonous round of toils, for a subsistence, never see nor hear anything of the world around them. Improvements in the useful arts and sciences, and an increase of the conveniences of life are not known among them. In the place where their fathers lived and died, they toil and pass away, to be succeeded by another generation in the same manner. The towns, and even the villages, which are noted in the old maps, we found as delineated; unchanged, except by decay, and unimproved in any respect. The people possess few of the comforts of life; neither table, chair, nor any article of furniture, was to be seen in the houses of the poorer classes. No prospect of amelioration for them appears, but in the liberalizing and happy influence of Christianity. This delightful province might then become the abode of millions of happy inhabitants. But now, and for ages, they have been excluded from that best boon, which the Almighty ever gave to man, and without their own consent. They have an indisputable right to call for the knowledge of the Christian religion, which was given to man by God, and no government may justly hinder them from possessing it. They call for religious knowledge, not indeed, as appreciating its full and eternal importance, but as presenting a host of moral maladies, which need relief; and, it will ever be the happiness of those, who aided in this expedition, to know that nearly four thousand volumes, containing much of the Holy Scriptures, were left in Shan-tung. What the result of that little beginning will be, is to us unknown. To the truths of the books themselves, and to the influence of the God of truth on their minds, we leave the work, not expecting that it will be wholly in vain.

CHAPTER XVIII.

PROCEEDINGS IN KEANG-SOO PROVINCE.

VOYAGE TO THE SOUTHWARD — ARRIVAL AT WOO-SUNG — APPEARANCE
OF THE COUNTRY — RECEPTION ON SHORE — JOURNEY TO SHANG-HAE
— INTERVIEW WITH THE OFFICERS — BOOKS DISTRIBUTED — ARRIVAL
OF THE CHIEF MAGISTRATE — REFUSAL TO STAND BEFORE HIM —
DISCUSSION ABOUT CEREMONIES — REASONS FOR DECISION — AT-
TEMPT TO ENTER THE CITY — UNPLEASANTNESS AT PARTING —
OPERATIONS AMONG THE JUNKS — REMARKS ON WOO-SUNG — AND
ITS INHABITANTS — ARRIVAL OF A GENERAL — DESCRIPTION OF THE
MILITARY — AND FORTIFICATIONS — VISIT OF ONE MANDARIN — CUN-
NINGNESS OF ANOTHER — UNSUCCESSFUL VOYAGE — PLEASANT TOUR
— THE PEOPLE EAGER FOR BOOKS — AND THE SOLDIERS FOR GAIN —
DIFFICULTIES AND DISAPPOINTMENTS.

On the first of October we set sail, with a light breeze,
to the southward: for two days we were becalmed;
and on the fourth, had strong head winds, and a heavy
sea, with much rain. It being the Lord's day, we held
service in the cabin, and towards evening the wind
grew more moderate and fair. The sea, however, still
continued high.

The next day we enjoyed a fair wind, and held on
our course to the southward. On the sixth we made
the Choo-san archipelago, and came to an anchor off
Gutzlaff's island. The day following, notwithstanding
the gloomy and rainy weather, we got under weigh;
but the tide setting us on the edge of a sand-bank, we
were obliged to come to, after running about twenty

Landing at Woo-sung.

miles.   Our situation at this period was by no means agreeable, or even safe; almost out of sight of land, and yet in such shallow water, that we were in great danger of grounding every moment; the waters of the Yang-tsze-keang, sweeping along at this point into the sea, had been carrying down for ages vast quantities of mud, which forming into shoals, rendered navigation dangerous and intricate.   The channel between the banks was not above a mile wide, and shoaled on each side, to one and two fathoms. The fog, which prevailed at the time, increased our perplexity ; and had it not been for the excellent chart constructed by Captain Rees, and the vigilant assiduity of our commander, aided by the superintending providence of God, we should most likely have been overwhelmed by the difficulties which surrounded us.

On the eighth, the weather was still dark and gloomy, in the midst of which we set sail, and arrived about noon off the forts at the mouth of the Woo-sung river, leading to Shang-hae, where we came to an anchor. The fog prevented the Chinese from seeing us, till we were close in ; but as soon as we were discovered, the batteries commenced firing blank cartridges, from each side of the river ; their powder, however, must have been badly mixed, as at the distance of only a few hundred yards, the report of their cannon was not louder than that of a musket.   The nearest fort was very much out of repair, having the foundation undermined by the late inundations, and a great part of the front wall fallen in.   We did not observe any guns on this fortification, but there were a few pieces of ordnance, without carriages, placed on the top of the mud embankment adjoining it.   The defences on the south side appeared to be in better repair.

The waters of the river, and indeed of the whole channel, were very turbid, and of a yellowish hue. They tinged the copper of our vessel, so that all the dashing of the waves against it, till our return to Lintin, did not wholly remove the colour.   A tumbler of the water soon deposited a sediment of soft yellow mud, one twentieth of its whole bulk in thickness.   The contrast between the hilly province we had just left, and the level and rich fields of Keang-soo, was most striking.   Trees and foliage here were abundant, and nature seemed to be profuse of her gifts.   But owing to the extremely unfavourable weather during our stay, and to other events beyond our control, we saw comparatively little of this fertile and thriving region. Enough, however, was seen to convince us of the great accuracy and value of Mr. Lindsay's observations, in his journal.   He has not only, in a manner, opened the way to this great city, but has collected more information of various sorts respecting it, than another can hope soon to do.   Owing to the violence of the prevailing storm, no vessels were seen passing out or in, and the river about a mile above us was filled with a numerous fleet, waiting for fair weather to go to sea.   The tides were strong, and the rise and fall two fathoms.

When the rain abated a little, we went up to the town of Woo-sung, off which there were about one hundred junks lying at anchor.   On landing, we observed a number of Fŭh-këen sailors, distinguished by their blue-jackets and cheerful looks, just going into their boat.   These we hailed in their native dialect, and were answered with all the heartiness peculiar to that people. We told them, that we had books for circulation ; and as they appeared to be accustomed to such distributions, they came eagerly forward to receive them. The people standing on shore, influenced by their example, also applied for tracts ; and we began dealing out our publications, when two mandarins accosted us, and asked us to step into a house. This we declined, till our business was done, when we promised to give them every satisfaction. The mandarins, however, went with us into the village, and stood by, while we distributed our tracts, keeping the people quiet, so that each one received his portion in an orderly manner. After two or three standings, at the corners of different streets, the books in our bag were expended ; and we went into the temple of the " queen of heaven," where we sat down to talk to the mandarins and people. After answering their enquiries, as to our voyage, business, &c., we took the opportunity of explaining to them the main doctrines of the Gospel, and our object in visiting their town, viz., to propagate the principles of truth and righteousness, by means of books. The mandarins assented to the propriety and goodness of our enterprize, and the people approved of what they heard. On learning that this was our first visit to Woo-sung, they asked how we came to know that there was such a place, and the way to approach it. We told them, that we followed the tracts of previous travellers, and could find our way by means of instruments and charts, without the aid of a pilot.

Having returned to the boats, we directed the remainder of the tracts to be given out, and as the people were a little too eager in grasping after them, one of

the mandarins became angry, and seized two persons,
to make examples of them.   We immediately interfered, and told the officers, that the supposed offenders
must be liberated; for, seeing that they had got into
trouble, on account of our affair, we should consider
anything done to them, as a mark of disrespect to ourselves.   The mandarin said, that since we came thither
with such kind intentions, to give away good books
among the people, it was unpardonable that these fellows should behave so unreasonably, and snatch them
out of our hands in such an unceremonious manner;
it was therefore necessary to make an example of them.
This was done under colour of protecting us from the
rudeness of the populace; but, had these same people,
pelted us with stones, there is little doubt that the mandarins would have been glad of it.   However, we persevered in requiring the release of the men; and, out of
respect to us, it was complied with.   This town was a
close, muddy place; but we saw a number of respectable
people in it, who, by their satin boots and decent
clothes shewed themselves to be somewhat above the
vulgar.   On returning to the vessel, we were headed by
a strong wind and heavy sea, which nearly swamped
our little skiff; but by the good hand of God aiding
our exertions, we were enabled to reach the brig.
About evening, a junk dropped down, and anchored
close by us, probably with the view of watching our
motions.

On the 9th of October, we started in the long-boat,
for Shang-hae; which, though a city of the third rank,
is one of the greatest emporiums of commerce, on the
east coast of China.   It communicates, immediately,
with the rich districts of Soo-chow, and Hang-chow,

receiving the rich brocades from that arcadia of China, and conveying thither, the inventions and commodities of the western world. The trade of this place is equal, if not superior to that of Canton, and the appointment to district magistrate, or superintendent of customs, at Shang-hae, is considered exceedingly lucrative, and highly important.

The day was stormy, and we were in doubt about the propriety of undertaking so long a journey, in such dark and rainy weather; but the value of time, and the necessity of getting up to the city, before any opposition was organized against us, determined us to proceed as soon as possible. The boat in which we were embarked was a bad sailer; and being without an officer, our men little heeded our directions, each one doing that which was right in his own eyes: notwithstanding which, we got up to the city, in little more than three hours. The river was about a mile wide, lined on each side by high embankments, beyond which the country appeared low and marshy, but by the industry of the Chinese, rendered serviceable and productive.

The vicinity of Shang-hae was marked by the forest of junks, which lay off the city, and which, according to the testimony of an officer of customs, amounted to upwards of a thousand in number. As the weather was dark and rainy, our approach to the city was not observed, till we got up among the junks; and even then, so few persons were abroad in the rain, that we passed along for some time, without much notice; when suddenly the hue and cry was raised, that a foreign boat had arrived, and immediately every window and door was crowded, and the sides of the junks lined with spectators. All wore a smiling aspect, and no one seemed alarmed or displeased at our sudden entry.

Passing on, we soon descried the temple of the Queen of Heaven, spoken of by Gutzlaff and Lindsay, where we landed, amidst a great crowd of spectators, and were just getting up our bag of books to commence the work of distribution, when, suddenly we heard behind us, a clattering noise on the granite pavement, produced by the thumping of long bamboos; and on looking round, we saw the people give way, right and left, and two officers appeared, who greeted us with a friendly aspect; and invited us to repair to the temple hard by. Being perfectly willing to respond to their invitation, we ordered a sailor to follow us, with a bag of books, and made towards the temple, through an immense crowd, who opened a way for us to pass, while the lictors went before, crying out Kìh lae, "the visitors are come."

In the temple, we sat down opposite the two officers, one of whom was Wang Laou-yay, a lieutenant-colonel in the army. After a short conversation, cakes and tea were served up, and the books were produced, which were accepted both by the mandarins and their attendants.

The rain continuing to fall, the officer requested us to delay giving out books among the people, till the weather cleared up. Perceiving that their intention was to hinder our work, and put it off to an indefinite period, we thought it best to divide our forces, and whilst the author engaged the officers in conversation, Mr. Stevens went to the boat, to distribute the tracts. He was not long in dealing out the contents of two boxes, amongst a dense crowd of eager and anxious

applicants. The police runners who followed, endeavoured, by their staves, to keep the people from crowding round, but it was impossible to restrain them; and
the beadles, in the attempt, were some of them borne
down and overthrown.

Mr. Steven's account of the transaction, is as follows: " Breaking open a box of books, I stood in the
boat and attempted to hand them out singly, to the multitude that thronged the shore. By moving from place
to place, this measure partially succeeded, till the contents of the first box were finished. The petty officers
then, with upraised hands, implored me not to distribute any more but seeing, as I did, such crowds assembled, that not one, in fifty, could obtain a volume,
and thinking that no other opportunity might occur,
I was obliged to be inexorable, and opened the second
box. Such a press was now made, upon the boat, that
I found it impossible to do better, than merely scatter
the books indiscriminately over the heads of the people,
letting them fall into their upraised hands, till a thousand volumes were given among the myriads of Shang-
hae. In the bustle, unavoidably occasioned by the
simultaneous moving of such a mass of human beings,
the officers' clubs were sometimes seen playing over
their heads, and again officers and cudgels were borne
down together."

In the meantime, the author was engaged in a
conference with the mandarins, an account of which,
penned at the time, may not be interesting.

" The party was now joined by another mandarin,
named, Chin Laou-yay, employed in the custom-house
department, who wore an European boat-cloak, made
of broad-cloth, with a velvet collar. He was a hearty,

rough-looking man but had a keen eye, and a voluble tongue. Immediately after his arrival, he took the lead in the conversation, and asked whether we had not been in Shan-tung, and had communication with some great officers there ? This question led me to think, that the news of our operations further north, had already reached Shang-hae; though twenty days had scarcely elapsed since our interview with the general, at Ke-san-so. He enquired after Messrs. Lindsay and Gutzlaff, and wished to know, whither we intended to proceed. I told him, that the gentleman alluded to were well ; and with respect to ourselves, we could hardly tell in what direction we should go ; quoting a Chinese proverb, ' We know not to day, what will take place to morrow.' ' But,' I continued, ' as your native conjurers are reckoned very clever, they may perhaps be able to tell you.' ' I am conjurer enough for that,' said Chin ; ' but what is your profession ?' I told him, that I was a teacher of religion, having been engaged in diffusing instruction, for a number of years ; in addition to which, I should be glad to administer medicine gratuitously, to any who were in need of it. ' Very well,' said he, stripping up his sleeve, ' feel my pulse, and see what is the matter with me.' He was told that there did not appear to be much the matter with him, as his looks indicated good health. ' Then I see,' replied he, ' that you do not understand the science of medicine, for I am troubled with asthma.'

" After a little time, a great noise was heard outside, and the arrival of the chief magistrate of the city was announced ; when several officers came in, and requested me to go and see his worship, the mayor. He was seated in the central hall of the temple, with a large

retinue of officers standing by his side.   He appeared
to be a middle-aged man, with a smooth face and fair
complexion, but he assumed a stern aspect, immediately
I entered. Without regarding his austere looks, I paid
him the usual compliments ; and finding a chair placed
opposite, I thought it was intended for myself, and
took my seat accordingly. This disconcerted him much ;
and as soon as he could recover himself, from the surprise and indignation which overcame him, at seeing a
barbarian seated in his presence, he ordered me to come
near and stand before him ; while all the officers around
called out, ' Rise! rise!' I rose accordingly, and asked
whether I could not be allowed to sit at the conference ?
and being told that I could not, I bowed and left the
room.   Many voices were immediately raised to call me
back, but I paid not the slightest attention to them, and
did not stop, till I had reached the apartment to which
I was at first introduced.

" I was soon followed by Chin and Wang Laou-yays,
who tried every effort to persuade me to return ; this,
however, I stedfastly refused to do, unless I could be
allowed to sit, as others of my countrymen had done in
like circumstances.   The Laou-yays observed, that the
native-officers were accustomed to stand, in the presence
of their chief magistrate, and why should a stranger
refuse to do the same ?   ' You stand,' I replied, ' because you are paid by the Chinese government ; and
as subjects of the empire, you ought to comply with
the imperial regulations ; while a stranger and a guest
should be treated with some degree of respect.'   ' But
among us,' they said, ' when a commoner appears before
one of our superior officers, he is obliged to kneel.'
On this being strenuously objected to, they asked,

2 H

'Well, if you will not kneel, will you stand?'   'No,' said I, 'I come as a friendly stranger, and am invited by you to a public conference. I have committed no offence, nor broken any laws; and therefore will not submit to stand as a culprit, before any mandarin in the empire. Messrs. Lindsay and Gutzlaff,' I continued, 'were allowed to sit at the conference to which they were admitted, and the same privilege was now expected.' Wang Laou-yay, who pretended to have been present at the conference to which those gentlemen were admitted, declared, that they had been compelled to stand. Such an unblushing falsehood was repelled by an appeal to the journal of Messrs. Lindsay and Gutzlaff, from which it appeared, that they had been treated with all due respect. I further observed, that I had been admitted to a conference with the military superintendent of the province of Shan-tung, and a governor of a city of the second order, when I was allowed to sit for several hours in their presence; and that I was not now going to stand before the magistrate of a city of the third order, with whom no high military officer was associated.

" They said, that those officers might have been great in their district, but their chief magistrate was the greatest Chinese in Shang-hae. 'Well then,' said I, 'and the individual who now addresses you, is the greatest Englishman in Shang-hae, and does not choose to compromise the honour of his country, or risk the success of his enterprise, by submitting to be treated as a barbarian, or contemplated as an offender. I have no petition to present, and no favour to ask; and if the chief magistrate does not wish to see me in a proper manner, I will not wait on him at all.' ' He wishes to see you,' said they, ' to put some questions to you.' ' Well,' said I, ' he can depute you to ask me any questions he pleases, and I will answer them.' They then endeavoured to persuade me by fair speeches, and said, if I would but go in, and state who I was, and that I was a teacher, and distributor of books, come on a benevolent enterprize, to diffuse knowledge, and promote happiness, doubtless he would then allow me to sit down. ' No,' I replied, ' I must be seated at the commencement of the conference, and will not consent to receive civility in the shape of condescension from any man ; so that you may cease your endeavours, as I am determined not to stand.' Finding that I would not be persuaded, they went to inform the mayor of my determination, to see whether he would comply with my desire ; but they soon returned, saying, that the present chief magistrate Kwan Laou-yay, was more rigid than the former one, who presided at the time of Mr. Lindsay's visit, and that he was resolved not to swerve in a single instance from the regulations of the celestial empire ; further, that if I would not comply with the usual ceremonies, I was at liberty to return to the vessel. I replied, that it was my intention to return when the wind and tide were favourable ; but that as I came in a friendly, and not in a hostile manner, I was not to be driven away, as an enemy or an evil doer."

It may appear to some fastidious, and to others pertinacious, that a missionary should stand so much upon trifles in his intercourse with the authorities of pagan lands ; and that to gain an object, a man should waive all personal and national considerations, and consent to stand, or even kneel for hours, if by that means he could but induce a heathen ruler to listen to the truth, or to permit the circulation of Christian knowledge throughout the land.   But the question is, would the object be gained by such a timid policy, and by such plastic obsequiousness?   The experience of ages has proved, that in negotiating with the Chinese, nothing would tend so effectually to defeat the end in view, as a ready compliance with their demands.   Finding their first requisition acceded to, they would immediately propose another, still more humiliating; and instead of abating the rigour of their terms, in consequence of our yielding, they would only rise in their demands, just in proportion to our voluntary humiliation.   After giving up, therefore, one after another, every point of ceremony, we should find ourselves still farther from adjustment than at the beginning ; and attempt in vain to gain the position from which we had willingly receded.   Besides, the matter in debate, though trivial in our estimation, is by no means unimportant in theirs ; every subsequent negotiation with the same individual, or with others of his nation, would hinge upon the first reception ; and attention to his message, or disregard to his declarations, throughout the land, would depend very much on the position which a missionary might maintain in his first conference with the mandarins. The Chinese assume to be, not only the greatest nation under heaven, but *the only* civilized and powerful nation in the world.   All others are either vassels under the imperial sway, or barbarians beyond the pale of civilization, and incapable of being influenced by the common principles of reason and humanity.   If now we admit the justice of their pretensions, we must either confess ourselves vassals, subject to their dominion, and liable to be bambooed at pleasure ; or irreclaimable savages, incapable of reflection, and consequently not very suitable persons for illuminating the subjects of the celestial empire. Should we acknowledge our vassalage, they would put us upon a level with the filthy Coreans, or naked Siamese, who sometimes visit their shores; and should we admit the appellation of barbarians, we should be ranged by them with the mountain tribes of their own country, who are said to be adorned with tails. Neither Christian humility, therefore, nor Christian prudence, would lead us to submit to Chinese encroachments; and regard for the success of our enterprise, as well as compassion for the souls of the poor benighted Chinese, would induce us to maintain a firm dignity and uncompromising policy, with such an encroaching and overbearing people. It must be remembered also, that the apostle of the Gentiles once stood on his rights as a citizen, and sent word to the magistrates, bidding them to " come themselves and fetch him out of prison."

The author having been joined by Mr. Stevens, we proceeded to converse more familiarly, and to deliver out books to the officers and their attendants, as well as to some strangers that were present, till they were all gone. We had already given a list of a few fresh provisions that were wanted, to Wang Laou-yay, which we requested him to purchase for us, and we would pay for them. By this time the articles were brought in, which they offered to give us as a present; and seeing that there was no other way of settling the question, we resolved to accept of the articles, and to send them some consideration in return.

Whilst engaged in the arrangement of these matters, the chief magistrate observed our native servant, a boy from Paulo Nias, off the island of Sumatra (whose portrait appears in the frontispiece), passing by before the hall; upon which he sent for him, and as he could not obtain the master's obedience, was determined to make the servant stand, and be catechized before him. He insisted on it, that the boy was of Chinese origin, as his features somewhat resembled those of the Chinese: but after much questioning and examination, they found that the youth was entirely ignorant of any dialect of the Chinese language, and consequently could not belong to the celestial empire.   Had they succeeded in getting a word or two out of him, they would doubtless have denounced him a Chinese traitor, or us kidnappers of celestial children; but his ignorance of the language confounded them, and compelled them to let him go.

The rain having moderated, we rose to take a walk, and proceeded towards the boat, where the sailors were busy eating their dinner, while thousands around eagerly stretched forward, to " see the lions fed."   One man who had pressed through the crowd to get a sight of the strangers, immediately began rubbing his eyes, and then took a second look, that he might be certain it was not a dream.

Wishing to enter the city, we turned off in that direction, but were stopped by the officers and their attendants, who actually blocked up the way, and would not allow us to proceed a step further; urging, that as we had refused to wait upon the chief magistrate, he had issued positive orders that we should not be allowed to enter the city.   The opposition they now manifested was so determined, that we saw there was no way of overcoming it but by a resort to force; which not being disposed to do, we thought it most advisable to give up the point, and reluctantly returned to the temple. We regretted afterwards that we had attempted, or that, having attempted, we had not persevered in the endeavour ; for we did not find the mandarins one whit the more civil on account of our compliance, but rather the contrary.

After another hour's conversation, they brought on the table two great heaps of cakes, expecting us like " hungry barbarians," to fall to work, and devour them ; but not liking the unceremonious manner in which they were offered us, we refused to partake of anything, unless they served up dinner in a regular way ; upon which they brought in a dish of rice, and different kinds of stews, which we partook of, in conjunction with the mandarins, and departed.

On coming down to the boat, we found that they had heaped up the fowls, and other articles of provision, in our boat, to go down with us to the vessel ; but as our bark was already overloaded, and as we apprehended much difficulty in getting down the river ourselves, we thought it better to have the presents taken out, and sent by another conveyance. On the steps, we observed a basket, nearly full of straw, and on the top, about half a dozen books, torn in pieces, and about to be burnt. On enquiry they told us, that these were a few that had been torn in the scuffle, and in order to prevent their being trodden under foot, which the Chinese consider a great evil, they were about to burn them. We immediately recollected, however, having heard Chin Laou-yay giving directions to his servants to keep one or two of the books which fell to his share, and to do something with the rest ; but what it was, we could not tell; and it now occurred to us, that he had directed them to be burnt in our presence, in order to vex and degrade us, in the eyes of the people. On the torch being applied to the basket, therefore, we took the presents which were lying by, and placed them on the fire, by which means, the flame was extinguished; but the Chinese, taking off the articles, applied the torch again, whilst we repeated the former operation; to shew them, that if they despised our presents, we also disregarded theirs. Finally, the basket was thrown into the river, and we departed very much displeased at the insulting conduct of the mandarins. The books thus destroyed, were only a few which had fallen into the hands of the officers, while a thousand others had been distributed among the people, which the authorities could neither discover nor destroy.

On our return, we found the wind directly against us, so that, after wasting an hour, and not getting out of sight of the town, we were obliged to take to the oars, and assisted by the tide, we gently dropped down the river. Fearing lest we should not be able to reach the vessel before the tide made up again, and thus be kept out all night, we applied to the masters of several junks, requesting them to give us shelter; but our application was vain. They were so alarmed at our sudden appearance, that they scarcely knew what to answer, and appeared mainly anxious to get us out of their vessels as soon as possible.

Night soon came on, with rain, and as there was no officer in the boat, the men gave vent to their vexation, in horrid oaths and blasphemies, which, added to the inclemency of the weather, rendered our external and internal sensations alike uncomfortable. The profanity and ribaldry of these men exceeded anything we had ever heard; and, having been for many years unaccustomed to such language, it the more shocked and grieved us. The Chinese, though idolatrous, and sceptical, never indulge themselves in the use of profane expressions, and spend their rage in railing on men, without blaspheming the gods. It is reserved for Christians, so called, to outrage decency and common sense, by mixing up profane language with common conversation. Surely, we never heard any so fervent in prayer for blessings, as those wretched fellows appeared to be in imprecating curses on their heads; and made us feel, that, while attempting to evangelize China, our own countrymen needed our most zealous and unwearied efforts for their conversion. In all future expeditions of this kind, however, it will be necessary to obtain a crew, at least, decent in their external deportment, if not hearty in the promotion of the good cause.

At length, by persevering endeavour, we arrived at the vessel, wet, cold, and tired, a little before nine o'clock, at night; thankful that we had been preserved from all dangers, and were free from sickness; having been enabled to circulate about one thousand volumes among nearly a million of people.

On the 10th, we went round to distribute a load of books among the native vessels, lying off the town of Woo-sung. Almost all the people, on board the junks first visited, received books readily; but we had not been long occupied, before we observed a custom-house boat going round, and giving orders against trade and intercourse, which had the effect of inducing some to demur about receiving our publications.

After having supplied a goodly number, however, we went towards the town, and landed up a creek, which communicates with the main river. The shore was lined with hundreds of people, who greedily received our books, and prevented our distributing them regularly and judiciously, by diving their hands into the bag, and helping themselves; struggling, at the same time, which should have them first. Having exhausted one bag full, we sent the sailor for a second supply; but the man was nearly overpowered by the crowd in coming up the bank, and was several times pushed down, bag and all, by the pressure; he finally succeeded in reaching the place where the multitude was assembled; when the contents of the bag quickly disappeared. In the meanwhile, Mr. Stevens was employed in giving out books from the boat, which could be done more deliberately, as the people not being allowed to come on board, were easily restrained from disorderly scrambling. When the books were nearly expended, the mandarins, whom we had seen on our first arrival, came again amongst us, and shewed a little disapprobation at the outrageous eagerness of the people, but did not otherwise find fault with what we were doing.

Having gone through the task of distributing these little messengers of mercy, we walked through the streets, followed by the mandarins, and a large crowd of people. We found that the town was much larger than we had at first imagined, consisting of one long principal street, and several other subordinate ones, and containing altogether about four or five hundred houses. The people were unwilling to sell us anything, on account of the prohibitions and presence of the manda-

rins; but we told them, that we must have the necessaries of life, for which we were willing to pay; upon
which they acceded to our purchasing a few provisions.
The shops were nearly cleared of the goods, as we
passed along, and in one street, they were altogether
shut up, so that it looked like a Sunday at home. The
people seemed in general well fed, and the women
were better looking than those we had seen in Shan-
tung. The more respectable females wore a fillet of
black silk or cloth round their heads, which kept their
hair back, and which was sometimes pointed downwards in front, between the eye-brows, so as to give
the countenance a singular, but not an unpleasing appearance. We observed several tea shops, were people met to regale themselves, but which, from other
circumstances that came under our observation, did
not appear to be of the most correct character. Liquor
shops were also frequent, and in one place we saw
a distilling apparatus at work.

In the centre of one of the streets, we met with a
notice to the following effect : " By the order of the
chief magistrate, you shop-keepers and people are informed, that if you dare to trade and barter with those
barbarians, you will be apprehended, and severely
punished." On reading this, we turned round to the
officer who was following us, and told him that we
were not barbarians, but a civilized people; and, therefore, did not choose to have such insulting epithets
applied to us. To this he replied, that he had nothing
to do with the notice and was not answerable for it.

On coming out of the village, we observed a line of
military, drawn up on the embankment by the side of
the river, discharging a round of musketry, while a

salute was fired from each fort, in honor of the lieutenant-general of the district, who was just coming over from Tsung-ming. On looking out upon the river, we perceived the general's barge passing up, with the character Sae, or "general," written on a flag, suspended from the mast-head. The troops appeared to be kneeling as he went by, for they rose after he passed. About five and twenty war junks followed in the general's train, who all fired blank cartridges immediately they came abreast of the brig, to infuse terror into the minds of the "crafty barbarians." These war vessels were about sixty tons burthen, and carried a four or six-pounder, on a pivot at mid-ships, and sometimes one at each gangway, with a number of swivels along the rail. Some of these junks appeared better built, and more neatly fitted up, than ordinary Chinese vessels. Two of them carried the flags of Tsan-tsëangs, or colonels.

When the general had passed, and the war junks had all anchored, instead of being alarmed at their demonstration of force, we walked up to the soldiers, to inspect their military bearing and efficiency. The corps consisted of about one hundred men, standing in single file, fully six feet apart, to make those at a distance believe that their numbers were greater than they really were. At each end of the line, were a couple of small tents, capable of containing about half a dozen men each; and at the head of the company, stood two officers. The men were dirty beggarly-looking fellows; some with matchlocks, others with swords and basket-shields; a few with spears, and the remainder with no weapons at all. We passed along in front of the line, examining their arms, and commenting on their slovenly appearance, without the least restriction. Their matchlocks

were longer in the barrel than common muskets, but
they were exceedingly thin, and rendered much thinner
by rust, which had actually eaten holes on the sides, in
various parts, so that the powder might escape at more
places than one. The only wonder is, that these matchlocks do not burst every time they are fired off, and
their standing can be accounted for only, on the supposition, that the powder they employ is too weak to
burst anything. The cartridge box consisted of a case,
containing half a dozen small bamboos, about the size
of a thimble, with only a small quantity of coarse powder in each. We spoke to the officers at the head of
the line, on the unsoldierlike appearance of their men;
to which they replied, that they could not help it, as
the emperor did not provide the troops with better arms
and accoutrements. They did not attempt to interfere
with our inspection of the men, and we could not help
smiling, to think that all this military parade was intended to strike terror into our breasts, while we were
allowed to pass in front of their line, and comment on
their deficiencies without molestation. The general of
this division was lodged in a temple, by the river side,
in front of which we passed, on our way to the boat;
but, as he did not seem disposed to court our acquaintance, we did not seek a conference with him.

Having returned to the ship, and replenished our
stock of books, we made a second excursion, in the
afternoon, to the northern fort, which has been before
alluded to, as so much out of repair. We had here an
opportunity of examining the utter desolation into which
this fortification was brought, by the violence of the
waves; one half of it being already in ruins, and the
other half in such a tottering condition, that it was not

safe to walk round the ramparts, lest the whole should fall down by the weight of a single individual. On the embankment, adjoining the fort, were four long eighteen-pounders, placed on low frames, which were formed by two thick planks, lying edgewise on the ground, and joined by a few cross-pieces, on which the cannon was placed. One of these planks had already given way, and the gun lay on the ground, while the rest were nearly as immoveable. We went into the barracks, by the side of the fort, and were soon surrounded by a few officers and people, who received our books with great willingness. One old man remembered Mr. Lindsay very well, and said that that gentleman had been several times in his dwelling, and had fired off his fowling piece to amuse him. The rain now pouring down, in torrents, we were obliged to return on board, and close the operations of the day.

On the morrow, we had a visit from an officer, with a crystal button, Tsaou Laou-yay, who said, he was deputed by the general, to come and pay his respects to us; and fearful lest we should be gone out of the harbour, before he could get an opportunity of so doing, he came in the rain to visit us. Of course this was only a civil way of asking us to go; but as he spoke in such a friendly manner, we felt inclined to treat him with equal civility. We, therefore, asked him to step down into the cabin, and gave him tea, when we entered into conversation on the nature of our visit to the country. He said, that European vessels had been there previously, but that the laws forbad all trade, except at Canton. We told him that we came not to trade, but to distribute books; that we were sent by a religious society, whose object was to spread instruction, and make men acquainted with the way of salvation; thus we did not offend against the prohibition which forbad trade elsewhere than at Canton. He said, the distribution of books was a good thing; he had seen some of them on shore, and thought them excellent. Here his attention was taken up with the red curtains before our bed places, and he asked whether those were our altar pieces, dedicated to the worship of the gods? We told him that we worshipped only one God, the maker of heaven and earth, who, being a spirit, required to be worshipped in spirit and in truth; but that the places he referred to, were our sleeping berths. We went on to give him some account of Christianity, but he seemed to have no heart for it, and turned off the conversation to something else. He said, he had frequently been on board Mr. Lindsay's ship, and had received presents from him, of a spy-glass and a piece of broadcloth; wishing, perhaps, that we might be equally generous; but seeing no reason to lavish our gifts on a mere sycophant, we were dull in taking his hint. He then asked, when we intended to depart, and we told him that we could not think of it, until the wind and weather were more favourable. To this he assented, saying, it was impossible to go out in such a mist as then prevailed. He was particularly anxious to ascertain whither we intended to go, but could get no positive information from us. He informed us, that an overland dispatch had been received from Shan-tung, containing an account of our visit there, and stating that we had fifty men on board. We said that he probably alluded to some other vessel, as we had only eighteen hands; but he persisted that it was the same vessel, as the names and circumstances all agreed.

After his departure, we went to the fort on the south side of the river, where we were met, on landing, by some soldiers, who gladly received our books; and in a few minutes, an old fat mandarin, with a promiscuous crowd of followers, came running from an adjacent hamlet, to see what the strangers wanted. The old mandarin took some books, but appeared desirous of preventing our journey to the village, telling us, that the inhabitants were a bad set, who would rob and murder us, if we went amongst them. We said, that we would run all the risk of that, and were about to persevere in our journey, when the wily fellow sought to detain us, by engaging us in conversation, and requesting us to explain some of the books which had been given him. With this view, he held up one of the tracts, and said, " This is a very pretty book, and must be very interesting; please to explain a page or two in my hearing." We said that we had no time, but would willingly comply on our return. On his repeating the request, we were half inclined to gratify him; when it struck us, as such an unusual thing for a mandarin to express any curiosity about our books, that we could not help thinking he had some sinister object in view; and the result proved that our suspicions were not unfounded; for on breaking from him, and going towards the village, we found that he had sent forward one of his people, to remove the plank which was laid over the stream, by which means we were prevented from proceeding further. Finding that he had deceived and disappointed us, we called upon him to distribute the books among the people, with his own hands, as we were determined not to return till our work was done. Upon this, he gave five or six to one of his serjeants, and as many to another, for which he held them responsible. This mode of distribution, however, did not satisfy us, and we insisted that he should give them out, one by one, to as many as wanted books. This he objected to at first, but on our declaring that we would not return till he did, to our surprise he complied, and ordered his attendants to deal out the tracts leisurely and regularly, till a whole bag-full was expended. Thus we made a mandarin of the celestial empire, instrumental in distributing books among the people. The fort on this side of the river was in better order than the other; but the walls were just as thin, and the defences as ill contrived, as those on the opposite side. We could see no traces of anything like European art, in the erection of these forts; and concluded that they must have been the work of mere Chinese genius, without the aid of western science.

On the morning of the 12th, we undertook to sail over to Tsung-ming, an island about fifty miles long, and twenty wide, which has been formed by the deposits from the river Yang-tsze-keang, and is now inhabited by a million of people. As the weather appeared rather unsettled, and the estuary wide and rough, we thought it best to take the long boat, though experience had taught us that she was a bad sailer; yet we hoped she would be better adapted to a rough sea, than the smaller boat. We intended to start before four o'clock in the morning, in order to take advantage of the flood tide, which would carry us well to windward; but by some means or other, we did not get away till nearly five o'clock. Our course, in order to get to windward of the banks, that lay between us and the island, was due north, and the wind west north-west; but having got under weigh, we found that the nearest we could lay, was north north-east, and the tide having made to the east, was taking us fast to leeward; so that we were making but a north-east course of it. The sea also was rougher than we had calculated on, and we soon found, that the course we were going, would bring us directly on the southern shoal: having tried in vain to get nearer to the wind, we all judged it expedient to give up the undertaking, and put back to the vessel. On the other tack, we found that we could only lay south south-west, which would not enable us to fetch where we started from; and when morning dawned, we found that we were two or three miles to leeward of the brig, with a tide carrying us out to sea. Here we were much perplexed, to know what to do; for, if we remained on the beach, we expected that the boat would soon be stove in by the surf; if we put out into the stream, having no anchor, we felt that we should be carried a dozen miles to leeward before the tide turned; and pull or sail up against wind and tide, with a heavy unmanageable boat, was impossible. We therefore looked for some creek or cove, and at length discovered a small rivulet, into which we ran the boat; but as the tide was ebbing, it was evident she would soon be left aground, till the tide flowed again. This, however, was our only alternative; and being now on shore, our next thought was, how to turn our disappointment to the greatest advantage.

The people on this side, we had been told by the old mandarin, were extremely rude, and would be likely to beat us, if we went among them; but as we knew he was a deceiver, we took a bag of books, and started off through the villages. The path we took was about one of the dirtiest we had ever seen; but the people were exceedingly kind and friendly, and all anxious for books. The fields through which we passed, were fertile, producing rice, cotton and vegetables. The inhabitants were dirty, but most of them appeared to have sufficient clothes to keep them warm. When the report got abroad that we had brought books, they came flocking out of their houses, or running over the fields, to solicit tracts. Some waded up to their middle through dikes to get the volumes, and one man wanted to know, what he had to pay for them. Our bag was frequently replenished, but it was emptied nearly as soon as it was filled. We observed, every now and then, coffins above ground, made fast to stakes, in order to prevent their being washed away by the inundations which sometimes prevail. Passing on, we saw a number of jars, about a foot and a half high, which, on inspection, proved to be full of human bones, with the skull on the top. Hence we inferred, that they leave the dead bodies uninterred till they decay, and then collect the bones for further preservation. Whether this is on account of the dampness of the soil, which will hardly admit of graves being made under ground, or in consequence of the value of land, which induces them to give more to the support of the living, than to the accomodation of the dead, we were not able to determine. The natives, however, did not seem displeased at our examining the bones; and appeared to look upon these monuments of mortality with much familiarity, shewing that they regarded the commom lot of mankind with the utmost indifference. Having given out our books, we returned to the boat, which we found, as we expected, aground in the rivulet.

We now became anxious to get her afloat as the tide
would soon turn, and we wished to avail ourselves of it,
to get back to the vessel.   Being unable, however, to
move the boat ourselves, we applied to the natives,
and offered them cash if they would shove her off.
They said, they would not do it for money, but if we
would give them books, they would consent.   We accordingly promised them a tract each, but they stipulated
for two; and we finally agreed to give each man two,
and each boy one.   They then gave a shout, and set to
work some of them up to their middle in black mud,
and pushed the boat, with all hands in her, to the mouth
of the river; arrived at this point, they came to a stand,
demanding their books: but we refused to give out a
single volume, till the boat was fairly over the bar.
Hearing this they again set to work, and soon had her
out in deep water.   Upon this, we fulfilled our contract;
but the rogues contrived to steal two pair of shoes belonging to us; which depredations we did not discover,
till they were gone.

No sooner had we distributed our books, than some
mandarins and a party of soldiers appeared; upon which
the natives decamped, taking their books with them.
We now beckoned to the soldiers, and told them, that
if they would tow us along the beach, we would give
them money.   The bargain was accordingly struck, for
four hundred copper cash, which the soldiers required
to be paid before haned.

Notwithstanding experience has often proved, that it
is as bad to pay too soon, as too late; yet we thought
that the sight of the money would put new life into
them, and set them to work forthwith.   In this, however, we were mistaken; for no sooner was the money

in hand, than they found it necessary to sit down to count, and then divide the prize, before they could think of proceeding to active operation. Having settled this important business, they endeavoured to procure some people to tow us along, and got us ahead nearly a mile; when, tired of this slow mode of procedure, we cast off the rope, took down our masts, and having the tide with us, rowed towards the brig. In a few minutes we saw our vessel under weigh, intending to meet us near the island, according to previous appointment; upon which we exerted our utmost strength to get to the brig, but had the mortification to see her pass, within gun-shot, without observing us. At length, however, the people on board got sight of a signal which we made, and came to; but the vessel was then so far away, that, with the tide making against us, and without sail on the boat, we could not possibly reach her. Upon this we resolved to push for the nearest junk, where we might get purchase enough to hoist our mast, and thus endeavour to fetch the vessel. We now found the wind so strong, that the boat was nearly capsized, and at one time she went over so far, as to roll her gunwale about four inches under water. This obliged us to shorten sail; and after much wetting, fatigue, and danger, we finally reached the vessel, about two o'clock in the afternoon, thankful to our Divine deliverer, who had thus far brought us safely through.

We ascertained from the captain, that as soon as he began to weigh anchor in the morning all the war junks came down, ond anchored alongside of the brig, each one firing blank cartridges across the vessel's bows; after which, a boat-load of mandarins came on board, completely filling the quarter-deck. As soon as they came over the gangway, they asked for the missionaries, and were thunderstruck when they heard, that we were absent.   Having left the ship before daylight, we eluded the vigilance of their scouts, and some of the poor subalterns on guard, doubtless got severely punished for allowing us to escape them.   It is the practice of the Chinese mandarins to punish their inferior officers, for real or supposed neglect of duty, by boring their ears with a long bamboo, to which is affixed a flag, descriptive of the crime of the offender. Finding that the birds were flown, they were anxious to get the cage away also, and did not cease dunning the captain, till he had nearly got his anchor up, when they left him, and with their war junks, all returned up the river.   The trading vessels, however, seemed very anxious to have commercial dealings with us, for they called to us as they passed, desiring us to meet them outside.   On passing us, one of their navigators asked us, *what letter we intended to eat ?* by which he meant to enquire, what course we proposed to steer, in order that he might meet us in the offing.   Thus, it is evident, that if we had been disposed to buy and sell, an opportunity would have been afforded us for so doing, out of sight of the mandarins.

CHAPTER XIX.

OCCURRENCES IN CHE-KEANG AND FUH-KEEN.

DEPARTURE FROM KEANG-SOO — AND ARRIVAL AT KIN-TANG — VISIT OF
WAR-BOATS — OPERATIONS ON SHORE — PERISHING BOY — PROCEED-
INGS AT CHOO-SAN — EAGERNESS FOR BOOKS — COFFINS SCATTERED
ABOUT — VOYAGE TO POO-TOO — PICTURESQUE APPEARANCE OF THE
ISLAND — ITS CONSECRATION TO IDOLATRY — DESCRIPTION OF THE
TEMPLES — CHARACTER OF THE PRIESTS — CONVERSATION WITH NA-
VAL OFFICERS — LIBERAL VIEWS OF A MANDARIN — PROVIDENTIAL
ESCAPE — ARRIVAL AT NAN-YIH — APPEARANCE OF THE WOMEN — THE
TOWN OF TUNG-SAN — FREE DISTRIBUTION — DISORDERLY CONDUCT OF
A MANDARIN — AND SUBSEQUENT ALARM — SURPRISE OF THE PEOPLE
— RETURN.

ON the 13th of October, we left the mouth of the
Yang-tsze-keang, passing by Gutzlaff's island, with
some others, and anchored for the night, as we thought,
within a few miles of Kin-tang: but the next morning,
we found that we had mistaken our position, as the
charts of this region differ about sixty miles from each
other. Finding our water shoal suddenly, we were
obliged to come to; and on going ashore, at the nearest
island, we found that instead of Kin-tang, we had made
Fisher's island, one amongst the barren islets of the
northern Choo-san group, but thirty miles to the eastward of the place we sought; so that we had to steer
west a considerable way, and not reaching Kin-tang by
sun-set, were obliged to anchor for the night. Thus
we lost a day. On the morrow, we were becalmed, till
the afternoon; but were enabled to fetch Kin-tang by

the evening, off which we anchored, between that island and Ning-po.

On the morning of the 16th, six war-boats came
alongside, the commanders of which were very civil.
We supplied the crews with books, and conversed with
the officers, on the best things, for a considerable time.
One of them appeared to be rather an intelligent man,
and listened with attention to our discourse, approving
of our doctrines and proceedings. After remaining about
an hour, they observed a war junk heave in sight,
having on board the commander of the squadron, on seeing whose signal they all quitted us abruptly; and having anchored under our stern, commenced firing blank
cartridges; but whether to salute their colonel, or to
terrify the barbarians, we could not tell. We, however,
manned our boat, and went on shore at the island of
Kin-tang, whither none of the war-boats followed us,
so that we were left to carry on our operations unmolested. We landed at the head of the bay, on the north-
east side, and entered a town, where we found the
people uncommonly friendly, and where our books circulated with ease and rapidity. None of them were
snatched out of our bag, but the volumes were eagerly
caught at, by the surrounding multitude, as soon as we
held them up. All were cheerful and delighted; and
not a wry look, or an angry word, was seen or heard.
The women also came forward, soliciting books; and
the boys followed us to some distance, begging for
tracts. At one place, we were obliged to get upon a
wall, in order to avoid the crowd, and from that elevation dealt out our publications with the greatest facility.
Outside the town, we saw a poor boy, lying down in
the last stage of dropsy, and evidently dying. We had

no medicine with us, but we saw that, with the best
advice and care, it would have been impossible to save
him; added to which, he was lying on the cold ground,
exposed to all the winds of day, and dews of night,
which circumstance of itself, was enough to bring any
one to a speedy end. The poor boy had probably been
turned out to die in the streets, a practice very common
in China, to prevent persons dying in a house, and thereby polluting the dwelling for some time to come.

After having supplied this town with tracts, we went
over to Ta-ping-shan, an island opposite, where we
found a large plain, in a high state of cultivation, over
which we walked, distributing books to all. Scarcely
any refused our offer, and many came running over the
fields, as soon as we shewed them a book, eagerly
grasping at it, as though it were some highly valued
treasure.

Returning to Kin-tang, we ascended the hills, which
we found planted with firs; these hardy plants serve
the inhabitants for fuel, and appear to be the only production capable of thriving on the high lands; while
the plains are covered with waving grain, and yield a
rich produce. On the whole, we had a very good
day's work, and after a second excursion to another
bay, retired to rest, completely fatigued.

Apprehending much annoyance in going to Ning-po,
and not being willing to waste time in negociations, we
did not prolong our stay in this quarter; but set sail on
the 17th, through the Choo-san archipelago, followed
by two imperial junks, aud several war-boats, which
kept astern of us, for a considerable way, firing blank
cartridges continually; but without further troubling
us. After an intricate navigation, which our captain

conducted with much skill and care, amid rocks and shoals, altogether unknown, we arrived at Sin-kea-mun, on the east end of the great Choo-san island. Here we went on shore with a load of books, which were eagerly caught at by the people; indeed, they actually fought with each other to obtain them; and so fierce were their contests, that we found it impossible to take more than one bag-full of books up the beach; while the rest were distributed from the boat, to the crowds who pressed down to receive them. We were afraid that, in this way, the rabble only would obtain tracts, while the more repectable part of the population would come short; but on passing afterwards through the village, we found, that every shopkeeper had a book in his hand, and that they were all as regularly supplied, as if we had gone from house to house, distributing our publications.

We met with a number of Fŭh-këen people here, from the junks which had anchored off the village; these sea-faring men were remarkably friendly, and the more so, when they heard us address them in their own dialect. The war junks that followed us, anchored close alongside the brig, to the number of eleven; but did not give us any annoyance, neither did they deter the people from receiving our books. We observed an order stuck up in the village, issued by the chief magistrate of Ning-po, forbidding any commercial dealings with foreigners; but as the order seemed to be of an old date, and as we were not come to trade, we considered that it did not respect us, and therefore took no further notice of it.

The next day, being the sabbath, we remained on board, and held service in the cabin, at which some of

the sailors attended.   But in the afternoon, we went on
shore with a boat-load of books, which we commenced
distributing through the villages.   The people, old and
young, male and female, were all anxious to obtain
them ; and we went on delightfully and quietly in our
work of mercy.   In the retired hamlets, we found numerous opportunities for regularly and systematically distributing our pamphlets, without that boisterous scrambling, which prevailed in the town ; and, therefore,
preferred it.   But having gone through the villages,
and approached the town, we found a number of people,
congregated in front of a temple, clamorous for books.
We told them, that we would not distribute any, unless
they would consent to receive them quietly ; adding that
it was quite preposterous, in a civilized people like the
Chinese, to behave so rudely.   This they all acknowledged, and promised faithfully to forbear scrambling.
But no sooner was the mouth of the bag opened, than
they darted upon it, like birds of prey, and in spite of
all that we could do, they got it completely into their
own hands, and did not cease till they had emptied it
of its entire contents.   Our subsequent reproofs were
as unavailing as our previous stipulations, for they carried off their prize without regarding us.   Some by-
standers, who did not get any, said, that such conduct
was shameful ; and a few Fŭh-këen people declared that,
if we were in their province, we should be treated with
more civility ; but even among them, we afterwards
found that wherever a crowd was collected together,
scrambling was the order of the day.   We addressed
the multitudes who surrounded us, on the importance
of religion, and the necessity of attending to their best
interests, to which they paid some attention.

In the neighbourhood of the town, under a little hill, we observed a number of coffins, promiscuously thrown together; some new, and others decaying and tumbling to pieces. On asking the people, why they did not bury their dead, we were informed, that they had not money enough to buy a burial place, or to make the sacrifices usual on such occasions; on which account, they deposited the remains of their relatives and friends provisionally under the hill; until success in business, or a fertile harvest, should provide them with the means of performing the last duties towards them.

On the 19th of October, we weighed anchor, and intended to sail outside the archipelago, in order to reach Poo-too, which lay to the north-east; but discovering a narrow passage between the islands, we sailed through it, within fifty yards of a rock on one side, and as near to a dangerous shoal on the other. By this manœuvre, we reached Poo-too about ten o'clock, instead of spending 'the whole day about it, as we should otherwise have been compelled to do. As soon as we got under weigh, the Chinese fleet of war-junks followed us, firing off several guns, which salute we returned. By means of their superior knowledge of the passages between the islands, they saved much of the distance, and arrived at Poo-too as soon as we did, casting anchor at some distance from us. Without heeding them, we loaded our boats with tracts, and went ashore; where we commenced ascending those romantic heights, crowned by fantastic temples and enchanting groves, so glowingly described by a previous traveller in his account of this island. We soon found a broad and well-beaten pathway, which led to the top of one of the hills, at every crag and turn of which, we espied a tem-

ple, or a grotto, an inscription, or an image; with
here and there a garden tastefully laid out, and walks
lined with aromatic shrubs, diffusing a grateful fragrance through the air. The prospect from these
heights was delightful in the extreme; numerous
islands, far and near, bestudded the main; rocks and
precipices above and below; here and there a mountain
monastery rearing its head; and in the distant valley,
the great temple, with its yellow tiles, indicative of imperial distinction, basked like a basilisk in the rays of
the noon-day sun. All the aids that could be collected
from nature and art, were there concentrated, to render
the scene lovely and enchanting. But to the eye of the
Christian philanthropist, it presented one melancholy
picture of moral and spiritual death. Viewed by the
light of revelation, and in the prospect of eternity, the
whole island of Poo-too, with its picturesque scenery,
its hundred temples, and its six thousand priests, exhibited to the mind nothing but a useless waste of property, a gross misemployment of time, and a pernicious
fostering of error, tending to corrupt the surrounding
population, and to draw off their minds from the worship
of the true God, to the adoration of the phantom Buddha.
All the sumptuous and extensive buildings of this
island, were intended for no other purpose than to
screen wooden images from the sun and rain; and all
its inhabitants employed in no other work than the re-
citation of unmeaning prayers, and the direction of useless contemplations, towards stocks and stones : so that
human science and human happiness, would not be in
the least diminished, if the whole island of Poo-too,
with its gaudy temples, and lazy priests, were blotted
out from the face of the creation. The only thing we

heard out of the mouths of these dull monks, was " O-me-to Fŭh," or Amida Buddha. To every observation that was made, re-echoed, " O-me-to Fŭh;" and the reply to every enquiry was, " O-me-to Fŭh." Each priest was furnished with a string of beads, which he kept continually fingering, and while he counted, he still repeated the same dull, monotonous exclamation. The characters for this name met the eye at every turn of the road, at every corner of the temples, and on every scrap of paper : on the hills, on the altars, on the gateways, and on the walls, the same words presented themselves ; even the solid rocks were engraven with Buddha's titles, and the whole island seemed to be under the spell of this talismanic phrase, as if it were devoted to the recording of " *O-me-to Fuh.*" We were never so much disgusted with a phrase in our lives, and heartily wished ourselves out of the hearing and seeing of its sound and form.

The temples, which at a distance look pretty and interesting, lost much of their beauty on a nearer inspection ; and the caverns, which we thought would repay the trouble of exploring, proved to be mere holes, about eight or ten feet deep, with a few rude images, cut out of the rock, at the further end. The inscriptions on stone, by the road side, were most of them so shallow, and the disintegration of the granite, by the mere action of the rain water, so rapid, that the letters were nearly illegible ; the sculpture of the images, which here and there presented themselves, was likewise so badly executed, that it was difficult to conceive at times, what the artist had intended to represent, by the uncouth and unsightly figures produced. The smaller temples abounded at every turn of the road, and presented nothing remarkable; of large temples, there were two, very nearly resembling each other, and not much unlike the Josh-house at Honan, opposite the city of Canton, described in Davis's Chinese. These fanes consisted of a central range of buildings, one behind the other; flanked on each side by the dwellings of priests. The first of these middle structures was occupied by four colossal figures, which appear to have been placed as guards to the establishment: behind this building was the principal hall, with the three Buddhas in a very large size, surrounded by the eighteen disciples of the god; which, though in a sitting posture, were each about eight feet high. The third hall was dedicated to Kwan-yin, the mother of Buddha, and the goddess of mercy; while the fourth was occupied by three bearded images, with savage aspects, which appeared to be of Egyptian origin. In this latter hall, was the library of the establishment, containing several thousand volumes of religious books, relating the conversations of Buddha with his disciples, and embodying the prayers which are to be recited by his votaries. In the rear of the great temple, we found a school, taught by a disciple of Confucius, but the scholars were all young shaven-headed fellows, destined for the Buddhist priesthood. We asked, whether the priests ever taught the boys under their care, of which there are great numbers on the island; but were told, that the sole employment of these holy men was to recite prayers to, and employ themselves in contemplations upon, Buddha. Attached to the other great temple, we observed a refectory, where the holy brotherhood are supplied with their daily rations; for though they profess to live solely on a vegetable diet, they are not backward in securing to themselves all that a bounteous providence affords, among the various productions of the earth. Indeed, wherever we went, we found the priests busy in providing for their natural wants, since on on entering their dwellings, we almost invariably encountered them in the kitchen.

On asking to be admitted to the high priest, we were told, that he was engaged in reciting prayers to Buddha, but we rather suspect that he was taking an afternoon nap, for on approaching his chamber, an attendant had to go in and arouse him ; taking with him his garment, that he might not appear abroad in his dishabille. His conversation was as uninteresting to us, as ours was to him; and he appeared so absorbed in himself, or Buddha, that we found it necessary to take our leave.

Over the whole island, our books were readily accepted, and some were found that had been left there by Gutzlaff, a few years before: the people, however, did not solicit our publications, with tears in their eyes, as when he visited the island. On all sides, we were gratified by perceiving marks of decay, in the temples and adjacent buildings ; and earnestly hope, that future travellers will find these worse than useless structures level with the ground ; and the lazy drones who inhabit them, scattered abroad, or employed in promoting the welfare and intelligence of their fellow countrymen. The priests generally opened the doors of each temple as we approached, supposing that we came to worship at the different shrines ; but we told them, that our adorations were paid to the living God, the maker of heaven and earth, to whom alone they were due. One of the priests wished us to contribute something towards beautifying an image, which had lost its gilt coat, and

looked rather shabby; but we told him, that his was a
poor god, that could not furnish himself with clothes;
for our parts, when our apparel was worn out, we contrived to get a new dress by honest industry, and should
leave their god to do the same.

Being followed, from place to place, by one man in
particular, we suspected that he came from the war-
junks, to watch our motions; and on putting a few enquiries to him, we found that our surmises were true.
We therefore asked him, why he followed us so closely?
To which he replied, that he merely wished to prevent our trading, as foreigners were forbidden to traffic
any where but at Canton. We told him, that he had
quite mistaken our object, seeing that we came neither
to buy nor sell, but to distribute good books, for their
instruction and benefit.

On returning to our brig, we found the commodore
of the Chinese fleet, and one of his naval captains,
come to pay their respects to us. The former was
Te Laou-yay, with a blue button, filling the rank of
lieutenant-colonel; and the latter was Sung Laou-yay,
with a crystal button. The colonel was a sleek-faced,
easy sort of man, who said little and did less; but the
captain was very friendly and talkative. We asked
them, why we were honoured by the attendance of
their vessels from place to place? to which they replied,
that they merely came out to shew us the way, and to
see that we did not fall upon rocks and shoals; only
they happened to be astern, instead of ahead. We observed, that if their object were to prevent our trading,
they might spare themselves the trouble, as we were
not traders, but circulators of good books, which surely
they could not forbid. They said, they could perceive

that our object was a benevolent one ; but as there had been vessels in those seas before, engaged in the opium trade, which was not only illegal but immoral, they thought, at first, that we were embarked in the same traffic, and, therefore, came to prevent it.   As for regular intercourse, they confessed that it would be better for both countries, were it allowed ; and they complained that the laws of China were too severe, in prohibiting all commerce with foreigners, except at Canton.   They spoke highly of Mr. Lindsay ; and said, they felt for him, when they saw that he was obliged to depart from Ning-po, without having been able to effect his purpose.   Such candid and liberal sentiments did them honour, and we felt ourselves somewhat attached to the individuals who uttered them.   Our dinner being ready, we invited them to partake of our humble fare, to which they readily assented ; and, after having spent a pleasant afternoon, we parted good friends.   On the following day, we set sail, and left the Choo-san archipelago, when we were pleased to see, that the junks no longer followed us.

On the 21st, we tried to get into Shih-poo, but found that we were more than twenty miles to leeward of it, before we made the land ; so that, rather than spend much time in endeavouring to beat back, we thought it best to stand away, towards the province of Fŭh-këen.

After two days' sail, we came to a part of the coast, to us unknown ; and as the weather was threatening, we endeavoured to work into a bay, which opened out before us.   After spending the whole morning in beating to and fro, we, at length, came to an anchor, under the lee of a few islands.   We had scarcely dined, however, before we perceived, by the falling of the tide, an extensive reef of rocks, within a few hundred yards of us, with the breakers dashing over them, as high as the mast-head. Had we stood on, or altered our course, in the least, we should, inevitably, have been dashed in pieces. Thus we were again preserved from dangers, seen and unseen, by Him, who sees and knows all things. On enquiry, we found that the island near us, was one of the north-western, Nan-yïh (Lan-yeet), islands, belonging to the district of Poo-tëen, in the county of Hinhwa, and the province of Fŭh-këen. But the weather was so bad, and the sea so high, that we could not go on shore ; and the storm continuing for the two following days, confined us entirely to the vessel. On the 26th, we attempted to land, but were compelled, by the roughness of the sea, and the violence of the wind to return.

On the following morning, the weather having moderated a little, we set off in the jolly boat, and in a few minutes were completely drenched by the spray. We arrived, however, in safety at the beach, when the people flocked down to us like ants, and readily accepted our books. There was no hesitation manifested ; indeed we could not distribute the volumes fast enough for them, and it required no little adroitness, so to dispose of our stock, as to give each one a book, without allowing a few individuals to grasp more than fell to their share. After the people on the shore were satisfied, we commenced a tour through the villages, distributing as we went along; when we saw them hurrying across the fields, or running out of their houses, with their potatoe broth in their hands, while not a few followed hard at our heels, begging for books. The women, who were

2 K 2

particularly anxious to obtain our volumes, exhibited
more taste and skill in the decoration of their persons,
than their sisters farther north ; their heads were
adorned with artificial flowers ; their hair was tastefully
arranged, and around the knot was a circular ornament,
not much unlike a tortoise-shell comb ; which, with
their dangling ear-rings, and long hair pins, presented
quite a gay appearance.   Their pinks and roses looked
as bright and blooming, as if they had just been plucked
from the garden ; and those who could not afford flowers,
inserted a sprig of myrtle into their head-dress, which
had a very pleasing effect.   Some of them had their
hair twisted into a variety of bows and crests, whilst
others had fillets of black silk or crape, bound round
their foreheads, which tended not a little to set off their
pale complexions.   Their feet were the smallest we
had ever seen, even among the Chinese. We measured
the impression of one woman's foot in the sand, and
found it only four inches ; while some appeared to be
much smaller.   Owing to the compression of their
feet, their ankles were much swollen, and the lower part
of the leg was a little crooked ; however, they hobbled
along, and even managed to run, with their bodies
bent forward, much better than we could have expected.

   The soil seemed exceedingly poor, producing only
sweet potatoes, and ground nuts ; while the people subsisted mainly by fishing ; in the prosecution of which
occupation, they were very bold and daring, venturing
out to sea in the roughest weather, and sometimes
obtaining only a few baskets of small fish, about the
size of shrimps, for their pains.

   Their houses were built of stone, and generally
thatched ; but many were covered with tiles, and in

some instances, cemented together, in the same neat and compact manner, which we had observed at Shan-tuhg. On the roofs we espied a great number of stones, placed there to prevent the tiles being blown away, by the strong winds which prevailed. The inside of their dwellings was filthy, and the stench about them exceedingly offensive to strangers, though it appeared to give the inhabitants little annoyance.

Having returned to the vessel about two o'clock, we got under weigh the same afternoon, and steered for the southward. In four and twenty hours we came to an anchor in Tung-san (Tang-soa) bay, sheltered by Pagoda Island, when we immediately went on shore, to visit the town of Tung-san. The ship having anchored at some distance, and the boat not being perceived till we were close in, we came quite suddenly upon them; and landed at one end of the town, before the people could get out of their houses. We found two or three persons on the beach, to whom we gave books, and the news of the free distribution of tracts spreading rapidly, a great multitude soon assembled, every one clamorous for the gift. We clearly perceived, that it was impossible to give out our publications in the midst of the crowd; for though we reasoned with them on the propriety of patience, and said they should each have a book if they would but wait; yet no sooner was the basket opened, that each one, fearful lest he should lose the prize, made a dart at the volumes, and snatched them away in all directions. We therefore climbed up on a rock, about eight feet high, and began giving out the tracts, one by one, to the hundred hands stretched forth to receive them; but the more active natives soon mounted the rock from behind, and in

their eagerness to obtain what they sought, nearly
pushed the distributor off the rock, while they threw
the whole contents of the basket over the people's heads,
and in a moment every volume disappeared.   We kept
our station, however, and having got a fresh supply,
dealt them out as well as we could; and then a third,
talking to them in the meanwhile, and exhorting them
to study the tracts which they so eagerly desired. Having supplied the people round the rock, we perceived
that a greater crowd had surrounded the boat, and we
proceeded thither.   Here we dealt the books out as fast
as our hands could move, while the sailors were busily
engaged in keeping the people out of the boat, and
their hands out of the bag. It was pleasing to see how
the natives waded into the water, above their knees,
one party after another, greedily crying out for books,
and bearing them in triumph to their friends, till our
store was more than half exhausted.   Thinking now
that the people in this part of the town were well supplied, we judged it adviseable to go to the other end of
the settlement, in order to give the rest of the inhabitants an opportunity of obtaining books.   The crowd,
perceiving our intention, followed us along shore ; and
when we put the boat's head out to sea, in order to avoid
the rocks, the people supposing that we were about to
leave the place, came up to their middle in water, entreating us not to go away, till we had distributed the
rest of our books.

When we reached the further end of the town, we
landed in the midst of a multitude, and got into an
empty boat on shore, in order to give out the books
with greater ease ; but the crowd pressed so heavily
on each other, and rushed with such eagerness into the

boat, that we were afraid of being thrown down and trodden under foot. We therefore stood on one side, while the second mate, who was a powerful man, aided by one of the sailors, to keep off the crowd, took the books and distributed them leisurely amongst the people. Having finished one bag-full in this way, the mate climbed a high wall with another supply, and from thence handed out the tracts to the populace below. Unexpectedly, however, they got the bag from him, and were bearing it off in triumph, when he sprang in among them, and recovered the prize, which he did not let go again, till the books were all regularly distributed. About this time, hundreds of people thronged the place, and we were standing at a little distance, among the crowd, to observe how matters went on ; when suddenly we heard a clattering of bamboos about our heads, and thinking that the shed under which we stood was coming down, we instinctively moved on one side to avoid it. But we soon found that the noise was occasioned by two petty officers who came along with bamboo poles, sixteen or twenty feet long, battering about the heads of the populace, and making them fly right and left. Having scattered the people, we perceived one of the officers advancing towards the mate, with his bamboo, and knowing that if he attempted to strike him, a disturbance would ensue, we went up to the mandarin, and making him lay down his weapon, asked him what he meant by such disorderly conduct. He said, that having observed a tumultuous crowd assembled, and fearful lest an altercation should ensue, between our people and theirs, he wanted to disperse the mob. We told him that such a mode of proceeding would rather tend to an altercation than otherwise, and therefore advised him to resort to milder measures. As the books were now all distributed, we did not mind the dispersion of the crowd, and being addressed by another mandarin in a little more decent manner, we accepted of his invitation to go into the castle, and partake of some tea.

This castle consisted of a kind of tower, about twenty feet high, and as many broad, on the top of which was a room, just strong enough to bear the weight of the mob that followed us up. No guns were to be seen, and the only warlike instruments were a few spears, stuck up in the room just mentioned. Attached to the tower was a wall, about eight or ten feet high, and one foot thick, which stretched over the hill adjoining the fortress; this fence did not appear to enclose any habitations, while the place where the town was built, had no wall round it: as if the people, by some strange whim, had resolved to build their houses where there was no walk, and the government by as strange a caprice, had determined to construct a wall where there were no houses. The defences, however, were of the most flimsy description, being not even calculated to exclude a tumultuous rabble of their own countrymen, much less to resist the incursion of foreigners.

Whilst seated in the tower, surrounded by scores of soldiers, and hundreds of people, who might if they pleased have seized and imprisoned us, we were not a little amused at the consternation of one of the mandarins on observing the pretended anger of Mr. Stevens. The author was relating to his companion the circumstance of the petty officer having made use of the bamboo, by which he inadvertently struck the narrator; when Mr. S. got up, apparently much displeased, and with a fierce countenance, asked the officer, in English, how he could think of striking his fellow traveller. The mandarin, not understanding what was said, and imagining from the tone and manner of our friend, that he was displeased, turned as pale as death, and enquired of the author, with quivering lips, what was the matter? In order to calm his fears, and prevent a real misunderstanding, he was told that Mr. S. was merely in joke; when the mandarin resumed his wonted equanimity.

After conversing a short time with the officers, we proceeded to the market, in order to purchase provisions, to which no objection was made. We found the streets narrow, but the population overflowing, attracted principally by the desire of seeing the strangers, so that we could scarcely move along for the crowd; and when we stopped to purchase anything, the way was completely choked up with people, while many climbed up to the tops of the houses, and surveyed us from thence. The market was well stocked with all kinds of eatables, and the shops with different sorts of wares. The country around, however, was barren, and the promontory on which the town was built, exhibited the most bleak and sterile aspect that could be imagined; so that one might well wonder, how people could think of fixing upon such a spot for a residence, or how, when settled, the inhabitants could possibly obtain the means of subsistence.

The people were astonished at the exactness with which one of us spoke their dialect, being not only that of the province of Fŭh-këen, and the county of Changchow, but even of the district of Chang-poo, where their town was situated. This is sufficiently accounted for by the speaker having had a moonshe from the district alluded to, for several years in his employ. They were, however, much puzzled how to account for the circumstance. Some insisted on it, that the stranger was a native of that region; others imagined that his parents belonged to Chang-chow, and that he had acquired the dialect from his earliest infancy. But then they could not account for the light colour and curling nature of his hair. Still they thought he must be a Chinese, though of a strange make; but were satisfied when they heard, that he came from Batavia, where he had learned the language from some of their own countrymen residing there.

The next morning we went to the north-west side of the bay, where we had observed a group of villages, affording an excellent opportunity for distributing books. Here we were gladly received by the people, who were anxious for tracts, and who hailed us as friends, wherever we went. The petty officers on shore gave us no annoyance, and did not interfere with our distributing books, or purchasing provisions from the people. The women were forward also in begging books, and one said she wanted a volume to give to her son, as a school-book. Here we had frequent opportunities of conversing with the people on good things, who heard us the more readily, because we spoke their native dialect. Some were so delighted, that they scarcely knew how to express their joy, dancing with frantic wildness, and running before us, to get a more regular survey of the strangers. Altogether, we spent a most delightful morning, and coming on board a little after mid-day, as our books were exhausted, we immediately set sail for Canton.

Thus we have gone through various parts of four

provinces, and many villages, giving away about eighteen thousand volumes, of which six thousand were portions of the scriptures, amongst a cheerful and willing peo ple, without meeting with the least aggression or injury; having been always received by the people with a cheerful smile, and most generally by the officers with politeness and respect. We would here record our grateful sense of such long-continued and repeated manifestations of Divine goodness, to his unworthy servants, and pray that His blessing may descend on the seed sown, and make it bring forth an abundant harvest.

CHAPTER XX.

SUBSEQUENT OCCURRENCES.

RESTRICTIVE POLICY OF THE CHINESE—EXCLUSION OF FOREIGNERS—
ANGER AT THEIR INTRUSION—EDICT AGAINST THE HURON—APPEAL
TO THE BRITISH AUTHORITIES—COMPLAINTS AGAINST THE ENGLISH
—DISAPPROBATION OF OUR BOOKS—THREATS OF STOPPING THE TRADE
—LATE VOYAGE OF GUTZLAFF—TUNG-SAN BAY—DESCRIPTION OF THE
COUNTRY AND ITS INHABITANTS—BARREN REGION—EXTENSIVE VAL-
LEY—MOUNTAIN RIDGE—DESERTED VILLAGES—INTESTINE BROILS—
CHINESE TEMPLE—FERTILE SPOT—POPULOUS CITY—RAVENOUS LA-
BOURERS—CHARACTER OF THE MANDARINS—TSIN-KANG DISTRICT—
EAGERNESS FOR BOOKS—VISIT TO AMOEY—ANXIETY FOR MORE LA-
BOURERS.

THE Chinese government is characterized by restriction
and exclusion. Though they boast of their emperor,
as the " Son of Heaven," and consider " all within the
four seas," as subject to his dominion ; affecting to
believe, that all besides " the flowery nation" is barbarity and meanness, depending on the Chinese for the
necessaries of life, and existing only by their permission,—yet they are afraid of every petty horde on their
borders, and suspect every foreign nation of having designs on their country. They anticipate nothing but
disaster from the reciprocation of kind offices, between
their own countrymen and strangers, and as for the
mutual exchange of intelligence, it must, in their estimation, be " evil, only evil, and that continually." They
care not to be made acquainted with our discoveries in

the arts and sciences ; while they would doubly deprecate our obtaining any knowledge of the weakness of
their government, the discontent of their people, the
poverty of their resources, the inefficiency of their defences, the navigation of their rivers, the direction of
their roads, the fertility of their soil, or the secret of
their manufactures. In short, any statistical, political,
commercial, or general information, relative to the interior, falling into the hands of foreigners, would be
regretted by them, as leading others to covet and over-
throw their country : they have, therefore, resolved to
keep to themselves as much as possible.

This restrictive policy leads them to exclude all fo-
rigners from the interior of the empire, to order off all
vessels from any other than the authorized port, to disapprove of strangers landing elsewhere than in Canton,
to prevent their proceeding far in land, to require them
to depart as soon as possible, and to provide that shipwrecked mariners be forwarded, by the most expeditious means, to Canton, without being allowed to loiter
in the districts where they may be cast on shore. Formerly, a few foreign literati were entertained at court,
for the purpose of calculating eclipses, correcting the
calendar, and teaching mathematics, as well as with
the view of completing a geometrical survey of the
country : but as the Chinese think that they can manage these things alone, they abstain from employing
any foreign adherents, and exclude strangers, as much
as they can, from the country ; in order that they may
keep native information from leaking out, and foreign
opinions from creeping in.

Notwithstanding their prohibitions, however, they
are astonished and exasperated to find, that the catho-

lics still secretly maintain their footing, and increase the number of their adherents in the country; while protestant missionaries are perpetually attempting to diffuse their principles, by landing on the coast, and deluging the maritime districts with Scriptures and tracts. This has called forth the expression of imperial disapprobation on various occasions, and edicts have been published, denouncing such proceedings, in the most unmeasured terms. One very severe proclamation was issued in the year 1812, in which the diffusion of Christianity was declared a capital crime; and yet, in the very teeth of that order, Dr. Morrison and his brethren have been carrying on their operations, for a quarter of a century. When the Honourable Company's chartered ship, the Amherst, went up the coast, proclamations of various kinds were issued; and the most furious edicts have followed each successive voyage in the same direction, which, if collected, would fill a volume. No sooner had the enterprise, described in the foregoing pages, been concluded, than a dispatch arrived from Peking, addressed to the viceroy of Canton, expressive of the emperor's high displeasure, and requiring the governor to take measures to prevent such proceedings in future.

To those who are not familiar with Chinese edicts, the language of such proclamations may appear alarming. In the preamble the emperor says, that " immediately after the attempt of the Amherst and other vessels, to penetrate into the inner waters, he issued orders to all the civil and military officers, to be on their guard, and ward off, and obstruct foreign vessels, without suffering the least remissness." The stranger, on reading this, and imagining that commands are as punctually obeyed in China, as in Europe, would expect to find, that the strictest care was taken to discover foreign vessels on the coast; and that a force was everywhere provided, sufficient to ward off all attempts at intercourse; but when the author prosecuted his voyage, several years after the expedition of the Amherst, he found no such watch kept up, or guard maintained; while the vessel anchored at various ports, and the travellers went on shore, rambling through the villages, and conversing with multitudes of people, frequently without being discovered, much less impeded by the mandarins.

In the course of his proclamation, the emperor declares, that " the restrictive laws must be eternally obeyed, so as to render the dignity of the empire, in the highest degree, impressive, and effectually prevent future evils." On reading this passage, the uninitiated would be ready to conclude, that the laws of China are like those of the Medes and Persians, unalterable; and that henceforth the efforts of Christians to spread among the Chinese the knowledge of salvation, will be entirely unavailing; but the apprehension of the unchangeablenesss of the present state of things may be allayed, by considering, that the laws of China have been altered, and are altering every year. When a regard to self-interest on the one hand, and spirited remonstrances on the other, urge them, the celestials do not scruple to swerve from their eternally restrictive laws; and when the perseverance of foreigners has convinced them, that it is of no use any longer to hold out, they have been known, of themselves, to propose terms of accommodation. It is only for the propagators of Christianity to persevere in their efforts, to enlighten the people, and when the government find that they are unable to prevent it, they will consent, either to shut their eyes to what they cannot help ; or to admit that to be done regularly, which will be done irregularly without them.

But the emperor has already told the world, by this very edict, that he cannot prevent the introduction of Christian books into his dominions. He says, that "strict orders have been given to watch and ward off," and yet he acknowledges that "an English vessel is sailing about in an irregular manner, regardless of the laws." He assumes to have both a naval and military force on the coast, and yet, confessing the inability of the imperial troops to ward off the intruders, he applies to the "barbarian eye," the superintendent of British trade, at the port of Canton, to see that "the restrictive laws be eternally obeyed." If we should reverse the case, and suppose that an alien act had been passed in England, prohibiting all Chinese from landing on our shores, and if in spite of our enactments, these intruders were found landing at every port; what would strangers think of the "dignity of our empire," if unable to prevent the ingress of these foreigners, we should address a letter to the nearest Chinese officer, requiring him to see that the "restrictive laws were eternally obeyed?' and what greater proof could we give of our impotency?

The quiet attempt of the Huron to break through the "eternal restrictions," seems to have stirred up all the wrath of his imperial majesty ; so that he does not scruple, in the course of his proclamation, to indulge himself in the strongest invective against the "violent and crafty English." In order to exhibit them in the worst light possible, he recalls to memory all their former misdemeanours, and accuses them of " usurping possession of a quay, presumptuously sending in petitions and statements, clandestinely bringing up foreign females to Canton, and riding in sedan chairs with four bearers." The first of these charges alludes to the inclosure of a few feet of waste land, once a receptacle for rubbish, in front of the foreign factories at Canton, which the British merchants had converted into a small garden, that they might enjoy a very confined walk, on a summer's evening. The second item refers to the well-known and very justifiable practice of the foreign merchants there, stating their grievances in a calm and dispassionate tone, to the native authorities. The third offence of these " violent and crafty barbarians" is, that during the continuance of the Company's factory in the neighbourhood of the provincial city, the chief of the select committee, and other gentlemen, brought up their wives and daughters to their own dwellings, in order to enjoy the sweets of domestic life, when fatigued with the toils and cares of business ; and the last aggression seems to be, that these English merchants, during the heat of the summer months, rode about in sedan chairs, with four bearers, a privilege exclusively claimed by the mandarins of the celestial empire. These " turbulent and unusual proceedings," however, have since, with the exception of the right of petitioning, been discontinued ; but while they lasted, the missionaries had no share in them.

Not content with thus infringing the unalterable customs of the celestial empire, the emperor complains, that in the autumn of 1834, these same English " brought ships of war into the inner waters of Canton, and had

2 L

the audacity to discharge musquetry and great guns, keeping up a thundering fire on the forts." This is an allusion to the well-known affair of Lord Napier, when that distinguished nobleman, feeling that the persons and property of British subjects were insecure at Canton, ordered two English frigates to enter the port. On attempting to pass the Bogue, however, the Chinese opened a fire upon our men of war, from the forts on both sides of the river, which was returned by the commanders of those vessels, in such a way, as to silence their guns, and disperse their men. If the Chinese complain, therefore, of the " thundering fire," they have themselves to blame, as they were the first to commence hostilities. With this proceeding, however, the missionaries had as little to do, as in the seizure of the quay, or the introduction of foreign females to Canton.

But the " head and front of their offending" seems to have been " the distribution of foreign books, calculated to seduce men with lies ; a most strange and astonishing proceeding !" Strange, indeed, that barbarians should become acquainted with the language of the celestial empire, and even compose books in the same ; distributing them gratuitously, among a people who despise and vilify them. However, from this part of the emperor's proclamation, two encouraging inferences may be drawn. First, the British public may hereby see, that the missionaries have done what they were sent forth to : they have learned the native language, published books in it, and circulated them along the shores of China, to such an extent as to excite the attention of the emperor himself. Secondly, the friends of missions may see, that the emperor has not only received, but read, and understood our books ; for he has found out that they contain doctrines contrary to the received opinions, and calculated to mislead his people; that is, maxims which the Chinese sages did not teach, and which the ruler of that country will not approve of. Now it is matter of no small encouragement to the friends of truth to know, that Christian books have reached so great a monarch; and though from their foreign character, he may at first disapprove of them, yet the frequent repetition of such attempts, and the presentation of truth in new and more interesting points of view, may, under the divine blessing, produce an effect, in the first instance tolerant, and, ultimately, favourable to our objects.

The emperor, conceiving that these things could not be done, unless by the direction and appointment of the "barbarian eye," directs his viceroy "to issue explicit orders, to the English chief and others, on the subject; and to remind them, that their being allowed commercial intercourse at Canton, is a matter of extraordinary favour; but that, if the foreigners continue to sail about, in this disorderly manner, they must immediately be driven out of port, and no longer allowed commercial intercourse." This threat of the stoppage of the trade, may alarm some who are but little acquainted with Chinese politics. The deprivation of our silks and teas, will concern both old and young, and numbers will deprecate such a dire calamity coming upon them. But the apprehensions of all may be allayed by the consideration that the Chinese cannot stop the trade, without reducing themselves to the greatest extremities. The imperial treasury is exhausted, and the government is already involved in debt; while the people are ill at ease under the dominion of a foreign yoke,

2 L 2

which the Tartar dynasty is felt to be ; the stoppage of
the trade, therefore, would weaken those resources,
which are already too much circumscribed, and increase
the dissatisfaction of the people, by throwing millions
out of employ. The prohibition of foreign commerce,
being the cause of their calamities, would be the signal
for revolt; and the government would need larger supplies of troops, to keep down insurrection, with less
money to sustain them; in which case, ruin must be
the consequence. While the Chinese, therefore, are
lavish in their threats, they know too well the state of
their own country, to attempt to put the threat in execution. Besides which, as the Company's monopoly is
at an end, and as the trade is open to the energies of
private adventurers, the driving of our merchants out
of the port of Canton, would only be the driving them
into every other port in the empire ; and thus, instead
of a regular trade, which the authorities could control,
and from which they might derive a profit, they would
have an irregular traffic, to an unlimited extent, which
no authority (such as that which exists in China) could
restrain. The Chinese know that this would be the
effect of the stoppage of the trade, and though they
dislike the irregular proceedings of a few missionaries,
and the introduction of foreign books into the empire,
they would dislike still more the deprivation of the
immense revenue to the government, and the denial of
the decided advantage to the people, which the cessation
of foreign commerce would occasion. Of two evils, they
know how to choose the least; and will rather bear
with our feeble efforts, than procure their discontinuance
at such an immence cost.

Should the Chinese ever determine on stopping the

trade, it will be from a far different motive than the wish to exclude the Gospel. The determined perseverance, and the audacious daring, with which the opium traffic is pushed forward, to the real injury of his people, as well as the defiance of his authority, exasperates the emperor a great deal more than the distribution of tracts along the coast. Never was a weak and pusillanimous government more violently roused than the Chinese authorities appear to be, on the subject of the illicit traffic in opium. The native dealers in the drug, are obliged to flee into holes and corners, the foreign opium merchants have been required to leave Canton; the quiet anchorage of the receiving ships, at Kap-sing-moon, has been broken up, and the smugglers obliged to retreat to Hong-kong bay. In addition to all this, the admiral of the port has declared, that if the opium smugglers do not discontinue their illicit transactions, he will bring down thousands of war junks, which shall hem them in on every side, like the men on a chess-board, so that it will be impossible to escape. If the trade be stopped, therefore, it will be in consequence of the progress of evil, and not the efforts to do good, in China.

It has been apprehended by some, that such was the displeasure of the Chinese government, elicited by the voyage of the Huron, that it would be impolitic, if not impossible, to make any more attempts of the kind. Several voyages have, however, been undertaken since the return of the author to England, going over some of the same ground, and doing the very same thing, which appeared so much to exasperate the government before. An account of one of these expeditions, prosecuted a year ago, by Mr. Gutzlaff, may not be uninteresting to the reader. The object of the voyage was to ascertain the fate of some shipwrecked sailors, who were afterwards sent back by the Chinese government, with liberal presents, to join their countrymen. We make no apology for introducing this account here, as a sequel to the voyage of the Huron, and hope that the vein of cheerfulness, happily blended with piety, in the writer's style, will at once please and profit the reader.

The place visited by our enterprising friends, is the last which the author touched at, as described in the preceding journal, viz. Tung-sang, on the coast of Fŭh-këen; Mr. Gutzlaff, however, went further into the interior. He writes as follows :—

" Having been called upon to undertake a journey to Fŭh-këen, I provided myself with a considerable number of Bibles and tracts, and arrived on the 24th of October, in Tung-san bay. This is an inlet of many miles in extent, presenting a barren shore, and having the town of Tung-san at the south-western extremity. This bay contains sufficient shelter for a large fleet, but a great part of the inner harbour is dry at low water. Here, as every where else on the eastern coast of China, the ocean recedes from the land, and extensive estuaries are gradually changed into fertile rice fields.

" The next morning we proceeded on our journey, and skirting the shores of the bay, as high up as pos-possible, we landed at a distant village, having been in some danger of swamping our little skiff. Chinese ingenuity was here displayed to the greatest advantage : the people were in search of shell-fish ; and to obtain as many as possible, they had spread an immense net at the bottom of the water, which the fishermen dragged on shore, while some people in a boat, directed the motions, and telegraphed by signs their success or failure. Thus the bottom of the bay was swept quite clean, and the scaly tribes had no means of escape. A Chinaman puts land and sea under heavy contributions, and wherever he resides, no living animal or useful plant escapes his notice, but is made to constitute a part of his mess. I have seen them angling for little frogs in a flooded rice field, and periodically hunt rats, which serve for their table. Such are the effects of an over-crowded population.

" On landing we might have imagined ourselves in the deserts of Arabia. All was floating sand and gravel. By some means, however, the people had contrived to condense it, and from such beds they gained a scanty crop of potatoes and earth-nuts. Yet in many places the young plants were scorched, and the harvest in general was scanty.

" The village we entered consisted of a number of hovels, irregularly built, but so thickly inhabited, that we were soon surrounded by crowds of natives. The people notwithstanding their poverty, shewed themselves very generous, and invited us to a repast of rice gruel; which, however, we refused. I now commenced dealing out the inestimable treasures of the word of God. Addressing my auditors in a lively strain, and preaching Jesus Christ, of whom they had never heard, I perceived with pleasure that they thronged about me in increasing numbers. When both their curiosity, as well as avidity after books, were gratified, the sick made their appearance, of whom, even in this small hamlet, the number was considerable, and the diseases most loathsome. How many physicians would be ne-

cessary, in order to remedy human sufferings amongst
these myriads! May they soon come! wherever they
travel, they will find work, and a hearty welcome.
Having no medicine with me, we set forward to the
place of our destination, Chang-poo, a city about thirty
miles inland. Our guides took charge of our book
bags, while each of my companions took as many
volumes as he could carry.

"Five miles we had to walk, over an isthmus of barren sand, where there was neither shrub, nor grass, nor
any living creature, except man. The inhabitants of
this dreary spot had built themselves huts along the
strand, where there was not even fresh water to quench
their thirst, nor a potatoe bed to satisfy the cravings of
appetite. Notwithstanding all this, however, the people were cheerful. Seeing them look with wistful eyes
at my books I asked them if they could read; and
being answered in the affirmative, I tendered them a
volume gratis. This liberality called forth the population from the corners of their cottages, and in a place
where we supposed few only resided, crowds soon made
their appearance. So I went on distributing, and if I
happened to forget a single man, he would run after
me with great speed, crying out, 'a book, a book!' I
was at the same time in mental prayer, that the Saviour,
in much mercy, might bless his word to the souls of the
people. Since they have no worldly chattels, to lead
their thoughts astray from God, and have little to expect in this life, it may be presumed that they would
the more gladly seize upon the treasures reserved for
them in heaven. Yet even the most abject wretch frequently prefers a life of misery here, to the joys of the
future state ; and while dragging out his existence un-

der reiterated sighs, can never so much as raise his eyes
to heaven.   We are indeed a forlorn race, no matter of
what rank or nation.

    " With the conviction that the books were read, I
sped my pace over the desert, and occasionally met a
solitary wanderer, with whom I entered into conversation.   The name of Jesus entirely unknown, the most
obvious Christian truth hidden, and the mind enveloped
in impenetrable darkness, are obstacles sufficient to
frighten the most persevering teacher.   Thus, after
long and most impressive conversations, I had the mortification to learn, that my auditors had all the while
been intimately surveying my clothes, while they
scarcely heeded my exhortations.

    " A march of several hours, under a burning sun, had
brought on fatigue, and as soon as we espied the end of
the desert, we put off our shoes which by this time
were filled with gravel, and dined under the blue canopy
of heaven.   As our mess was duly seasoned with sand,
it did not prove very palatable, and therefore very
little delayed our journey.   We now emerged gradually
into an extensive valley, which had been gained from
the sea.   It might be about fifteen miles in circumference, and numbered more than thirty hamlets, large
and small.   It need not be told, that every inch of
ground was cultivated, and that all the articles planted
were, by means of manure, brought to the highest state
of perfection.   Whilst crossing the first village, I had
given away some books ; and as the tidings, that an
' exhorter of the world ' had arrived, gradually spread,
the people who were bringing in their potatoe crops,
speedily left off their work, and hastened towards us.
Many returned a heartfelt thank, whilst receiving the

sacred volume, whilst others cut off pieces of sugar
cane, and presented them in return.   It was a real fes-
tival for the whole valley, which will be long remembered by all the inhabitants.   Many mothers urged
their children to run after us, to get a book, which they
might read to them.   What would I have given, if one
of the supporters of the Chinese missions had been
present that day !   It was for me a day of real rejoicing ;
and though I feel that curiosity was the great spring of
such an eagerness, I was on the other hand persuaded
that God can bless the perusal of his word, even to the
curious reader.   When we approached the first borough
we had not a single volume left.   This place consisted
of a mass of houses, surrounded by a wall, about fifty
feet high, provided with loop-holes and parapets.   It is
rather extraordinary, that such a paltry place should
have been defended by such a substantial wall.   But
it ought to be remembered, that the Chinese are very
fond of similar protections, and believe them impreg-
nable against every assault.

" In all parts of the country one may find these
structures, either entire or dilapidated, often enclosing
a space of more than ten miles in circumference, with
nothing but small hamlets within the enclosure.

" As the people thronged around us, and became
boisterous, my companions (the sailors) got alarmed,
and stood upon the defensive.   But on my addressing
the populace, every body was silent and peaceful, to the
great astonishment of my fellow travellers.

" Stretched out under a few shady trees, in order to
refresh our weary limbs, we looked with considerable
anxiety to the dark mountain ridge, which we had to pass.
Here, as well as in all other parts of China, the hills

have an undulating form, probably assumed at the time of the deluge, when the mighty waters impressed this shape upon them. Upon a nearer approach, they presented a most fantastic appearance, remarkable for the immense rocks, which seem to be piled up by art. The barrenness is so great, that only in a very few places does the dwarf fir tree thrive, and even those stand very scanty. Yet there grow many curious plants and flowers, between the cliffs, and wherever there is a little earth. As I am, however, no botanist, I cannot regale my readers with a number of Latin names of the plants I discovered. My whole science extends to trees which bear savoury fruits, and flowers of a sweet smell, including kitchen vegetables; and as I found neither, I remained in happy ignorance.

" As we advanced, the appearance of the country grew worse, and we observed, to our great astonishment, whole patches uncultivated. For this we could discover no reason. We moreover espied several hamlets in ruins, whilst the inhabitants passed us in gloomy silence; a rare thing with a Chinaman, who has generally a smile in store, and is never parsimonious of his good wishes. We finally came to a hamlet which was nearly deserted, and inhabited only by old women and children. Having on our road perceived some very large castles, which were, however, nearly fallen into ruins, we made enquiries of a gentleman, whom curiosity had brought into our company. He readily explained to us, that these fortifications had been erected during the sway of the Mongols, when the country was nearly as much disturbed, as Germany in the twelfth and thirteenth centuries. Our conversation then turned upon the many dilapidated houses we had seen, when all at once our visitor became eloquent. ' These evils,' he said, ' have been occasioned by war. Two rival clans, Wang and Chin, have risen in open hostilities against each other. Behold,' he continued, pointing to an extensive encampment, surrounded by some entrenchments, ' their fortifications; and the field of battle upon which they fought only a short time ago. It is on this account that the region around has been laid waste, and that many inhabitants have fled, or are roving about as desperadoes! The government, during the heat of the contest referred to, did not dare to interfere; but since the fury has abated, the chief magistrate at Chang-poo has just made his appearance, to extort fines and apprehend some of the guilty. For this unseasonable officiousness, several of his myrmidons have been killed, and things are again ripe for a revolt. The whole populace, in the meanwhile, are ready to rise in arms, and most of the peasantry have provided themselves with matchlocks and swords.'

" Notwithstanding the exhortations of our informant, we hastened towards the mountain passes; when evening began to fall. Having procured a sedan, we were enabled to pursue our journey with the greater facility. When we entered among the mountains, which might be about three thousand feet above the level of the sea, the scenery assumed a most romantic cast. Over-hanging cliffs, deep ravines, gurgling streams, and fantastic rocks, looking just as if the chisel of a human artist had been at work with them, were all objects of curiosity and wonder. It was a fine moon-light night, and if we had not been too weary, so as to stumble over the rocks in our path, we might have enjoyed this evening still more. For many miles there was not a

single human habitation to be seen, nor was the voice
of man heard.   It was the Lord's silent temple, where
the heart becomes most disposed to worship the Maker of
heaven and earth ; cherishing such thoughts, and occasionally raising my heart towards the Creator, we
arrived near a small but fertile valley, where we
expected to find human beings.   Our guides ushered
us into a temple, hard by, where we sunk exhausted on
the ground.   The keeper was a poor man, and greatly
alarmed at our appearance ; for an European is a far
greater curiosity there, than a Chinaman could be in
Europe.   He would gladly have run away and left us
in possession of the house and idols, had not our
Chinese companions persuaded him that we were
peaceful people.   Having therefore lighted a fire, with
a little straw, he took no further notice of us, while we
stretched ourselves upon the pavement in front of the
idols.

   " Plagued by musquitoes, and disturbed by the
numerous visitors in the next room, none of us could
enjoy sleep.   Often did I pace the premises, and when
I looked upon the images most fervently pray, that the
Lord, in his mercy, would soon break down these
monuments of Satan's power, and bring this great and
interesting people to his fold.   May we not hope, that
the gracious hearer of prayer will bend his ear to the
supplications which were uttered in sight of the abomi-
nations of Paganism.   Being the leader of the train, I
roused my companions about midnight, supposing, on
account of the bright moon, that it was already morning.   We wound our way through mazes of rocks and
ravines, stumbling and falling, and laughing over our
misfortunes.   The further we went, the more inac-

cessible the mountains became, and, in some places, we
had to crawl up and slide down on the opposite side.
Having surmounted the pass, we found human habitations, and cultivated patches of ground, of which we
had seen nothing the day before.   At length, when we
almost despaired of getting to the end of our journey,
we were greatly rejoiced when, turning off at a by-road,
we crossed a small stream in a ferry boat, and emerged
into a very extensive valley.   This is the most fertile
spot I have ever seen in China.   The sugar cane and
wheat grow here, to such a height, that even in Siam
I have seen nothing equal to it.   The neat order in
which every thing was planted formed an entire contrast
with their habitations.   In the latter all is confusion,
filth, and wretchedness.   This valley, which might
contain about forty square miles, was one large, beautiful garden, with the city of Chang-poo in its centre.

" At this place we arrived while it was still early, and
when the slumbers of the inhabitants were disturbed
by none but night revellers.   We therefore sat down at
the gate, and looked at the brilliant moon, which shone
in all her lustre.   The first thing which struck our
fancy was a moveable cook-shop, where we breakfasted
for one penny a head.   Then commenced the noisy hum
of carriers and farmers; the former performing all the
services of our beasts of burden.   The street was soon
thronged with people, dragging huge loads of cotton and
paper, with the strength of packhorses.   Then appeared
the shopkeepers and other tradesmen, and, before five
o'clock, the city was one living bee-hive.   In numbers,
as well as pursuits, the Chinese may fitly be compared
to ants.   The land is filled with men; the houses are
not inhabited, but stuffed with human beings; and every

one of them tries to get through the world as well as
he can.   Of their readiness to listen, I had manifold
proofs.   The people were unwearied in their questions,
delighted with the answers given, and anxious for more
information.   Oh that one soul might be saved!

" The great crowd forced us to retire to a house,
which was built upon poles. There, however, the throng
became so great, that we began to fear the whole
would fall, and we be smothered in the mud below.
We were well treated by the owner of the house, who
seemed of all others the least inconvenienced by such a
crowd of visitors.   As neither of my companions nor
myself were able to walk, I procured sedan chairs, and
thus we moved on in an imposing procession.   The
bearers themselves appeared to be the lowest of the low,
clad in a few rags, and looking as emaciated as if just
ready to fall down dead.   But under this unseemly
exterior they hid great strength.   I believe that a well
fed horse would not have been able to carry some of us
over the craggy mountains, without sinking under the
load; but these men walked on briskly and sure-footed,
and ascended declivities with greater speed, than we
could have done in walking.   They were a cheerful
and boisterous race, as hungry as wolves. To satisfy
their craving appetites, I bought more than ten pounds
of pork, and had some buckets full of rice and vegetables
prepared in an adjacent tavern.   This mess, which
thirty Europeans would not have been able to consume,
disappeared from the table as if by magic.   I had sat
myself down, in a separate apartment, and was taking
up the chopsticks to taste a little rice and salt beef, and
though tolerably expeditious in this work, my guests
had finished the whole before I had tasted a few mouth-

fuls. After this treat they were loud in my praises, and performed the journey with redoubled speed. They actually ran, and made every body get out of the road. Of the scanty livelihood upon which the poorer classes, and indeed nine-tenths of the nation are obliged to live, it is difficult to form an idea. The wages are so low, that a man who has worked hard from morning to evening, gains about four pence to maintain his wife and children. Their sufferings are therefore indescribable ; but a Chinaman is armed against them all by the obtuseness of his nerves.

" I hope a missionary will soon be sent to this district. As long as he avoids the presence of the higher mandarins, and does not force himself into notoriety, there is some hope of his effecting a residence ; but he must be versed in the art of the leech ; a devoted man of God ; and ready to suffer and die for the Saviour. The farther from the coast, the more the moral condition of the people appears to improve, and the greater the interest the natives take in our books. They receive them respectfully, and do not forcibly tear them out of our hands. A regular tour through these villages, to exhort and console, displaying a love for the souls of our auditors, would certainly be attended with the best results. The prospect of thus establishing a mission in China, is not utopian ; but we have not, yet, men who are sufficiently conversant with the language, and who have become Chinese, in order to win Chinese to Christ.

" In this whole trip, we have not seen any mandarins ; and the farther we are out of their atmosphere, the better, for their very touch is contaminating, and when in their company the people are shy and suspicious of us. To make friends with them, I have long given up as a hopeless task. The more intimate the terms upon which we stand with the mandarins, the more circumscribed is the sphere of our usefulness. They are, from their very calling, opposed to every thing good and laudable, and perfectly steeled against the truth.

" We returned the next evening late to the ship, and had to recount numerous acts of kindness which we had received on our journey. The following day, I performed another tour; the country was equally unpromising, and the inhabitants poor, but not without their wonted cheerfulness. Having circulated all my tracts, I commenced the distribution of Scriptures, of which I had a great quantity. Whenever I entered a village, all business was suspended, and old and young sped towards the distributor of books.

" We finally weighed anchor, and arrived at Tsinkang district. Here it would be impossible to describe the joy with which the inhabitants, who knew me, received their old friend. After the first expressions of gladness had passed, they asked for books, which I was obliged to produce, and, whether I would or not, to part with the sacred volumes. Long before we reached the village, almost the whole stock taken on shore was expended; and new demands being made upon me, I had to refuse the applicants with a sad countenance.

" The next day we took a large boat-load of books, anxious to perform a long tour, among ten or twelve villages. On landing, however, I was met by urgent applicants, who upbraided me with having been so long absent, and considered it a shame that I did not satisfy their demands immediately. Such arguments had peculiar force; I supplied them plentifully with the word

2 M

of life, and proceeded onward, at the head of five bearers, with a sack on my own shoulders. But we were soon stopped by new crowds, equally as boisterous as the former; and, as they quoted precedents, I had to conform to their wishes, and all our burthens vanished.

"We fetched a new investment from the boat, and being now determined to go over to some of the villages beyond, we set off to travel through an extensive marsh; but had scarcely proceeded half a mile, when we were overtaken by a fresh set, who craved from us the divine gift, and another load disappeared. My bearers, who saw their burthens vanish, in the twinkling of an eye, were struck with astonisment, having never in their lives witnessed a similar scene. I ordered up a fresh supply; but by this time the villagers were in motion, and as this was a general thoroughfare, the crowds became denser than ever. The books were, however, distributed with much regularity; and we thought now to proceed to a distant village, determined not to be hindered on any account. The new comers, however, importuned us so eagerly, that we couldnot refuse them. Thus a new investment was circulated. I sent for more, but received for answer, that not a single leaf was left; and I had to regret unavailingly, that I had not laid in a larger supply.

"I subsequently visited Hea-mun, (Amoey) the place which received me as a naturalized citizen, when I was astonished to see that I was generally known, even more than in my own native place. There was no end of pointing me out to strangers, and speaking of my pursuits, and the present object of my voyage. Often a man, wiser than the rest, mingled in the conversation, and explained my parentage and pedigree.

" We traversed, in this manner, a great part of that large city, rejoicing to find that the vigilance of the mandarins had considerably abated, since I visited the same spot, only four years before. May the Lord soon grant us an entrance, were it only into one province!

" Oh! may the ardour in behalf of the good cause grow! May hundreds engage in this blessed work, and devote their lives to the spread of the Gospel, in this extensive country. The Lord our Saviour is with us, and will certainly not withdraw his hand as long as we trust in him the Rock of ages. Let us therefore go on in his strength, and work till the last breath."

CHAPTER XXI.

CLASS OF LABOURERS REQUIRED FOR CHINA.

COMPARATIVE CLAIMS OF CHINA — NEED OF MORE LABOURERS—FOR THE COLONIES—AND THE COAST — OFFERS INVITED—OBJECTIONS MET— REGARDING THE CLIMATE — AND THE LANGUAGE—THE ORAL AND WRITTEN MEDIUMS—COMPARED WITH THE ENGLISH—EXHORTATIONS TO ENGAGE—EDUCATIONAL AGENTS NEEDED—SCHOOLS FOR SCHOOL-MASTERS REQUIRED—PIOUS PHYSICIANS—EFFORTS ALREADY MADE— OPHTHALMIC HOSPITAL—MORE PRACTITIONERS WANTED—THE PROBABILITY OF THEIR SUCCESS — SPEECH OF SIR H. HALFORD — MORAL INFLUENCE OF PHYSICIANS — DEFERENCE PAID THEM — INTERESTING ANECDOTE—IMPORTANCE OF MEDICINE TO MISSIONARIES — INFERIORITY OF CHINESE PRACTICE—UNION OF THE CLERICAL AND MEDICAL PROFESSIONS—PERSONS WHO SHOULD OFFER.

No one, we presume, after the perusal of the foregoing pages, will hesitate to admit, that the Chinese stand in need of conversion; and no one, believing the Christian scriptures, will doubt the future and final triumph of the Gospel, in that populous and important empire. The only question is, what are the best means of bringing about so desirable an end. We do not wish other parts of the world to be neglected, and this alone cared for; but we desire that China may receive that attention which her population and influence demand. The London Missionary Society has sent out, during the last thirty years, twenty missionaries to labour for the benefit of China; while India and the South Seas, have each had one hundred labourers employed in their different fields. It is true, that success has cheered us in the one; and free intercourse, accompanied by British protection, encourages us to persevere in the other; but the command of Christ, and the woes of the perishing heathen, render the call of duty as imperative, where prosperity does not gladden, nor security defend, as where both these are withheld, and the labourer is required to toil in the very fires, without witnessing the full result of his endeavours. While China, therefore, enjoys only one-fifth of the interest, which either India or Polynesia receives, no one will say that her three hundred and sixty millions have obtained more than their due share of attention.

We hope, however, to see the dawn of a better day for the Chinese empire, and that the society which has sent out a Morrison and a Milne, will not allow their labours to be lost, and their successors to be discouraged, for want of needful assistance. The London Missionary Society, having purchased an interest in China, at the expense of some most valuable lives, and many thousand pounds; having been the first of all protestant institutions to enter the field; having gained much experience, and possessed itself of very important facilities, for the vigorous prosecution of the work; will not now, that success begins to crown its efforts, and increasing openings invite it to proceed, draw back, or be slothful in this interesting undertaking.

But should it be asked, what is still needed to make an impression upon China, that shall tell upon thousands, and extend to future generations? we answer, in a word, *men*. God works by instruments, and generally apportions the end to the amount of means employed. What effect, then, can we hope to produce on so vast an empire, by the employment of half a dozen

individuals at a time? As well might we attempt,
with a feeble wire, to move a solid rock, as with so
small a band, to instruct and influence so vast a multitude. In order to benefit the Chinese, two kinds of
labour are requisite, stated and desultory; the one to
be employed in the colonies, where the emigrants reside, under European protection; and the other to be
resorted to on the coast, where, at present, only occasional visits can be paid. For the first, we require all
the strength we now possess, and much more; as the
stations already occupied are but half supplied, and
other islands and countries where the Chinese dwell,
invite our attention; for the second, we need an additional number of pious, enterprising, and zealous men,
well acquainted with the language and habits of the
people, who will go forth on missionary expeditions,
and employ themselves in carrying the Scriptures and
tracts, to every part of the coast of China. Such men
ought to be in a state of preparation, ready to avail
themselves of all the openings which now exist, and to
embrace every new opportunity which may occur. Without men, we can neither make new discoveries, nor
follow up those attempts which have been made. The
Christian public having got the idea, that China is
shut, must retain their opinion, until we can get men
of God to open it.

We need, therefore, a larger supply of missionaries,
not only to carry on the labours of our various stations,
in the colonies, but to prepare for more extended efforts
on the coast. Besides which, the pen must be kept at
work, and new works written and published, calculated
to inform and improve the mind of China. The acquisition of a good Chinese style, is a most difficult thing,

and unless our publications be drawn up in an intelligible and idiomatic form, they will not be read. Such a habit of writing can only be the result of years of study, and unless a beginning be made, no advance can be anticipated. The philosophical speculations and absurd superstitions of the natives must be grappled with, while the doctrines and duties of Christianity, with its evidences and effects, must be set forth, in a way that will affect and convince the mind of a Confucian or a Buddhist; and unless pious, talented, judicious, ardent, and persevering men be obtained, the work must, for a time, stand still. Should the agents employed, possess an acquaintance with science, and be able to instruct and benefit the Chinese, by imparting some of the late discoveries in natural and experimental philosophy, they would be so much the more useful in the mission.

Let those whose minds are deeply affected with the condition of the Chinese, and who burn with a desire to diffuse Christianity in that empire, offer themselves, with an especial reference to China; and if their qualifications be such as would justify their being employed, they will doubtless be sent forth, and the religious public, feeling the call for extra exertions imperative, would contribute additional means for their support. Let such as are yet young in years, and therefore more likely to stand the fatigue; those also who possess the imitative faculty, and a retentive memory, which would enable them readily to acquire the language of China, offer themselves; and should there be any mentally and morally, what Saul was physically, " a head and shoulders higher than any of the people," let them be first and foremost in an undertaking, which would re-

quire and exhaust the best talents and most devoted
energies.

Lest any should be deterred by minor considerations,
the author will here add a few suggestions, relative to
the climate and the language.   With regard to the former, it may be observed, that China, lying without the
tropics, is fully as salubrious, but by no means so
changeable, as England.   At Canton, the summers are
hot, but the winters are bracing.   In the latitude of
Peking, the thermometer is sometimes below zero.   No
peculiar diseases infest the celestial empire, while many
invalids repair thither for the benefit of their health.
A missionary, stationed at Canton and Macao, or voyaging along the coast, has nothing to dread from the
influence of climate.   The Malayan archipelago, where
our brethren must first reside, in order to acquire the
language from the Chinese emigrants, though situated
in the vicinity of the line, being favoured with land
and sea breezes, is comparatively cool ; and even Batavia has been found to be more healthy than either of
our Indian presidencies.

The language of the celestial empire has been considered, by some, an insuperable difficulty, and many an
ardent labourer has been appalled by it.   No one can
deny, that the acquisition of the Chinese tongue will
require all possible attention and diligence.   It is confessedly a singular language, but by no means beyond
the compass of ordinary powers to attain.   Moderate
capacities and due diligence, aided by the increased
facilities which now exist, will enable a man to converse fluently in the course of two years, and in double
that time, to compose intelligibly in the native dialect.   The vernacular tongue is acquired by Chinese

infants, just as soon as our children begin to prattle English; while the tones and accents, which, in Chinese, denote the variation of one word from another, are picked up by the native youth, just as readily as we learn to distinguish articulate sounds. Were men therefore, to set about the study, with the simplicity and teachableness of children, there can be no doubt but that they would be equally successful.

Much has been said about the arbitrary nature of the Chinese language, when, in fact, it is no more arbitrary than our own, There is as much connection between the sound *má*, and a certain animal that goes on four legs, and draws carriages, as there is between the same quadruped and our English word *horse;* and with the same ease whereby we learned to affix the sound *horse* to the animal in one country, we might learn to append *má* to it in another. So with regard to abstract as well as simple terms; the same effort of memory, that would enable us to retain them in one language, would render us equally successful in another.

The nice distinction of tones observable in the Chinese language, being unknown among us, have led some to doubt whether they could ever acquire it. But with proper attention, the student can learn to distinguish as readily between varieties of intonation, as differences of orthography. The same effort of mind, that would make us masters of the difference between the sounds *horse* and *scold*, would enable us to mark the distinction between the acute *má* and the grave *mà*. Thus the acquisition of a *copia verborum*, in Chinese, is not more difficult, in the nature of things, than the storing of our minds with English words.

The written language of China constitutes indeed a

difficulty, but not such an insuperable one as has been imagined. The main difference between their written medium and our own consists, in the degree of connection between the figure exhibited and the sound attached to it. Strictly speaking, there is no more connection between a triangular shape and the sound of the letter *A*, than there is between a certain Chinese character and the sound *má*; and so on, throughout the alphabet. The sounds attached to our letters are as arbitrary as those affixed to any given Chinese symbol; but our arbitrary signs amount only to a few tens, while those of the Chinese amount to several thousands. The difference then is one of degree, not of principle; inasmuch as we have adopted the same arbitrary mode in our own written medium, though confined to the letters of the alphabet. Having attached articulate sounds to a certain number of arbitrary signs, we have further learned, by the combination of several, to form compound sounds, or words. This the Chinese have not reached, but have gone on multiplying signs for each particular word, till their symbols have amounted to thousands. Hence theirs has become a hieroglyphic, while ours has remained an alphabetic language.

It is, however, not always adverted to, that the orthography of our own tongue, notwithstanding its alphabetic base, is almost as arbitrary as the Chinese. Far from fixing a definite sound to each particular letter, we have been in the habit of attaching five or six sounds to most of our vowels, and three or four to some of our consonants; while these sounds are interchanged, without the least intimation of the variation, or the smallest reason for the difference, but use and custom. Some persons have calculated that the word *scissors* may be spelled eleven hundred different ways, and that to the word *phantom* as many various pronunciations may be given, without departing from the acknowledged sounds of the letters, in other words of the English language. Thus a foreign student of our own tongue may be at a loss, when he hears a word pronounced, to know how to write it; or when he sees any thing written, to know how to read it, until instructed in the usual mode of spelling or enunciating the word in question. Having such an arbitrary mode ourselves, what reason have we to complain that the Chinese written medium exhibits no connection between shape and sound; when there is not a word in our own language, that a stranger, acquainted with the powers of our letters, would be able to spell or pronounce, without being instructed by a pedagogue? and what need has a person, capable of mastering the arbitrary orthography of the English language, to fear that he shall never conquer that of China?

But the want of connection between shape and sound is not the only difficulty in the way of acquiring the Chinese character, for the complex nature of the character itself confounds some so much, that they despair of acquiring it. And is the Chinese character, indeed, more complicated than the written words of our own tongue? we believe not. Take the word *benevolence*, for instance, and compare it with the Chinese character for the same idea, and it will be seen, that while the former contains eleven letters, the latter exhibits a simple symbol of only four strokes. Perhaps it may he urged, that our words, though apparently complicated, are reducible to a few elements; but this, we may reply, is precisely the case with the Chinese characters. The most difficult hieroglyphic, which the Chinese use, is composed of only six different kinds of strokes, while each character is reducible to a few simple elements, which constitute the radicals of their language. When a student is once acquainted with the two hundred and fourteen radicals, he ascertains immediately how a character is formed, and writes it accordingly. There is no more difficulty in remembering the elements of any given Chinese character, than in calling to recollection the letters of any particular English word: the difficulty is the same in kind, and varies only in degree, inasmuch as the Chinese elements exceed those of the English. Thus the formidable obstacles, which have hitherto frightened so many of our English students, are considerably reduced by a comparison with the peculiarities of our own language, and would vanish entirely before the patient assiduity of the determined scholar.

Let our young men of piety and talent, therefore, who are longing to employ their energies in a way that shall have the most extensive bearing upon the destinies of the human family, turn their attention towards China, and they will find the improvement and evangelization of that great empire an object worth living for. Let our educated youth, our students of theology, and the rising ministry consider the claims of that numerous people, and foregoing in some degree the ease, convenience, sympathies, and elegancies of home, let them go forth to spread amongst these Gentiles the unsearchable riches of Christ. If it be asked, who are the agents called upon to embark in this undertaking, we may safely say, to every well-qualified and unfettered individual, " Thou art the man." And if the enquiry be, what is the most suitable time for engaging in the enterprise, we would instantly reply, *now*.   The Saviour's command, " to preach the Gospel to every creature," had no reference to political arrangements, or apparent facilities; it was a direct order to " go;" and if we be actuated by the right spirit, we shall immediately and vigorously set about the undertaking. It is of no use waiting for extensive openings, effected by political arrangements, or changes brought about by internal convulsions.   When the rulers of this world open the door, they take care to admit only those who may be least likely to interfere with their wealth and aggrandizement : and when revolutions take place in a heathen country, it is only the change from one despot to another; while the empire may be shaken to its very centre, before any advance be made towards the attainment of civil and religious liberty. Our duty, therefore, as well as wisdom, is to go forward ; let us call forth our men, and plant them on the borders of the celestial empire, and assuredly the time is not far distant, when even China shall stretch forth her hands unto God.

In addition to preachers of the Gospel, we need a band of educational agents, to improve the mode of tuition adopted among the Chinese.   The attention of missionaries, from the very first, has been directed towards the young. The establishment of schools in the empire of China, has been found to be difficult, if not impossible ; but among the emigrants, extensive efforts have been made to benefit the rising generation. About seven hundred Chinese children are daily taught in the various settlements of the Indian archipelago ; but though Christian books are introduced, and daily or weekly examinations held, yet the improvement of the children is not such, as the friends of education and Christianity could desire. Among the causes leading to this, may be enumerated, the origin of the children; who, being sprung from Chinese fathers and Malayan mothers, speak Malay as their mother tongue, and have to acquire the Chinese as the language of business. Then, the nature of the Füh-këen dialect presents another difficulty. The people of that province have a reading and a colloquial idiom, differing essentially one from the other, so that a person residing amongst them, may be able to understand everything that is said in conversation, without comprehending a single syllable of what is read from a book; and may acquire by rote whole volumes in the reading dialect, without being able to express one sentence in the colloquial medium. The practice of the Chinese schoolmasters is, to make their pupils learn by heart the whole text of the Four Books, without explaining a single syllable; so that the boys remain in utter ignorance of the meaning of their author, while they are committing his words by wholesale to memory. The amount of knowledge acquired, therefore, is not to be estimated by the number of pages learned: and much labour is undergone, with little profit to the scholars. It is true, that the Christian books put into the hands of the children, are all assiduously explained by the missionaries; but the schoolmasters being heathen, and constantly with their pupils, are likely to undo, in a moral and religious sense, what the missionary has been attempting during the brief interval of his visit.

In order to make our schools efficient and useful, therefore, it will be necessary to train up a race of schoolmasters, acquainted with a better system, and imbued with holier principles, who will train up the native youth to be useful and happy. For this end, we need a few devoted young Christians, to go out from this country, with talent enough to acquire the native language, and humility sufficient to devote their acquisitions to the education of children; and after having qualified themselves to become schoolmasters in the native tongue, to seek to raise up others to be teachers in their turn. It will be necessary for such, to make themselves familiar with the standard writings and complex characters of the Chinese, so as to be able to compete with the native schoolmasters, and by their superior tact and method in conducting the work of tuition, to beat the original pedagogues out of the field. Beginning with half a dozen, and going through all the drudgery of scholastic business, for the first few years, the educational agent may, in the course of time, succeed in training a number of vigorous and intelligent young men, whom he may appoint over different seminaries; and then, commencing the work of superintendence, he will feel himself at the head of a range of schools, from which hundreds of well-taught children may proceed, to enlighten and bless the next generation. The man who will devote his energies to such an enterprise will, in the present state of things, be labouring as effectually for the conversion of the Chinese, as the writer of books, or the preacher of the Gospel. The inferior light in which schoolmasters have been unjustly viewed, may perhaps deter some from undertaking this work; but the hope is fondly cherished, that some who enter with spirit into the business of tuition, will on learning the wants of China come forward, and consecrate themselves to the improvement of schools, for the greatest of pagan nations.

Amongst the individuals most essentially needed, to aid in the introduction of the Gospel into China, must be enumerated, pious physicians and surgeons, who, combining science with benevolence, will be able to make both tend to the diffusion and establishment of truth and righteousness in the world. The healing of human maladies has frequently been connected with, and rendered subservient to, the spread of Christianity. In evangelized countries, gratuitous medical assistance to the poor, has often been of essential service to religion ; but in heathen lands, where prejudices and obstructions abound, the co-operation of pious surgeons with devoted missionaries, is very desirable, and would be most effective. The vast population and debasing superstitions of China, are calculated to affect the sympathies of the Christian mind. That land is, however, fenced round by restrictions, so that the disciples of the Saviour can hardly gain access to the mass of the population. Missionaries have laboured assiduously among the Chinese emigrants, and have spread divine truth extensively along the shores of the mother country ; but they have not been able to secure for themselves the privilege of a quiet residence in the interior, to propagate the Gospel through the length and breadth of the land. It has occurred to them, that an amicable intercourse might be cultivated, and existing restrictions more speedily removed, by the employment of benevolent efforts, in conjunction with pious endeavours to diffuse the Gospel. They have, therefore, attempted on a small scale, to relieve the more common maladies of the heathen around them, and have availed themselves of the opportunity thus afforded, to inculcate moral and religious truth on the minds of their patients. But these desultory efforts have been circumscribed and ineffectual, owing to the limited knowledge of the missionaries, who have longed to see persons better qualified employ their time and talents to the undertaking. Happily such individuals have been found, and the results of their well-directed efforts have been such, as to encourage others to engage in the same duties. The Chinese have begun to esteem our medicines, and to place themselves willingly under European treatment, while the character of English physicians, for skill and benevolence, has been firmly established, and native prejudices gradually removed.

In 1805, Dr. Pearson introduced vaccination into Canton, which the natives readily adopted; in the course of twelve months thousands were vaccinated, the practice spread to the neighbouring provinces, and Chinese practitioners undertook to disseminate the vaccine matter for their own reputation and emolument. The next effort for the temporal benefit of the Chinese was made by Dr. Livingstone, followed by T. R. Colledge, Esq., surgeon to the British factory, who, in the year 1827, opened an opthalmic hospital in Macao, and within five years from its establishment relieved about four thousand indigent Chinese, while upwards of one thousand eight hundred pounds were contributed towards the object, by the European inhabitants of Canton and Macao, aided by the subscriptions of several respectable Chinese. Some very delightful letters of thanks were received from those who had been restored

to sight and health, shewing not only the gratitude of
the Chinese for the benefits conferred, but the extent to
which the physicians' fame had spread throughout the
empire.

The last attempt to benefit the Chinese physically,
and thus to pave the way for their moral and spiritual
amelioration, was made by the Rev. Dr. Parker, an
American missionary and physician, who, in November,
1835, opened an opthalmic hospital in Canton ; at
which, within the space of two years, three thousand
patients were relieved, including many cases of opthal-
mia, amaurosis, cataract, and entropia; besides some
very distressing and alarming instances of tumours,
which were removed with success.   One man had his
arm amputated at the shoulder joint, which was the
first instance in Canton of a native's voluntarily submitting to the removal of a limb.   The people have
been remarkably eager to avail themselves of the
benefits of the institution, and have been very grateful
for the assistance imparted.   Persons from different
provinces have applied for relief.   No opposition is
excited ; while the hospital has been known to, and
approved of, by the native government.   One of the
private secretaries to the chief magistrate of Canton
has been restored to sight, and has indited a poem to
the praise of his benefactor.   Dr. P. is still prosecuting
his important labours, and the Canton public have
testified their sense of the importance of this mode of
operation, by contributing three thousand dollars to the
object.   In addition to the opthalmic hospital already
established, other departments of surgical labour are
equally needed, each of which would fully occupy the

time and talents of one individual, while wider fields are still opening, where the most skilful and devoted may find full scope for all their energies.

" The men who go forth on this enterprise," observes Dr. Parker, " should be masters of their profession, conciliating in their manners, judicious, disinterested, truly pious, and ready to endure hardships and sacrifice personal comforts, that they may commend the gospel of our Lord and Saviour, and co-operate in its introduction among the millions of China. Exclusive as that country is, in all her systems, she cannot exclude disease. nor shut up her people from the desire of relief. Does not the finger of Providence then point clearly to one way, which we should take with the Chinese, directing us to seek the introduction for the remedies of sin itself, by the same door through which we convey those which are designed to mitigate or remove its evils. At any rate, this door seems open; let us enter it. Loathsome disease, in every form, has uttered her cry for relief, from every corner of the land. We must essay its healing. None can deny, that this is a charity that worketh no ill to his neighbour, and our duty to walk in it seems plain and imperative."

Medical and surgical practitioners seeking to benefit the natives of the east, may safely reside in all the. islands of the Malayan archipelago, in Burmah, and Siam, as well as on the borders of China. Should a skilful and successful practitioner, after having become known by his benevolent efforts, attempt to effect a permanent residence in any of the northern or eastern ports, the inhabitants of the place would see it to be their interest to screen and shelter him; and the probability is, that he would be left unmolested longer than those whose objects are more directly missionary. For though the law which excludes the preacher, operates equally against the practitioner, yet the incipient departure from the letter of the enactment would be more likely to take place in the case of the dispenser of health, than the reformer of morals; simply because the Chinese feel their need in the one case, and not in the other. It is true, that in order to promote the conversion of souls, we must employ the preaching of the gospel, in dependance on the Holy Spirit; but it is also true, that we cannot adopt a more effectual means for promoting the introduction of evangelical instruction into China, than by making medicine the pioneer of religion.

It is gratifying to see that this subject has begun to attract attention in high and influential quarters. In the beginning of 1838, Sir Henry Halford, President of the Royal College of Physicians, delivered an address on " the results of the successful practice of physic," before a meeting of that body, which was attended by several of the present and former ministers of the crown, some of the highest dignitaries of the church, and the principal nobility of the land; in the course of his speech, the benevolent baronet expressed himself to the following effect:—

" In laying before you some of the rewards of a successful practice of our profession, I do not intend to advert to the pecuniary fruits of our toil, nor to the honours awarded to physicians. No. I contemplate the moral influence, which the cure of bodily ills has upon the minds of our patients. I allude to that deference to the physician's judgment, and to that gratitude and attachment, which is the sweetest reward of our anxious and laborious life.

" It is your peculiar privilege, my brethren, in the daily exercise of your calling, to go about doing good; and it ought to be a gratification and encouragement to you to recollect, that the great author of our salvation, first conciliated the attention and good will of the multitude, by healing their sick.

" Nor is it possible to find a happier moment, to create and establish a confidence and regard in the heart of a sick person, than this, in which his hopes and fears hang upon the physician's counsel and decision.   Should a patient recover, how enviable the feelings of the practitioner ! how grateful those of the restored !   How impossible is it for him not to respect that judgment, which proved so correct and successful in the hour of peril !

" The physician will also manifest a kind and friendly interest in the sick man's comfort, by suggesting, at a proper moment, the necessity of 'setting his house in order ;' and availing himself of a fit occasion for calling the patient's attention to a future state, and the consideration of his spiritual concerns ; and if the suggestion be presented with a sound discretion, and at a proper moment, it will assuredly be accepted with good will and thankfulness.

" Should we turn to history, for a verification of this position, we shall find passages in Homer, strongly expressive of the attachment of the Grecian heroes to their medical attendants ; and several instances in the life of Hippocrates, are demonstrative of the regard and admiration of his countrymen.   Our own times furnish us with a striking example of the deference paid to a physician by the highest potentates.   When Dr. Jenner first made known the benefits of vaccination, the king of Spain fitted out an expedition, to carry the vaccine matter to every part of his dominions, and even introduced the preservative to the remotest parts of Asia and China.   The emperor of Russia also transmitted fresh matter into the latter country ; so that the Spanish and Russian expeditions reached different points of the celestial empire at the same time.   Buonaparte, even in the plenitude of his power, accorded freedom from bondage to no less than nine captives, at the request of Dr. Jenner ; while the rulers of Austria and Spain paid equal homage to the benevolent author of so important a discovery.

" But the anecdote most flattering to the medical profession is, the establishment of the East India Company's power, on the coast of Coromandel, procured from the great mogul, in gratitude for the efficient help of Gabriel Boughton, in a case of great distress.   It seems that in the year 1636, one of the princesses of the imperial family had been dreadfully burnt, and a messenger was sent to Surat, to desire the assistance of one of the English surgeons there, when Boughton proceeded forthwith to Delhi, and performed the cure. On the minister of the great mogul asking him, what his master could do for him, to manifest his gratitude for so important a service, Boughton answered, with a disinterestedness, a generosity, and a patriotism beyond my praise, ' Let my nation trade with yours.' ' Be it so,' was the reply. A portion of the coast was marked out for the resort of English ships, and all duties were compromised for a small sum of money.* Here did the civilization of that vast continent commence—from hence the blessed light of the Gospel began to be promulgated, amongst a hundred millions of idolators, since subjected to the control of British power.

" This happy result of the successful interposition of one of our medical brethren, suggests to my mind a question of the expediency of educating missionaries in the medical art, as the earliest object of their studies. I propose this question with great diffidence, particularly in the presence of that part of my audience, with whom it may rest, to direct the preliminary education of this useful body of men; but I know that the candour of these venerable personas, is equal to their high dignity, and that they will receive my suggestions in good part. We know what the Jesuits have accomplished, in the pursuit of this object, wherever they have found admittance; and I am sanguine enough to believe, that even the proud and exclusive Chinese, would receive those who entered their country with these views, without that suspicion and distrust, which they never fail to manifest, when they surmise that trade is the object of the stranger's visit, or some covert intention to interfere with their institutions.

" The Chinese received vaccination kindly ; and since that time, have allowed a missionary from America, to establish an ophthalmic institution and general dispensary, for the sick poor of Canton. Dr. Parker continues to operate most astonishing cures, and other physicians have already arrived at Bankok and Sincapore. By endeavouring thus, to benefit both the body and the soul, some favourable impression may be made on the minds of that people, and the comforts of the Gospel be given to three hundred millions of the inhabitants of our globe.

" The Chinese practice of physic is so meagre and inadequate, as

* On the payment of three thousand rupees, a government license for an unlimited trade, without payment of customs, in the richest province of India, was accorded.—Mills' British India, vol. 1. p. 70.

to give an easy superiority to the commonest pretensions of European knowledge. You will agree with me, in this opinion, when I
tell you what their physiology and pathology is, and what are their
resources under disease. It seems that they know nothing of the
doctrine of the circulation of the blood. They believe that the human
body is composed of five elements—water, fire, wood, metal, and
earth; that, as long as the equilibrium between these is maintained,
people enjoy health, but as soon as one of them predominates, sickness ensues; that all diseases arise from disturbing the equilibrium
of these parts, and that the art of healing consists in restoring their
mutual relation. They know nothing of chemistry; their medicines
are almost all vegetable, and ginseng is their panacea. Detesting the
sight of blood, the abstraction of it is almost unknown among them :
and their utter aversion to any surgical operation, reduces them to
the necessity of depending upon the efficiency of internal remedies in
surgical cases.

" With those who practice upon such a system, if system it can be
called, the English surgeon must come into competition with the
greatest advantage in his favour. His knowledge of anatomy, his
acquaintance with chemistry, and all the other resources of his art,
will give his patients a greater confidence in his judgment, than in
that of a feeble native practitioner. Be it understood, however, that
I do not claim your acknowledgment of his superiority for an Englishman of superficial knowledge only. And it is on this conviction, that
I humbly propose, that those who are to be educated as missionaries,
after having had their minds thoroughly imbued with moral and religious principles, in their first scholastic discipline, shall then attend
to anatomy and chemistry, and the other courses of medical lectures,
so as to qualify them for the practice of physic and surgery, as much
as if they were to prosecute our profession as a means of living.

" With minds so exercised, men are surely not ill prepared to go
forth amongst the heathen, to expound the sacred truths of religion.
Some seem disposed to keep the medical and clerical characters distinct, and think that while the physician gains credit by the good he
does, the missionary may avail himself of the opportunity to impart
religious instruction. But confidence is not transferable; and it does
not follow that the impression of gratitude and attachment, which the
medical man shall have made, by his successful administrations to
disease, will be given necessarily, and of course, to a stranger, introduced to explain what is required for the salvation of the soul. I

hold it, therefore, far preferable, that the two offices should be united in those, whose zeal for the benefit of mankind may carry them to that remote part of the world.   Of this union, we know several respectable instances at home, and it cannot be forgotten that Linacre, the first president of this college, took orders in the latter period of his life, and died in the exercise of those sacred functions."

We have taken the liberty to quote, thus largely, from the foregoing speech, because, coming from such a source, and delivered before such an audience, it shows that the amelioration of China, by the united influence of medicine and religion, occupies the attention of the most learned, most pious, and most exalted in our land; while it augurs well for the cause of that populous and interesting empire, being taken up generally and vigorously by the people of this country. What Sir Henry has observed, respecting the union of the two offices, in one person, is appropriate and just; where the practitioner of physic is able to fulfil the duties of the minister of the Gospel, we hail the combination with delight and satisfaction.   The length of time, however, that is necessary to qualify persons for the successful and efficient discharge of the duties of both professions, would be unfavourable to the acquisition of the native language, which is not so easily attained after the meridian of life is passed; while some danger exists of former acquirements being forgotten, during the years devoted to philological studies. By attempting too much, therefore, we may spoil all, and render our agents skilful in nothing.   The division of labour in this, as well as every other department, will be adviseable, and excellencies of various kinds should be brought to bear on the one great object. Let our medical men be eminent in their profession,

and skilled in every branch of the healing art; but let
them, at the same time, be deeply pious, thoroughly
imbued with a missionary spirit, and sound, though not
profound divines. Then let them use their professional
attainments only as a means to an end, and as soon as
they can effect a residence, or gain any influence over
the minds of the natives, let them consecrate every
advantage to the diffusion of the Gospel.   Our missionaries, also, should not only be proficient in classical,
theological, and biblical learning, but should have some
acquaintance with medicine, so as to render very
important aid to their medical brethren.   Such labourers, sent two and two, along the coast of China, may
succeed, under the Divine blessing, in making a useful
impression on that hitherto impenetrable country.

Let those, therefore, who have acquired the necessary
qualifications, and whose souls burn with a desire to
accomplish lasting and effectual good, consider, whether
they can possibly devise an undertaking more likely
to result in the purest gratification to themselves, the
most extensive usefulness to their fellow men, and the
greatest glory to God our Saviour, than the object now
proposed. The relief they would afford to suffering
humanity, and the grateful acknowledgments which
they would so frequently receive, must spread a delight
through the mind, of which those only who know the
luxury of doing good can have the least conception;
while the result of such labours, in tending to open the
vast and populous empire of China, to the efforts of
missionaries, will be greater than any that could be
produced by pious and philanthropic labours in any
other part of the world. Instead of benefiting a village,
or a generation, such individuals would be the means

of blessing the greatest of nations, and that to the latest posterity.

Those who propose to engage in this undertaking, should be men of ardent piety and orthodox sentiment⁼, willing to go forth, with the same views, and under th ꞓ same regulations, as other missionaries. They should make the propagation of the Gospel the business of their lives, connect all their operations with a dependance on the Divine blessing, study accurately the native language, and embrace every opportunity of imparting religious instruction to their patients and others.

Besides having received a thorough medical education, and possessing extensive practical experience, the candidate for such an office should be fully informed on physiology and pathology, therapeutics and pharmacy, clinical and operative surgery, with obstetric medicine. Some months might then be allowed him to devote himself to biblico-theological instruction, and the elements of the Chinese language ; after which he might go forth, in the capacity of " the beloved physician," to evangelize and bless the nations.

CHAPTER XXII.

DESIDERATA FOR THE CHINESE MISSION.

TRANSLATION OF THE SCRIPTURES — DIFFICULTIES IN THE WAY — EF-
FORTS ALREADY MADE—NEED OF A REVISION—OPINIONS OF CHINESE
CONVERTS—AND EUROPEAN STUDENTS—RESOLUTION OF THE BIBLE
AND MISSIONARY SOCIETIES—STEPS TO BE TAKEN—IMPORTANCE OF
THE SUBJECT—CHINESE PRINTING—MOVEABLE TYPES—MODE OF PRE-
PARATION — NECESSITY OF PUNCH-CUTTING — AND CASTING — DYER'S
FOUNT—PARISIAN TYPE-FOUNDING—VARIOUS COST OF BLOCK, STONE
AND METAL TYPE PRINTING — WITH THE ADVANTAGES AND DIS-
ADVANTAGES OF XYLOGRAPHY — LITHOGRAPHY — AND TYPOGRAPHY
—SUPERIORITY AND IMPORTANCE OF THE LATTER.

ONE of the greatest achievements of the protestant
mission to China is, doubtless, the translation of the
whole Bible into the language of that country. This
work will immortalize the names of Morrison, Milne,
and Marshman, who being dead yet speak. In undertaking however, to give the mind of the Spirit to the
millions of south-eastern Asia, they attempted a great
task. The first difficulty to be overcome was, the attainment of the language, which for a long time, was
considered beyond the compass of ordinary capacities
to acquire ; its numerous and complicated hieroglyphics,
together with its extremely nice distinctions of accent,
were sufficient to appal any but the most ardent and
persevering minds. The fact of several thousand Chinese traders at Canton learning English, and scarcely
an English merchant there mastering Chinese, seemed

to indicate, that the latter language was vastly more unattainable than the former. This herculean task was, however, commenced, and the ability to speak and write in Chinese rewarded the toil of the first labourers. But familiarity with the language tended only to shew how widely it differed, in its whole structure, from that of the rest of the world. The Chinese having branched off from the great human family, very soon after the dispersion, and holding little or no intercourse with other nations, have grown up a distinct people, as isolated as if they had been the inhabitants of another planet. Their minds appear to have been cast in a different mould ; and their thoughts arranged in a manner peculiar to themselves. Unlike the languages of Europe, that of China is hieroglyphic and monosyllabic, and " so devoid of grammatical construction, that it seems the very copy of the forms of thought expressed in signs by the deaf and dumb." Hence the difficulty of translating from a foreign tongue into Chinese, and *vicé versa ;* a difficulty felt only by those, who have attempted to make the writings of eastern and western nations mutually intelligible to each other.

Again, the situation of China tends to increase the difficulty. Its inhabitants are utterly ignorant of the Gospel history, doctrines, terms, and allusions. Every feeling in the country is inimical to foreigners ; they suspect and despise barbarians, and repudiate whatever emanates from countries beyond their own. Under these circumstances, to produce a version, that should be at once faithful and idiomatic, conformable to the original text, and yet intelligible to the Chinese, must be a matter of some difficulty.

This difficult enterprise was, however, undertaken; and in order to facilitate the attempt, Dr. Morrison took out with him to China, a manuscript copy of a Harmony of the Gospels, the Acts, and the Pauline Epistles, which he always " stated explicitly, was the foundation of the New Testament in Chinese, completed and edited by him, with such alterations, as from the knowledge which he then possessed, he thought necessary."

A few years after his first arrival, he printed the Acts, and in seven years the whole New Testament was published. Being then joined by Dr. Milne, they proceeded together to the translation of the Old Testament, which in six years more was completed. This they " gave to the world, not as a perfect translation, but contemplated its improvement at some future period, expecting that they should be able to sit down together and revise the whole. This expectation was never realized, for in 1822, Dr. Milne died; and though in subsequent years, Dr. Morrison made it his study to find out and correct errors in the version, yet, with the exception of some verbal alterations, it does not appear to have undergone any considerable improvement; so that the New Testament remains substantially the same that it was in 1814, and the Old in 1820. Towards the decline of his life, however, Dr. Morrison felt the necessity of a thorough revision, and proposed that his son should undertake that work, sustained by the American Bible Society. In the meantime, the venerable missionary died, and Mr. J. R. Morrison succeeding to his father's post, as translator to the superintendents of British trade, had less time than before to devote to this object.

Being the first English missionaries that ever attempted the study of this most difficult language, and having been but a few years engaged in it, before they commenced the work of translation, though much credit is due to them, for the skill and perseverance displayed in the task, it is not to be supposed that they could at once produce a perfect version. All first efforts are necessarily defective, and it will not appear strange if this should be found capable of improvement. As, however, the Chinese must be considered best acquainted with their own language, we shall here introduce the opinions of some of them respecting it; not with the view of detracting from the praise justly due to the devoted missionaries who led the way in this herculean undertaking, but in order to stir up their successors to equal diligence in improving what they have so laudably begun. The Chinese evangelist, Leang Afǎh, writing on the subject, says—

" The style adopted in the present version of the scriptures, is far from being idiomatic, the translators having sometimes used too many characters, and employed inverted and unusual phrases, by which the sense is obscured. The doctrines of scripture are in themselves deep and mysterious; and, if in addition to this, the style be difficult, men will be less likely to understand the book. I am a Chinese, and know the style most suited to the Chinese mind; let us endeavour, therefore, to render the version more idiomatic, and then print as many books as we please. The belief or rejection of the scriptures rests with those to whom we send them; but it is our duty to render the sacred volume as intelligible as possible. Although I am a dull scholar, yet I know whether the style of a book be native or foreign; and perceiving the version to be unidiomatic, I feel the necessity of attempting its correction. I have, therefore, gone through some of the books of scripture, rejecting the redundant particles, and amending the inverted expressions, with the hope that my countrymen may the more readily comprehend them; thus the grace of God, in sending Jesus into the world to save sinners, will not be frustrated, and the kind intentions of Christians in com-municating the Gospel to the Chinese, will not be entirely in vain."

Lew Tse-chuen, a Chinese literary graduate, and a Christian convert, writes in the following strain:—

" From the time that I first met with the holy book of God, I saw that it contained mysterious doctrines, which could not be understood without deep attention. But the Chinese version exhibits a great number of redundancies and tautologies, which render the meaning obscure. It is possible that the sacred books are in themselves thus stiff and unbending, or is it the effect of the translation ? When they are distributed among the people, I perceive that there is no unwillingness to accept them, but failing to comprehend their mean-ing, they frequently throw the work aside. Like the flesh of do-mestic animals, though originally good for food, if presented in a raw state, it would not be tasted; and if not tasted, its qualities would not be known : thus the Bible is not esteemed, because it has not been tasted; and it has not been tasted, on account of its unfinished style. I have frequently wished to correct the style of these books, that people at one glance may comprehend them, but I find it exceedingly difficult; perhaps the best plan would be, to take the meaning of each chapter, and make another chapter of it, in an easy style, after the perusal of which, men would be able to under-stand the old version."

Choo Tih-lang, a Chinese transcriber, now in Eng-land, (whose portrait appears in the frontispiece) thus writes on the subject:—

" Having perused the present translation of the scriptures into Chinese, I find it exceedingly verbose, containing much foreign phraseology, so contrary to the usual style of our books, that the Chinese cannot thoroughly understand the meaning, and frequently refuse to look into it. It ought to be known, that in the Chinese, phrases have a certain order, and characters a definite application, which cannot be departed from with propriety. In order to illustrate offences against idiom, it may be observed, that the Chinese are accustomed to say, ' You with me come along !' while the English say, ' You come along with me !' Now it appears to me, that the present version is in Chinese words, but in many respects arranged according to English idiom. In a translation, the sense ought certainly to be given, according to the original; but the style should be conformable to native models: thus every one will take up the book with pleasure, and read it with profit. If the translation be not revised, I fear that the efforts of missionaries in China, will be unproductive, and a mere waste of money—will not this be lamentable?"

Messrs. Dyer and Evans, of Malacca, are of opinion—

"That a revision of the Chinese scriptures is necessary, and that the late Dr. Morrison's glorious effort may be vastly improved upon for the benefit of China."

While Mr. Kidd, now of London University College, says—

" Were I to assert that there are no defects in the old version, I should excite unmixed wonder; since it is a first version into a difficult language, and must needs be susceptible of much improvement. Its chief imperfections are, a too literal adherance to the order of the original, where equal faithfulness might be secured, by a more idiomatic disposition of the words: and also inattention to some minutiæ, in arranging antithetic words and phrases, to which the Chinese attach great importance. Sometimes by ommitting or supplying a word or two, the euphony of the sentence could be improved, without impairing its fidelity to the original," &c. &c.

From the opinions and statements before quoted, it would appear that the revision of the Chinese version is an important desideratum, in aiming at the evangelization of that great empire. The Committee of the Bible Society have therefore passed a resolution, " requesting the Directors of the London Missionary Society to take the necessary steps for procuring such a revision of Dr. Morrison's work, as appears to have been contemplated by the Doctor himself; with the understanding that, of a verson thus revised, and duly accredited by them, all the reasonable expenses will be

defrayed by the Committee of the Bible Society."
This Resolution bears date December 5, 1836, and
having been discussed before a full meeting of the
Directors, on the following February, it was resolved to
"take the recommendation of the Bible Society into
their serious consideration, in the hope of securing a
careful revision of the existing version, at as early a
time as may be practicable." Since then it does not
appear that any effectual steps have been taken, though
doubtless something is in contemplation, or in progress. As a preliminary measure, the Directors
may have requested some of their number, who are
deeply versed in Biblical learning, to draw up a few
principles of translation, which would be serviceable, not only to the missionaries in China, but to all
those engaged in evangelizing the heathen, in every
part of the world. They may bring the subject earnestly
and affectionately before their agents, in the various
stations, urging unanimity and co-operation, recommending them to ascertain the real character and genius
of the Chinese language, and charging them to acquaint
themselves thoroughly with the letter and meaning of
Scripture, in order that they may express the truths
of revelation in the most suitable, exact and idiomatic form. They may furnish their missionaries
with all the necessary helps, in this important undertaking; providing them with lexicons, polyglots, commentaries, illustrations, and the results of Biblical
criticism on the several parts of Scripture, which have
been published in this improving and enquiring age.
They may direct each of their missionaries to prepare
separate revisions, according to the best of their judgment, having respect to the known views of their
coadjutors, and the wishes of the Bible Committee; and

while they study fidelity in the first instance, aiming to make it intelligible and useful to the Chinese; when all is completed, they may authorize the missionaries to meet together, compare their several productions, in the presence of learned and converted natives, and decide upon the renderings to be adopted in each particular passage. This done, they can recommend the whole to the Bible Society, and multiply copies equal to the utmost demands of China.

Something has already been attempted, by several of the missionaries, as well as by the native converts; but for want of a well-digested plan of combined co-operation, these efforts have been unproductive of permanent good. The subject is here brought forward, to invite the attention of the friends of China, and to press it on the consciences of all concerned in the evangelization of that empire, to unite in one determined and judicious effort, to make the word of God plain and profitable to a numerous people, constituting nearly one-third of the human race. When viewed in the light of eternity, this undertaking appears of incalculable magnitude, and nothing should be left undone, that would tend to the clearing up of God's holy word to so vast a portion of his intelligent and accountable creatures.

Next in importance to the perfection of the Chinese version of the Scriptures is, the improvement of the means of printing in that language. The native mode of printing has been described in a preceding chapter. It has, however, notwithstanding its simplicity, great disadvantages. These have been felt by the Chinese themselves; and the emperor Kang-he, in the year 1722, ordered an assortment of moveable types to be prepared, of copper, which he called " congregated pearls ;" these were afterwards, in a season of necessity, melted down for coin, and two hundred and fifty thousand wooden types were cut in their stead.

Foreigners, seeking to introduce religion into China, or to communicate to their own countrymen some knowlege of Chinese literature, have resorted to the use of moveable types. At the College of St. Joseph, in Macao, there is an assortment of such types, with which various religious works, and a Portuguese and Chinese Lexicon, have been printed. When Dr. Morrison's Dictionary was put to press in Macao, it was found necessary to combine the Chinese character with the Roman letter, and for this end a steel mould was prepared, in which the body of the type was cast, after which each separate character was engraved on the face of the metal, as needed. In this way, a complete assortment of Chinese types was obtained, suited for the printing of philological works, but not adapted for the publication of voluminous religious books, in Chinese. About ten thousand of these were selected and sent down to Malacca, which were afterwards greatly increased by successive additions, till the fount was sufficiently large for printing small tracts, and a few numbers of a native newspaper. Its unevenness and incompleteness, however, have prevented its being brought into general use. The Baptist missionaries, at Serampore, have cut or cast a fount of moveable types, sufficient for printing the Scriptures; and several editions of the Chinese version, executed by them have been thus published. This fount, however, though of a small and convenient size, is not so elegant, uniform, and purely native as could be wished.

Another method of obtaining metal types was invented by Mr. Dyer, who prepared a number of wooden blocks, and then causing a set of stereotype plates to be cast from them, each the height of common letter, he sawed the metal into squares, and thus obtained moveable metallic types, the very *fac-simile* of the blocks. He counted the number and variety of characters in fourteen authors, some historical, some moral, and some foreign, in order to ascertain how many different symbols would be required. As the result he ascertained, that three thousand two hundred and forty varieties would be necessary; that of these the greater number would occur only two or three times, while some would be met with several hundred times in the course of a few pages. Altogether thirty thousand types would be needed to constitute a fount, which would require two hundred wooden blocks to be engraved, some of which must have several successive casts made from them, in order to give a due proportion of each character.

Some objections were, however, found to this system: the chief of which was that the inferior material was made the basis of the superior. Engravings on wood, executed by rough artists, never could be so neat as those made on metal. Owing to the soft texture of the wood, and the carelessness of the Chinese in cutting, some of the finer strokes of the character were imperfectly executed; and then all the errors and defects, unevenness and discrepancies of the block were, in the stereotyping, transferred to the plate, and finally appeared in the separate type. Again, it was ascertained, that a fount would last only five or six years, when it must be re-cast, and the model blocks be recut. So that, after due and patient consideration, it was deemed adviseable to proceed at once to punch-cutting.

Mr. Dyer's chief reason for this was, because a punch was the foundation of perpetuity: the punches once cut, matrices could be struck, and types and founts multiplied to any extent. The mass of the language was found to be about one thousand two hundred characters, for which punches might be made; and the rest, occurring but seldom, might either be cut on the face of the metal, or stereotyped from blocks, in the way before described: but there was every probability, if the work was once commenced, of our being able to form punches for all. A method was also devised for dividing the Chinese character, and joining the component parts of several symbols, so as to form distinct wholes. Some punches, it was ascertained, by a little alteration, could be made serviceable for other characters; so that the work of casting a complete assortment of moveable types did not appear so formidable, as was at first imagined.

The expense of preparing these punches turned out to be less than was apprehended. Instead of paying a guinea for each punch, Mr. Dyer found that he could get a Chinese workman to engrave characters in steel, for about two shillings and ten pence each. Thus the cost of three thousand punches would be four hundred and twenty-five pounds; and of casting one thousand pounds weight of metal type, at two shillings per pound, would only amount to one hundred pounds, for each fount of Chinese characters. So great were the advantages likely to result from this undertaking, and so small the expense, (only one-tenth of what Dr. Milne calculated on twenty years ago) that Mr. Dyer was encouraged to proceed ; some friends in England and America raised considerable sums to sustain him, and he is now engaged in casting three or four complete founts of moveable metallic types, for the various missionary stations in the east.

Specimens of the types have been exhibited, and they are such as to afford entire satisfaction. The complete Chinese air they assume, so as not to be distinguishable from the best style of native artists, together with the clearness and durability of the letter, would recommend them to universal adoption. There is, however, one drawback upon their utility, and that is, their size. They are cast on two-line pica, and will, of course, occupy much room. They are very little smaller than the characters employed in the octavo edition of Morrison's Bible, which amounts to twenty-one volumes; while Marshman's, printed in a smaller type, occupies eight volumes. Situated as missionaries are, on the borders of China, and aiming to introduce the Christian religion, by the quiet diffusion of Scriptures and tracts, it is necessary, so long as the government opposes our efforts, and continues to account Christian books contraband, that we should bring them into as small a compass as possible : both for the convenience of carriage, when voyaging along their shores, and for concealment, when the books are placed in the hands of the natives.

Another attempt to found Chinese moveable types has been made in Paris, under the direction of M. Pauthier, member of the Asiatic Society there. From some specimens of these which have been published, it appears, that they are much smaller than Mr. Dyer's types, being about the size of great primer ; and being cast by one of the most expert type founders in France, they are, as it respects fineness of stroke, and exactness of height, superior to anything that Asiatic workmen can produce. The form of some of the characters is a little stiff, and disproportionate, owing partly to inexperience, and partly to the attempt which the French have made, to split and combine the elements of various characters, so as to prevent the necessity of cutting a new punch for each separate symbol; but on the whole they are exceedingly neat and handsome.

In the prospectus, which accompanies the specimen, the projectors ascribe the little interest which the study of the Chinese language has excited, to the want of native types, wherewith to publish European books, illustrative of that tongue. " The same difficulty," they say, " existed in Sanscrit, before the munificence of the king of Prussia gave a fount of Sancrit types to the learned world." They then proce d to observe —

" We desire to enjoy the same advantage in the Chinese, and thus enable all sinologues, colleges, and printers, to procure either a fount, or the copper matrices of the types we announce. M. Pauthier, in order to encourage Chinese literature, formed the design of publishing a translation of the principal philosophical works of that country, with the original text on the opposite page : and desirous of giving to these editions all the typographical perfection which can now be obtained in Europe, he addressed himself to M. Marcellin Legrand, who for the interest of science, was willing to cut steel punches for two thousand of the most common Chinese characters, to be increased from time to time, as occasion might require. The dimension of these characters being only *fourteen points* on each side, they could be used with ordinary letter-press, without injuring the neatness of the page.

" But it was not sufficient to have an elegant fount of Chinese types, it was also necessary to find out a method of composing and distributing them. For this purpose, the characters have been arranged under the two hundred and fourteen radicals of the Chinese language, each one having the number given to it in this classification cut in the nick, so as to enable the printer, whatever may be his degree of intelligence, to compose Chinese, with as little difficulty as numerical figures."

Attached to a beautiful specimen of the characters engraved by him, M. Marcellin Legrand has the following remarks :—

" Of all the languages in the known world, the most difficult to represent by moveable types, is, without controversy, the Chinese ; having hitherto baffled the most skilful European typographers. The Chinese have determined, after trying in vain to render each of their numerous characters moveable, to retain their primitive engraving on wooden blocks. Almost all the trials which have hitherto been made in Europe, to engrave Chinese characters, had in view the union of a greater or less number of those characters, which were most frequently engraven on wood, without ever forming a rich and commodious fount. It was necessary, therefore, to make something more complete and definite ; and to solve the problem of representing the figurative language of China, with the fewest possible elements, without, however, altering the composition of the symbols.

" Under the direction of M. Pauthier, who has obligingly assisted me in the choice of models, I have, I believe, resolved this problem, and have undertaken to engrave on steel, and cast a complete fount of this most difficult language. The greater part of the Chinese characters are composed of two elements, one of which represents the idea, and the other the sound. The result of this very remarkable composition is, that by the combination of these two elements, we have been able considerably to reduce the number of punches, and to produce all the characters contained in the imperial dictionary of Kang-he, while the classification and composition of the symbols has been rendered as easy as possible."

These types are divided into three series ; first, a group of three thousand characters, sufficient for composing the works of Confucius ; secondly, a group of four thousand six hundred, by means of which the Bible, and the dictionary of P. Basile could be printed;

and thirdly, a group of nine thousand, which by their combinations would produce characters enough for the Chinese Imperial Dictionary. The price of the first of these series is, three francs and a quarter, for each rough copper matrix; for the second, three francs; and for the third, two francs and a half: on the obtaining of which, types could be cast to any amount, for all religious and learned bodies. The engraver expects to have a set of matrices ready by the middle of 1838; and it is only for the benevolent public to supply the means, and we can obtain facilities for printing in two sizes of Chinese character, viz., that cast by Mr. Dyer, and the fount produced by M. Legrand.

Perhaps it may lead the friends of Christianity and education more readily to a decision on the subject, were we to state the proportionate cost of the different modes of printing, which have been adopted for the Chinese, viz., xylography, lithography, and typography. And in order to this, we must take a definite number of some large work, say two thousand copies of the Chinese Bible, in octavo; by considering the cost of which, as printed in wood, stone, or metal, we may be able to form a just estimate of the subject.

1. By Block Printing, at Malacca :—	£.	s.	d.
The passage of nine workmen, to and from China . .	72	0	0
Two thousand blocks, at £1. per hundred	20	0	0
Tools, gravers, &c	10	0	0
Transcribing 2,689 pages, at 9d. per page.	100	16	9
Engraving, 1,160,548 characters, at 1s. 3d. per hundred	725	6	10
Printing and binding 5,378,000 pages, at 1s. 8d. per thousand	448	3	4
Two hundred and ten peculs of paper, at £2. 10s. per pecul	525	0	0
	£1901	6	11

The foregoing is the charge generally made for work done at Malacca, Batavia, and Singapore; in China, the prices to Europeans are about two thirds of the above; but as we cannot now print with safety at Canton, we are obliged to take the estimate of work done in the colonies. The time occupied in the above undertaking, by nine type-cutters, and five printers and binders, would be somewhere about three years.

2. By Lithography, at Batavia :—

	£.	s.	d.
For two lithographic presses, with stones	100	0	0
Materials, repairs, &c.	100	0	0
Transcribing 2,689 pages, twice over, at 9d. per page .	201	13	6
Printing, 5,378,000 pages, at 1s. per thousand pages. .	268	18	0
Binding the above, at 3d. per thousand pages	67	4	6
Paper, the same as in the first statement	525	0	0
	£1262	16	0

The above is the charge for printing by lithography, at Batavia, where labour is cheap. The folding and collating would cost less for sheets worked off at a press, than for separate pages printed by the hand, according to the Chinese mode. The time occupied in the work, by one transcriber, four pressmen, and one binder, would be two years.

3. By Typography :—

	£.	s.	d.
Cost of three thousand punches, or matrices, furnished by Mr. Dyer	425	0	0
Ditto of one thousand pounds weight of metal, at 2s. per pound	100	0	0
One iron press, cases, furniture, &c.	100	0	0
Composition of 2,689 pages, at 2s. per page	268	18	0
Printing 5,378,000 pages, at 6d. per thousand pages .	134	9	0
Binding the above, at 3d. per thousand pages	67	4	5
For 168 peculs of paper, at £2. 10s. per pecul . . .	420	0	0
	£1515	11	6

Mr. Dyer's types being somewhat smaller than those used in the octavo edition of the Bible, less paper will be required. If, however, the French types be used, not only will the original cost be less, but a saving of one half the price of paper be effected. The time required for the punch cutting cannot be precisely stated; but supposing the types ready, the printing of two thousand copies of the Chinese Bible would occupy four compositors, two pressmen, and one binder, one year.

Thus the entire cost being reckoned, the balance will appear at first in favour of lithography, but permanently in that of typography; in addition to greater speed and superiority of execution. When the first two thousand copies are struck off, if executed by means of xylography, we possess a set of blocks adapted for printing the scriptures alone, already much worn, and capable of working only five more editions, at one half of the original cost. If the work be performed at a lithographic press, we possess after its completion, only the presses and the stones, very much the worse for wear. But if metal types be employed, we have, when the work is done, a set of punches and matrices, from which millions of types may be cast, sufficient to supply the whole world; besides an iron press, and a complete fount of types, from which fifty more editions can be taken, at a lower rate, than that at which each edition could be printed from the wooden blocks.

We shall now subjoin a few of the advantages and disadvantages of the three systems, independently of the cost.

Of xylography, the advantages are—that it is suited

to the nature of the Chinese language; while it possesses all the advantages of European stereotype, except durability. It is adapted for printing in different forms and sizes of the character. It requires no complicated machinery, or expensive apparatus. The blocks once cut, need no further correction; though they are capable of it, if necessary. New editions may be frequently printed without trouble; and in travelling, a few blocks may be packed in a small compass, and printed from at every stage.

But the disadvantages of block-printing are, that it is not adapted for ephemeral works, or miscellaneous pieces: neither is it calculated for expedition, in engraving or throwing off copies. The same character must be cut over again, if it should occur ten thousand times. It is difficult, by such a system, to combine other languages with the Chinese. The blocks, after a certain number of copies have been struck off, are of no use but for fire-wood; while they are liable to be destroyed by white ants, before they are worn out. In addition to this, they occupy much room. The blocks for the octavo edition of the Scriptures would occupy sixty-seven cubic feet. If one block be lost or injured, the whole edition is spoiled, unless a type-cutter be at hand, to supply the deficiency. By means of wooden stereotype, the earliest and most inferior works of missionaries are perpetuated, when years of experience, and more extensive knowledge of the language, might enable them to produce something better. Besides which, the type-cutters are troublesome men, very difficult to be kept in order, and should they be prohibited from quitting their native land, our work must come to a stand.

Of lithography, the advantages are,—that small

editions may be printed, according to the demand, while every successive edition is capable of improvement. Periodical publications may be struck off at a very short notice : and each small station might be furnished with a lithographic press, which a single individual could manage. Further, this mode of printing is adapted for any language, or any form of the character, while pictorial illustrations might be introduced, so pleasing to the natives of the east.

The disadvantages are, slowness of execution ; liability to failure, on account of climate, ignorance, or inattention ; and the irregular appearance of a book thus printed.

Of typography, the advantages are,—that it is equally adapted to large and small editions : the types are calculated to last long, and when worn out, may be re-cast, or sold for old metal. Metal types, when well executed, appear much more beautiful than wooden blocks. By adopting this mode, we become entirely independent of the Chinese. In typography corrections and improvements are easy. Moveable metallic types may be combined with European letters in the printing of Dictionaries, &c. The space occupied by separate characters is not so great as the room taken up by wooden blocks. Nine symbols will fit into a square inch, and a frame one foot square will contain a thousand : thus four pairs of common printing cases will hold thirty thousand characters. The white ants cannot destroy metal types. The speed with which letter-press can be worked off is double that of wooden blocks ; and there is a considerable saving of paper.

The disadvantages of typography are, that it would require an European printer, acquainted with the

Chinese language. Should unusual characters occur in the course of printing, or should the pages run upon sorts, the press must stop until the necessary characters can be cut or cast for the purpose ; while two sets of types will be needed, one large and the other small, to serve for text and commentary. These, however, are procurable, the former at Malacca, and the latter at Paris.

Thus, upon a review of the whole, it will appear, that printing by means of metal types is greatly preferable to every other method. The obtaining of them is easy. Mr. Dyer has nearly completed the engraving of his punches for the large size, which he expects will cost about four hundred pounds ; after which he can furnish founts of three thousand varieties, and thirty thousand number, for one hundred pounds each. The Paris printer will soon be ready with his matrices, in a smaller size, prepared with mathematical exactness, for the same money, from which as many founts can be cast as are required for missionary and educational purposes.

The religious and scientific public are perfectly able to provide both these sums, and a subscription for that purpose ought to be immediately begun. Furnished with metal types, and European presses of the latest construction, we can produce Scriptures and tracts to any amount, equal to the most enlarged wishes of the religious public, by which a reading people may be furnished with the means of evangelization, and China be gradually brought acquainted with the Gospel. This is one of the most important objects that was ever presented to the attention of the Christian world, which, if left undone, for the want of a few hundred pounds, will occasion the expenditure of thousands, in order to get the same quantity of work accomplished by the present mode. China is open to the distribution of books ; the myriads inhabiting the maritime provinces are ready to receive the word of life, and the lever that shall move this moral world is undoubtedly metal-type printing.

Having obtained the means of multiplying books, with speed and neatness, we next require increased facilities for circulating them. With an archipelago studded with islands, a line of coast thousands of miles in extent, and hundreds of commodious harbours, we have a field for operation larger than any which the whole world presents elsewhere. To avail ourselves of the native craft would be dangerous, to sail in opium-smugglers inconsistent, and to hire ships on the spot, expensive. The only alternative is to have a vessel devoted entirely to the object ; but as we have before alluded to this matter, we shall not now enlarge, further than to observe, that by recent intelligence it appears, that the result of the effort made in America in 1835, on this subject, is the fitting out of a vessel for one year, by which it is supposed, the sum of five hundred pounds has been contributed to missionary objects. The voyage referred to has been made, and the year is now expired, so that at present no vessel is on the ground, nor any certain conveyance available to missionaries, who wish to carry the Gospel along the shores of China, Cochin-China, Corea, and Japan, with the islands and countries scattered throughout the Yellow, China, and Java seas. Is it too much to say, therefore, that increased facilities for circulating scriptures and tracts are included among the desiderata for the Chinese mission ?

In conclusion, the author would earnestly appeal to the benevolent and devotional feelings of the Christian public. Funds, of no ordinary amount, are needed for this great object; and should be given with an unsparing hand. If missionaries will subject themselves to much personal risk and inconvenience, for the sake of the cause, surely it is not asking too much of those who enjoy the ease and gratification of home to contribute of their substance to the accomplishment of the same end. Let the rich and the poor, in this respect meet together, and each one consecrate of his substance, according as God hath prospered him, in sums proportionate to the magnitude of the object, and the amount of personal responsibility and obligation. And oh, if ever, the fervent and importunate cry of the sympathizing Christian should ascend to God, on behalf of a lost and degenerate world, if ever the disciples of Christ should pray " thy kingdom come," then how incessant and earnest should be the supplications of modern believers on behalf of China. Time was when ignorance of their state, and inability to reach them, might have led Christians "to restrain prayer" on their behalf; but now that their real condition is set before the public mind, and the mode of benefiting them plainly pointed out, who is there, that longs to "see of the travail of the Redeemer's soul," that can withhold his strong crying and tears, on behalf of a class of nations constituting within themselves one third of the human race, and one half of the heathen world.

A BRIEF SKETCH

OF

CHINESE CHRONOLOGY,

ACCORDING TO NATIVE DOCUMENTS.

FABULOUS PERIOD.

Pwan-koo, was produced after the first division of heaven and earth, and the settlement of chaos.

Tëen Hwang-she, "Imperial Heaven," settled the years.— His rule lasted 18,000 years.

Te Hwang-she, "Royal earth," fixed the months.—His rule lasted 18,000 years.

Jin Hwang-she, "Sovereign man," divided the land.—His rule lasted 45,600 years.

Yew-chaou-she, the inventor of dwellings.—Gen. iv. 20.

Suy-jin-she, the inventor of fire.

TRADITIONARY PERIOD.

Fuh-he, taught hunting and fishing, invented the diagrams and music, and established marriage. He was assisted by a female called Wa; probably Chawah, or Eve.—Gen. iii. 20.

Shin-nung, taught husbandry and medicine.—Gen. iv. 2.

Hwang-te, invented the cycle, and letters, discovered the silk-worm, made implements and boats, and wrought in metals.—Gen. iv. 2.

Chun-kŭh. About this time, divine and human personages mixed together, and produced confusion.—Gen. vi. 2.

Te-kwŭh.

HISTORICAL PERIOD.

Dynasties.	Emperors.	When began to reign. Year.	Cycle.	B.C.	Reigned Years.	Remarkable Events.
Hea	Te Yaou	41	5	2356	102	B. C. 2296. A great inundation occurred.—Gen. vii. 11.
	Te Shun	23	7	2254	50	Astronomical instruments formed, and the planets observed.
	Yu	13	8	2204	8	Wine discovered and repudiated.—Gen. ix. 21.
	Te Ke	21	8	2196	9	B. C. 2192. A dragon seen; perhaps one of the Saurian tribe.
	Ta-kang	30	8	2187	29	This prince was fond of hunting.—Gen. x. 9.
	Chung-kang	59	8	2158	13	B. C 2158. Oct. An eclipse of the sun was seen in $\beta \check{\epsilon}\tau\eta$ of Scorpio. He and
	Te Seang	12	9	2145	28	Ho, the astronomers, were drunk, and did not observe it; hence, they were
	Shaon-kang	40	9	2117	61	punished. P. Gaubil says, that an eclipse really occurred, in the constella-
	Te Choo	41	9	2056	17	tion referred to, B. C. 2155.
	Te Hwae	58	10	2039	26	
	Te Mäng	24	11	2013	18	
	Te Sëeh	42	11	1995	16	
	Te Püh-kang	58	11	1979	59	
	Te Shang	57	12	1920	21	
	Te Kin	18	13	1899	21	
	Te Kung-këä	39	13	1878	31	This emperor was vicious and disorderly, on which account his servants
	Te Kaou	10	14	1847	11	rebelled.
	Te Fah	21	14	1836	19	
	Këä-kwei	40	14	1817	52	This emperor was deposed on account of his tyranny, and the dynasty changed.
Shang	Ching-tang	32	15	1765	13	B. C. 1765. Commencement of a seven years' drought. The sovereign ascribed
	Ta-këä	45	15	1752	33	the calamity to his own misrule, and while confessing his sins, the rain fell
	Yüh-ting	18	16	1719	29	in torrents.—Gen. xli. 54.
	Tae-kang	47	16	1690	25	
	Seaou-shin	12	17	1665	17	
	Yung-che	29	17	1648	12	
	Tae-süh	41	17	1636	75	Two trees grew up in the palace, in one night: which were considered calami-
	Chung-ting	56	18	1561	13	tous signs. The emperor, however, cultivated virtue, and in three days, the
	Wae-jin	9	19	1548	15	trees died away.

Dynasties.	Emperors.	When began to reign. Year. | Cycle.		B. C.	Reigned Years.	Remarkable Events.
Shang	Ho-tan-kёä	24	19	1533	9	The course of one of the rivers stopped and changed.
	Tsoo-yih	33	19	1524	19	
	Tsoo-sin	52	19	1495	16	
	Yŭh-shin	8	20	1489	25	
	Tsoo-ting	33	20	1464	32	
	Nan-kang	5	21	1432	25	
	Yang-kea	30	21	1497	7	
	Pwan-kang	37	21	1490	28	This prince changed the name of the dynasty from Shang to Yin.
	Seaou-sin	5	22	1372	21	
	Seaou-yih	26	22	1351	28	
	Woo-ting	54	22	1323	59	B. C. 1293. The Tartar country was subdued, called the "land of devils."
	Tsoo-kang	53	23	1264	7	This prince was vicious, and the dynasty began to decline.
	Tsoo-kёä	60	23	1257	33	
	Lin-sin	33	24	1224	6	
	Kang-ting	39	24	1218	21	Images invented, and the inventor struck dead by lightning.
	Woo-yih	60	24	1197	4	
	Tae-ting	4	25	1193	3	
	Te-yih	7	25	1190	37	B. C. 1175. An earthquake.
	Chow-sin	44	25	1153	32	Great tyranny and oppression. The tyrant slain.
Chow	Woo-wang	16	26	1121	7	The country delivered by Woo Wang, who encouraged learning.
	Ching-wang	23	26	1114	37	B. C. 1108. The mariner's compass invented.
	Kang-wang	60	26	1077	26	For forty years, no punishments inflicted or needed.
	Chaou-wang	26	27	1051	51	This prince attempting to cross a river, in a boat glued together, was drowned.
	Mŭh-wang	17	28	1000	55	
	Kung-wang	12	29	945	12	
	E-wang	24	29	933	25	
	Heaou-wang	49	29	908	15	B. C. 895. A great hail storm.
	E-wang	4	30	893	16	
	Le-wang	20	30	877	51	Le-wang was a tyrant; and the people rebelled. [xxiv. 1.
	Seuen-wang	11	31	826	46	The emperor numbered the people, which was displeasing to heaven.—2 Sam.
	Yew-wang	57	31	780	11	B. C. 777. A great earthquake, and three rivers stopped in their course.

Dynasties	Emperors	Year	Cycle	B.C.	Reigned Years	Remarkable Events.
Chow	Ping-wang	8	32	769	51	At this time, the dynasty was called Eastern Chow.
	Hwan-wang	59	32	718	23	Confucius's history commences here.
	Chwang-wang	22	33	695	15	B.C. 717. An eclipse of the sun, in March. } Of these, 36 are recorded in the preceding history, but this was the greatest for the last 1000 years.
	Le-wang	37	33	680	5	B.C 686. The stars disappeared, and
	Hwuy-wang	42	33	675	25	meteors fell like rain.
	Seang-wang	7	34	650	33	Learning encouraged. The probable time when Buddha lived.
	King-wang	40	34	617	6	At this time, the Chinese wrote on bamboos, with an iron style.
	Kwang-wang	46	34	611	6	Sacrificing at the tombs commenced about this time.
	Ting-wang	52	34	605	21	
	Këen-wang	13	35	584	14	Wars and commotions.
	Ling-wang	27	35	570	27	B.C. 549. Confucius born.
	King-wang	54	35	543	25	Laou-tsze lived about this time.
	King-wang	19	36	518	44	B.C. 499. Confucius obtained office.
	Yuen-wang	3	37	474	7	B.C. 477. Confucius died.
	Chin-ting-wang	10	37	467	28	
	Kaou-wang	38	37	439	15	Mang-tsze, or Mencius, flourished.
	Wei-lëĕ-wang	53	37	424	24	
	Gan-wang	17	38	400	26	
	Lëĕ-wang	43	38	374	7	The authority of the emperor, at this time, was merely nominal.
	Hëen-wang	50	38	367	48	B.C. 359. A comet appeared in the west.
	Shin-tsing-wang	38	39	319	6	
	Lan-wang	44	39	313	59	B.C. 302. A comet appeared.
	Tung-chow-keun	43	40	254	8	B.C. 303. Another comet, and an eclipse of the sun.
	Chwang-seang-wang	51	40	246	1	
	Seven rival states	52	40	245	25	The dynasty terminated.
Tsin	Che Hwang-te	17	41	220	12	The books burned, and 460 literati buried alive. The great wall built.
	Urh-she	29	41	208	3	Cruelties soon brought this dynasty to a close.
Han	Kaou-te	32	41	205	12	The Han dynasty was founded by a private individual.
	Heaou-hwuy	44	41	193	7	
	Kaou-how	51	41	186	8	An empress seized the reins of government.
	Wǎn-te	59	41	178	23	This emperor was frugal and plain.

Dynasties.	Emperors.	When began to reign. Year.	Cycle.	B.C.	Reigned Years.	Remarkable Events.
Han	King-te	22	42	155	16	The empire prosperous.
	Woo-te	38	42	139	54	Learning encouraged.
	Chaou-te	32	43	85	13	About this time foreign merchandize began to enter China.
	Seuen-te	45	43	72	25	The day divided into twelve periods, of two hours each.
	Yuen-te	10	44	47	16	This emperor was talented and learned.
	Ching-te	26	44	31	26	This ruler was given to wine.
	Gae-te	52	44	5	6	The dynasty Han began to decline.
	Ping-te	58	44	A.D.1	4	The emperor slain by an usurper.
	Too-tsze-ying	2	45	5	4	A youthful emperor on the throne.
	Sin-wang	6	45	9	14	The throne usurped.
	Hwae-yang-wang	20	45	23	2	
Tung-Han	Kwang-woo	22	45	25	33	The fortunes of Han revived.
	Ming-te	55	45	58	18	This emperor sent messengers to India, to look for "the holy man of the west," and to bring his books and religion into China. From this time, Buddhism was introduced.
	Chang-te	13	46	76	13	
	Ho-te	26	46	89	17	
	Shang-te	43	46	106	1	The eunuchs began to acquire influence.
	Gan-te	44	46	107	19	Another empress usurped authority.
	Shun-te	3	47	126	19	The Han dynasty again declined.
	Chung-te	22	47	145	1	The literary title of Ken-jin invented
	Chih-te	23	47	146	1	
	Hwan-te	24	47	147	21	The Arabians began to trade at Canton.
	Ling-te	45	47	168	22	Chairs were now introduced, on which they sat cross-legged.
	Heen-te	7	48	190	31	This prince was deposed by an usurper.
How Han	Chaou-lëë	38	48	221	3	The empire was divided into three states, but the preference is given, by historians, to the lawful descendants of Han.
	How-choo	41	48	224	41	
Tsin	Woo-te	22	49	265	25	The three kingdoms united into one.
	Hwuy-te	47	49	290	17	Paper money began to be used at funerals.
	Hwae-te	4	50	307	6	The literary title of Sew-tsae introduced.
	Min-te	10	50	313	4	This emperor was murdered.
Tung Tsin	Yuen-te	14	50	317	6	A.D. 321, April. A dark spot was seen in the sun
	Ming-te	20	50	323	3	An intelligent prince.

Dynasties.	Emperors.	When began to reign. Years.	Cycle.	A. D.	Reigned Years.	Remarkable Events.
Tung Tsin	Ching-te	23	50	326	17	A. D. 328. A comet appeared.
	Kang-te	40	50	343	2	
	Müh-te	42	50	345	17	About this time Buddhism widely spread.
	Gae-te	59	50	362	4	
	Te-yĭh	3	51	366	5	Stamp duty, on the sale of houses and lands, introduced.
	Këen-wăn	8	51	371	2	
	Heaou-te	10	51	373	24	A. D. 393. A comet was seen in Capricornus.
	Gan-te	34	51	397	22	
Pih-Sung	King-te	56	51	419	2	This emperor deposed the prince of the preceding dynasty, and reigned in his stead.
	Woo-te	58	51	421	1	
	Ying-yang Wang	60	51	423	30	This prince put to death his best ministers.
	Wăn Te	1	52	424	11	A. D. 454. A comet appeared.
	Heaou-woo Te	31	52	454	1	
	Fei Te	42	52	465	7	
	Ming Te	43	52	466	4	
	Chwang-yu Wang	50	52	473	2	
Tse	Shun Te	54	52	477	4	These two emperors were slain by Taou-ching, who founded the Tse dynasty.
	Taé-tsoo	56	52	479	11	
	Woo Te	60	52	483	5	
	Ming Te	11	53	494	2	
	Tung-hwun How	16	53	499	1	This prince was vicious, and soon slain.
	Ho Te	18	53	501	48	Much confusion.
Leang	Woo Te	19	53	502	2	During this dynasty, five colleges were opened.
	Këen-wan Te	7	54	550	3	
	Yuen Te	9	54	552	2	People began to sit on chairs, with their legs hanging down.
	King Te	12	54	555	3	Short and troublous reigns.
Chin	Woo Te	14	54	557	7	
	Wăn Te	17	54	560	2	
	Fei Te	24	54	567	14	
	Seuen Te	26	54	569	6	An ambassador was sent to Cambodjia.
	How Choo	40	54	583		Persons began to be hired to weep at funerals.—Jer. ix. 17.

Dynasties.	Emperors.	When began to reign. Years.	Cycle.	A.D.	Reigned Years.	Remarkable Events.
Suy	Wăn Te	46	54	589	16	
	Yang Te	2	55	605	13	
	Kung Te	15	55	618	2	
Tang	Kaou-tsoo	17	55	620	7	The first ruler of Tang attacked the disorderly Tse, and in six years the whole empire was subjugated.
	Tae-tsung	24	55	627	23	
	Kaou-tsung	47	55	650	34	The public examination of literary candidates began.
	Chung-tsung	21	56	684	27	The throne was usurped by an empress.
	Juy-tsung	48	56	711	2	
	Heuen-tsung	50	56	713	44	Books bound up in leaves about this time.
	Süh-tsung	34	57	757	6	At this period education flourished most.
	Tae-tsung	40	57	763	17	The dynasty began now to decline.
	Tÿh-tsung	57	57	780	25	
	Shun-tsung	22	58	805	1	The feast of lanterns commenced.
	Hëen-tsung	23	58	806	15	This emperor was slain in contending with the Tartars:
	Müh-tsung	38	58	821	4	And this one was murdered by his eunuchs:
	King-tsung	42	58	825	2	Who raised Wăn-tsung to the throne.
	Wăn-tsung	44	58	827	14	This was a courageous prince, much to be pitied.
	Woo-tsung	58	58	841	6	
	Seuen-tsung	4	59	847	13	An extravagant and licentious ruler.
	E-tsung	17	59	860	14	Two meteors shot across the heavens, intersecting each others tract.
	He-tsung	31	59	874	15	
	Chaou-tsung	46	59	889	16	The literary title, Chwang-yuen, was introduced.
	Chaou-seuen	2	60	905	2	The founder of this dynasty was formerly a robber.
How Leang	Tae-tsoo	4	60	907	6	This prince killed his own father, and afterwards destroyed himself.
	Choo-chin	10	60	913	10	This emperor was formerly a private soldier.
How Tang	Chwang-tsung	20	60	923	4	The custom of binding the women's feet introduced.
	Ming-tsung	24	60	927	7	A.D. 924. Printing was invented by Fung-taou.
	Min Te	31	61	934	1	The founder of this dynasty was a foreigner.
	Fei Te	32	60	935	2	Charms to drive away evil spirits began to be used.
How Tsin	Kaou-tsoo	34	60	937	6	
	Chŭh Te	40	60	943	4	

Dynasties.	Emperors.	When began to reign. Years	Cycle	A. D.	Reigned Years.	Remarkable Events.
How Han	Kaou-tsoo	44	60	947	2	The founder of this dynasty was also a foreigner.
	Yin Te	46	60	949	2	Three hundred priests sent from India to China.
HowChow	Tae-tsoo	48	60	951	3	The founder of this dynasty was of mean parentage, and soon murdered.
	She-tsung	51	60	954	5	
	Kung Te	56	60	959	1	
Sung	Tae-tsoo	57	60	960	17	The founder of this dynasty was raised to the throne in a state of intoxication.
	Tae-tsung	14	61	977	21	
	Chin-tsung	35	61	998	25	A. D. 1005. A predicted eclipse did not appear, upon which the astronomers congratulated the emperor.
	Jin-tsung	60	61	1023	41	Canton was walled in, as a defence against the Cochin Chinese.
	Ying-tsung	41	62	1064	4	
	Shin-tsung	45	62	1068	18	
	Ché-tsung	3	63	1086	15	This emperor was guided by his mother, a virtuous woman.
	Hwuy-tsung	18	63	1101	25	
	Kin-tsung	43	63	1126	1	
	Kaou-tsung	44	63	1127	36	
	Heaou-tsung	20	64	1163	27	Choo-foo-tsze, the commentator on the Four Books, flourished.
	Kwang-tsung	47	64	1190	5	
	Ning-tsung	52	64	1195	30	
	Le-tsung	22	65	1225	40	Cannon first used against the Tartars.
	Too-tsung	2	66	1265	10	
	Kung-tsung	12	66	1275	2	Marco Paulo, the Venetian traveller, visited China.
	Twan-tsung	14	66	1277	2	Cotton cloth made about this time.
	Te Ping	16	66	1279	1	
Yuen	She-tsoo	17	66	1280	15	The founder of this dynasty, was a Tartar; the famous Coblai Khan.
	Ching-tsung	32	66	1295	13	Stone throwing engines, or cannon were employed.
	Woo-tsung	45	66	1308	4	
	Jin-tsung	49	66	1312	9	
	Ying-tsung	58	66	1321	3	The religion of Buddha prevailed, during this dynasty, while the books of Taou were burned.
	Tae-ting Te	1	67	1324	5	
	Ming-tsung	6	67	1329	1	
	Wǎn-tsung	7	67	1330	3	

Dynasties.	Emperors.	When began to reign.			Reigned Years.	Remarkable Events.
		Years.	Cycle.	A. D.		
Yuen	Shun Te	10	67	1333	35	A. D. 1344. The grand canal was dug.
Ming	Hung-woo*	45	67	1368	31	The founder of this dynasty was originally a barber, and afterwards ruled over China.
	Këen-wăn	16	68	1399	4	
	Yung-lŏ	20	68	1403	22	
	Hung-he	42	68	1425	1	The Japanese frequently pillaged the coast.
	Seuen-tîh	43	68	1426	10	Various fire arms were in use.
	Ching-tung	53	68	1436	14	No regard was paid to rank; merit and talent alone secured advancement, during this dynasty.
	King-tae	7	69	1450	7	
	Tëen-tsun	14	69	1457	8	
	Ching-hwa	22	69	1465	23	
	Hung-che	45	69	1488	18	
	Ching-tîh	3	70	1506	16	
	Këa-tsing	19	70	1522	45	A. D. 1554, foreigners came to Macao.
	Lung-king	4	71	1567	6	
	Wan-leîh	10	71	1573	47	Muskets and leaden bullets were introduced.
	Tae-chang	57	71	1620	1	
	Tëen-ke	58	71	1621	7	
	Tsung-chin	5	72	1628	16	A Chinese general invited the Tartars to assist him against the rebels.
Ta Tsing	Shun-che	21	72	1644	18	The Tartars again occupied China, and required the Chinese to shave their heads.
	Kang-he	39	72	1662	61	
	Yung-ching	40	73	1723	13	The Chinese subjugated Formosa.
	Këen-lung	53	73	1736	60	Coxinga, the famous Chinese pirate, submitted to the emperor.
	Këa-king	53	74	1796	25	
	Taou-kwang	18	75	1821		

* To these emperors, the national, instead of the sacred title, is given; because the former is better known.

APPENDIX, No. II.

LIST OF BOOKS

PRINTED AT

CANTON AND MALACCA.

Names of Books.	Authors.	When Printed.	Size.	Number of Pages.	Number of Copies.
Acts of the Apostles	Morrison	1810	8vo.	65	1,000
Luke	Do.	1811	8vo.	60	100
Pauline Epistles	Do.	1812	8vo.	155	50
Tract on Redemption	Do.	1811-19	8vo. & 12mo.	6	12,550
Assembly's Catechism	Do.	1811-19	Do.	30	7,500
New Testament	Do.	1813	8vo.	537	2,000
Genesis	Do.	1814-19	8vo.	125	2,000
Psalms	Do.	1814	8vo.	148	500
Short Abstract	Do.	1814	8vo.	1	1,800
Farewell Letter	Milne	1814	12mo.	3	2,000
Life of Christ	Do.	1814-19	8vo.	70	1,500
Old Testament History	Morrison	1815-19	8vo.	9	3,900
New Testament	Do.	1815-19	12mo.	537	3,420
Chinese Magazine	Milne	1815	12mo.	33	725
Do.		1816	12mo.	73	815
Do.		1817	12mo.	83	800
Do.		1818	12mo.	81	500
Do.		1819	12mo.	84	1,000
Do.		1820	12mo.	84	2,000
Do.		1821	12mo.	86	2,000
Do. (odd nos. various years)		1815-18	12mo.	7	25,860
Strait Gate	Do.	1816-33	12mo.	7	5,500
Tract on Lying	Do.	1816-19	12mo.	7	5,800
New Testament	Morrison	1817	12mo.	537	100
Youth's Catechism	Milne	1817-19	12mo.	37	6,600
Hymn Book	Morrison	1818-22	12mo.	27	500
Liturgy	Do.	1818	18mo.	30	400
Miscellaneous Essays	Do.	1818	12mo.	17	2,000
Tour of the World	Do.	1818	8vo.	29	
Exposition of the Lord's Prayer	Milne	1818-19	12mo	37	1,900
Tract on Idolatry	Do.	1818-19	12mo.	7	8,500
Tract on Justice	Do.	1818-19	12mo.	10	7,500
Twelve Short Sermons	Do.	1818-19	12mo.	12	13,000
Deuteronomy	Do.	1819-20	12mo.	91	600
Joshua	Do.	1819-20	12mo.	61	600
Psalms	Morrison	1819-20	12mo.	148	600
Isaiah	Do.	1819	12mo.	136	800
Tract on Gambling	Milne	1819	12mo.	13	6,000
Dialogues	Do.	1819	12mo.	20	2,000
					134,390

Names of Books.	Authors.	When Printed.	Size.	Number of Pages.	Number of Copies.
Brought forward .					134,390
Sacred History . .	Milne.	1819	12mo.	71	2,500
Tract on Calamity . .	Do.	1819	12mo.	13	2,000
Geographical Catechism .	Medhurst	1819	12mo.	27	1,100
Miscellaneous Essays . .	Afăh	1819	12mo.	37	2,000
New Testament . .	Morrison	1820	12mo.	537	500
Exodus . . .	Do.	1820	12mo.	104	500
Luke and Isaiah . .	Morrison	1820	12mo.	196	500
Three Pearls . .	Milne	1821	12mo.	33	1,000
Jeremiah . . .	Morrison	1822	12mo.	164	
Ezekiel . . .	Do.	1822	12mo.	132	
Hymn Book. . .	Do.	1822	12mo.	50	
Homily on Scripture .	Do.	1822	8vo.	12	
Sketch of the World .	Milne	1822	12mo.	30	
New Testament .	Morrison	1823	12mo.	537	1,000
Psalter and Liturgy .	Do.	1824	12mo.	178	
Complete Bibles .	Morrison & Milne	1824	12mo.	2689	272
New Testament . .	Morrison	1824	12mo.	537	200
Village Sermons. .	Milne	1824	12mo.	70	500
New Hymn Book .	Morrison	1824	12mo.	50	1,000
Tract on Regeneration. .	Collie	1824	8vo.	50	1,500
Brown's Catechism .	Col.Students	1824	12mo.	10	1,500
Sheet Tracts .	Collie	1824	folio	29	1,000
Commentary on Ephesians	Milne	1825	8vo.		Number
Essay on the Soul .	Do.	1825	12mo.		printed
Help to the Scriptures .	Collie	1825	12mo.		not as-
Christian School Book .	Do.	1825	8vo.		certain-
Portals to the Seminary .	Do.	1825	12mo.		ed.
Astronomical Catechism .	Do.	1825			
Commentary on Phillippians .	Do.	1825			
Treatise on Regeneration .	Do.				
Sheet Tracts .	Do.			20	13,000
Brown's Catechism .	Students				
Hymn Book .					
Complete Bibles .		1826	8vo.	2689	125
Testaments . .		1826	8vo.	537	200
Tracts . .		1826	12mo.	20	3,600
Sheet Tracts .		1826	folio	1	11,000
Introduction to the Scriptures .					
Complete Bibles . .	Mor.& Milne	1827	8vo.	2689	375
New Testament .	Morrison	1827	8vo.	537	2,600
Religious Tracts (various) .		1827	12mo.	10	24,000
Essay on the Soul .	Milne	1827	12mo.	200	500
Com. on the Ephesians .	Do.	1827	12mo.	150	1,400
Bogue's Essay .	Collie	1827	12mo.	180	500
New Testament .	Morrison	1830	8vo.	537	100
Gospel of John .	Do.	1830	12mo.	57	1,000
Psalter and Liturgy .	Do.	1830	8vo.	178	1,000
Essay on the Soul .	Milne	1830	12mo.	200	500
Tracts (various) .	Various	1830	12mo.	20	13,000
Scripture Lessons .	Morrison	1832	12mo.	150	500
Complete Bibles .	Do. & Milne	1832	8vo.	2689	130
Separate Gospels .	Morrison	1832	12mo.	60	2,000
Chinese Dialogues .	Milne	1832	12mo.	20	2,500
					229,492

Names of Books.	Authors.	When Printed.	Size.	Number of Pages.	Number of Copies.
Brought forward .					229,492
Life of Christ, in rhyme .	Collie	1832-3	12mo.	20	800
Com, on the Lord's Prayer .	Milne	1832-3	12mo.	37	2,000
Village Sermons . .	Do.	1832	12mo.	70	500
Milne's Four Tracts . .	Do.	1832-3	12mo.	40	3,500
Three Character Classic .	Medhurst	1832-3	12mo.	17	1,200
Domestic Instructor . .	Morrison	1832	8vo.	400	100
Com. on the Ten Commandments	Medhurst	1833	8vo.	90	2,200
Scripture Extracts . .	Collie	1833	12mo.	50	800
Strait Gate . .	Milne	1823	12mo.	10	1,000
Catechism . .				20	100
Comparative Chronology .	Medhurst	1833	8vo.	30	1,000
Prayers and Hymns . .	Morrison	1834	18mo	66	10,000
Sheet Tracts . .	Do.	1834	folio	1	60,000
Separate Gospels . .	Do.	1833	12mo.	60	1,000
Tracts and Books . .	Various	1834	12mo.	20	10,000
Whole Bibles . .	Mor. & Milne	1835	8vo.	2689	600
Testaments . .	Morrison	1835		537	150
Single Gospels . .	Do.	1835		60	17,800
Tracts . . .	Various	1835		20	40,956
Whole Bibles . .	Mor. & Milne	1836	8vo.	2689	573
Tracts . . .	Various	1836		20	66,698
					450,469

LIST OF BOOKS PRINTED AT BATAVIA,

WRITTEN BY

W. H. MEDHURST,

IN THE CHINESE LANGUAGE.

Names of Books.	When Printed.	How Printed.	Size.	Number of Leaves.	Number of Copies.
Monthly Magazine	1823-26	Xylography	8vo.	6	83,000
Child's Primer	1825-36	Do.	12mo.	14	2,200
History of Java	1825-34	Do.	8vo.	85	1,630
Doddridge's Rise, 1st part	1826-34	Do.	8vo.	40	3,577
Tract on the New Year	1826-34	Do.	8vo.	7	2,000
Feast of the Tombs	1826-34	Do.	8vo.	7	2,510
Sayings of Jesus	1826-36	Do.	8vo.	7	2,000
On Feeding the Ghosts	1826-34	Do.	8vo.	8	2,514
On the Sailor's Goddess	1826-33	Do.	8vo.	5	2,325
Exposition of the Moral Law	1826-35	Do.	8vo.	90	3,563
Various Reprints	1827	Do.	8vo.	18	12,000
Three Character Classic	1828-35	Do.	8vo.	17	5,210
Miscellaneous Pieces	1828-35	Do.	8vo.	50	2,376
Fraternal Dialogues	1828-34	Do.	8vo.	26	1,100
On Walking over the Fire	1828	Do.	12mo.	5	500
On Walking over the Fire	1833-35	Lithography	12mo.	8	1,800
Various Reprints	1829	Do.	8vo.	30	3,000
Various Reprints	1830	Xylography	8vo.	20	4,000
Tract on Redemption	1829-35	Do.	8vo.	30	4,453
Village Sermons	1829-32	Do.	8vo.	39	700
Important Selections	1834	Do.	8vo.	32	500
Gospel of Mark	1836	Lithography	8vo.	35	1,000
School Book	1828-32	Do.	12mo.	16	1,200
Comparative Chronology	1828	Do.	8vo.	40	1,000
Assembly's Catechism	1832	Do.	8vo.	20	300
Scripture Prints	1832	Lithography	4to.	19	1,000
The Divine Attributes	1833	Do.	12mo.	100	3,000
The Fall and Recovery of Man	1834	Do.	12mo.	100	1,000
Harmony of the Gospels	1834-36	Do.	8vo.	200	3,000
On the Being of a God	1834	Do.	32mo.	8	4,500

IN THE MALAY LANGUAGE.

Names of Books.	When Printed.	How Printed.	Size.	Number of Leaves.	Number of Copies.
Catechism of Nature	1832	Lithography	8vo.	112	500
Ditto, Roman character	1835	Typography	12mo.	50	1,250
Scripture Catechism, by Mrs. M.	1832	Lithography	24mo.	208	1,000
Ditto, Roman character	1833	Typography	8vo.	16	1,000
Introduction to the Scriptures	1833	Lithography	8vo.	32	500
Scheme of Christian Doctrine	1833	Do.	8vo.	76	1,000
Malay Primer	1834	Do.	8vo.	48	500
Discussion with Mahomedans	1834	Do.	8vo.	186	1,000
Search for Sin	1835	Do.	8vo.	42	2,000
Ditto, Roman character	1835	Typography	12mo.	50	2,000
Persuasive to Public Worship	1836	Lithography	8vo.	24	952

168,660

Tracts printed at Batavia, written by various Authors:

In Malay, by Mr. Thomsen.

Names of Books.	When Printed.	How Printed.	Size.	Number of Leaves.	Number of Copies.
Malay Prayer . .	1828	Lithography	8vo.	8	200
Good News for the Sons of Adam	1835	Do.	8vo.	96	2,000
Catechism . . .	1835	Do.	8vo.	18	1,000
Parables . .	1834	Typography	8vo.	34	1,000
Life of Christ . .	1834-5	Lithography	8vo.	45	2,000
School Book . .	1834-6	Do.	8vo.	24	384

In Malay, by Mr. Robinson.

Way of Salvation . .	1828-33	Lithography	8vo.	48	1,300
Hymn Book . .	1834	Do.	18mo.	98	500
Life of Bunyan, Roman char. .	1834	Typography	18mo.	48	1,300
Geography . .	1835	Lithography	8vo.	94	300
Arithmetic, Roman character .	1835	Typography	18mo.	56	1,250

In Malay, by the Sourabaya Society.

Dutch and Malay Catechism	1834	Typography	18mo.	60	500

In Lettinese, by Mr. Luyke.

Lettinese Catechism . .	1830	Typography	18mo.	8	500

In Javanese, by Mr. Bruckner.

On the Divine Attributes .	1834	Typography	12mo.	24	3,000
Catechism of Nature .	1834	Do.	12mo.	124	1,000
On the Gospel Plan .	1834	Do.	12mo.	28	2,000
On the Son of God .	1834	Do.	12mo.	58	1,500
Three Javanese Tracts .	1835	Do.	12mo.	90	3,000
					191,394

LIST OF BOOKS PRINTED AT PENANG.

	1834	1835	1836
Malay Poems, by a Native . .	2000	2000	2000
Ditto Catechism, by Mr. Beighton . .	1500	1500	
Ditto Hymns	1500	3000	
John Knill (Malay) . . .		1000	
Religion of the Bible (ditto) . . .		1500	
Fourth Commandment (ditto) . . .		2000	
Ten Commandments (ditto) . . .		2000	
Beatitudes (ditto)		2000	
Believe on the Lord Jesus (ditto) . .		2000	
Tract on Heaven (Chinese), Mr. Dyer . .		700	
Scripture Lessons (ditto) . . .		3500	
Easy Lessons (ditto) . . .		2000	
First Lessons for Schools (ditto) . .		7000	
Matthew vi. and vii. (ditto) . .		1200	
Scripture Catechism (24 pages) Malay .			1500
Abdullah and Sabat ditto . .			1000
Life of Christ (36 pages) ditto . .			1000
The Mystery, by a Native ditto . .			1500
Malay Sheet Tract			1000
	5000	30,900	8000
			30,000
			5,000
			43,900

LIST OF BOOKS PRINTED AT SINGAPORE.

1824.	A Selection of Hymns, in Malay.	
	A Spelling Book, Do.	
	A System of Arithmetic, Do.	
1825.	The Gospel of Matthew, Do.	
	Assembly's Catechism, Do.	
1826.	Malay Tracts . . .	25,000
1827.	Watts's First Catechism, Malay.	
	School Lessons, Do.	
	Three Tracts, Do.	
	Missionary Hymns, in English.	
	Malay Hymns.	
	A Bugguese Tract.	
1828.	A new Malay Do. in the Roman character.	
	Two Ditto, Arabic do.	
	Watts's First Catechism, in Malay.	
	School Lessons, Do.	
1829.	Malay Tracts	8,000
	Scripture Tickets, Do. . .	4,000
	Abdullah and Sabat, Do.	
	Sermon on the Mount, Do.	
	Good News for the Children of Adam, Do.	
1830.	Malay New Testament . . .	2,000
	Matthew, in Malay . . .	2,000
1831.	Bugguese Tract	500
	Three Malay Do.	6,000
	One Siamese Do.	1,000
	Three School Books, in Malay.	
1832.	Several Malay Tracts reprinted.	
1833.	Six Malay Do.	15,000
	Two Bugguese Do. . . .	3,000
		66,000

Many of the works printed at Malacca, Penang, and Singapore, have not been regularly reported, or the record of the work done is not to be found in this country; so that it is difficult to ascertain, at this distance, the number of pages, or the quantity printed of several publications specified in the foregoing lists: still, as far as the account can be made up, it appears that there have been printed, from the year 1810 to the year 1836,

At Malacca and Canton	450,469 books and tracts.
At Batavia	191,394 ,,
At Penang	43,900 ,,
At Singapore	66,000 ,,
	751,763

Including 2,075 complete Chinese Bibles, 9,970 New Testaments, and 31,000 separate portions of Scripture; with 2,000 Malay Testaments, and 2,000 separate Gospels in the same language. If the number of pages of each work be reckoned, with the amount printed off, it will be seen that the brethren in the Ultra-Ganges missions have issued from their presses, in those regions, upwards of eight million pages of religious publications in the Chinese and Malayan languages.

LONDON:
PRINTED BY A. SIMPSON, WARWICK LANE,
PATERNOSTER ROW.

DATE DUE